AGRARIAN POWER AND AGRICULTURAL PRODUCTIVITY IN SOUTH ASIA

Sponsored by the
JOINT COMMITTEE ON SOUTH ASIA
of the
SOCIAL SCIENCE RESEARCH COUNCIL
and the
AMERICAN COUNCIL OF LEARNED SOCIETIES

Agrarian Power and Agricultural Productivity in South Asia

EDITED BY
MEGHNAD DESAI
SUSANNE HOEBER RUDOLPH
ASHOK RUDRA

UNIVERSITY OF CALIFORNIA PRESS
Berkeley   Los Angeles   New York

University of California Press
Berkeley and Los Angeles, California

University of California Press, Ltd.
London

Published in India
by Oxford University Press

© 1984 by Oxford University Press

Printed in the United States of America

1 2 3 4 5 6 7 8 9

Library of Congress Cataloging in Publication Data
Main entry under title:

Agrarian power and agricultural productivity in South
    Asia.

    Bibliography: p.
    Includes index.
    1. Agriculture and state—Asia, South—Addresses,
essays, lectures.   2. Agricultural productivity—Asia,
South—Addresses, essays, lectures.   3. Local government
—Asia, South—Addresses, essays, lectures.
I. Desai, Meghnad.   II. Rudolph, Susanne Hoeber.
III. Rudra, Ashof.
HD2065.3.Z8A37   1985   338.1′854   84-16333
ISBN 0-520-05369-9

Contents

Acknowledgements

This volume owes its origins to the decision of the Joint Committee on South Asia of the Social Science Research Council (SSRC) to launch a subcommittee on South Asia Political Economy. It in turn created three working groups, the first of which was the group on agrarian power and agricultural productivity. Michelle McAlpin, Department of Economics, Tufts University, served as the first chair of the South Asia Political Economy Subcommittee and Veena Das, Professor of Sociology at Delhi University, as the second.

The initial planning was the work of Dr David Szanton of the SSRC. Funding in the United States was provided by the SSRC from grants it received from the National Science Foundation and the Ford Foundation. In India, the Indian Council of Social Science Research, under the direction of Professor T. N. Madan, Member Secretary, provided financial support from its resources. Dr Veena Oldenburg of the SSRC dealt with the complex international logistics of coordinating papers and planning the meetings.

Introduction

SUSANNE HOEBER RUDOLPH

Intellectual Genealogy of the Volume

The intellectual genealogy of this volume extends back to several exploratory meetings convoked in 1977 by the Joint Committee on South Asia of the Social Science Research Council (SSRC). These meetings, attended by an interdisciplinary and international group of social scientists, addressed the question: given the state of the social sciences in the 1970s, how can and should problems of South Asian political economy be explored? It defined a number of research agendas, one of which is addressed in this volume, while others are addressed in companion volumes.

The group that assembled to define the project (Ludden 1977) and the working groups that eventually emerged to implement it, differed significantly from those responsible for the seminal efforts launched by the SSRC in the early sixties to understand political development in new nations (SSRC, Committee on Comparative Politics 1963–75). They differed in their composition. The 1960s working groups consisted mainly of American political scientists. The 1970s group reflected the greatly increased participation of scholars from Asia and from several disciplines in defining the research agendas for understanding how to achieve equity and growth in Third World countries. The 1960s groups believed that Western patterns of social and economic change could be taken as predictive and prescriptive for the non-Western world. The 1977 groups questioned the extent to which the historical sequences, value premises and social forms that dominated development in the West were relevant or desirable for Third World countries. The 1960s group considered political institutions and behaviour critical for development, and found congenial structural-functional or behavioural perspectives. The 1970s groups were more concerned about how economic power and exploitation affected development. The 1960s and late 1970s efforts also differed in the financial and institutional patronage that sustained them. The Indian Council of Social Science Research (ICSSR) co-sponsored the project and collaborated with the SSRC in funding a significant portion of the meetings and expenses of the endeavour.

The working groups that prepared the shared papers for three years, with a series of small international conferences, were cross-national communities of scholars encompassing the varying, even conflicting, environments and agendas of the participants. We believe that non-ethnocentric social science is most likely to emerge as the social product of such communities.

In the planning stage of the South Asia Political Economy Project (SAPE), proposals focused on the need to delineate an approach from 'within' to South Asia political economy. The planning group noted that economics has commonly been formulated with a degree of universality unparalleled by other social science disciplines. The conceptual assumptions of neo-classical economics in particular have been exceptionally immune to evidence of social and temporal variation. Other social science disciplines have been more hospitable to such evidence, reshaping their concepts and explanatory frameworks to accommodate anomalies.

In the effort to approximate a more contextual understanding of economic processes, the planners envisioned a research alliance. On the one hand, they would find anthropologically oriented scholars attuned to 'indigenous conceptual systems as bases for understanding, explaining and interpreting South Asian institutions and behavior' (Social Science Research Council 1978: 6). On the other hand, they would find scholars who recognized that political economy was known and practised by John Stuart Mill and Karl Marx as well as Adam Smith. These founders of political economy spoke for it from 'without', from more universal and systemic conceptual systems. Collaboration on common problems by those who saw them from 'within' and from 'without' would be fruitful. It would 'link careful delineation of indigenous conceptual systems, goals, and institutions with systematic observation and analysis from external perspectives' (4).

Creating social science concepts relevant to South Asia was to be advanced also by a self-conscious effort to address appropriate levels of action. Levels that fall *between* what economics conventionally deals with, micro and macro, between individual preferences and choices on the one hand and public choices and systemic outcomes on the other, were identified as most promising. Some SAPE workshops would focus on family and locality because they provided contexts of decision and action in which indigenous formulations were most likely to constrain or challenge the more universal formulations of political economy. The significance of the indigenous was to be extracted by focusing on such contexts, especially collective micro-contexts. In them, it was believed, the indigenous was most likely to be clearly articulated. Behind this strategy lay the implicit notion that, given the nature of the modern world and its communications networks, macro-contexts are invariably 'contaminated' by universal categories.

The interest in local forms was not only motivated by methodological concerns. It was also abetted by the empirical situation of South Asia. Unlike scholars working in Latin America, for example, who see the problem of political economy as mainly influenced by the international environment, scholars working on South Asia tend to view political economy as strongly affected by local and regional power structures as well as by the imperial legacy. While most social theory would predict that the hold of locality and its power structure would be transient, the most striking aspect of the Indian case is the slow pace at which the hold of locality has declined. Rural–urban population proportions have been stationary at about 80/20 since the beginning of the century. Change in South Asia may diverge so radically from change in Europe that that factor alone would render European social theory inapplicable. The focus on local areas, therefore, is warranted by empirical considerations as well as by the light they shed on indigenous formulations.

On the other hand, while local power systems are thought to play a powerful role in South Asia's political economy, it was recognized that linkages between levels and to actions originating outside local arenas make localities units in a chain of technical, financial and policy initiatives reaching to village from region, nation and international arena. International interest rates, Middle Eastern oil prices, the world market for wheat, and the decisions of the central government and its Agricultural Prices Commission bear heavily on the structure of opportunity at the local level.

After the intellectual agendas of the planning group had been adapted to the reality principles of funding and to a search for appropriate contributors, three small, multidisciplinary international working groups were formed. SAPE I, on the relationship between local power structures and agricultural productivity, assembled historians, economists and political scientists, combining systemic views of political economy with regional and local perspectives. SAPE II, on health and nutrition at the household and family level, accommodated a concern for anthropological orientations and local decision making. SAPE III focused on societal responses to crises. The group on local power and agrarian productivity, of which this volume is the product, met in 1979 and 1980 in Delhi to discuss evolving drafts contributing to the topic.

Any intellectual production should be understood in the first instance by reference to its substantive findings, and we shall presently suggest the kind of findings and research agendas this volume embodies. But sociology of knowledge is so pervasive a concern among social scientists, and the question of who can help create a non-ethnocentric social science has so greatly occupied scholars working on South Asia, that it is appropriate to suggest the disciplinary and national provenance of the participants. That is by no means easy: the group constitutes part of the increasing cadre of scholars whose experience is local, national and international.

The working group consisted of three scholars teaching in India, Sukhamoy Chakravarty, B. B. Chaudhuri, and Ashok Rudra; two teaching in England, Meghnad Desai and Hamza Alavi; five teaching in the U.S., Ronald Herring, David Ludden, Susanne and Lloyd Rudolph, and T. N. Srinivasan; and one teaching in Canada, Donald Attwood. All of these, except Alavi and Srinivasan, have contributed essays to the volume. It consisted of four economists, Chakravarti, Rudra, Desai and Srinivasan; two economic historians, Ludden and Chaudhuri; two anthropologists, Attwood and Alavi; and three political scientists, Herring, and Lloyd and Susanne Rudolph. The group cuts vertically through the arenas of economic action. Rudra, Alavi, Herring and Attwood have done significant fieldwork in local contexts—villages and districts; Ludden, the Rudolphs and Chaudhuri have focused on specific provincial and regional contexts; the rest are macro-theorists. The disciplinary labels overstate the extent of identification—Desai does mathematical models but edits economic history; Alavi is a social theorist as well as an anthropologist; economists Chakravarti and Rudra are also concerned with economic history and statistics respectively. What the group had in common was a certain disdain for the boundary maintenance function of disciplines. The national locations also convey more exclusive identities than is warranted. Srinivasan has spent many years in India thinking about macro-economics, and some years at Yale; the Rudolphs spend every fourth year in India; Alavi and Desai have and maintain dual roots, on the subcontinent and in Europe.

The group encompassed a variety of cosmologies, pluralist, neo-classical, Marxian, in various shades of each. Ideological boundary maintenance was no more stringent than disciplinary boundary maintenance. The cross-cutting cleavages produced curious align-ments: at some moments and on some topics, the 'other social sciences' thought the differences among Marxian and neo-classical economists were less than their linguistic and conceptual unity *qua* economists.

We did not attempt to settle on agreed-upon methodological or conceptual frameworks. To have done so would have proved im-possible and destroyed the differentiations that made our exchanges worthwhile. We did infiltrate one another's perspectives, expanded one another's conceptual language and empirical base, and created a universe of common discourse. Our discussions were not always harmonious. While in some Indian conceptual systems consensus is regarded as necessary for community, Alvin Gouldner's writings (1964) remind us of a different sociological tradition that asserts con-flict creates community. In our interactions as colleagues, we hewed closer to Gouldner than to consensual traditionalism. National, generational, disciplinary and ideological cleavages supplied the ground for conflict, which was by no means avoided. Our eventual capacity to work fruitfully as colleagues may safely be referred in part to conflict theory.

The other element in our unity, the systematic practice of com-mensality, also fits awkwardly into South Asian conceptual systems, although the SAPE II authors of 'The Food of Well-being' would not be surprised at the social function of meals. We ate together a great deal, which led to talk that was not always to the point of our common enterprise. Meals allowed us to explore each other's per-spectives in contexts not ruled by chairmen's gavels, and with respect to world views and tastes on subjects other than agrarian political economy. The process has created durable collegial relations that are likely to survive the conferences and the volumes.

The title of our project, 'Agrarian Power and Agricultural Pro-ductivity in South Asia', suggests that we were to examine the possibly reciprocal relationship between local power structures on the one hand and the generation, allocation, appropriation and disposal of resources in agriculture on the other. This relationship has provided the main focus for two state-of-the-art papers, one by Sukhamoy Chakravarti from the perspective of the economic tradition, and one by Ronald Herring from a more political perspective. These papers, together with Ludden's extended literature review of the economic history of agrarian power structures, suggest the major issues and controversies affecting this field. They create research agendas even while they offer interpretive perspectives on the literature. The other papers take up particular substantive issues that clarify agrarian power, productivity, or the relationship between the two. Below, we will try to suggest some of the general themes that animate the volume: political economy; power; the reciprocal effects of power and productivity; linkages.

Political Economy

The contributors to the volume speak in different languages, in response to different theoretical and disciplinary agendas, and in the light of different normative commitments. Hence it is not surprising that the notions of political economy implicitly or explicitly animating different papers vary. For us political economy was more an approach than a concept around whose definitions we could unite.

Many of the major writers on economics, such as James and John Stuart Mill as well as Marx, have had something to say about India. But theirs was not a tradition that worried about 'indigenous categories'. They lived in the heyday of 'universal history', for which Europe had the template. *The* central phenomenon shaping their thinking was the process of European commercialization and industrialization which they lived to experience. This was as true of Marx as of Mill, although Marx' discussion of pre-capitalist power generated some concepts that are more relevant to our enterprise. However, neither Marxian nor liberal economic theory takes into account the nature of the production process, and how it is related to variations in crops, ecology, family, food habits and the social organization of work processes.

Both classical and Marxian economists tend to assume a political economy in which power is reflexive of economic relations. Engels' assertion speaks for both traditions: 'Political economy in the widest sense is the science of the laws governing the production and exchange of the material means of subsistence in human society' (1954: 203). Not only has political economy shown a propensity to place material forces in the forefront, it more or less assumes the congruence of determinants of power: class, status, ideology and control of state institutions are assumed to be summed or congruent, and ultimately referable to material forces. It is possible, on the other hand, to work with a notion of political economy in which power is seen as relatively autonomous. For the Marx of the 18th Brumaire, state power was not merely reflexive of material forces but acquired a certain detachment from them. When Binoy Chaudhuri in this volume notes the constraints nineteenth-century British legislation imposed on zamindars, he is noting the effects of a bureaucratic state that is not embedded in local society and has considerable autonomy. Political economy also need not assume the congruence of determinants. It becomes an empirical rather than a theoretical question whether class, status, ideology and control of state institutions are congruent or incongruent. In logic, the very conception of society that does not accept a static set of relations, that envisions social change or revolution, must assume some incongruence, else there would be no way out of the constant cycle of 'reproduction' of given relations. In the possibility of incongruence lies the prospect that other forms of power can be a countervailing force to economic power.

But these are familiar intellectual agendas. Some participants in the working groups thought that regardless of whether the adjective or the noun in the compound phrase 'political economy' took precedence, political economy was too narrowly conceived, too barren of history and culture, especially the latter, to respond adequately to South Asian relations. One aspect of the agenda was to expropriate the oligopolistic holdings of the two disciplines that have established hegemony over the concept of political economy, politics and economics. Another was to encourage both to share with history and cultural anthropology the task of conceptualization and of certifying what data is relevant. Several articles in this volume are addressed to this commitment. SAPE II and SAPE III will carry further the project of creating formulations and agendas for political economy that are more sensitive to diverse cultural categories and contexts.

To the extent that classical economics wrote the original agenda for political economy, and European history wrote its typical scenarios, we have diverged from the original agenda. Urbanization and commercialization were powerful facilitators of agrarian development in Europe. The persistent and powerful hold of locality in South Asia, the slow and uneven growth of urbanization and commercialization, make much neo-classical theory inapplicable to the case of Indian agriculture. The growth of British agriculture after the enclosures is the paradigmatic Western historical case for agricultural development, and, as Chakravarty points out, it is a commercial model. Attwood's account of the Maharashtra sugar cooperatives suggests such rapid commercialization also affects parts of India, but they are a sport even within Maharashtra, where noncommercial dry land cultivation and low growth are the norm. In Punjab, too, commercialization has grown rapidly. But Rudra's Bengal survey and Herring's Kerala account suggest cases in which commercialization is slow, and in terms of area and population covered, these areas are more characteristic.

The project of infiltrating political economy with an understanding for configurations unique to South Asia merged into an older and less country-specific critique of the data-proof nature of neo-classical assumptions. As Herring writes here and elsewhere: 'Clearly it is possible to factor out, under the covering *ceteris paribus caveat*, much of the "noise" in the system, gaining parsimony and deductive power at the expense of complexity and explanatory power; analysis in the general equilibrium model of traditional economics typically does just this' (Herring 1980). But 'such operations are misleading and inadequate; political economy paradigms must reflect the same structural unity of the processes which they seek to explain' (4).

A number of papers demonstrate persistent empirical divergence from neo-classical assumptions: the absence of a competitive labour market, the absence of free contractual labour, differential prices to big and small farmers, and fragmented credit markets. The pervasive assumption of the existence of markets is selectively negated in the South Asian setting—selectively, we say, because regions differ radically as to the extent to which they approximate initial assumptions. Chakravarti notes that the differentiation of markets is itself differential in India. In some regions, villages normally distinguish between crops grown for sale and crops consumed in the village. It is so in the Northwest, where commerce and marketing have proceeded far. In yet other regions, there is no such distinction. Attwood, picturing the Maharashtra canal areas and their sugar crop, suggests an open and mobile economy in which seasonal and permanent migration from dry to wet areas are the rule, creating a competitive labour market. Rudra, on the other hand, presents data for a set of villages among which mobility of persons and information is so low that each village constitutes a separate and self-contained labour market. He also adds that the absence of a market is not a universal for all functions. The exchange of products is much less affected by locality than the market for labour; products move out into trans-local, regional and national markets. These findings are contrary to the assumption that the impact of commercial forces is universal, easily dissolving previous relationships. They suggest the existence of lags, resistances, and the compartmentalization of economic spheres, producing outcomes in which *ceteris* is in most cases not *paribus*. A more historically and culturally sensitive political economy can say so.

Power

The same consideration—divergence of methodological cosmologies —that led us to avoid a common definition of political economy, led us to avoid a common definition of power. However, in order to discuss the variety of meanings implicit in the essays, it is useful to begin with a definition that is frequent in the social sciences, notably in the literature of organizations. We can say that power is the capacity to impose one's will upon another, so that he is obliged to do what he would not otherwise do, or so that he is prevented from doing what he would otherwise do. This definition is deceptively simple. The phrase 'he would not otherwise do' does not specify the nature of the will that 'would' or 'would not'; it does not confront the philosophical problem of what is voluntary; it does not specify the conditions of changing consciousness and false consciousness. In a psychological world, mature persons are expected to tame the raw desires engendered by the pleasure principle. In an anthropological world, persons are moulded by culture to want to do what they have to do. In this sense, Rudra points out, social institutions and ideologies are power. Their power is exercised at the stage of socialization when a will is being created. Where this exercise is successful, the preferences of the socialized person are its residues, and appear as voluntary intent rather than as compliance with power.

Neither psychologically nor culturally is socialization ever so complete and all-encompassing that one can predict reliably what a fully socialized person 'would' do. The world is full of adapters who want to do what a particular cultural definition has told them to want. The same adapters stand ready, with all appearance of willingness, to fit into environments which demand new things of them. One of the functions of fresh ideologies is to make people want things which previous ideologies told them they didn't want.

Volition, for the equilibrium economist, means acceptance of the structure of opportunity offered by the market. A 'voluntary contract', says Desai, is settled when one can 'show that it is in the interest of both parties to a contract to enter into it', interest meaning that 'neither party [is] worse off than he would be without the trade.' 'Will' or 'volition' is given by economists that peculiar signification which some German philosophy developed, in which volition is structured by the acceptance of necessity.

Power defined as the capacity to impose one's will upon another is not confined to those located in formally superior positions in status or economic hierarchies. Power in this sense is also exercised by formal inferiors via a variety of strategies such as withdrawal of efficiency, work to rule, or sabotage—forms of power which are more often preventive than imperative. 'Embezzlement' of grain, manure, and working time by agricultural workers and share-croppers are exercises of the power of the inferior.

Different conceptualizations of power arise depending on whether authors have in mind a neo-classical world in which there is no power; a neo-Marxian world of structurally generated economic power, where power is mainly reflexive of economic relations; or a partly Weberian world of politically generated power, where power arises in a realm that is partly or wholly autonomous of economic relations. The definition offered above does not envision the 'powerless' universe of the classical economists. The neo-classical world posits a frictionless equality among buyers and sellers; nobody wins and nobody loses, and asymmetries do not convey power in the absence of market imperfections. As T. N. Srinivasan put it, '. . . in the competitive model, no agent has economic power in spite of . . . asymmetry. The reason is that each employer is in (actual or potential) competition with numerous other similarly placed employers for the services of his employee so that the asymmetry of hiring or firing does not confer any power [on] him in the sense of his being able to strike a deal more favorable than the market would allow' (1981).

'Would not' by contrast is a concept implying friction. People are seen as wanting to do all sorts of things, or not do all sorts of things, that the market mechanism enables or disables them to do. Desai intends to work with a definition of choice processes which accommodates the notion of friction (i.e., power): 'If my product and consumption activities are voluntarily chosen (albeit subject to budget/technology constraint) then we are in a situation where power does not matter. Once I can be forced to do things involuntarily, we depart from the powerless situation.' Srinivasan responds to this attempt by pointing out, as I do above in connection with the definition of power as the imposition of will, the slippery nature of the idea of voluntarism and involuntarism. (Does a contract in which I accept restrictions because of my economic weakness create a voluntary situation?) Yet though there is much indeterminancy in the conception of voluntarism—'true' intent, 'false' consciousness, changing understanding and interests—can a normative social science do without it? Or even a purely empirical one?

Others too pursue the concept of friction. For Rudra, power is a social phenomenon generated by institutions and ideologies. Power operates on the economic system by preventing markets from coming into existence (i.e., *causing* non-existence of markets) and by preventing markets from becoming perfect (as defined by economic theory). The non-existing labour market among the adjoining villages which he surveyed arises from their institutional nature as autonomous units. The persistent hold of local networks illustrates the role of institutional frameworks in generating the power that restrains the emergence of markets.

The modes of conceptualizing power vary along a continuum that emphasizes purely economic factors at one end and purely political at the other. Desai and Herring both employ the idea of the surplus as a measure of power, but in ways that suggest the contrasting conceptualization of an economic and political emphasis. Desai sees the surplus as 'the distance between actual consumption and subsistence consumption'. It is his measure of the relative power of the client versus the landowner. A second measure is 'the gap between the rates of return earned by the different parties'. These are measures that assess power as arising from *within* the process of production and exchange. For Herring, by contrast, it is not the *size* of the surplus, but the capacity to *control* the surplus which is the measure of power. While this conception suggests power is in its origins economic (accumulation of surplus), it is in its exercise—disposition of the surplus—affected by social structural and political local and translocal forces, forces exterior to the production process. The Rudolphs start yet further toward the other end of the continuum, with the possibility that power can be generated by forces that are at least partially autonomous of local economic relationships. It can be mobilized by social solidarities, political leadership, and translocal political and administrative networks that are not grounded in or generated by local economic relations.

Power and Productivity

The central problematic for this volume was how local power structures impinge upon levels of and changes in agricultural production or productivity. The focus on local agrarian structures quickly expanded to suggest the relevance of translocal forces as well. But the question remained, do some power relations obstruct productivity? Do others facilitate it? 'The interesting question that needs to be looked into,' writes Chakravarti, 'is whether differences in power structures have played an important causal role in the region-specific success of the [green] "Revolution".' There are some possible answers: 'Absentee landlordism has not been a characteristic feature of the regions which have experienced the sharpest rates of increase. Secondly, owner cultivators have a much larger role to play in [green revolution] regions as compared with tenant cultivators who operate largely on the basis of oral leases which are virtually renewed every year, a characteristic which is typical of the Eastern Gangetic region.'

This line of argument has been pursued elsewhere by Harris (1980), Bhaduri (1973) and Prasad (1975) and several Planning Commission policy documents, and been rebutted by yet others, such as Bardhan and Rudra (1978, 1980, 1981). It has especially taken the direction that 'semi-feudal' configurations block the transition to a technically progressive capitalist agriculture. But it has also taken a more general form, voiced by the Indian Planning Commission's Task Force on Agrarian Relations in 1973, that local power structures are 'insurmountable hurdles in the path of the spread of modern technology and improved agricultural practices' (Government of India, 1976).

Our authors, by contrast, find the relationship between power structures and productivity highly variable. Chakravarti suggests the general reluctance of our contributors to commit themselves to sweeping propositions that transcend the data. In contrast to the assertions that 'semi-feudal relations' obstruct productivity he points to the considerable literature that suggests Bihar and Bengal over-lords are not necessarily blocked from technical innovation by their 'semi-feudal' status. The growth of wheat agriculture as well as innovative crops such as summer paddy and potato in Bengal in 'semi-feudal' conditions suggests limits on the formulation of strong causal connections. Chaudhuri articulates a similar stance when he shows the great difficulty of formulating general propositions about the effects on agrarian production of Bengal zamindars and *jotedars*. Their impact on production and productivity has fluctuated widely over time in ways that suggest local power structures must always be placed in their contexts. Productivity depends also on demographic change, price levels, legislative interventions—all circumstances beyond the reach of local power structures.

Finally, Attwood's observations in the Maharashtra sugar area lead him to a more radical conclusion which denies that in his area control of land is relevant to productivity. In sugar cultivation, he asserts, human capital is more important than physical capital or land. Control and quality of cultivation, not land, is the central feature. Attwood's Saswad Malis typically rent in lands, and soon move on to new rented lands. They do so at their choice, not the will of the rentier. For Attwood, a 'truly' maximizing perspective may be expressed through such serial tenancy rather than land control.

We do formulate some general propositions. On the one hand, the disproportionate concentration of scarce resources—water, extension information, credit—on the powerful agriculturists, often at the expense of the less powerful, diminishes the productive potential of small farms, even though their telescoping of management with higher quality family labour often makes small farms more productive users of inputs. On the other hand, as Herring notes, concentrated economic and political power permits risk-taking in investment, breakthroughs with respect to administrative bottlenecks that prevent productivity, and (to the extent it is combined with superior education and information) better management.

The association between productivity and power is shaped by variations in regional and ecological circumstances. Thus Chakravarti notes that in the Eastern Gangetic plain declining yield rates and growing man–land ratios point toward what Geertz in Java called agricultural involution. Agricultural involution in the region is associated with highly asymmetrical social profiles and more oppressive power structures. Chakravarti suggests the association but declines to specify the direction of causality. Ludden suggests a somewhat different and more sweeping distinction between the agrarian structures of wet and dry areas and their association with productivity. The wet may be associated with steep social profiles, high class conflict, slow agricultural growth and immiseration of a class of servile labour. The dry may be associated with less steep social hierarchies, less class cleavage, greater agricultural growth and more cultivator's own labour. The Rudolphs note that the wet areas and steep social hierarchies are in some cases associated with the propensity for mobilization. Areas such as sections of Thanjavur and Palghat often have a high proportion of landless labour to owners, facilitating organization and mobilization from below *if* leadership is available.

There are limits, however, to the usefulness of such macro-distinctions. Many areas escape the typologies: Punjab is wet, with high agricultural growth and a high proportion of self-cultivating labour. As Binoy Chaudhuri shows, ecologically similar lands and structurally similar power relations may produce quite different outcomes depending on the nature of the crop—as when *jotedars* (masters of share-croppers) bear the costs of investment in cash crops but not in subsistence crops. Or again, as the Rudolphs point out, in the Eastern Gangetic plain one would predict greater mobilization because hierarchies are steep and the proportion of landless labour is high. But in the absence of leadership, mobilization has been weak. Still, the attempt at typologies that unite ecological and sociological elements suggests hypotheses concerning the complex associations between region, ecology, agrarian structure and productivity. Because regularities are elusive does not mean they cannot be approximated.

Another important element in the discussion of power and productivity is the debate over the connection between large size and inefficiency as against small size and efficiency which has been hypothesized for South Asia. Rudra in earlier work questioned such an association—without, however, claiming much for the reverse (1968a, 1968b, 1976). Herring argues that there may be a shift over historical time in the nature of the association. In the initial phases of the green revolution, smaller size holdings may indeed have been more efficient due to the unification of 'labour' and 'management' that characterizes such small-scale production. On the other hand, when new technology is combined with economies of scale, small farmers may lose their advantage.

A leading implication of the power/productivity nexus has been that increased productivity requires changes in agrarian power structures. If the relationship between power and productivity is indeed as variable as this volume suggests, it becomes more ambiguous which power structures under which circumstances favour productivity. The studies in this volume indicate that the relationship is complex, contextual, and not easily captured in large generalizations of the kind represented by the 'semi-feudal' formulation. If this is so, the case for altering the power structure has to rest mainly on political and equity grounds.

Linkages

Another concern of this volume is with linkages. As Ludden suggests, the history, politics and anthropology of agriculture has set individual scholars mining disparate and often incomparable sets of data in particular localities. It is often hard to piece these together and establish the general meaning of major constellations of phenomena. Economists, on the other hand, 'because of their data, methods and polemical heritage . . . prefer to focus on the aggregate, not local phenomena'. Most of the studies in this volume mean to supply the linkages required to integrate the value and relevance of aggregate and specific formulations. They do so along both vertical and horizontal dimensions. The problem of the vertical is how the study of one level elucidates the study of others. 'Level' can refer to geopolitical locations (the centre, state, district, village); to degrees of empirical specificity or theoretical abstraction; and to the extent to which data are or are not contextualized.

To take first the geo-political dimension of the vertical, our contributors stress the extent to which layers of action constrain each other. It is a commonplace of South Asian social science that local power structures have a propensity to divert, redirect, and appropriate to their own purposes whatever policies national and state legislation mandated. It is a commonplace that partly dictated the problematic of this volume. Numerous studies by official and non-official authors have confirmed this perspective in connection with panchayats, credit and marketing cooperatives, and in relation to the impact of tenancy, ceiling and other agrarian legislation (Rosenthal 1977; Weiner 1968; Brass 1966; Carras 1972; Narain 1976). It would be inappropriate, however, to narrow the lens to a purely local focus. Higher levels also constrain local power; system levels affect each other reciprocally. In Herring's formulation, the effective enforcement of the Kerala Agricultural Workers Act of 1974, an instrument of the state political process, effectively removed decisions about the hiring and firing of agricultural labour from the local arena by giving labourers permanent rights to their jobs. Binoy Chaudhuri shows the constraints on local power, specifically on the Bengal zamindars' capacity to act, by British legislation regulating rent enhancement. On the other hand, we know that in other situations local power is determinative: ceilings and tenancy legislation in many states remained unenforced because not backed by powerful political forces such as those in Kerala, or by a relatively 'autonomous' state, such as that of the raj in Bengal.

The linkage between 'levels' as a problem in specificity and abstraction is illustrated by the spectrum covered by the economists contributing to this volume. At one end of the spectrum is Rudra's radically empirical study of 39 Bengal villages, testing the 'usual assumption' concerning the existence of a market for labour—which he disconfirms. At the other end is Desai's model of a theory of power and productivity. In between is Chakravarti's middle level review, straddling theory and context, of the fit between historical and regional data on the one hand and neo-classical assumptions on the other. All three contributors work with agendas set by neo-classical economics, though their relationship to these agendas is more critical than supportive.

The level of abstraction is revealed as *the* problematic of the neo-classical framework in the South Asian setting. Local level data pervasively negate the 'usual assumptions'; Desai's model attempts to link the modes of abstract reasoning native to econometric methods to the prevailing South Asian empirical realities. His model treats the power relations typical of South Asian local systems as a central assumption rather than as peripheral, a market imperfection.

The third problem of the vertical concerns linkages between contextual and non-contextual data. Much of our understanding of South Asian agrarian reality derives from macro-aggregative time series such as those prepared by the census and the National Sample Survey. While such data are useful for estimating magnitudes and trends, their level of abstraction is such that it cannot easily capture specific power configurations, and the prospects for action. As the Rudolphs suggest, the overall growth in numbers of agricultural workers cannot help with predicting their propensity for mobilization. The aggregative figures obscure, for example, the difference between *tehsils* where such workers constitute 60 per cent and others where they constitute 20 per cent of the agricultural work-force, quite apart from the problem that objective realities do not translate automatically into motives for action.

The problem of the horizontal is less a matter of linkages than of comparison and contrast. What can a study of Puddokottai tell us about Meerut? Can both cases be captured meaningfully in a common analytic framework? Alternatively, why must a researcher resist the impulse to apply findings in Bengal to Gujarat? The ecological frameworks already mentioned and employed by the Rudolphs and Ludden help provide a common framework. Certain geographically scattered regions exhibit similar features—in the structure of agrarian relations and the organization of production. The East Gangetic Delta and Thanjavur are sufficiently alike that the fact of stagnation in one and rising productivity in the other, or the lack of mobilization of agricultural workers in one and effective mobilization in the other, needs to be explained.

On the one hand, it is necessary to seek out common frameworks. On the other, it is important to resist the impulse to generalize. Again and again the discussion of findings in this volume forced us into the enterprise of contrast. The findings for the Maharashtra sugar area depict utterly different social phenomena than do findings for Kerala and Bengal. In a country that has greater cultural and ecological diversity than Europe, it is essential to recognize that different political and administrative subsystems (the political constellations of particular states), combined with strongly differentiated cultural and historical traditions, create different outcomes. Elsewhere Paul Brass (1973), contrasting the implementation of particular programmes in Bihar and Punjab, has shown that similar policies and legislation produce highly diverse results in the two states. In this volume, Attwood advances such a contrast by comparing the different outcomes for sugar growers' productivity of Maharashtra's vertical integration between sugar cooperatives and sugar mills and the lack of such integration in U.P.'s government founded mills.

The notion that conclusions about agriculture generated in Southern Spain may not apply to North Germany is self-evident. The notion that conclusions generated in Puddokottai may not apply to Meerut has still to be learned. The propensity to deduce the future of Indian agriculture, or even of Andhra agriculture, from 'my tehsil' dies hard.

The themes suggested in these introductory remarks are suggestive, not exhaustive, of the problems addressed and conclusions reached in the volume. We have attempted to give readers some sense for the state of the art; to suggest what lines of inquiry have yielded enough information that one can confirm or disconfirm prevalent hypotheses; to divert researchers from some false paths; to suggest the complexity and differentiation of agricultures' socio-ecological arenas; and to use critique and reformulate middle range and macro-theory. Throughout, we have sought to guide our enterprise toward a political economy that is more comprehensive and sensitive to culture and history.

REFERENCES

Bardhan, P. and A. Rudra (1978), 'Interlinkage of Land, Labour and Credit Relations: An Analysis of Village Survey Data in East India', *Economic and Political Weekly*, Vol. 13, Nos. 6 and 7.

—— (1980), 'Terms and Conditions of Sharecropping Contracts: An Analysis of Village Survey Data in India', *Journal of Development Studies*, Vol. 16, No. 3.

Bhaduri, A. (1973), 'A Study in Agricultural Backwardness under Semi-Feudalism', *Economic Journal*, Vol. 83.

Brass, Paul (1966), *Factional Politics in an Indian State: The Congress Party in Uttar Pradesh* (Berkeley: University of California Press).

—— (1973), 'The Politics of Ayurvedic Education: A Case Study of Revivalism and Modernization in India' in Susanne Hoeber Rudolph and Lloyd I. Rudolph (eds), *Education and Politics in India: Studies in Policy, Organization and Society* (Cambridge, Mass.: Harvard University Press).

Carras, Mary C. (1972), *The Dynamics of Indian Political Factions* (Cambridge: Cambridge University Press).

Engels, Friedrich (1954), *Anti-Duhring: Herr Eugen Duhring's Revolution in Science* (Moscow: Foreign Language Publishing House).

Gouldner, Alvin (1964), *Patterns of Industrial Bureaucracy* (New York: The Free Press of Glencoe).

Government of India, Ministry of Agriculture and Irrigation (1976), *Report of the National Commission on Agriculture* (New Delhi).

Harris, John C. (1980), 'Contemporary Marxist Analysis of the Agrarian Question in India', Madras Institute of Development Studies Working Paper No. 14 (Madras).

Herring, Ronald (1980), ' "A Paddy Field is not a Factory," Production Relations and Redistributive Policy in South India' (Wisconsin Conference on South Asia, November, mimeo).

Ludden, David (1977), 'Rapporteur's Report: The Planning Meeting for a Subcommittee of the Joint Committee on South Asia on "South Asian Political Economy" ' (13–15 June).

Narain, Iqbal (ed.) (1976), *State Politics in India* (Meerut: Meenakshi Prakashan).

Prasad, P. H. (1975), 'Limits to Investment Planning' in A. Mitra (ed.), *Economic Theory and Planning: Essays in Honour of A. K. Das Gupta* (Delhi: Oxford University Press).

Rosenthal, Donald B. (1977), *The Expansive Elite: District Politics and State Policy-making in India* (Berkeley: University of California Press).

Rudra, Ashok (1968a), 'Farm Size and Yield per Acre', *Economic and Political Weekly*, Vol. 3, Nos. 26–28 (July).

—— (1968b), 'More on Returns to Scale in Indian Agriculture', *Economic and Political Weekly*, Vol. 3, No. 43 (26 October).

Rudra, Ashok and G. Mukhopadhyaya (1976), 'Hiring of Labour by Poor Peasants', *Economic and Political Weekly* (10 January).

Social Science Research Council, Committee on Comparative Politics (1963), *Communications and Political Development*, edited by Lucien Pye (Princeton: Princeton University Press).

—— (1963), *Bureaucracy and Political Development*, edited by Joseph LaPalombara (Princeton: Princeton University Press).

—— (1964), *Political Modernization in Japan and Turkey*, edited by Robert E. Ward and Dankwart A. Rustow (Princeton: Princeton University Press).

—— (1965), *Education and Political Development*, edited by James S. Coleman (Princeton: Princeton University Press).

—— (1965), *Political Culture and Political Development*, edited by Lucien Pye and Sidney Verba (Princeton: Princeton University Press).

—— (1966), *Political Parties and Political Development*, edited by Joseph La-Palombara and Myron Weiner (Princeton: Princeton University Press).

—— (1971), *Crises and Sequences in Political Development*, edited by Leonard Binder *et al.* (Princeton: Princeton University Press).

Social Science Research Council, Joint Committee on South Asia (1978), 'Proposal for South Asian Political Economy' (April).

Srinivasan, T. N. (1981), 'Comments on Meghnad Desai's Paper, "Political Power and Agricultural Productivity" ' (September, mimeo).

Weiner, Myron (1968), *State Politics in India* (Princeton: Princeton University Press).

Capital and the Transformation of Agrarian Class Systems: Sugar Production in India

DONALD W. ATTWOOD

Why do some agrarian systems generate more economic growth than others? Why do some undergo structural transformations leading to further growth, while others stagnate?

In parts of western India, the cultivators are renowned for their high yields of sugar cane and for their rapid expansion of cane production in several spurts over the last 100 years. These cane growers are also renowned for having established and managed numerous cooperative sugar factories with considerable efficiency, thus changing the whole organization of sugar production in this region. The cultivators in other parts of India, such as Punjab, have shown a similar entrepreneurial spirit, while those in yet other regions cling to old techniques and relations of production. How are these differences in economic growth and organizational dynamism to be explained?

This question is often discussed in terms of the different kinds of agrarian class systems which may either promote or inhibit economic innovation. But this approach tends to assume that class systems are somehow self-determining. Are not class systems also reshaped by economic forces in the processes of production and distribution? The argument of this essay is that such forces may be found in the different levels of capital investment and managerial skill required for different kinds of production systems.[1]

[1] I am very pleased to be able to thank the following for their comments on earlier versions of this essay: D. Aronson, S. Bandopadhyay, B. S. Baviskar, D. Kumar, R. F. Salisbury, P. C. Salzman, D. Von Eschen, R. Attwood and the

The question why some class systems generate growth and change was at the heart of nineteenth-century sociology, especially in the works of Karl Marx and Max Weber. This tradition has been carried forward in recent times by Barrington Moore (1966) and Jeffery Paige (1975), both of whom argue that certain kinds of class systems facilitate economic change, while others inhibit it. This tradition has been broadened recently by greater attention to ecological variables, which are seen to shape these contrasting types of agrarian systems (e.g. Popkin 1979).

In the interpretation of Indian history, the significance of ecological variables is just beginning to be recognized. Sporadically, anthropologists have drawn attention to the importance of rainfall and irrigation in shaping population densities and social structures (cf. Mencher 1966; Béteille 1974: Ch. 5; Beals 1974). Most of India gets its rain during just a few months of the year, and half the continent gets 30 inches or less (Lewis 1970: 18). Consequently, water supply is the critical constraint in Indian agriculture. Those areas more favoured by the rains evolved systems of wet-rice production, which historically supported denser populations and more complex social structures, including more elaborate hierarchies and larger proportions of landless labourers (Stein 1980; Ludden 1984). Such elaborate hierarchies may impede economic innovation, in part because the local landowners withdraw from active management of crop production, the work being left in the hands of tenants, share-croppers, or dependent labourers (Stokes 1978: Ch. 10; Ludden 1984). Consequently, those who have the resources to invest in new technologies lack the skills or incentives to do so efficiently.[2]

On the other hand, when dry areas, such as Punjab, become irrigated, they seem to respond more dynamically to new markets and new technologies. For one thing, the previous low productivity of the soil meant that a dense population of dependent labourers or

---

members of the SAPE conference. The research for this essay was made possible by grants from the Social Sciences and Humanities Research Council of Canada, with additional funding from the Shastri Indo-Canadian Institute, the Center for Developing Area Studies (McGill), and the Faculty of Graduate Studies and Research (McGill).

[2] In a related argument, Lewis (1970: 22–7) has stressed that high population density is an impediment in its own right to economic growth, since this makes it difficult to free up land from staple foodgrain production for experimentation with new crops and techniques.

share-croppers could not be maintained. Consequently, the local landowners were experienced cultivators and were prepared to try new crops and new technologies with a 'hands on' approach (Stokes 1978).[3] Moreover, since irrigation multiplies the productivity of the soil, the effective land area is multiplied; and with population densities already relatively low, the dry-land people then have less worry about feeding themselves and can afford to specialize more in the production of crops for the market (Lewis 1970).

Thus recent research suggests that ecological variations shape agrarian class systems, which in turn shape opportunities for economic change. This essay confirms the ecological approach, as far as it goes. The historical analysis presented here concerns the impact of a new cash-crop regime in an area of low rainfall and low population density, concluding with a discussion of the contrasting impact of the same crop in a region of higher rainfall and population.

However, this essay is concerned with another question besides the ecological and social preconditions for economic growth; the focus is rather on the economic processes which reshape the production system, including the system of class relations. The argument is that a cropping system which demands heavy capital investment also stimulates a high demand for human capital—that is, for skills to manage the investment efficiently. Efforts to improve managerial efficiency then stimulate technical and organizational innovations which provide something of an internal engine for growth and structural transformation. Stated more explicitly, the argument runs as follows:

(1) Assume, first, that capital is very scarce (even scarcer than land in the dry, low-density regions) and thus very expensive (entailing high interest rates and opportunity costs) and very risky to use.

(2) Assume, next, that the cultivators must invest a lot of capital in order to produce an expensive new cash crop for the market. (They might need to do this either because labour is scarce, or because the technical requirements of the crop make it necessary, or for both

[3] Under premodern conditions, according to Stein (1980: 27–8), the most skilful managers were the dry-land cultivators who also held small patches of garden land under well or tank irrigation, since they had to experiment with a range of options concerning what crops to grow with what amounts of water. Stein's analysis applies to medieval south India, but it also specifies perfectly the group of cultivators who transformed the agrarian system of the Bombay Deccan through their technical and organizational innovations in the twentieth century.

reasons.) Such an investment puts the cultivators in a high-risk situation.

(3) Consequently, they will be forced to try to reduce their risks and costs by learning to manage the new crop as efficiently as possible.

(4) As a result, they will seek to adopt new technologies, in order to reduce costs per unit output. They may, for example, invest in fixed capital (such as machinery) in order to save expenditures on working capital (for example, on the cost of labour).

(5) As another result, non-cultivators will be unable to seize control of the production process (or of the profits, which amounts to the same thing), since they lack the skills necessary to manage the new capital investments on their own account, and since those who have the skills will not undertake the risks without a share of the rewards. Consequently, the cultivators will assume and retain control of production and a good share of the profits.

(6) As a further result, the cultivators will be able and motivated to enhance their control over the relations of production and distribution by reorganizing them when opportunities arise.

(7) Finally, in a region where the second assumption (of high demand for capital) does not apply, these results (skilful management, technical innovation, cultivator control, and organizational innovation) are less likely to follow.

The Cost of Sugar Cane Cultivation in the Bombay Deccan

In the semi-arid plateau region known as the Bombay Deccan, along the western side of the Indian peninsula, population densities were relatively low during the nineteenth century,[4] and land could be rented at reasonable rates. Most villagers cultivated their own plots; there were not many landless labourers or share-croppers (see Fukazawa 1983; McAlpin 1983: Ch. 4). Agriculture was a 'gamble in the rains' and the rains (averaging only about 20 inches per annum in the driest areas) were sparse and uncertain. Water was scarcer and more valuable than land. In the drier areas, wells often had to be sunk as deep as 40 feet or so, costing as much as Rs 1,000 or 1,500 to dig and line with masonry (Indian Irrigation Commission [IIC] 1902: 221). These wells were able to irrigate, at best, only about four acres

[4] In 1881 the population density of the Bombay Deccan was 144.1 persons per square mile (Baines 1882: Vol. I, p. 2).

apiece; and they were expensive to use, costing something like Rs 30 per acre per year for labour, repairs, bullock feed, and so forth (Taylor 1856). These wells were used to protect the staple grain crops against drought and to water small patches of garden crops, including sugar cane. However, when the rains failed altogether, as happened about once every five years or so, the wells dried up too, so this region was considered the most famine-prone in India.

To provide some protection against famines, the Bombay government began constructing large-scale canal irrigation systems in the late nineteenth century. Because there were no snow-fed rivers in peninsular India, the rivers dried up in the worst droughts; consequently, the new Deccan canals required large storage dams at their heads, to catch rainwater during the brief monsoon season and release it gradually during the subsequent dry seasons. These storage works were built in the coastal mountains, where the monsoon never failed, and they made the Deccan canals from three to six times more expensive than the canals of northern India, where snow-fed rivers ran all year round (IIC 1902: 225). The high cost of canal water was one reason that the cultivators along the Deccan canals were reluctant, at first, to use the new water on a regular basis (ibid.; cf. Attwood 1980).

In the 1890s, however, new cultivators belonging to the Mali (gardener) caste migrated from their native town of Saswad, near Poona, to the new canal tracts. These Saswad Malis were experienced in growing garden crops on well irrigation, and they soon found they could make handsome profits by raising sugar cane along the canals. Given the soils and climate of the region, sugar cane was the only crop which grew well under canal irrigation and also fetched a good price on the market (Inglis and Gokhale 1934; Attwood 1980). Consequently, it seemed to be the only crop which could stimulate a regular demand for water from the canals, and the whole system of canal administration was redesigned to suit the needs of this crop and of the innovators who were growing it (Visvesvaraya 1903). From 1890 to 1903, the area under cane on the largest canal, the Nira Left Bank Canal, rose from less than 300 to 8,500 acres. By 1928 there were 40,000 acres on five canal systems (Inglis and Gokhale 1934: 34–5).

This rapid growth of sugar cane production entailed much more than a simple change in the normal cropping system, because cane was far more expensive than other crops. Sugar cane demanded both fixed capital investments (in levelling the land, purchasing stronger bullocks and heavier implements, etc.) and also heavy working capital expenditures to cover the recurrent costs of cultivation. As mentioned, the canal water itself was quite expensive. Sugar cane was a thirsty crop, demanding regular irrigation every ten days or so, all year round. After 1900, the rate for year-round canal irrigation was set at Rs 27 per acre (Visvesvaraya 1903: 12). This was no less than three-and-a-half times the *total* cost per acre of growing staple foodgrains on dry land (Mann and Kanitkar 1921: 76, 80).

However, the cost of irrigation was by no means the heaviest charge on the cultivators' working capital. The largest share of the costs (some 45 to 50 per cent) went for farmyard manure, oilcake fertilizer, sometimes chemical fertilizer, and seed cane—a total cost of about Rs 230 per acre around 1910 (Knight 1914: 33; Inglis and Gokhale 1928: 15).

Additional heavy charges went for hired labour and the hiring or upkeep of bullocks. Before planting, the crop required three ploughings interspersed with harrowing, then manure spreading, ridging and furrowing. Planting was followed by five weedings, by another manuring, and by earthing up (or mounding earth around the young plants to prevent lodging later on). In addition, labour was needed every ten days all year round for irrigation. And finally, a large team effort was required for cutting the cane, carting it to the crushing mill, crushing it, boiling the juice, and making it into *gul* or crude sugar, which was then carted off to the nearest market. Sugar cane deteriorates rapidly once it is cut, so it must either be processed on a small scale in the fields or delivered promptly to a large-scale factory for manufacture into white sugar. Until the 1930s, there were almost no white sugar factories along the Deccan canals, so the cane growers manufactured *gul*, using bullock-driven cane crushers and big, shallow iron pans for boiling the syrup. The cost of all these operations (several of which included hiring bullocks as well as men) came to a total of about Rs 160 to 220 per acre around 1910, or 35 to 40 per cent of total recurrent costs (Knight 1914: 33; Inglis and Gokhale 1928: 15).

The small-scale cane grower could do many of these operations (such as ploughing, spreading manure, weeding and irrigating) with his own family labour and his own bullocks, thus reducing his cash expenditures. However, there were several big operations (ridging and furrowing, earthing up, and cutting, carting, crushing and boiling) which were better done by contract teams, costing a total of at least Rs 135 per acre (Knight 1914: 33). Labour costs were high, not only because the crop demanded a lot of work in certain crucial periods, as well as regular attention throughout the year; but also because labour was hard to get in this region of low population density, especially during the harvest season.

In addition to all these running costs, the cultivators needed improved implements, stronger bullocks, better cane crushers and boiling furnaces. These they could either rent or purchase as fixed-capital investments. Investment costs are discussed in the next section; for the moment, we may note that the rental cost of a bullock-driven cane crusher was about Rs 8 per acre in 1905 (Knight 1905: 14). The rental cost (and presumably the depreciation) for machinery, then, was not very high compared to other running costs (such as those for labour and fertilizers). This provided a strong incentive for any fixed capital investment which might reduce working capital expenditures.

To summarize, in the rapid expansion of sugar cane production before World War I, average working capital costs ranged from Rs 300 to 500 per acre, which was something like 50 to 70 times the cost of growing foodgrains on dry land. At that time, sugar cane in the Bombay Deccan was probably the most expensive crop grown in India. Cane was also an expensive crop in other regions, compared with foodgrains or cotton, for example. However, in the northern provinces where most of India's sugar cane was being grown at that time, the average cost of cane cultivation was at most about Rs 100 per acre, or 20 to 30 per cent of the cost in Bombay (Sahasrabudhe 1914: 5).

There were two main reasons why costs in the Bombay Deccan were so much higher. First, there was much less rainfall in the Deccan than in Bihar and eastern U.P., where most of the northern cane was grown; consequently, much more irrigation, with more expensive water, was required in the Deccan. Second, the local variety of cane required a lot of fertilizer, especially when grown on canal irrigation. The canal-irrigated valleys were low-lying, with heavy black soils which became sticky and waterlogged under copious irrigation; consequently, large doses of organic manure were needed not only for their supply of nitrogen (which was also critical) but to maintain the physical quality of the soil (Knight 1914: 12–13). As we shall see, many growers actually applied far too much irrigation and fertilizer to their cane crops. However, careful experimentation by the Department of Agriculture established that at least Rs 138 worth of fertilizers per acre were required for a good yield. The other costs (for labour, bullocks, and equipment) were in proportion to this amount. Even with the most thrifty methods, the cost of cultivation would still have been about Rs 320 per acre (ibid.: 34)—still well in excess of the requirements for other crops, or even for sugar cane itself in other provinces. Consequently, we may wonder whether the unusual capital demands of this crop also entailed special managerial skills, or exerted special pressures on the organization of production and distribution.

Management of an Expensive Crop

One argument of this essay is that a capital-intensive crop demands increasingly careful management in order to reduce costs and risks. An indication of careful management is the willingness to adopt new seeds, methods and implements, in order to economize on running costs.

The local variety of cane gave good yields under intensive cultivation; and until the 1920s, the central cane-breeding station at Coimbatore concentrated on improving varieties for north Indian conditions, where most of the sugar cane was grown (Indian Sugar Committee [ISC] 1921: 381–95). Thus markedly improved varieties did not appear in the Bombay Deccan until the 1930s, when they spread fairly rapidly (Agricultural Marketing Advisor [AMA] 1943: 12).

Meanwhile, the cane growers found other avenues for improvement. From about 1880, heavy iron ploughs came to replace the indigenous wooden type over much of the canal areas. The iron plough, which cost about Rs 45 in 1905, turned the soil deeper, improving its texture under heavy irrigation. The iron harrow, which cost about Rs 100 to 200 by 1914, was better for mixing manure into the soil. The iron plough required three teams of bullocks to draw it, but it did the work two or three times faster than the wooden plough, saving on the cost of labour (Knight 1905: 4; 1914: 6–11).

Crushing the sugar cane, boiling the juice and making *gul* were operations where careful management and improved equipment paid good dividends. The quality and market value of the *gul* depended in large part on the timing of the harvest and the care with which the *gul* was made (Knight 1914: 30–1); and *gul* made in the Bombay Deccan was known for its high quality (ISC 1921: 278). As the Saswad Malis migrated into the new canal areas, they brought not only better equipment but more efficient methods of organizing contract teams to do the harvesting and processing operations— methods which were then copied by the local cultivators (Patil 1928: 17). An improved furnace, for example, was adopted along the canals, saving about Rs 30 per acre in the cost of fuel for boiling the juice. Other furnace improvements were designed and publicized by the Department of Agriculture (Knight 1914: 26–7; Patil 1927: 1). The cost of building such a furnace was Rs 45 for the size needed to process about five acres of cane (Patil 1928: 15).

The adoption of new cane crushers was quite rapid. In the late nineteenth century, most of the indigenous crushers were wooden, though old stone crushers were also found here and there. Bullock-driven iron crushers became common along the canals, however, by 1906. The Department of Agriculture, again, promoted their use and helped to improve their design (Patil 1927: 4–7). The advantages of these iron crushers were that they extracted about 14 per cent more juice from the cane, they worked faster, and they saved labour (Knight 1914: 25). By 1927, these iron crushers cost about Rs 200 to 300 (Patil 1927: 7–8).

As we have just seen, all this new equipment was relatively moderate in cost, compared with the normal running costs of cultivation. Consequently, the growers were eager to adopt these new technologies, making fixed capital investments (or obtaining equipment on hire) in order to reduce their working capital expenditures as much as possible. Even heavier machinery was adopted by some growers.

Cane crushers powered by oil engines were expensive per unit, though not per acre for the larger growers. Power crushers were introduced by the Agriculture Department: in 1914 there were only three or four in the whole Bombay Deccan, but by 1927 the number was more than 45 (ibid.: 18). These power mills saved a lot of human and bullock labour, as well as fodder for the bullocks, and they extracted about 10 per cent more cane juice than the bullock-driven crushers (ibid.: 10–11; Knight 1914: 26). Power crushers were really necessary for growers with more than 20 acres of cane, but the capital cost was too high for a smaller grower. A small power crusher, along with multiple furnace and other equipment suitable for processing 20 to 45 acres of cane, cost about Rs 6,100 in 1927. Larger units ranged up to Rs 14,200, with enough capacity for 100 acres (Patil 1927: 14).

There was clearly, then, a tendency for different factor proportions to be used on different sized holdings, the larger ones becoming more capital-intensive and the smaller ones remaining more labour-intensive. All the new equipment enabled the cane growers to save on the cost of human and bullock labour. The larger growers, who depended much more on hired than family labour, found this economical not only because hired labour was costly, but because it was sometimes hard to get at all. Most of the harvest and *gul*-making labour was supplied by migratory contract teams, consisting of cultivators with their bullock carts, from the dry villages outside the canal tracts. However, when the rains were good, these cultivators preferred to stay home tending their own crops and were not available to the cane growers, not even when *gul* prices were high and wages too (Patil 1927: 10). By the same token, wages sometimes rose when *gul* prices fell, catching the cane growers in a painful squeeze (Patil 1932: 22). Consequently, the cane growers used family labour, or substituted capital for labour, in whatever quantities they could manage.

Investments in fixed capital were not simply motivated by the high cost of labour, however. The new equipment also improved the efficiency of manure, bullock power, and fuel, as well as the extraction of cane juice. Research by the Department of Agriculture on the experimental farm in Manjri village, near Poona, showed that different methods of cultivation could bring even more savings. Wider spacing of furrows would enable the crop to be weeded and earthed up by bullock-driven implements instead of by hand, and larger cane growers probably adopted some of these suggestions to save labour. There were other aspects of the Manjri method, as it was called, which were neutral to scale: that is, equally beneficial to small and large cane growers. In particular, the method entailed more careful irrigation with about half the total quantity of water used by most of the cultivators (ISC 1921: 163, 170–1). Less irrigation would require less fertilizer, since the cultivators applied very heavy doses to counteract both the leaching of nutrients and the damage to soil texture caused by heavy irrigation (Knight 1914: 12–13). Research at the Manjri farm had shown that more careful irrigation, with less fertilizer, would actually provide yields equal to those achieved with more lavish use of these inputs (ISC 1921: 170; Inglis 1927b: 16). However, the cane growers did not pay much attention to this aspect of the Manjri method until the late 1920s, when they were forced to economize on fertilizers by falling *gul* prices (Inglis and Gokhale 1928: 11–13). Excessive irrigation, meanwhile, was causing heavy damage to low-lying areas due to waterlogging and salination (Mann and Tamhane 1910; Inglis 1927a).

Why were the cane growers slow to economize on the use of water and fertilizer? Did this indicate a lack of careful crop management? There were several reasons for their dilatory adoption of the new method.

In the first place, it was not feasible for the canal administration to measure the volume of water delivered to each field, so the cultivators were able to flood their fields to whatever depth they pleased without having to pay extra. There was no direct monetary pressure to economize on water, and many cultivators living on this dry, dusty plateau probably believed that 'more' was always 'better' when it came to water. Second, it would have required more skilful labour and supervision (which were both costly) to irrigate more carefully (Inglis and Gokhale 1928: 12). Third, the intervals between waterings along the canals were sometimes irregular. A delay of five days or so could damage the crop, especially during the hot season. The cultivators tried to prevent this by soaking the soil more heavily, a technique which sometimes saved the crop at the expense of long-term damage to the soil (ibid.: 9, 12).

In addition to these technical reasons for heavy irrigation, there were also reasons connected with the organization of production and with the economic climate of the time. The Saswad Malis who migrated into the new canal areas had a get-rich-quick attitude. Land rents were cheap, canal water was abundant, and *gul* prices were buoyant. As a result, the Malis adopted the habit of renting lands for short periods, working the soil as hard as possible, then moving on to new holdings and new canal tracts (ibid.: 8; Patil and Patwardhan 1926: 40)—an entrepreneurial style reminiscent of sugar booms in other times and places (Wallerstein 1980: 161–2). The Malis took repeated cane crops from the same fields, instead of rotating with other crops; these repeat crops were less expensive but they exhausted the soil (Patil and Patwardhan 1926: 40; Knight 1914: 22–3). Many local cultivators, who were not tenants, probably copied the Malis without knowing better.

Finally, since Bombay was such a dry province, the demand for *gul* outstripped the local supply. This created a favourable market for the cane growers, who undoubtedly aimed at producing the maximum yields per acre with a view toward earning the maximum *total* profits, even at the expense of diminishing marginal rates of profit. Again, this approach was reminiscent of sugar booms elsewhere.

The growers stuck to this approach, then, until the market was glutted with *gul* in 1923, when they were forced to reduce expenditures on fertilizer and were apparently surprised to learn that the Agriculture Department was right: yields did not decrease as a result (Inglis and Gokhale 1928: 9–12). The more prolonged and serious fall of *gul* prices which began in the late 1920s forced them to economize even more. Whether it also made them more careful irrigators has not yet been ascertained.

What can we say, then, about the general level of management skills employed on this crop? Clearly, these skills varied from one cane grower to the next. Although they criticized the growers for excessive use of water and fertilizer, Inglis and Gokhale (1928: 3–5, 13) stressed that the skill of the grower was a more important determinant of variation in yields and profits than the type or condition of the soil. The methods for measuring 'skill' used by Inglis and Gokhale may have been circular; though at one point they imply that caste (Malis vs. others) was used as a proxy for skill (ibid.: 10). If this was their independent measure of 'skill' (apart from the profits or yields which the skill was supposed to explain), then their results do show a consistently higher performance by the skilful cultivators (ibid.: plate VIII). There was no question that the Saswad Malis, and some of their imitators, were very good at making profits.

There were probably many local cultivators who tried to imitate the lavish methods of the Malis. By the early 1930s, the prolonged drop in *gul* prices had forced many to become stricter in their methods. Those who were slow to adjust were saddled with heavy debts, and some were forced to sell off their lands. However, it is interesting to note that cane production fell off more sharply along the newer canals, where the Mali tenants were concentrated (Inglis and Gokhale 1934: 34–5). Along the older Nira canal, where local cultivators had taken over after the Malis moved on, the area under sugar cane remained remarkably stable. This suggests that most of the local cane growers were able to economize well enough to keep going. Considering that they were caught in an extremely tight squeeze, this seems tribute enough to their managerial abilities.

The point of this section has been to suggest that a capital-intensive crop both demands and stimulates careful management, innovative techniques, and fixed capital investments in order to reduce working capital expenditures. Certainly, these cane growers were renowned for their high yields, comparable to some of the best anywhere (Knight 1914: 1; Patil 1927: 2; Sahasrabudhe 1914: 5), as well as their heavy investments and their high profits. As we have seen also, there is good evidence for the rapid adoption of new technology—using fixed capital investments to economize on working capital and to raise the productivity of labour. Granted, the evidence in this section is not all on the side of careful management, but we have to allow for the excesses of early growth. So long as there was no monetary pressure to economize on the use of land and water, the Malis adopted a wasteful approach to these resources. Among the local cultivators, this approach was perhaps copied carelessly; but the main determinant for all the cane growers was their goal of maximum profits under the given technical and market conditions.

The Organization of Production and Distribution

Another argument of this essay is that the heavy capital and managerial requirements of this crop exerted a strong influence on the organization of production and distribution—or, in other words, on the class relations in this agrarian system.

What relations emerged between the suppliers of land, labour, capital, and human capital? It is a long-standing belief of Marxists and Third World nationalists that the rise of a cash-crop sector within a peasant economy necessarily entails the coercion or displacement (or both) of the indigenous peasantry (cf. Lenin 1956; Patel 1952; Mukherjee 1957; Roseberry 1976). Similarly, a basic assumption of the 'world system' perspective is that the commercialization of agriculture outside the core states of northwestern Europe both depended on and stimulated the rise of coercive labour control systems, such as the second serfdom in Eastern Europe, the slave plantations of the West Indies, and the haciendas of Central

America (Wallerstein 1974: 86–101). Certainly, there were many cases of this type; but one theme of this section is to show that there is no necessary connection between commercialization and coercion of the peasantry or the labour force.

First, consider the suppliers of land. In the late nineteenth century, land was largely in the hands of local cultivators, who did not at first recognize its commercial potential when canal irrigation became available. They were glad to rent it to Mali immigrants at rates which seemed princely but which amounted to only about four or five per cent of the costs of cane cultivation for the Malis. At a rental rate of about Rs 25 per acre in 1914 (Knight 1914: 33), land was simply not the most expensive or scarcest factor of production. Consequently, mere control of the land did not provide effective control over the production of sugar cane. The most enterprising cane growers (the Malis and their imitators) were tenants, renting land both from local villagers and also from a few scattered Rajas in the area. Because control of the land did not provide control of production, these Rajas were only able to collect fixed, monetary rents at moderate rates, just like anybody else. There was no hint of a second serfdom (in part because the Rajas had little influence on state policy towards agriculture). The Rajas, instead, tended to play a progressive role, to the extent that they played any at all. They promoted the spread of irrigated cash cropping, they sponsored new cooperative credit and marketing societies, they also sponsored educational institutions and the establishment of sugar factories (Attwood 1974a; 1974b).

If the Mali tenants were in control of cane production, why did they not demonstrate this control by buying land? The answers are very simple. First, they expected to exhaust the land and move on, so long as there were new canal tracts being opened up. Second, buying land would have meant tying up their working capital. Working capital on the order of Rs 500 per acre was much harder to obtain than rented land at the rate of Rs 25 per acre; so what temptation could there be for a profit-oriented cultivator to sink his capital into land? The pattern of renting rather than buying also prevailed among the Malis' most successful imitators until the 1930s, when new canal tracts were no longer being opened up. (Renting land also had the advantage that the tenants could easily reduce their operations when prices fell, without leaving idle large fixed investments.)

Second, consider the suppliers of working capital. Some cane growers financed themselves out of last year's profits; others had to borrow from *gul* brokers in the market towns and share more of their profits with them (Patil 1932: 21–2). Though they have been accused of cheating the growers, it would be a mistake to assume that these brokers were able to take effective control of the production process and to rake off all the profits through high interest charges, brokerage commissions, creative accounting, and so forth. (This assumption is extremely common in the literature; see, for example, Whitcombe 1972: 171.) Living and working in town, as they had to, the brokers could not supervise the day-to-day production of the crop. On the other hand, without such supervision, lending large amounts of working capital to a partner who did not expect to share in the profits would have been foolhardy. Consequently, the management of the crop (along with its attendant risks and potential profits) had to be left in the hands of the actual cultivator. Would any cultivator have assumed the burden of such management, if all the surplus was extracted by the broker? (The convenient alternative for the cultivator would have been just to grow subsistence crops, thus vastly reducing his credit needs and reliance on the moneylender.) Good management was essential in the growing of this expensive new crop, and managerial skills were scarce. Could these then have gone unrewarded? This argument leads to a seeming paradox: *the larger the credit needs of the crop, the more control the cultivator will have over its production, and the more likely he is to take a large share of the profits.*

What evidence is there to support this reasoning? Direct evidence on the sharing of profits and losses between moneylenders and cultivators is always extremely difficult to obtain. However, the indirect evidence seems conclusive. Many of the small cane growers, for example, were able to expand their scale of operations, in a few cases to areas of 500 acres or more (see Attwood 1979). Moreover, many were also able to invest in new cattle, implements, cane crushers, irrigation wells, houses, business enterprises, and so forth.[5] In these cases, at least, it is evident that the *gul* brokers did not extract all the surplus from cane production.

We might also note that the brokers did not attempt, or were not able, to parlay their control of credit into control of land: that is, they did not become big rentier landlords. The reasons have already

[5] Research in progress includes long-term rates of investment among landholders of different sizes. See note 7 below.

been suggested: ownership of the land alone did not mean control over cane production; and, as in other parts of India, the money-lenders did not want to tie up their working capital in land—not even at the artificially low prices which might be obtained by foreclosing on mortgages (cf. Musgrave 1978). It was not the direct cost which inhibited them, but rather the opportunity cost.

This leads to an interesting conclusion. If the brokers, who had access to capital and who could have taken over plenty of land (especially during the great depression), did not become the dominant class in this production system, this must have been because *human capital was more important than physical capital or land*— that is, it was a stronger determinant of variations in yields and profits (cf. Schultz 1964). This rather abstract formulation undoubtedly had good social visibility, due to the outstanding entrepreneurial abilities of a particular caste, the Saswad Malis. The crucial importance of expertise in managing large amounts of capital in the production process meant that cultivators, not money-lenders or landlords, emerged as the class in control of cane production.

Third, consider the suppliers of labour. For the Malis, the supply of labour came initially from their own families, supplemented to an increasing extent (as production expanded) by hired labour. Some of this labour was hired by the day (for weeding, for example), some by the year (for irrigating or tending cattle), and some in contract teams for specific operations (for earthing up or harvesting and making *gul*). Share-cropping, an option used frequently even today for other crops, was never employed in cane cultivation, since whoever was risking the capital wanted to maintain close supervision over the crop.

As the cultivation of sugar cane expanded, so did the demand for labour, stimulating seasonal and permanent migration from the surrounding dry villages. Most of the seasonal migrants were land-owning cultivators, who brought their bullocks and carts along for the harvest operations. As a consequence, they were not dependent labourers, subject to ready coercion. As mentioned earlier, in a good season these workers often preferred to stay at home tending their own crops, regardless of the high wages offered by the cane growers. On the other hand, droughts brought them flocking to the canals in large numbers, forcing them temporarily into a more precarious economic position.

That the labour market was more competitive than coercive is shown by the trend in wages. Cash wages for agricultural labour nearly tripled between 1900 and 1922, while real wages (that is, cash wages deflated by the cost of living index) rose by 45 per cent (Shirras 1924; cf. Keatinge 1912: 68–73; Patil 1932: 3). Part of this increase was undoubtedly due to the expansion of cane cultivation along the canals.[6]

The low levels of coercion in the labour control system are most dramatically illustrated, however, by the careers of some families of immigrants, who came to the canal areas initially as construction workers and daily labourers. After a while, some were hired on annual contracts, and some of these were later promoted to foremen. Later still, in the Great Depression, when some of the largest cane growers could not shake off their debts, they encouraged their foremen to become tenants. Eventually, a number of these tenants bought out their landlords and became cane growers in their own right (Attwood 1979).

These striking cases of upward mobility not only bear out the lack of coercion in the labour system, they also reinforce the point that human capital was the most crucial factor of production. While working on annual contracts, and then as foremen, *these labourers were acquiring skills in the management of cane production*, skills which were the basis of their subsequent upward mobility (and which were also beneficial to those who hired them along the way).

This leads to another interesting point. Some of the hired labour was supplied by small cultivators living in the irrigated villages. The new methods, equipment, seeds, etc., adopted by the larger cane growers were experienced first-hand, then, by the small cultivators who worked for them on a part-time basis. As a result, it is quite possible that some successful innovations were transmitted most rapidly from the large cane growers to the smaller ones, leaving the independent 'middle peasants' lagging behind. This may help to explain why the small cane growers not only survived under intense

[6] In recent decades, the position of the migrant harvest workers seems to have deteriorated (cf. Breman 1978–79), probably for two main reasons. First, the growth of population has been very rapid since 1920. Second, the rapid expansion of factory sugar production after 1950 made the more skilled operations of the harvest workers (that is, *gul* making) obsolete. However, the still more rapid expansion of cooperative factories in the 1970s has created a shortage of harvest workers, enabling the workers to unionize and negotiate for somewhat higher wages (Abraham 1980).

economic pressure, as well as intense population pressure in the period 1920–70, but were able, on average, to buy more land (both absolutely and proportionately more) than the medium and large-scale growers (Attwood 1979: 503).

This brings us to the more general question of class relations between the small and large cane growers. Again, it is often assumed that commercialization must result in the differentiation, or class polarization, of the peasantry. From what we noted earlier about different factor proportions on different sized holdings, this process might have seemed inevitable. We might also note a study of data collected in 1914–18, which found that average profits per acre of cane were twice as high for holdings over three acres than for those which were less (Inglis and Gokhale 1928: 4). These bits of data suggest that the small cane growers were due to be driven out of business by the larger, more capital-intensive operators. Yet nothing of the kind occurred. Why not?

Early in the Great Depression, Patil (1932: 22) observed that cane growers depending on hired labour were caught in a much tighter cost–price squeeze than those who relied more on family labour. Consequently, we should not assume that the larger cane growers had all the advantages all the time. (It is, in any case, nearly impossible to make realistic assessments of the 'profits' accruing to small cultivators who rely mainly on unpaid family labour.)

Obviously, some cane growers became very wealthy, while others ran into debt and were forced to sell their lands. However, a careful study of family histories from 1920 to 1970 in one cane-growing area reveals no tendency for the smallholders as a class to be displaced into the landless proletariat, nor for the large landowners to expand their holdings indefinitely. On the contrary, there was mobility in all directions for holdings of all sizes, and the aggregate results were that the large landowners sold the most land, while the smallholders bought the most (Attwood 1979). The best indicator of the economic strength of the small cane growers is that they survived, and they even invested in new lands, cattle, equipment, houses, businesses, and so forth.[7]

What we have found in this section is that control of sugar cane production fell into the hands of a broad class of cultivators—not

[7] Preliminary results of research into long-term investment patterns show that smallholders invested much larger amounts per acre than medium or large-scale landholders between 1970 and 1978 (see Attwood 1984).

into the hands of the brokers, or the feudal landlords, nor even a narrow stratum of big cane growers. The argument is that the capital and managerial requirements of the crop itself made this inevitable. Labour was not coerced because it was scarce and because the policies of the state were not favourable to organized coercion.[8] Small peasants were not displaced, on the whole, because they could become successful cane growers and because irrigation expanded the effective land area, making small holdings more viable (Attwood 1982).

Before leaving this point, however, we must also consider the question from another angle. Why were the small cane growers not wiped out by competition from central sugar factory estates as happened so often in the Caribbean (cf. Guerra y Sanchez 1964)? In the first place, such factories could not run at a profit in the Bombay Deccan (with its expensive cane) until after the sugar tariff of 1932. After the tariff was enacted, nine factories were established along the Deccan canals by industrialists from Bombay. These followed the Malis' example by leasing their estate lands from villagers in the newer canal tracts. It should be noted that the Indian Sugar Committee (1921: 294–303) had considered at length whether to recommend compulsory acquisition of lands by the government for leasing to factory estates. (The Government of Bombay had even done this in a single case.) However, political conditions and the general climate of administrative tradition were not favourable to such coercive measures, and the Sugar Committee recommended against them. Consequently, the industrialists had to await favourable market conditions before colonizing the Deccan canals.

The new central factories did quite well during the 1930s and forties. However, the local cane growers were already an established interest group, and they sensed new opportunities in their favour after Indian independence (in 1947). Within two decades, the cane growers were able to compete economically with the central factories and had them politically on the defensive. How this occurred is described in the next section.

Reorganization of Production and Distribution

The previous section outlined what might be called the initial core

[8] The ideologies and interests affecting state policy on agriculture deserve an analysis in their own right, but this must wait for another opportunity.

of class relations among the suppliers of land, labour, capital and human capital—relations shaped by the need to invest large amounts of both capital and human capital in the production process. Another argument of this essay is that subsequent changes in this class system were shaped by the same influences, or, to put this another way, that high capital requirements stimulated organizational as well as technical innovations.

To present this argument in full would require a book-length analysis (now in progress), so this section must suffer from compression. This is perhaps more tolerable because the reader has access to an excellent description of the reorganization of production in Chapter 2 of the *Politics of Development* by B. S. Baviskar. Here we shall merely sketch these changes.

First, of course, came the initial effort to grow sugar cane in a largely non-commercial, peasant economy. Before the rise of cane production, most villagers grew mainly foodgrains for local consumption, using family labour and the minimum of purchased inputs or borrowed capital.[9] Cane cultivation required the mobilization of hired labour and borrowed capital, the adoption of new methods and equipment, and the organization of new relations of production, as described in the preceding sections. The government provided the initial fixed capital, in the form of irrigation canals and railroads, as well as some assistance in technological innovation. All other changes, however, were made on the initiative of the cultivators.

Second, the cane growers exhibited a willingness to experiment further with their relations of production and distribution. Many of them joined the credit and marketing cooperatives which were sponsored by the government from 1910. Some cooperatives failed, especially later in the Great Depression; but the rates of success were good compared to other parts of India. Many cane growers learned how to cope with the government bureaucracy through these institutions, which paid off handsomely with the later rise of cooperative processing units. Another early innovation was a private sugar factory, established along the Nira canal in the early 1920s. Local cane growers bought shares in this factory and supplied the cane. However, the factory was faced both with high *gul* prices,

---

[9] Cotton became an important cash crop in parts of the Bombay Presidency in the middle of the nineteenth century; however, these were not the areas where the Deccan canals were later built. Canal-irrigated sugar cane was the crop which caused the commercial transformation of these latter areas.

limiting cane supplies, and with competition from white sugar from Java, so it closed within two years. On a more individual basis, one large-scale cane grower tried to improve his access to the market by setting up his own *gul* brokerage shop in the nearby market town. Others obtained cane supply contracts with the new factories which sprang up in the 1930s. All these activities demonstrated a willingness to seek more efficient relations of production and distribution as opportunities arose.

Third, after the government enacted a protective sugar tariff in 1932, and capitalists from Bombay city established several new factories along the canals, the Saswad Malis managed to organize their own factory in 1934. Though not registered as a cooperative society, this factory was probably the first in India to be organized along cooperative lines: that is, as a factory owned and operated by the cane growers. This was the second major turning point (after the start of large-scale cane cultivation) in the agrarian class system of the Bombay Deccan: the growers gained access to a new market (white sugar instead of *gul*), in which they had a certain amount of direct investment and control. This was the first step towards vertical integration of the cane growers into the white sugar sector (since the other factories relied as much as possible on cane from their own estates), and this step was initiated entirely by the cane growers themselves. In 1941 another factory was organized by a consortium of very large-scale cane growers, but the Saswad Mali factory, which incorporated a cross-section of growers of all sizes, provided the real model for the reorganization which was to occur after Independence.

Fourth, the cane growers from other castes and locations were also eager to gain access to the white sugar market, so some followed the Mali example by organizing a cooperative factory, which began operation in 1950. This venture was supported financially by the government; but the initiative and managerial control (after the first few years) came from the local cane growers. Once this factory got off to a successful start, it was quickly copied by others all over the Deccan canals. By 1982 there were 67 cooperative factories in the region (now the state of Maharashtra), some very successful and others not (due to a period of too-rapid expansion in the 1970s). Cooperative sugar production in Maharashtra has expanded, in just three decades, to a 32 per cent share of total white sugar production in India (and India is the third largest producer of cane sugar in the world). The technical efficiency of the better cooperative factories is as good as that of the nearby private factories, much better than most sugar factories in other provinces, and comparable to some of the best in the world.

One of the main reasons for this success is that cooperative organization is one solution to the cane supply problem, which has long been recognized as the main impediment to efficient white sugar production in India (cf. Sahasrabudhe 1914; ISC 1920: 291–321). As we shall see in the next section, it is very awkward for a private factory to negotiate a regular cane supply with thousands of independent growers. This was one cause of the failure of the Nira valley factory in the 1920s—an event which caused Bombay investors to avoid the problem as much as possible by setting up factory estates in the 1930s. The factory estate system could only spread, however, where land and water were temporarily under-utilized. In the established cane areas, other methods had to be found for coordinating local growers with factory operations; and the cooperative factory, as pioneered by the Malis, was the most efficient model (Attwood 1982).

The cooperative factories have provided a number of direct welfare benefits (such as schools, dispensaries, support for other co-ops, etc.) to their members and nearby communities; but their main achievement has been the efficient integration of nearly all cane growers along the canals into the production of white sugar. Among other activities, these factories help to arrange crop loans through affiliated credit societies; promote lift irrigation societies; provide extension services; organize the harvest and transport workers; and produce the sugar, store it, and sell it.

It should be stressed, again, that these factories were established and managed on the initiative of the cane growers—helped and supervised, to be sure, by the government. Part of their success is due to political influence, though to discuss that aspect would require another essay or two (see Baviskar 1980; Rosenthal 1977). In any case, political influence alone is not sufficient to create an efficient economic organization, as we shall see in the next section.[10]

[10] The cooperative factories now enjoy political advantages over the local private factories, and some of the latter are planning to sell out. However, there was never the remotest possibility that the sugar sector would be able to operate free of political interference after Independence, and some institution was surely needed to represent the interests of the cane growers. The cooperative factories are so effective at this that they have become politically unpopular with other interest groups, particularly with the urban middle classes.

The success of these cooperative factories is consistent with the argument of this essay, which suggests that there is a high premium on managerial skills in the production of a capital-intensive crop. These skills obviously contributed to the successful management of many cooperative factories by directors elected from among the cane growers who are their shareholders.[11]

In this section, I have glossed over a large array of political, social and institutional factors which had a direct influence on the changes just outlined, in order to present a simple argument about economic innovation and efficiency. The argument is that high capital costs in cane production forced the growers to seek organizational as well as technical innovations, and that the success of these innovations is due to the managerial skills engendered by capital-intensive crop production.

Contrasts with North Indian Sugar Production

Fifty years ago, the sugar industry of northern India had several advantages over the Bombay Deccan; and it was in the north that the main growth of the industry was occurring at that time. However, these same advantages led the northern industry into organizational problems from which it now seems unable to fight clear. Perhaps because growing cane was relatively easy and inexpensive in the north, the growers lacked the incentive and the experience required to reorganize efficiently.

The northern sugar industry is concentrated in the states of U.P. and Bihar, which together in 1920 were producing 60 per cent of the sugar cane in India and had 13 of the 18 sugar factories (ISC 1921: 35–6, 61–2, 291). After the tariff of 1932, this industry expanded rapidly, accounting for 109 out of 140 factories and 83 per cent of sugar production in India by 1937 (Indian Tariff Board [ITB] 1938: 18–22). In U.P. these factories obtained most of their cane by purchase from the local cultivators (Amin 1981). In Bihar, with its different land laws, some of the factories had their own estates and some obtained cane from European 'planters' who grew the crop on a large scale. Even so, many of the Bihar factories also depended on

[11] Cooperative management does not always run smoothly, since the directors and would-be directors often get embroiled in factional conflicts. However, these are not as damaging to economic efficiency as might be thought (see Baviskar 1980).

local cultivators for their cane supply. Broadly speaking, the same organization of sugar and cane production—that is, factories owned and operated by industrialists buying cane from thousands of independent growers—prevails in the north today.

Cane production in this region had several advantages over the Bombay Deccan: more abundant rainfall, more abundant labour, and thus much lower costs for growing cane. Costs per acre were about 70 to 75 per cent lower, and even costs per ton of cane were definitely lower. Around 1910, for example, cane cost about Rs 6.67 per ton to grow in the north, as compared with Rs 8.75 in the Bombay Deccan (Sahasrabudhe 1914: 5). In 1930, the cost was about Rs 7.50 per ton in many parts of the north, as against Rs 17.75 per ton in Bombay (ITB 1931: 55–9). Since 1930, this disparity in costs per ton has been considerably reduced, probably for two reasons. First, improved cane varieties were available in the Deccan only after 1930, more than ten years after they began to spread in the north. Second, the cooperative factories helped to improve cane production and reduce costs after 1950. In the 1930s, however, the large supply of cheaper cane in the north stimulated the greatest expansion of factory production in that region.

Compared to the Bombay Deccan, where average cane yields were about 26 tons per acre in 1920, yields in the north were only about 10 tons per acre (ISC 1921: 36, 61, 160). Cane yields were lower in the north for two main reasons. First, cane is a tropical crop and the north is a subtropical region, with cool winters which inhibit growth and shorten the growing season. Second, the average annual rainfall is more than 40 inches in eastern U.P. and Bihar; consequently, irrigation was much less necessary and less expensive than in the Bombay Deccan.[12] As a result the crop was grown on a more casual basis, with less manure, equipment, labour, irrigation, working capital, and supervision (ISC 1921: 39–41, 65–6; AMA 1943: 6–7).

Inexpensive and non-intensive cane cultivation seemed a blessing for the northern industry before the 1950s. Nevertheless, the non-intensive cultivation pattern posed problems which were bound to

[12] In western U.P. rainfall was scarcer and labour less abundant than in the wet-rice zones to the east. Consequently, sugar cane was grown more often on irrigation in the west, resulting in both higher costs and higher yields per acre (ITB 1938: 21–22; AMA 1943: 6). Western U.P. is thus an intermediate case between the Bombay Deccan and the northeast (that is, Bihar and eastern U.P.). The contrasts outlined in this section apply more strongly to the latter region.

grow more serious as the industry aged and faced new competitors. First, a shorter growing season meant a shorter crushing season, with the factories forced to stand idle for longer portions of the year. Second, the northern cane was of poorer quality; that is, it had a lower sucrose content. This meant that the factories had to crush larger amounts of cane to make a ton of sugar. Third, lower cane yields and lower sucrose content together meant much less sugar produced per acre. (Currently, sugar production per acre in the north is about 35 per cent of the amount in Maharashtra [Indian Sugar 1979–80: 19].) This in turn meant that the factories had to obtain sugar from a much larger number of growers over a wider area in order to operate at full capacity, which made their cane supply problems more complex. A steady supply of fresh-cut cane is absolutely critical for efficient factory production; and cane supply was long considered the most serious problem for Indian sugar factories (ISC 1921: 291–321). This problem was exacerbated, more-over, by the ability of the cane growers to process their crop into *gul* if they were not satisfied with the prices offered by the factories. Even today, about 60 per cent of the cane grown in the north is used for making *gul* or other 'artisan sugars', while the proportion has fallen to just 15 per cent in Maharashtra (Cooperative Sugar 1980: 491). This reflects the awkward and conflict-ridden nature of nego-tiations over cane prices in the north. Some of these problems have been mitigated by the formation of cane supply cooperatives. However, these cooperatives mainly serve to implement government dictates (Hirsch 1962: 102–18); they cannot be described as organiza-tional innovations managed by the cane growers.

The northern industry has now become, by universal agreement, a 'sick' industry and a battleground between the government, the growers and the factory owners. From producing 83 per cent of the white sugar in India in 1936–37, the north now produces just 30 per cent (Cooperative Sugar 1983: 39). Most of the northern factories are now old and decrepit, since capital investments to improve them have not been forthcoming from the owners. The reasons for this are manifold: the government holds down sugar prices to benefit urban (middle class) consumers, while it raises cane prices to benefit the growers and saddles the industry with very heavy taxes (Smith 1978: 109). Meanwhile, the *gul* trade, which is not burdened with any taxes or price controls, competes with the factories for their cane supplies. The factory owners obviously feel they are caught in a political squeeze; and some would be glad to close down entirely, if the government would let them.[13]

In 1978–79, twenty-three mills were taken over by the government, forcing them to stay open and pay the cane growers at the rates the government dictated (Franda 1979: 8). The question of nationalizing the industry has been debated heatedly for years. What seems striking, in comparison with Maharashtra, is that the whole question seems to be treated more as a political battle than as a search for more efficient economic organization. The interests of the cane growers seem to act mainly through pressure on the government rather than through organizational innovations of their own.

Given that so much of the northern cane is still processed into *gul*, there might be ample scope for new cooperative factories in the region. However, by 1981 only 11 per cent of the northern white sugar was produced by cooperatives, compared with 90 per cent in Maharashtra (Cooperative Sugar 1983: 39). There seems to be less enthusiasm for cooperative factories among the northern cane growers. The growers in one area were invited to take over a private mill and run it as a cooperative, but they refused (Hirsch 1962: 58).

Some problems of the northern sugar industry stem directly from the non-intensive system of cane cultivation, which exacerbates the general problem of cane supply for factories dealing with multitudes of independent growers. Other problems stem from the unresolved conflict of class interests between cane growers, factory owners, urban consumers, and the government—a conflict which grows directly out of the cane supply problem. It is interesting to note that the rise in political power of the cane growers as a class led in Maharashtra to an efficient cooperative factory system, while in the north it led to a seemingly perpetual struggle entailing a great deterioration in economic efficiency. A number of historical and institutional factors (which have been glossed over in this account) could be invoked to explain this contrast. The argument of this essay, however, is that the northern cane growers are seeking to

---

[13] Of course, many of the same problems of government control are faced by the factories in Maharashtra—in fact, sugar prices are held very much lower in this region. However, the cooperative factory directors enjoy a much more comfortable relationship with their state government (Baviskar 1980; Rosenthal 1977), and investment in these factories has been heavily subsidized by government loans. Moreover, since these factories are owned by the cane growers, there is no struggle to minimize the price paid for cane, and thus much less trouble in securing a steady supply.

accomplish through purely political means what they may be unable to do through economic innovation, simply because they never had the opportunity to manage capital-intensive enterprises. They appear to lack confidence in the idea of running their own cooperative factories; and on this reading perhaps they have reason.

This argument, based on the importance of capital and expertise, is intended to complement, rather than displace, others based on ecology, history and social structure. In eastern U.P. and Bihar, the villages are dominated by 'a petty landlord class, driven close to the soil but still continuing to exploit it through lower caste sub-tenants and predial labourers' (Stokes 1978: 239). Stokes suggests that systems of status discrimination endure in the northeast despite economic changes which render them ever more inefficient. He also suggests that those who disdain manual labour and aspire to petty landlordship are ill-equipped to become enterprising farmers, a point which fits with the argument of this essay. Thus the social and historical setting, along with the abundance of labour and rainfall (which made non-intensive cane growing easy), may have rendered capital-intensive agriculture improbable in the northeast.

We should also allow some weight to the timing and momentum of changes in the industry. Small cane growers in the Bombay Deccan were not fully incorporated into the white sugar industry until after 1950, when the cooperative factories were assured of financial and political support from the government. In this region, private investors considered it too risky to set up factories dependent on cane purchased from independent growers. They rejected the north Indian system in the 1930s, at a time when that system was rapidly incorporating many of the northern cane growers. Once that incorporation was effected, it locked the factories and the farmers into a relationship of mutual antagonism and dependence which has been difficult to reorganize in subsequent decades.

Conclusion

As we noted at the start of this essay, social scientists (especially non-economists) tend to explain divergent paths of economic growth or stagnation in terms of the influence of social structure on the process of production. This approach tends to leave in limbo the complementary question of how economic forces in the production process may reshape the social structure, setting in motion an internal engine of growth. The object of this essay has been to show that such a complementary approach may open up a range of questions that were not otherwise apparent.

In particular, this essay has argued that a cropping system which requires heavy capital investment will stimulate a search for increasingly careful management methods which, in turn, will stimulate the adoption of both technical and organizational innovations—the latter including efforts to mobilize new sources of capital, gain access to new markets, and experiment with new forms of vertical integration. The high demand for managerial ability also tends to stimulate a demand for education (quite visible in the form of voluntary education societies in the Bombay Deccan)[14] and a supply of expertise for the management of new enterprises such as cooperative sugar factories.· Even more fundamentally, this high demand for human capital makes it impossible for landlords or moneylenders to manage the new crop system by remote control, so the cultivators emerge as the dominant class in the new agrarian system.

[14] Much could be written about the role of voluntary education societies in the spread of rural education in this region. My impression is that much more progress was made by private, voluntary institutions than in most other provinces; but this remains to be substantiated. In any case, the considerable activity along these lines testifies to the perception *by the rural people themselves* of the importance of education for upgrading their skills (Attwood 1974a).

REFERENCES

Abraham, Amrita (1980), 'Another Patchwork Agreement for Sugar Workers', *Economic and Political Weekly* 15: 2007-8.

Agricultural Marketing Advisor [AMA] (1943), *Report on the Marketing of Sugar (Including the Various Kinds of Gur and White Sugar) in India and Burma*, Marketing Series No. 39 (New Delhi: Government of India Press).

Amin, Shahid (1981), 'Peasants and Capitalists in Northern India: Kisans in the Cane Commodity Circuit in Gorakhpur in the 1930s', *Journal of Peasant Studies* 8: 311-34.

Attwood, D. W. (1974a), 'Political Entrepreneurs and Economic Development', unpublished Ph.D. dissertation, McGill University.

—— (1974b), 'Patrons and Mobilizers: Political Entrepreneurs in an Agrarian State', *Journal of Anthropological Research* 30: 225-41.

—— (1979), 'Why Some of the Poor Get Richer: Economic Change and Mobility in Rural Western India', *Current Anthropology* 20: 495-516, 657-8.

—— (1980), 'Irrigation and Imperialism: Water Distribution and the Origin of

Enclave Capitalism in Rural Western India', Paper presented at the Harvard Institute for International Development.

—— (1982), 'Class Interests and Changes in the Organization of Production in the Indian Sugar Industry', Paper presented at the annual meeting of the Social Science History Association, Indiana University.

—— (1984), 'Poverty, Inequality and Economic Growth in Rural India', in J. Galaty and T. Bruneau (eds), *The Social Impact of Development* (in press).

Baines, J. A. (1882), *Imperial Census of India: Operations and Results in the Presidency of Bombay, Including Sind* (Bombay: Government Central Press).

Baviskar, B. S. (1980), *The Politics of Development: Sugar Co-operatives in Rural Maharashtra* (Delhi: Oxford University Press).

Beals, Alan R. (1974), *Village Life in South India* (Chicago: Aldine).

Béteille, André (1974), *Studies in Agrarian Social Structure* (Delhi: Oxford University Press).

Breman, Jan (1978–79), 'Seasonal Migration and Co-operative Capitalism: The Crushing of Cane and Labour by the Sugar Factories of Bardoli, South Gujarat', *Journal of Peasant Studies* 6: 41–70, 168–209.

Cooperative Sugar (1980, 83), *Directory and Yearbook* (New Delhi: National Federation of Cooperative Sugar Factories).

Franda, Marcus (1979), *All is Not Sweet in Indian Sugar Politics*, Hanover, N.H.: American Universities Field Staff Reports, No. 21, Asia.

Fukazawa, Hiroshi (1983), 'Western India' in Dharma Kumar (ed.), *The Cambridge Economic History of India*, Vol. 2 (Cambridge: Cambridge University Press), pp. 177–206.

Guerra y Sanchez, Ramiro (1964), *Sugar and Society in the Caribbean* (New Haven: Yale University Press).

Hirsch, Leon V. (1962), *Marketing in an Underdeveloped Economy: The North Indian Sugar Industry* (Englewood Cliffs, N.J.: Prentice-Hall).

Indian Irrigation Commission [IIC] (1902), *Minutes of Evidence: Bombay Presidency (Including Sind)* (Calcutta: Government Printing, India).

Indian Sugar (1979–80), *Yearbook* (Calcutta: Indian Sugar Mills Association).

Indian Sugar Committee [ISC] (1921), *Report* (Simla: Government Central Press).

Indian Tariff Board [ITB] (1931), *Report of the Indian Tariff Board on the Sugar Industry* (Calcutta: Central Publication Branch).

—— (1938), *Report of the Indian Tariff Board on the Sugar Industry* (Delhi: Manager of Publications).

Inglis, C. C. (1927a), 'Note on Irrigation on the Block System in the Deccan Canal Tracts', Bombay Public Works Department, Technical Paper No. 16 (Bombay: Government Central Press).

—— (1927b), 'Note on the Effluent Farm near Poona (1918–19 to 1925–26)', Public Works Department, Technical Paper No. 17 (Bombay: Government Central Press).

Inglis, C. C. and V. K. Gokhale (1928), 'Note on the Outturn and Profit from Sugarcane Crops Grown in the Deccan Canal Tracts', Bombay Public Works Department. Technical Paper No. 21 (Bombay: Government Central Press).

—— (1934), 'Development of Irrigation in the Deccan Canal Areas', Bombay Public Works Department, Technical Paper No. 49 (Bombay: Government Central Press).

Keatinge, G. (1912), *Rural Economy in the Bombay Deccan* (London: Longmans, Green).

Knight, J. B. (1905), 'Sugarcane', Bombay Department of Land Records and Agriculture, Bulletin No. 25 (Bombay: Government Central Press).

—— (1914), 'Sugarcane, Its Cultivation, and Gul Manufacture', Bombay Department of Agriculture, Bulletin No. 61 (Bombay: Government Central Press).

Lenin, V. I. (1956), *The Development of Capitalism in Russia* (Moscow: Foreign Languages Publishing House).

Lewis, W. Arthur (1970), 'The Export Stimulus' in W. Arthur Lewis (ed.), *Tropical Development 1880–1913* (London: George Allen and Unwin), pp. 13–45.

Ludden, David (1981), 'Agricultural Development and Social Change in India: Some Considerations from Agrarian History', in J. Galaty and T. Bruneau (eds), *The Social Impact of Development* (in press).

Mann, Harold H. and N. V. Kanitkar (1921), *Land and Labour in a Deccan Village: Study No. 2* (London: Oxford University Press).

Mann, Harold H. and V. A. Tamhane (1910), 'The Salt Lands of the Nira Valley', Bombay Department of Agriculture, Bulletin No. 39 (Bombay: Government Central Press).

McAlpin, Michelle Burge (1983), *Subject to Famine: Food Crises and Economic Change in Western India, 1860–1920* (Princeton: Princeton University Press).

Mencher, Joan P. (1966), 'Kerala and Madras: A Comparative Study of Ecology and Social Structure', *Ethnology* 5: 135–71.

Moore, Barrington Jr. (1966), *Social Origins of Dictatorship and Democracy: Lord and Peasant in the Making of the Modern World* (Boston: Beacon Press).

Mukherjee, Ramkrishna (1957), *The Dynamics of a Rural Society* (Berlin: Akademie).

Musgrave, P. J. (1978), 'Rural Credit and Rural Society in the United Provinces, 1860–1920' in Clive Dewey and A. G. Hopkins (eds), *The Imperial Impact: Studies in the Economic History of Africa and India* (London: Athlone), pp. 216–32.

Paige, Jeffery M. (1975), *Agrarian Revolution: Social Movements and Export Agriculture in the Underdeveloped World* (New York: Free Press).

Patel, Surendra J. (1952), *Agricultural Labourers in Modern India and Pakistan* (Bombay: Current Book House).

Patil, P. C. (1927), 'Sugarcane Mills and Small Power Crushers in the Bombay Presidency', Bombay Department of Agriculture, Bulletin No. 139 (Poona: Yeravda Prison Press).

—— (1928), 'The Organization and Cost of *Gul* (Crude Sugar) Making in the Deccan Sugarcane Tracts', Bombay Department of Agriculture, Bulletin No. 147 (Poona: Yeravda Prison Press).

—— (1932), 'Preliminary Studies of Important Crops in the Bombay Deccan in the Post-War Period', Bombay Department of Agriculture, Bulletin No. 168 (Bombay: Government Central Press).

Patil, P. C. and V. G. Patwardhan (1926), 'Some of the Promising Exotic Sugarcane Varieties of the Manjri Farm', Bombay Department of Agriculture, Bulletin No. 125 (Poona: Yeravda Prison Press).

Popkin, Samuel L. (1979), *The Rational Peasant: The Political Economy of Rural Society in Vietnam* (Berkeley: University of California Press).

Roseberry, William (1976), 'Rent, Differentiation, and the Development of Capitalism among Peasants', *American Anthropologist* 78: 45–58.

Rosenthal, Donald B. (1977), *The Expansive Elite: District Politics and State Policy-making in India* (Berkeley: University of California Press).

Sahasrabudhe, G. N. (1914), 'Note on Indian Sugar Industry and Modern Methods of Sugar Manufacture', Bombay Department of Agriculture, Bulletin No. 60 (Bombay: Government Central Press).

Schultz, Theodore W. (1964), *Transforming Traditional Agriculture* (New Haven: Yale University Press).

Shirras, G. Findlay (1924), *Report on an Enquiry into Agricultural Wages in the Bombay Presidency* (Bombay: Government Central Press).

Smith, Dudley (1978), *Cane Sugar World* (New York: Palmer Publications).

Stein, Burton (1980), *Peasant State and Society in Medieval South India* (Delhi: Oxford University Press).

Stokes, Eric (1978), *The Peasant and the Raj* (Cambridge: Cambridge University Press).

Taylor, Meadows (1856), *A Statement and Remarks Relating to the Expenses of Irrigation from Wells in the Deccan, Khandesh, etc.* (Bombay: Bombay Education Society's Press).

Visvesvaraya, M. (1903), *Irrigation on the Block System* (Bombay: Bombay Works Department).

Wallerstein, Immanuel (1974), *The Modern World-System: Capitalist Agriculture and the Origins of the European World-Economy in the Sixteenth Century* (New York: Academic Press).

—— (1980), *The Modern World-System II: Mercantilism and the Consolidation of the European World-Economy, 1600–1750* (New York: Academic).

Whitcombe, Elizabeth (1972), *Agrarian Conditions in Northern India* (Berkeley: University of California Press).

Productive Power in Agriculture: A Survey of Work on the Local History of British India

DAVID LUDDEN

> Man's power over Nature turns out to be a power exercised by some
> men over others with Nature as its instrument.
>
> C. S. Lewis

Because agriculture means controlling land, labour, and capital, and
because politics in any agrarian society means competing for the
fruits of the earth, many historians of South Asia have turned their
minds toward the politics of agricultural production. But like countless little lights pointing into the darkness of rustic ages past, South
Asian agrarian history today is less a unified discipline than a galaxy
of individual inquiries. To draw conclusions from the literature,
therefore, we must first scan the galaxy as a whole, to identify its
major constellations, and to probe what holds constellations together, as well as apart. Having done so, we can proceed to formulate
some general and comparative propositions about power and productivity in the agrarian localities of British India.[1]

[1] This essay is both bibliographic and analytical. The notes refer to salient
material at each stage of the argument, avoiding excessive repetition, and group-
ing references so they might be more useful to readers wishing to pursue particular
subjects. Drawn from the bibliography, the notes do not exhaust the material
therein. The bibliography is not comprehensive, by any means, but indicates the
variety of relevant work. Certain genres of published material have not been
included, or have been included very selectively, for the sake of space and
coherence. These include many older polemical and official tracts, unpublished
dissertations, and many studies of contemporary conditions. Some items in the
bibliography have not been available at the time of writing, and the references

On Doing Agrarian History

Scholars have discovered a vast array of data,[2] so much, in fact, that the very diversity of sources and the technical demands of working with them impel historians to keeping working each in their own region and chosen set of problems. Difficulties of method thus exacerbate our over-arching conceptual dilemma, that is, how to piece together very fragmentary evidence, about various dimensions of agricultural life, over long stretches of time, in countless localities, to generate some reasonable and meaningful picture of 'the whole'.

Though limitations and virtues of data differ according to time and place, they almost always force historians to address social science questions in peculiarly historical terms. For instance, agricultural statistics are as a rule as flawed as they are old.[3] Data on output—most of it indirect, being records of cultivated acreage, cropping, and irrigation—generally suffice to portray gross production trends,[4] but not trends in yields per acre,[5] per capita, or per inputs of labour, capital, or water. Discussions of productivity, therefore, must rest for the most part on measurements of agricultural expansion and intensification. Concerning local politics, we cannot hope to find sufficient data for many detailed local studies. Bits and pieces of local detail must be interpreted in light of wider

---

in it concentrate purposefully on the regions of British India where the literature is fullest. Several readers have made critical contributions to this essay, most notably, Gyan Prakash, Veena Oldenburg, Ratna Ray, David Rudner, Ashok Rudra, and Susanne Rudolph. The entire SAPE contingent has been most helpful and stimulating during the process of writing and revision.

[2] Atchi Reddy (1978), Barrier (1974b), Crane (1963), Divekar (1978), Gordon (1980), Goswamy (1975), R. Guha (1974), Gustafson and Jones (1975), Hagen and Yang (1976), Henningham (1979), S. Islam (1977, 1978), Kessinger (1967, 1975), Kling (1966: 198, n5), A. R. Kulkarni (1976), Perlin (1978), Low and Wainwright (1969), Ludden (1978), Ratna Ray (1978: 257–9), and M. Siddiqi (1973).

[3] Bagchi (1976: 265), Blyn (1966: 39–56), A. V. Desai (1978), Dewey (1974, 1978), Heston (1973, 1978), Kessinger (1975).

[4] Blyn (1966: 128–301) argues that acreage expansion, multicropping, irrigation, etc. were the most important sources of increased output under the Raj.

[5] Soil exhaustion, erosion, deforestation, waterlogging, disease, lowered bovine/human ratio, and other consequences of expansion and intensification make indexes of output less than adequate as indicators of increased yields per acre. See Bagchi (1976: 265–6), B. B. Chaudhuri (1969a), and Whitcombe (1972: 61–119).

patterns and trends. Gathered mostly for political and policy purposes, most social data is, moreover, highly biased by its official
character. To illustrate this bias it is enough to point out that we
know far more about localities in which political disruptions of some
sort did occur than about those that were quiet. Historians, consequently, work within wide parameters of interpretive discretion,
for instance, in selecting local details to colour their regional portraits. They must approach questions of power and productivity by
considering the agrarian system at various levels of scale and abstraction, using one level to illuminate others.

To find, analyse, and interpret their primary material, historians
have approached the countryside from different directions, with
different goals. There are now five major methodological traditions,
each with its own perspective on local power and productivity. By
far the oldest began with questions about land tenure and land policy
at the imperial and provincial levels, and has shifted in the last few
decades to a broader concern with the land system conceived politically, economically and socially.[6] With this shift, and consequent
diversity, this tradition has lost much of its coherence, except in as
much as its adherents look for systematic patterns in people's relation to land. By contrast, the remaining four traditions continue to
be quite coherent, because of their essentially disciplinary character.
Political historians—a large tribe—focus on authority, on upheavals
and revolts, on nationalism, on obedience, coercion, and conflict.
Politics shades into economics, but economic historians remain distinct in their concern for statistics on agricultural performance, on
the distribution of wealth, and on living standards. Because of their
data, methods, and policy-oriented heritage, they prefer to focus
upon aggregate more than local phenomena. Finally, there are the
still small, but growing and important bodies of work in historical
geography, an offshoot of strong geography departments in both
India and Great Britain; and in what we can call 'historical anthropology', by anthropologists who do history to understand change
today.

Cross-cutting these traditions, there are the distinctive modes of
reasoning that historians use to produce generalizations. Different

[6] Bandopadhyay (1978), H. Banerjee (1977, 1978a, 1979, 1980), B. B. Chaudhuri (1958, 1975a), Cohn (1969), S. C. Gupta (1960, 1963), R. Kumar (1968a),
Ludden (1978a), G. Mishra (1978), K. M. Mukherjee (1971, 1977), J. Raj (1965,
1978).

modes can be combined, and often are, but many scholars do so unwittingly. Widespread inattention to the limits imposed upon generalizations by the modes in which they are reached has had the effect of making much secondary literature useless for local history, and much of what passes for scholarly debate but meaningless misunderstanding.

Some scholars prefer arithmetic reasoning. They discuss aggregates, averages, and trends. For them, localities are variations, usually considered with respect to one variable at a time. The best quantitative studies enable a reader to break down aggregates spatially and temporally; the worst leave only a flat, lifeless image of large territories over long periods of time. Because much of what is important cannot be quantified, however, and because much of what could be often cannot be historically,[7] many scholars prefer structural reasoning. Rather than seeking an average or trend, they look for inner organizational features in social relations. Some elements of structure can be quantified, others cannot. Important structural concepts, like the mode of production, contain both types of elements, but it remains debatable whether structural generalizations must be grounded, or can be refuted, empirically. In structural, in contrast to arithmetic, reasoning, furthermore, the domain or scale of analysis is not merely a matter of convenience: local power structures and production relations cannot be simply added up or averaged out to create a picture of the whole. Spatial levels of structure must be systematically related to one another, a feat to date not accomplished by many historians.[8] Debates over data and computations among quantitative scholars are replaced among structural historians by arguments over theory and interpretation.

Two modes of reasoning have assumed increasing importance in recent years because they combine both arithmetic and structural approaches; so they can employ a great diversity of data. One looks at networks of relations and traces lineal connections between types of social actors at each spatial level of structure, for instance, merchant networks spreading outward from cities to towns and villages,

[7] For problems of quantification in non-economic studies, see the brief discussion in Barrier (1974b).

[8] For a critique of the object of structural analysis, see Perlin on Kessinger (Perlin, 1975). For dialogues on Marxist items in structural analysis, see Schoer (1977), Moffatt on Gough (Moffatt 1979 and Ludden 1979a), and the debate in Rudra et al. (1978).

and downward from regional to local levels. Political historians have moved along these lines of work more than others, so we know much more about political networks than about economic ones in British India. Another relatively new strategy is to compare structures at comparable levels of scale, not only to measure variations and make typologies, but to explore the mechanisms whereby regional structures emerge and generate, in turn, divergent local structures. Such comparative work began to appear in 1973,[9] whereas systemic analysis developed rapidly after Irfan Habib's pathbreaking publications in the 1960s, and both arithmetic and structural scholarship have roots in the nineteenth century.

Regional specialization is another potent force guiding research and keeping students of agrarian South Asia in different orbits. The richness of work has been improved dramatically by our focusing on linguistic, cultural, and political regions,[10] though coverage is still far from complete. Some regions have been studied very much more than others. Native states are still neglected, relatively speaking, as are Bangladesh, Madhya Pradesh, Bihar, Burma, and all tribal territories; whereas West Bengal, Punjab, Maharashtra, Uttar Pradesh and Tamil Nadu receive lots of attention. Richness of regional detail has not always paid off in fuller understanding, however, especially concerning local agrarian relations in the subcontinent as a whole. Political and economic historians use their relatively uniform tools of thought to fit together regional bits of the historical puzzle; but for historians of localities and agrarian relations there is today a profound confusion of tongues. Local words for weights and measures, tenures, rents, and forms of labour often make detailed local studies impossible to understand, let alone translate into terms comparable with other places and times. We await what will surely be a long effort at a rectification of terms,[11] and, ironically, efforts along these lines to date have oft-times made matters worse. Terms like 'landlord', 'peasant', 'caste', 'bondage', and 'rent', for

[9] Darling (1925) was the first to pursue a comparative approach, and is unrivalled today. Recent work includes that by Arnold, Jeffrey, and Manor (1976), Bagchi (1976), Bandopadhyay (1978), H. Banerjee (1979), Ludden (1978a, 1978b, 1979b), Mencher (1966), Ratna Ray (1979), and Washbrook (1973, 1976).

[10] For discussions of regionalism in history and historical research, see Barrier (1974b, 1979), Beck (1979), Broomfield (1966), Cohn (1971), Smith (1976), Thapar (1963).

[11] D. Kumar (1963) makes brief mention of terminological problems. No serious discussion has occurred since.

instance, have been used in a great variety of ways, obscuring local custom in the veneer of social science terminology. There is even as yet no comparative analysis of the baffling array of zamindari tenures![12] The reason for all this muddle is not hard to find. Scholars of different disciplines studying the same region, in whatever period, have more contact with one another and more shared sense of purpose than agrarian historians studying exactly the same problems, in the same period, but in different regions. A young scholar frustrated by all this might be forgiven for muttering, 'Where is old Baden-Power now that we really need him?'

But archaic official scholarship aside, the major conceptual bridges across regions, across modes of reasoning, and across methodological traditions are now built within modern schools of historical interpretation. Ironically, disagreements among the three major schools today are perhaps most acute on questions relevant to power and productivity. Though imparting some coherence to work on the subject, therefore, schools divide the secondary literature into largely non-comparable chunks of processed primary data, and divide historians into factions of mutual non-comprehension. Very loosely organized, but with identifiable institutional centres, leading lights, and theoretical moorings, each school tends to talk at rather than to the others, though in fact they all contribute mightily to our collective understanding.[13]

Like the others, the oldest school is internally divided. Its unifying theoretical framework is Marxist, suffused with nationalism,[14] not only because most of its adherents are South Asians, but because Marxists take imperialism, class, and national struggles to be key elements of theory, not merely empirical issues. As a cluster of intellectuals, this group is fundamentally concerned with the means and modes of exploitation, and they have, more than the others, focused on power in the production process. Though they have done

[12] For varieties of zamindari organization, see n. 33 and the discussion below.

[13] These three schools do not exhaust or define the entire field. Rather, they are major constellations of intellectual coherence. Four historians deserve special mention as individual focal points for considerable work in recent years, work not easily subsumed within major schools. They are D. A. Low, Dietmar Rothermund, R. E. Frykenberg, and above all, Binay Bhushan Chaudhuri, the only senior historian to have concentrated his entire career on specifically agrarian history. Bayly (1979) provides a brilliant overview of some recent Indian historiographic problems.

[14] B. Chandra (1966) gives a brilliant account of formative nationalist thinking.

few local studies, they have done much of the best agrarian history.[15]

Led by political historians critical of both Marxist and nationalist styles, the so-called 'Cambridge School' took shape after 1970. It is positivist, neo-Namierite, and not much concerned with theory. These scholars insist on detailed description of the political competition and self-aggrandizement that pervades city and country life. Their efforts to explain specific events have helped us understand who got what, when, where, and how in British India. Though they have looked at localities, and at political networks, in great detail, they have not produced much work on agrarian relations. What they have done is extremely rich, and provocative.[16]

Finally, there is the diffuse 'American School' rooted in American regional studies programmes, and centred at the University of Chicago. Explicitly non-Marxist and non-materialist in theoretical predilection, it is heavily influenced by Anglo-American anthropology. Scholars in this school of thought emphasize culture, indigenous conceptual systems, and the authority dimension of politics; they downplay inequality, coercion, conflict, and exploitation. Their major contribution to agrarian history has been to portray the meanings, motives, institutions, and social interactions that shape agrarian life. Their major weakness is a principled inattention to agricultural production.[17]

Shared Conceptions, Pervasive Themes

The aforesaid should suffice to establish that South Asian agrarian history is anything but a unified system of knowledge. Recent efforts,

[15] Important efforts in Marxist agrarian history include Alavi (1975), Bagchi (1972), J. Bajaj (1972), J. Banaji (1977), Bhadhuri (1973, 1976), B. Chandra (1979), Ghosh (1980), Gough (1976, 1978), Jassal (1980), R. Mukherjee (1957), Omvedt (1973, 1978, 1980), Pandey (1978), Perlin (1975, 1978, 1980), Prasad (1976, 1979), and Rudra *et al.* (1978).

[16] Programmatic statements from the Cambridge School appear in Gallagher (1963) and Seal (1973). Major works with agrarian content include those by Baker, Brown, Washbrook, and Stokes.

[17] For programmatic statements, see Cohn (1968, 1970), Cohn and Marriott (1958), and Crane (1963). Work in this genre includes Adas (1974), Appadurai and Breckenridge (1976), Broomfield (1966, 1976), Cohn (1961, 1971), Dirks (1976), Fox (1971, 1976), Hardgrave (1965), Irschick (1969), Metcalf (1979), Moffatt (1979), Neale (1962, 1969), Price (1979), Lloyd and Susanne Rudolph (1967), S. H. Rudolph (1971), Singer and Cohn (1968), and Stein (1969, 1980). Tom Kessinger is the only adherent of this school who considers production.

58 DAVID LUDDEN

nonetheless, have begun to forge some intellectual unity. These include critiques by members of one school directed at another,[18] sweeping surveys,[19] and provocative theoretical work.[20] But more important, there has slowly emerged tacit agreement on basic issues. For example, we all seem to have faith in intensive, descriptive studies. By doing them we have discarded haunting images about the agrarian past—images we all inherit—with subtler concepts that better locate the locality in the history of South Asian civilizations. The mythic image of the isolated 'village republic' has finally been laid to rest.[21] Today we seek to situate localities within networks of agrarian relations, within a wider agrarian system. We also know that change under the Raj occurred within systems that already had long and complex histories, with trajectories of development that shaped processes of change under British rule.[22] Networks of trade,[23] worship,[24] royal authority,[25] kinship, and caste[26] enmeshed a charac-

[18] See Bagchi (1978) on Baker (1976b) and Washbrook (1976); Pandey (1980) on Stokes (1978); Irschick (1975) and Spodek (1979) on the Cambridge School; Washbrook (1975) on Hardgrave (1969); and Perlin (1975) on Kessinger (1974).

[19] B. Chandra (1979: 1–37, 144–70, 328–67), Habib (1975), Maddison (1971), Moore (1967), Rajat Ray (1977), S. K. Sen (1979), and Weisskopf (1977).

[20] Alavi (1975), Bhadhuri (1973), Cohn (1968, 1970), Gallagher (1963), Perlin (1978), Rudra et al. (1978), Seal (1973), Schoer (1977), A. K. Sen (1976, 1981), Stein (1980), and Stokes (1978).

[21] Darling (1925), Dutt (1874, 1901), Moreland (1929), Maddison (1971), Mann (1967), R. Mukhejee (1957), Neale (1962), and, implicitly, R. Kumar (1969) start from assumptions about village isolation, equality, and/or ahistoricity in 'traditional' South Asia. Dewey (1972) has an account of this imagery as itself an historical phenomenon.

[22] Major accounts of pre-modern agrarian systems include Appadurai and Breckenridge (1976), A. C. Banerjee (1980), Banga (1978), S. Chandra (1976), Dirks (1976), Fox (1971, 1976), Frykenberg (1963), Gordon (1980), A. Guha (1966), Gunawardana (1971, 1978), Habib (1969, etc.), Ludden (1978a, 1978b, 1979), Murton (1973, 1975, 1977), Perlin (1978, 1980), M. C. Pradhan (1966), Ratna Ray (1975), and Stein (1969, 1980).

[23] On pre-British commercial complexity and the integration of politics and trade, see Chicherov (1971), S. Chandra (1976), Habib (1960, 1963b, 1969), P. C. Jain (1978), Ludden (1978a, 1979b), Richards (1981), K. Singh (1966), and Stein (1969).

[24] For temples in the South Indian agrarian system, see Appadurai and Breckenridge (1976), Gunawardana (1978), Ludden (1978a), and Stein (1960). Each has references to much more work.

[25] For state involvement in local economies, see, for example, Dirks (1976), Fox (1971), Gordon (1980), Gunawardana (1971), Habib (1963b, 1969), Ludden (1978a, 1978b), Perlin (1978), and M. C. Pradhan (1966).

[26] Beck (1976), Fox (1971, 1976, 1977), Ludden (1978a, 1978b), Perlin (1978, 1980), M. C. Pradhan (1966), A. J. Qaisar (1974), and Stein (1969, 1980).

teristic South Asian village in 1750 within a web of social relations that was essential to agricultural production. One interesting thread of work has looked at the productive roles of major pre-British integrative institutions and their associated elites in agricultural development, a theme to which I will return in a moment.[27]

But before doing so, it is worth emphasizing here that historians take very seriously the assertion that agriculture is a way of life, not just a business. To understand power in productive decisions, and productive effort in power relations, we must consider both power and production to be elements in the everyday social life of agricultural communities.[28] One instructive step in that direction is to imagine how agrarian folk in centuries past might have construed these elements themselves. Literary and ethnographic evidence suggests that power—in nature, over nature, in people, over people, in gods, in places, and over land—was important indeed to ordinary people, especially as it concerned matters of life and death. And agriculture was for most a matter of life and death. Productivity (I search in vain for an equivalent in a South Asian language) was probably conceived in terms of prosperity, health, wealth, and auspiciousness; and in terms of good things, like rice, children, water, mosques and temples, festivals, as well as bountiful, magnificent rulers. Powerful people would therefore seem to have been thought both cause and effect of agricultural prosperity: they were protectors, arbiters, ritualists, and also embodiments of wealth. A good king, by the nature of things, would rule a prosperous land; would be generous, mighty, and just. Sharp lines thus do not seem to have run through popular thinking to divide economic, political, and moral categories; so we would be wise not to assume such lines exist in social life, when we discuss decision-making, resources, and transactions.

From this perspective, two aspects of British India stand out in high relief. First, the British themselves defined 'productivity' much more narrowly. For them, productive people, activities, and institutions were only those that contributed directly to increased output. Yet for government, as for our imagined villagers, agri-

[27] On the debate concerning productive roles among Mughal nobility (*mansabdars*), see S. N. Hasan (1973) and Richards (1981) for the affirmative; and Moreland (1929) and Habib (1963) for the negative.

[28] Discussions of intermeshing power, economic, and social relations in village communities before British rule include those by Breman (1974), Charlesworth (1978), Dhar (1973), Fukazawa (1974), Hjejle (1967), D. Kumar (1965), Ludden (1978a), Moffatt (1979), Murton (1977), and D. Singh (1979).

cultural prosperity was a matter not only of economics, but also of morality, legitimacy, and justice. Logically enough, by the late nineteenth century, official wisdom held that many social nodes of power and authority in the native population were arch enemies of productivity. Moneylenders, rajas, temples, zamindars, landlords, priests, and banias, all were vampires sucking dry the only truly productive people in village India, the peasant farmer. Significantly, nationalist historians turned the tables on men like Lord Curzon, who declared himself a great patron of the peasantry, by indicting the government itself as the cause of agricultural distress. R. C. Dutt even argued that zamindars had been unfairly maligned; while, from Madras to Mysore to Bengal and Punjab, native dignitaries scrambled to become model modernizers. In short, popular thinking about prosperity is, in part, a morality play, one that many social actors take quite seriously. Though as descriptions of reality the character portraits in such plays may be distorted, or false, they can still be influential in both mundane affairs and academic analysis. In British India, by 1947, there were more than enough villains to go around. Fingers pointed everywhere.

The second prominent aspect of the Raj pertinent here is that the resources that people with power could use in agriculture underwent drastic change. Under Pax Britannica, armies and armed conflict lost their ancient stature as a major means to garner investable wealth. Coercive force remained critical in agrarian relations, but throughout the subcontinent little kingdoms lost their military muscle, and with it much of their coherence as agrarian domains.[29] Ceremonial honours also lost much of their potency in the agrarian system.[30] Local systems of authority and status were thus undermined (see Rajat Ray 1977). At the same time, the extractive and executive powers of non-local, bureaucratic authorities steadily increased, as did the sway of markets. Agriculture more and more meant dealing in cash, and coping with imperial rules to access to resources. The potentially productive role of people with money, legal skills, and official positions increased accordingly.

The value of land itself, moreover, rose dramatically, not only from commerical and institutional changes, but because South Asia became a much more crowded place. There were in Travancore, in

---

[29] Price (1979) has the best sustained discussion of old martial strategies at work in a zamindari domain under the Raj. See also B. B. Chaudhuri (1958), Metcalf (1979), and Ratna Ray (1974, 1979).

[30] Hazelhurst (1976) has an interesting argument along these lines.

1830, an estimated one thousand square miles of open, uncultivated, paddy land, so much that if 'a man wished to leave the joint family, waste land was free and abundant' (Jeffrey 1976: 30). During the nineteenth century, about one hundred miles northwest of Delhi, 'almost the whole of Sirsa District was a waste land with very few permanent villages' (H. Banerjee 1979: 145). Nomads roamed what became the Canal Colonies in Punjab. Bangladesh and Assam remained agricultural frontiers even in the twentieth century, Malaria continued until the 1920s to take a regular toll in West Bengal, and the Bengali population continued its steady drift eastward. In 1941, after a decade in which the rate of population growth was triple that of the 1920s, densities in the east finally equalled those in the west.[31] Everywhere in British India, per capita cultivated land declined steadily after 1921.[32]

In the light of these trends, it is obvious that local land relations and the productivity of powerful people should be major themes for research. Today there are large bodies of work on zamindars,[33] moneylenders,[34] and export crop merchants;[35] on the integration of

[31] S. P. Chatterjee (1949: 30–4). M. M. Islam (1978: 188, n6) presents an estimate that in 1793 from one-third to two-thirds of Bengal was cultivable waste.

[32] See M. B. Desai (1948: 13–14) and *Census of India*, 1941. For more on the spatial process of agricultural expansion, and on land hunger and population growth, see Adas (1974), Blyn (1966), B. B. Chaudhuri (1969a, 1976a), A. Guha (1967, 1968), Hunter (1877, 1897), Klein (1972, 1973, 1974), A. Mukerji (1979), Rajat Ray (1973), Rothermund (1977), A. K. Sen (1976), and A. Siddiqi (1973).

[33] Punjab: H. Banerjee (1978a, 1978b, 1979, 1980). Madras: Baker (1976a), Ludden (1978a), Price (1979), G. N. Rao (1973, 1977). United Provinces: Cohn (1969), S. C. Gupta (1959, 1960, 1963), Jassal (1980), Kolff (1979), Metcalf (1969a, 1969b, 1979), Musgrave (1972, 1979), J. Raj (1965, 1978), A. Siddiqi (1973), M. Siddiqi (1978), Stokes (1978: 63–89, 185–204, 205–27). Bengal and Bihar: Abdullah (1980), B. B. Chaudhuri (1958, 1975a, 1977), Day (1908), Ghosh (1980), R. K. Gupta (1979), Henningham (1979), S. Islam (1979), J. C. Jha (1964, 1968), J. S. Jha (1966, 1972), Mahmood (1962), K. M. Mukherji (1968, 1977), N. Mukherji (1975), Ratna Ray (1974, 1979), Raychaudhuri (1969), Robb (1979), K. K. Sengupta (1970, 1971, 1974), R. N. Sinha (1968), S. Taniguchi (1978), and Yang (1976, 1978, 1979c).

[34] Adas (1974), H. Banerjee (1978a), Catanach (1970), Charlesworth (1972, 1978), B. B. Chaudhuri (1969b), Cheng (1968), Choksey (1945), Cooper (1960), Darling (1925), Day (1908), Hunter (1897), M. M. Islam (1978, 1980), S. Islam (1974), Jack (1916), Kolliner (1975), R. Kumar (1968a), Lakshmi (1980), G. Mishra (1978), Mudie (1931), Musgrave (1978), S. S. Nehru (1932), J. Raj (1978), Robert (1979), Stokes (1978: 243–64), Whitcombe (1972).

[35] Bagchi (1972), Baker (1976a, 1976b, 1978), Buchanan (1934), Charlesworth (1972), B. B. Chaudhuri (1964, 1970), Cheng (1968), Day (1908), Fisher (1978), A. Guha (1967, 1968, 1977), Hardgrave (1969), Hunter (1897), Jack (1916),

localities into imperial political[36] and economic[37] systems; and on that enigmatic character, the rich peasant, about whom more shortly. Most of this work posits, at least implicitly, a set of functional and causal connections between local power and productivity; and about the nature of localities in the agrarian system. Broadly stated, the propositions are as follows. Because productive investments require command over resources, and in turn generate social power, social nodes of power are also nodes of savings, wealth, and hence investable resources. Agricultural prosperity thus depends upon the productive activity of people with power, and power depends on controlling resources critical in production. Locally, resource control does not derive from local conditions alone—decreasingly so, over time—yet for power to be productive, it must be exercised locally, in the face-to-face world of agricultural operations. Links between local and supra-local realms have thus become central in discussions of agrarian political economy under the Raj.

Patterns of Productive Power

There remain, of course, huge realms of darkness waiting to be explored. We know precious little about the production process locally, in specific agro-technological milieus. There is very little work on networks of exchange in the daily necessities of farming. We have no historical accounts of trade networks in foodgrains, or in the whole range of non-export commodities. How did dominant caste networks pertain to agriculture? How did migration, non-agricultural employment, and commercial investment effect resource utilization on farms? A thousand questions remain. Many can be

---

Kling (1966), R. Kumar (1968a), G. Mishra (1978), D. Mitra (1958), C. Palit (1975), Ponniah (1940), Rajat and Ratna Ray (1973), and Whitcombe (1972).

[36] Arnold *et al.* (1976), Baker (1976), Broomfield (1966, 1976), Dhanagare (1975a), Frykenberg (1963, 1965a, 1965b), Gallagher (1973), A. Guha (1977), Hardiman (1981), Hauser (1961), Irschick (1969), S. Kumar (1980), Low (1977), Pandey (1978), Rajat Ray (1977), Washbrook (1976), Washbrook and Baker (1975).

[37] On merchant-cultivator relations and the issue of capitalist domination, see Alavi (1975), Arnold (1979a, 1979b), Bagchi (1976, 1978), Baker (1976a, 1976b, 1978), J. Bajaj (1978), J. Banaji (1977), H. Banerjee (1977), B. Chandra (1979), Ghosh (1980), Harriss (1979), Lakshmi (1980), Ludden (1978a), McAlpin (1975a), S. Mukerji (1970), Omvedt (1973, 1980), Rudra *et al.* (1978), Schoer (1977), S. K. Sen (1979), Sivakumar (1978), and Washbrook (1976, 1978).

answered, at least in part. Many, however, point to the great difficulty
that will always remain in documenting the mundane activities of
ordinary people. Current scholarship is thus strongest in assessing
who was most powerful locally, and much weaker in showing how
people with various amounts of power carried on in daily life.

This is, nonetheless, a significant strength. It enables us to locate
nodal points of savings, authority, and directive power in the countryside, and to sketch the dynamics of conflict over resource control.
The outcomes of such conflicts determined who could invest in
agriculture; and many investments had visibly political implications.
Two types of investment were involved in raising output in British
India, direct and indirect. Most directly, investing in agriculture
meant applying more labour to more land more often, to clear and
plant, to shorten fallow, to introduce new crops, and to increase
inputs that enhance yields, mostly water and fertilizer. Indirect
investments were also important, in transportation, credit, storage,
processing, irrigation, drainage, and protection. For all investments,
however, labour was the key: everything depended on what was done
by hand. The social distribution of resources that could effectively
direct labour power thus determined who could make what investments and benefit from them. The matrix of control varied greatly
from place to place, and over time, but some noticeable patterns
emerge from the literature.

First it is important to note that productive power can be exerted
at various levels of the agrarian system, and that it has distinct
characteristics at each level. Power at high levels, exercised over
wide stretches of territory, depends upon control of very moveable
resources, like money, credit, ritual honour, loyalty, armies, or
bureaucratic authority; whereas at low levels, locally, power derives
above all from an ability to command immoveables, like land, and
to control resources difficult to manipulate over distance, most
importantly, irrigation water, animals, human labour, and complex
social bonds. Under the Raj, the imperial elite had some power over
a large part of the globe; they were, at that level, very powerful
indeed. Their participation in production, however, was limited by
the economic character of the Raj itself. Decisions in London,
Calcutta, New Delhi, and provincial capitals shaped conditions of
agricultural production throughout the subcontinent. But for the
vast majority of localities, power radiating outward from major
centres in the world system had very indirect, indeterminant, and

highly mediated effects on production relations, productive decision-making, and politics.

At the other end of the productive power spectrum, there were locals deeply embedded in agrarian relations, in control of very local resources, both moveable and immoveable. From an imperial or subcontinental perspective, such people were inconsequential—the faceless 'peasants' of Curzon's imagination. Many, if not most, even lacked official designations within the imperial scheme of things. But their enterprise and power in agricultural communities has become increasingly apparent to historians. Productive activity, and control, were in their hands in the day-to-day workings of agriculture. But who were they? And how did they manage their operations? How did they grapple with the conditions presented to them by the changing agrarian system?

Consider first the case of zamindars. Zamindari domains under the Raj evolved from arenas of control that had focused upon rajas and officials during the eighteenth century. As local royalty, pre-British zamindars had been founts of patronage and authority for the provision of public goods. They regulated access to forests and to uncultivated land; they patronized irrigation, roads, temples, mosques, and shrines. The larger of their domains had been forged amidst always-shifting political alliances, and had been held together in part by ceremonial honours. Smaller domains could be and often were grounded in very direct local control, but the larger ones always worked through various intermediaries who connected royalty to villagers. Such domains remained integrated by balancing the ruler's claim for tribute and obedience with subordinates' ability to migrate, to change sides, or to fight back, given the wide availability of land and military technology.[38]

Designated by law as landlords in 1793, the zamindars stood henceforth, in theory, 'as the focal point for the local accumulation of capital in cash and kind' (Whitcombe 1972: 6). Officials, academics, and politicians would evermore ask why these landlords, with 'monopoly control of land',[39] did not, as expected, invest in agriculture. But the question itself confuses theory with reality, the

[38] See accounts in B. B. Chaudhuri (1958), Ludden (1978a), Price (1979), Ratna Ray (1975), A. Siddiqi (1973), and Stein (1980).

[39] The phrase is used by M. M. Islam (1978: 184–200), the most recent scholar to approach this question as a matter of landlords' economic rationality. See also Bagchi (1968: 265–6).

legal right to collect rent with the actual control of local resources
(Rajat and Ratna Ray 1975: 81). Where zamindars were not village
zamindars; or actually rich peasants, as in Punjab, where their
holdings averaged less than six acres (H. Banerjee 1975: 161–3);
turning a zamindari domain into a landed estate meant turning a
network of royal authority into an economic enterprise. To do so
required radically different management techniques, and closer control than ever before over local resources, all in the face of rigid, high
revenue demands and restrictions on zamindari power imposed by
the Raj itself (B. B. Chaudhuri 1958: 308–46).

Zamindari estates thus became agricultural enterprises to varying
degrees, and in various ways, depending upon the extent to which,
and the methods by which, zamindars sank firm roots in local
production relations. Locally, therefore, to be a zamindar meant
quite different things; as did being a subtenure holder, for instance,
a *thikadar*, who was, in the Hathwa Raj, in Bihar, a revenue con-
tractor closely controlled by the raja (Yang 1978), and who in Uttar
Pradesh operated in a fluid, shifting, and very competitive political
climate.[40] For village zamindars, to tap into production relations
was no problem. Even before the British Raj, they had roots in
village agriculture, though some were more productive and locally
powerful than others. The Rajputs among them were notorious
rentiers, who disdained both cultivation and cultivators; who,
always in debt (Darling 1925: 32–4), left their lands to managers and
hired labourers, and who lost thereby much of their potential income
from rents and profits (H. Banerjee 1979: 161–3).[41] By contrast, the
Punjabi Jats in Ludhiana, Ferozepore, and Jullundur districts invested their labour and capital in land, and 'did not hesitate to take
up the lands of unenterprising zamindars' (H. Banerjee 1978a, 1979:
161–3; also Kessinger 1974).

Relatively small zamindars could also forge working, profitable
estates. The sufi *pirs* and the moneylenders of Multan, having received land grants from Diwan Sawan Mal (1822–44), invested
directly in agriculture. They paid for wells and for expanding cultivation (Darling 1925: 101ff). The characteristic landlord among Arora
moneylenders, who as a group owned a quarter of all cultivated land

---

[40] Musgrave (1972), Whitcombe (1972: 7), and M. Siddiqi (1978: 5) make this
argument.

[41] See also S. P. Sharma on the Senapur Thakurs, Jaunpur District, U.P.,
quoted in Stokes (1978: 242).

in Multan, in 1925, 'carefully supervised his tenants, put up capital for investment, and searched for profitable investments, innovations, and fresh market opportunities. He was the well-sinker; the giver of sugarcane and vegetables and fruit' (Darling 1925: xiii). Though he could not be more of a cultural contrast, the thoroughly modern Jaykrishna Mukherjee of Uttapara, in the Calcutta vicinity, was comparably successful; because he bought up just the villages he could control effectively; he broke and coaxed his way through local circuits of power and influence; and he provided credit, induced cash cropping, and made various local reforms (N. Mukherjee 1975). Jaykrishna became not only the model 'improving landlord' of British dreams, but also a local model of the good zamindar, as portrayed by Lal Behari Day in *Bengal Peasant Life*, a novel composed for a contest sponsored by Jaykrishna himself.

For most large zamindaris, however, the Raj was an endless struggle to retain the aura of royal authority and to keep some control over estate resources. Many big zamindars lost even the indirect, yet still considerable, productive powers they seem to have enjoyed in pre-British times. A somewhat idealized account concerning northern Bengal in the mid-eighteenth century indicates that a great zamindar could then make publicly recognized contributions to agricultural prosperity, through the indispensable agency of local intermediaries. 'Throughout the vast area of the zamindar of Rajshahi, the well-remembered Rani Bhavani and her officials constituted government in the eyes of the people . . . the Rani's *paiks* maintained peace in the country, her revenue officials kept embankments in repair, her agents constructed numerous tanks, temples, and *serais* (inns), her munificence supported priests, teachers, and medical practitioners' (Mahmood 1967, quoted in Ratna Ray 1979: 34–5).[42] But after the Permanent Settlement, Rajshahi and many other estates fell into a vicious cycle of debt, dispossession, and fragmentation. Zamindari families who kept their estates whole and working seem to have done so through two major strategies, often in combination. They could increase their income by subordinating intermediaries, or they could maintain their royal stature by accommodating various local powers. Both strategies demanded zamindari patronage for public goods—and thus some indirect productive activity—as well as largesse for grand ceremonial occasions, to create the public image of enlightened rule and to retain at

[42] For the decline of Rajshahi after 1793, see B. B. Chaudhuri (1858: 308–14).

least the veneer of grandeur. Both also entailed continual conflict and negotiation with subordinate powers. Even small estates were racked with strife, in fact, as were those in the Chenab Colonies, where landlord–tenant relations were 'marked by endless dissension' so that zamindars never became the 'natural leaders of this tract', let alone 'enterprising landlords' (H. Banerjee 1979: 161–3); and where occupancy right disputes provoked severe disturbances in 1907 (Barrier 1974a).

Large estates that came under firm zamindar control seem usually to have done so through the intervention of government. The Hathwa Raj had been relatively centralized before British rule, but a period under the Court of Wards—'an institutional shelter' (Yang 1979c)—further tightened its administration. *Thikadars* put up bids for village revenue contracts, and were kept under close scrutiny; furthermore, they 'were generally the substantial raiyats and money-lenders of their localities' (Yang 1978a: 50; see also Ratna Ray 1979). Indigo planters fitted neatly into this scheme. As *thikadars*, planters paid top money for village contracts, so they could push up indigo cultivation by means of debt, revenue demand, and coercion (Yang 1978a: 35, 44–50; also G. Mishra 1978). They thus became 'improv-ing landlords' of sorts, but without title to land (Bagchi 1972: 200, 363). The Maharaja Lakshmishwar Singh of Darbhanga, who had received zero net income from his estate before its assumption by the Court, in 1860, returned to his durbar, in 1879, at the head of a tight bureaucracy. Under the Court, intermediary tenures had been eliminated, and many of his new administrators were now British, 'either former military or government personnel, or indigo planters' (Yang 1979c: 255). Estate revenues had soared, not without pain to cultivators, 25,000 of whom fled their land in 1974–75, in the face of drought and rigid rent demands.[43]

English educated, the Darbhanga raja patronized public goods in modern style. He funded dispensaries, schools, roads, irrigation, and, most lavishly of all, religious charities (J. S. Jha 1966: 126–8).[44] At least until 1850, even many old-fashioned rajas continued to make indirect investments in agriculture. Birbhum Raja financed tanks and persuaded Santhal tribal leaders to bring their people down to

[43] The actual figure is 5,000 families (Yang 1979c: 257).
[44] J. S. Jha (1966: 126–8). The Raja spent Rs 1,40,209 on public works from 1879 to 1887, out of an annual gross revenue of Rs 21,61,885. The Court of Wards had spent Rs 1,60,494 per year on public works from 1860 to 1879.

the plains, to extend cultivation. Begum Sumroo of Meerut dealt in cotton and sugar, selling her commodities as far afield as Delhi, and gaining for her estate a reputation of prosperity (R. K. Gupta 1977; also Whitcombe 1972: 6–7, 32). In Madras, too, some zamindars had long experience in cotton and grain markets, as did the rajas of Ettaiyapuram and Ramnad, who routinely distributed largesse in grand ceremonial occasions, and funded tanks and temples.[45]

But despite such expenditures, zamindars in Madras ruled domains that were less and less theirs; zamindaris had become by 1900 arenas for the rising power of more local landed elites, of merchants, and of bankers, whose money and minds turned ever less toward the raja's durbar and ever more toward market towns along railway lines. Collecting estate revenues in Madras became more and more difficult, and costly; the Great Depression ruined many estates altogether (Baker, 1976a). It seems that increasingly after 1850, estates had insufficient control over local resources to invest in agriculture. Zamindars could not collect the cash to invest; they could not put cash into localities to stimulate both increased productivity and a steady return for themselves. Instead, they collected what they could and tried to live in style. But even collection could be a vain struggle.[46]

In Uttar Pradesh, zamindars and talukdars struggled not only with one another, but with subtenure holders, too. One powerful group of tenants, called *pukhtadars*, had considerable clout in local circuits of credit and caste relations, so that even though they officially held a decreasing area of land, they amassed an increasing share of estate assets (M. Siddiqi 1978: 6, 14–15, 19–20). Conflicts between owners and tenants had various productive implications. A strong, wealthy estate owner could distribute largesse more lavishly than a weak one, to be sure; but would also tend to discourage many land improvements, like wells, because tenant investments in wells by custom provided a firm claim to occupancy rights (M. Siddiqi 1978: 68–71). Battles to establish local dominance, particularly where combatants were evenly matched, could soak up

[45] Price (1979) introduces the term 'largesse' into our vocabulary, and shows its importance to 'little kings'.

[46] Ludden (1978a) discusses Ettaiyapuram Raja, who expressed to me a great relief at Zamindari Abolition. The Raja had transferred a large proportion of his personal assets out of land following his difficulties from 1929 to 1935, which points to the important fact that zamindari estates, not necessarily zamindar families, were depleted as economic entities under the Raj.

valuable resources, and even disrupt agricultural operations. A very weak raja, on the other hand, might by his very inattention to local matters provide the *de facto* tenure security that would encourage local investment. In Sultanpur, for instance, the Amethi Raja's estate was said to 'swarm with warlike communities who think . . . that they have as good a right to the soil as the Raja, and who act on that belief'; such tenants built 80 per cent of the nearly 10,000 wells constructed in the zamindari from 1861 to 1864 (M. Siddiqi 1978: 69; also A. Siddiqi 1973: 94–6).

Having built and endowed a temple in Benares shortly before (Metcalf 1979: 352), the Amethi Raja may in fact have provided the credit needed to build the nearly 2,000 wells not attributed to his tenants in the early 1860s, because lines of credit in Uttar Pradesh under the Raj characteristically ran from talukdars and zamindars to *thikadars* and village headmen (*maliks*) (Whitcombe 1972: 167–8). These local powers in turn spun webs of credit ties around themselves. Indigo planters used loans, necessitated by the harvest cycle, to secure crops from cultivators, who seem to have accepted such debt peacefully. Credit and grain dealing also went hand in hand (Whitcombe 1972: 179–91). Hence there has emerged an argument among scholars as to whether moneylending in Uttar Pradesh tended 'to siphon off an increasing income from agriculture' (J. Raj 1978: 4), or rather tended to cement local bonds that were themselves part of the production process (Musgrave 1978).

There is no argument about the prevalence of debt, or its significance in agrarian political economy. In fact, strands of power, patronage, dependence, and obligation between lenders and borrowers have become basic diagnostic indicators of production relations in agriculture. But uneven coverage and inconsistent attention to this key transactional nexus make the social character of debt a hotly debatable subject. For example, though Reverend Day called 'the iron chest of the Mahajan' the extension of peasant savings; though Malcolm Darling said of the Punjab moneylender that 'by his assistance to agriculture for 2,500 years he has made life possible for millions who must otherwise have perished or never been born' (1925: 168); though Gerald Barrier called rural moneylending 'Punjab's largest industry' in the 1920s (1977: 215), Tom Kessinger's detailed study of a Punjabi village economy (1974) makes no mention of debt relations.[47]

[47] This omission is due to Kessinger's focus on peasant households and to the nature of the data at his disposal, which he makes clear in his Introduction.

Two trends in historians' thinking about debt are nonetheless notable. Whereas official thought under the Raj focused predominantly on the workings of urban and non-agriculturalist moneylenders, conceived as a distinctive set of specialists, today scholars appreciate that 'the moneylender' was not one but many people: poor widow, rich landlord, banker, foreigner, friend, oppressor, even saviour. Debt bonds were thus quite diverse, diffuse, and well-integrated into the social fabric; they were also, it seems, for the most part very local in their reach, though, as within zamindari domains in Uttar Pradesh and Bihar, they could be plucked out to tie locals to clever landlords, merchants, bankers, or planters. Secondly, whereas British officials saw pre-British Indian agriculture as non-commercial, and logically enough saw debt as an explosive issue—hence the Deccan Riots Commission Report and the Punjab Land Alienation Act (Barrier 1979)—scholars today appreciate more of the commercial complexity of agrarian relations before British rule, and have discovered the integrative, even conservative character of debt under the Raj.

In Bengal, by the late eighteenth century, at least, there had developed a 'complex of moneylending, money changing, and graindealing' around local landed families (*jotedars*), headmen (*mandals*), and other 'rich villagers who combined their activity with agriculture' (Ratna Ray 1979: 63). They were not upstarts. But they stood out increasingly in the course of commercial development, and they expanded their power during the disruption and desertion that followed the 1770 famine (Ratna Ray 1979: 59–60). Local webs of power around such people formed the core of production relations. A great variety of disturbances broke out between zamindars and combinations of these local leaders, whose aggressive activity produced court backlogs, tenant legislation, and subinfeudation in Bengal (K. K. Sengupta 1970, 1971, 1973, 1974). In some cases, zamindars and major tenants, like the iron-fisted *patnidar* of Burdwan, depicted by Reverend Day, reduced locally powerful men to the level of peons and ordinary raiyats.[48] But more commonly, these local folk either held on to their power or expanded at the expense of zamindars (Ratna Ray 1979: 275–9). Bonds of debt focused primarily on *jotedars* and *mandals*—not on zamindars (S. Islam 1974; B. B. Chaudhuri 1977)—and helped the locally rich to resist rent increases or pass them down to lesser folk. Thus the parts

[48] For types of tenancy, see K. M. Mukherji's work on Birbhum.

of Bengal where such local powers pressed hardest became the areas with the highest rental increases, little of which went to zamindar. Consequently, 'the shift of control to this group of privileged tenants (which was often reinforced by their control over rural credit) was a remarkable development in rural Bengal' (B. B. Chaudhuri 1977: 374).

In the midst of such struggles in Bengal zamindaris domains, 'it paid nobody to invest individually in improvement of land', for 'there was no viable mechanism of sharing the cost of land improvement collectively' (Bhaduri 1976: 48). Zamindars could not invest in local production when locals were bent precisely on keeping zamindars out. As economically integrated agricultural estates, therefore, these zamindaris rarely had a chance. Markets in land and crops as well as urban professions became standard investment alternatives for capital shut out of directly productive pursuits. Despite their theoretically 'monopoly control' over land, productive 'investments involved so many risks and uncertainties', including court and coercion costs, that zamindars looked for profits elsewhere (M. M. Islam 1978: 193). In addition, during the late nineteenth century, severe ecological disruptions from railway road building compounded investment problems in Bengal: malaria and cattle disease were epidemic; the river system was in drastic decline (B. B. Chaudhuri 1969a).

Zamindari problems in penetrating local circuits of power throughout South Asia under the Raj did not make it impossible for many to make substantial indirect investments; nor did it stymy local productive investments by others. Quite the contrary: the locally strong became stronger the more they invested in expanding cultivation, in wells, in cash crops, in credit, storage, marriage ties, and religious institutions. Ratna Ray argues that *jotedars* on the eastern edge of Bengali expansion had greater latitude for productive investments, which paid high dividends in local power (1979: 281–2). Where the internal organizational problems of zamindaris do seem to have hurt agriculture was in the provision of some key public goods, like small-scale irrigation and drainage works. Bunds and tanks were reported decaying in South Monghyr, Bhagalpur, Shahabad, and Shahadabad, due to zamindars' 'unwillingness to invest' (Narain 1965: 128–32; also Bagchi 1976; B. B. Chaudhuri 1969a: 188–9). Zamindars throughout Tamil Nadu had well-founded reputations for neglecting tanks (Price 1979; Baker 1976a; Ludden 1978a).

Though much more work on these issues needs to be done, scholarship to date suggests that patterns of local power and productive activity did not differ systematically between raiyatwari and zamindari South Asia. There was, it seems, but one defining difference: local circuits of power worked in the one under the imprint of both government and zamindar authority, and in the other under only that of the government. Conflicts over land control were therefore more localized, simplified, and politically insignificant in raiyatwari areas; they were confined to scattered, unconnected villages, and to the courts; they did not give rise to major pieces of legislation, nor to political organizations. But viewed in terms of strictly local patterns of productive power, raiyatwari and zamindari South Asia were strikingly similiar (see e.g. Nicholas 1968).

Research on Bombay and Madras Presidencies suggests that generally a minority of powerful people were dominant locally by the outset of British rule, in determining the distribution of productive resources. Land, credit, bullocks, carts, ploughs, grain reserves, and water supplies all gravitated toward their control. Their investments in agriculture, and the availability of investment opportunities for others less powerful, directed economic development locally and defined local power relations over time. As in zamindari areas, just how many and what sorts of opportunities emerged locally depended upon how specific agricultural milieus became enwrapped in developing markets. Who got what opportunities depended upon how their local politics of access worked out in the context of colonial legal and administrative operations. As in zamindari areas, too, numerous local struggles ensued, as those with power pursued economic opportunities and tried, at the same time, to monopolize key resources, while others pursued opportunities and sought increased access to the same key resources. In both zamindari and raiyatwari South Asia, the colonial market economy penetrated already commercialized local domains. In fact, market access became a resource to control like any other. Credit, and the local ties it helped cement, became increasingly tied to world prices for export commodities, and local decisions about investment were pegged accordingly (Baker 1978).

Changing conditions under the Raj reshaped local relations, in both zamindari and raiyatwari areas, but nowhere did the Raj dissolve the local circuits of power that defined the social character of production at the outset of British rule. Commercialization did not break up localities into swarms of individuals related to one another primarily through the market. Neither did political change obliterate the locality as an arena of power. In some respects, colonial administration enshrined localities with more institutional status than they had had in pre-British India, especially in raiyatwari and mahalwari areas. R. E. Frykenberg has shown how locals struggled to maintain their power in the decades of transition to Anglo-Indian administration (1963); and administrators believed in the authenticity of 'the village republic'. After 1920, local circuits of power became bases for electoral, agitational, and administrative alliances among dominant landowning castes.[49] The Raj effectively lopped off a layer of the eighteenth-century agrarian system, wherein zamindars, rajas, and agents of Emperors, Nawabs, and Peshwas had played significant local roles, partly as patrons of public goods.[50] Peasant and local landlord enterprise, therefore, became even more dominant under the Raj as the means of agricultural investment.

A final parallel between raiyatwari and zamindari areas is that in both there seems to have been, at least through the nineteenth century, noticeable slippage in social mechanisms to fund small-scale drainage irrigation. Rich farmers, merchants, bankers, and bureaucrats funded temples, roads, credit, storage, wells, and field irrigation, as did peasants and landlords locally. But tanks seem to have suffered pervasive neglect. Maintaining or rebuilding many tanks seems to have been beyond the means of locals and outside the priorities of government (Ludden 1979b). At this stage of research, it is not possible to make empirically solid comparisons between the 1800s and earlier centuries. But functionally speaking it appears that the rajas and revenue intermediaries of pre-British times were but imperfectly replaced by the colonial bureaucracy when it came to small irrigation works. Indeed, it may be that small tanks

---

[49] Examples of this phenomenon at work can be found in Baker (1976), Frankel (1978), Hardiman (1977, 1981), Jeffrey (1976), Washbrook (1976), and elsewhere.

[50] Gordon (1980) presents Peshwa records showing that local officials, in turn for land grants, repaired dams and recruited settlers in Khandesh to repopulate villages during the eighteenth century. R. K. Patil reports in the most recent issue of *Wamana*, a quarterly journal of water management, edited in Bangalore, that 'local influentials' built small diversion dams (*bhandaras*) in Nasik District, Maharashtra, in return for appointments to village office from the Mughals. Community-organized irrigation under these works was regulated under the British and reportedly continues to this day.

were best cared for precisely where local magnates best kept hold of
their former powers, that is, where the colonial administration was
least successful in replacing patrimony with bureaucracy. Possibly
R. E. Frykenberg's white ants, eating away at the edifice of empire
(1963), did some building, too. As for the general picture of small-
scale irrigation, Elizabeth Whitcombe's characterization of the U.P.
situation can be applied broadly to British India before 1900: 'The
giant public works dominated government's concern with the agricultural environment. Small-scale works were coordinated neither
within a framework of public works nor amongst themselves, for
such coordination implied a concept alien to the conduct of public
affairs and insufficiently developed even today. Added to this was a
chronic lack of agency and of means' (1972: 12).

Toward Comparing Localities

Historical work to date would thus seem to support two propositions
about productive power in agrarian localities under the Raj: most
agricultural investment, direct and indirect, occurred as transactions
within local circuits of power that existed before British rule; and
trends in agricultural development from 1750 to 1950 inevitably
effected local power relations built upon the control of productive
resources. It is therefore critical to explore the specific character of
localities themselves as arenas of productive power relations. To do
so, we must delineate key variables with which to describe social
relations at work in particular productive milieus, and thus to
compare change in localities over time. One means to approach such
comparative work is to posit fairly simple typologies (see e.g.
B. DasGupta 1975; Washbrook 1976; Ludden 1978; Bouton, forthcoming), which seek to reduce endless local diversity to manageable
terms, and thus to establish a framework within which to consider
the particulars of time and place.

   When we take a suitably long-term view of agricultural organization in South Asia, say 1750 to 1950, there does seem to be a cluster-
ing of key variables that differentiates patterns of productive power
in agrarian localities. Three variables stand out in the literature as
setting the range of possible productive opportunities: the man/land
ratio, agricultural technology, and commodity markets. Three other
variables seem critical in shaping patterns of local access to investable
resources: the division of labour, the distribution of landed property,

and the status of major caste groups. These variables are not determined locally, of course, but they combine locally, with definite implications for power and production. Their interaction would be something like this. Lower ratios of people to cultivable acreage increases opportunities to expand cultivation, while the technological means for doing so would set labour costs and organizational priorities, and commodity markets would set values on crops, labour, and capital. The division of labour would establish which groups would be most likely to pursue particular opportunities, while the distribution of land would define relative access to capital, and the status of castes would determine relative social mobility, hence the kinds of opportunities outside the locality available to those within it.

Some examples will illustrate how variables work together, and why simple propositions about political, economic, cultural, or ecological causality will not do. The availability of open land is not itself sufficient to create social mobility, as analogies with an idealized vision of the American frontier might suggest. If the land is jungle, as was most of eastern India, it takes lots of labour to clear, plant, and protect from animals. If it is dry scrubland, the same job can be done with very small groups, who nonetheless need to protect themselves, as well as to weather frequent droughts. Irrigated land, moreover, requires large initial and steady subsequent doses of organized labour for construction and maintenance, as well as an institutional mechanism to distribute water and to settle disputes, lest the system break down during the growing season. The specific technical requirements of any cultivation regime, therefore, combine with the natural tendency for farming populations to expand proximally to make it likely that one type of organizational structure will be reproduced throughout a particular type of terrain unless prevented from doing so. Pre-existing types of agricultural organization are thus more likely to be recreated on their respective frontiers than are radically new ones to arise, given no change in technology.

New technologies—both material and organizational—open new possibilities. Under the Raj, government works enabled farmers to organize irrigated agriculture on a new footing in the Canal Colonies and in the Krishna–Godavari delta. Since Independence, tubewells and motorized pumpsets have had the same effect. Thus irrigation itself has no single impact on production relations; rather, types of irrigation technology provide specific opportunities for the people who make them work. Whereas pre-British irrigation technology involved community control over water, based primarily on local means to build, repair, allocate, and arbitrate, more modern forms of government expenditure and bureaucratic control, combined with new types of irrigation-building and water-lifting apparatus, have increasingly freed farmers to exploit water as individuals. Thus, who gets how much access to local drainage and groundwater depends upon local politics, on the distribution of capital, and on available technology.

Similarly, commodity markets provide opportunities proportionately as people have the means to exploit them. Commercialization in general is less important than the character of specific markets. Under the Raj, export crop markets tended to be linear: a set of key intermediaries linked farmers to seaports and became social nodes of power within the marketing chain. Just who these people were, and what their relations to others in the chain entailed, depended upon the character of the agrarian relations penetrated by export markets, and upon the spatial spread of market integration. Markets in foodgrains, like those in land, labour, and credit, on the other hand, were not linear, and were, moreover, thoroughly enmeshed in long-standing local relations of resource control. Commercialization, or the development of agrarian capitalism, therefore, had not one but many local manifestations. The key problem becomes how to assess trends in market access and participation in particular types of localities.

With such complexities in mind, we might, following the lead of David Washbrook (1973, 1976), posit two broad categories of agrarian localities in South Asia, each comprised of many types and sub-types, but each nonetheless distinct as a category in contrast to the other. By 1750 each had a characteristic pattern of productive power relations, defined in very general terms, and each underwent distinctive processes of change under the Raj. For convenience we can call them 'wet' and 'dry' localities, because they developed in areas of sharply contrasting endowments of surface water usable in agriculture with pre-modern technology.

By the eighteenth century wet localities characterized much of Bengal and Bihar, as well as the western peninsular coast; they were abundant also along the eastern coastal plain, where they drew water from rivers and tanks. They depended upon relatively high rainfall and/or irrigation, to grow rice. Densely populated, and centres of traditional high civilization, they were dominated by non-cultivating, high-caste landowners, often Brahmans, who received obligatory patronage from native rulers, and who, as literate cultural elites, comprised a regional administrative and political elite group as well. Sophisticated and commercialized, such localities were not cut off from cities and towns by cultural, political, and economic differences often portrayed as definitive of 'peasant society'. Urban centres and trade networks were in fact dominated by the agrarian elite, whose opportunities for enterprise thus spread smoothly along caste, kinship, and factional lines from village to town to port city. Paddy cultivation was of course very labour- and capital-intensive; and agriculture went on within a rigid social distinction between the status of landowner and labourer. Agricultural labour was a low-caste, often untouchable, occupation, and thus the cultural evaluation of labour itself was low. There was a marked overlap of landlessness and labouring status; and of caste and class in the countryside.

By contrast, throughout vast stretches of the peninsular upland, in the Deccan, Punjab, and western Gangetic Plain, there were sparsely settled tracts, arid or semi-arid, whose main food crops were millets and wheat, and whose little irrigation was from wells. Carved from scrubby wastelands, or, as in Punjab, from rich land situated in the marches of invaders, these localities were the domain of rugged warrior castes, many of whom the British dubbed 'the martial races'. In 1750 there was still a lot of open land, as in Sirsa District, and a lot of fighting. Long-fallow dry-cropping and garden cultivation with wells were at the core of peasant subsistence strategies. Peasants, moreover, worked the land mostly with their own hands. There were certainly rich and poor among them, and an inner circle of dominant families in each locality. But there was no sizeable strata of landless agricultural labourers, and hence no clear correspondence of class and caste. Open land provided groups of ambitious or defeated warrior-peasants with many opportunites for new cultivation, for conflict over rights to land, and for military adventure. Fighting and farming went hand in hand.

Urban centres in regions covered with dry localities were strung out along trade routes surrounded by scrub, and needed constant protection. As centres of political power, located in favoured agricultural spots, and crowded with merchants and artisans, towns became quite distinctive social milieus. Their mercantile elites were different in caste from dominant landed groups in the countryside,

or, like the Shanars in southern Tamil Nadu, culturally estranged
from their rustic country cousins. As the abode of rulers, merchants,
and high culture elites, cities in dry tracts were a world apart from
the rugged villages all around. Here, much more than in wet regions,
there was a marked social gap between town and country.

Under the Raj, the local landlord status elite in South Asia's wet
localities seems to have retained its power. It was the stratum of
authority and economic power through which new commercial and
political opportunities entered the locality. Elite command of labour
and capital enabled them to expand their domains with the expansion
of cultivation. Though diversified labour markets provided some
new opportunities for people without land, the landed elite retained
its grip on labour through credit and rent, and through its power as
employers throughout the agrarian economy. The labouring castes'
very low social status, moreover, reduced their occupational mobility
to a minimum.

There was considerable circulation, however, within the elite
strata itself. Declining irrigation and decreasing reserves of land for
new cultivation drove many out of agriculture, into professions and
politics, where they pursued new resources based on their income
from land. Some of course did better than others in the village, too,
amidst struggles to garner bits of agricultural surplus. Individual
enterprise in the colonial context tended to make the rich among
them stand out more than ever before: they contracted for government public works, took on the mantle of local office, became cele-
brated politicians, and set up various business concerns: they
patronized temples and nationalist causes, gave huge weddings, and
set the pace in local society. Their less fortunate elite status peers
sank into the growing ranks of the landowning, educated middle
class, comfortable, sometimes precariously so, but quite respectable,
nonetheless. The poorest among this group, urban-employed for
generations, lost their contact with land altogether; today they are
clerks and hotel workers.

Whereas commercial, educational, and political trends did open
up new avenues out of agriculture, production trends in wet localities,
after 1900 at least, seem to have reduced options in landlord–labour
relations. Population growth, diminishing space for expanding cultivation, and few innovations in productive technique created greater
numbers of landless labourers, more pressure to apply their labour
more intensively, higher rents, lower wages, and increasing conflict.

In eastern India, the process embroiled whole tribal populations, as well. W. W. Hunter, for example, observed that in 1832–51 Santhals cleared and planted 12.7 square miles of jungle each year, in the Rajmahal valleys, only to be dominated thereafter by Hindu money-lenders, traders, and zamindars (1897: 222–5). The scenario was henceforth repeated many times (B. B. Chaudhuri 1969a). Many once-prosperous wet localities thus became in this century arenas of at best very slow agricultural growth, high class conflict, and pervasive immiseration of labour (see e.g. Bhaduri 1976; Bhattacharya and Roy 1977; Broomfield 1976; A. N. Das; Gough 1978).

Change under the Raj took quite a different path in dry localities, in warrior-peasant domains. Many of the most powerful warriors were eliminated from the local scene, either quickly, as in the Maratha Wars, or more slowly, as their domains of royalty decayed within zamindaris. Export crops, especially cotton, and new com-mercial crops, like groundnut, enabled cultivators to increase their cash income, and the best-placed among them took on key roles as market intermediaries. The internal structure of productive power clearly underwent more dramatic change in dry than in wet localities. But how to characterize that change remains controversial. Clearly the local power of moneylenders and merchants increased. But who were they? The Deccan Riots Commission believed they were alien forces who had fomented the riots by making demands on cultivators to repay loans in the face of falling cotton prices. Ravinder Kumar (1968a, 1968b) argues rather that the riots signalled basic structural changes in village society, typified by the growing power of indi-vidual rich peasants. Neil Charlesworth counters by questioning the significance of the riots as symptoms of anything other than food shortages. The Commission, in his view, blew these 'minor grain riots' out of all proportion, because of anxiety over agrarian unrest. Far from signalling great structural change, the riots were merely an exercise of power by violent rich peasants, who had been powerful long before the Cotton Boom, but who now flexed their muscles in the market (1972; also 1978, 1980). David Washbrook presents a similar view of dry localities in Madras (1974, 1978), where local magnates tightly controlled local access to land, credit, and cotton markets, in his view. But a contrary picture emerges for these same dry Madras localities from the work of J. S. Ponniah (1944) and Andrew Kolliner (1975), who see a very competitive market for cotton and credit, full of petty participants and no clear pattern of domination.[51]

It thus remains debatable how much and how fast commercial development produced a more open pattern of access to agricultural resources. Two related structural trends, both much less debatable, would seem to support the proposition that market participation expanded dramatically in many dry localities. First, commercial development in dry localities produced a great number of conflicts over access to social status and market goods. From tiny grain riots and violent crime (Arnold 1979a, 1979b), to fights between Shanars and Maravas in Tamil Nadu (Hardgrave 1969; Ludden 1978a), to the Deccan Riots and communal conflict in Punjab, a great many conflicts had the ethos of battles between money and landed interests, new power versus old. Second, there was an unmistakable dynamism in agriculture in many dry localities. New options opened up for people with land to make money, and to reinvest it in land. Rich peasants, who were certainly there before British rule, emerged decisively as peasant capitalists. Rustic folk, their vision of wealth focused less on genteel urban occupations than on the land itself. They put the proceeds of cash crop sales into new wells (Ludden 1978a); they used incomes from urban occupations, from the army, and from migrant labour to increase productivity on the farm (Kessinger 1974). Jats, Marathas, Reddis, and Gounders, they struggled with the land to make it pay, with a rationality perhaps more martial than economic (Nair 1979), and often in competition with non-dominant but commercially aggressive castes like the Shanars. New technologies furthered their success by opening new production possibilities. New irrigation works, and more recently hybrid varieties, tubewells, and motorized pumpsets, like cash crops, expanded investment opportunities for those with land. In time, farmers turned agrarian wealth into political power to challenge old urban elites in major capital cities.

Impressionistic, to be sure, this brief comparison of 'wet' and 'dry' locality categories reflects some trends depicted in more detail by others in this volume, particularly by Don Attwood, Ashok Rudra, and Lloyd and Susanne Rudolph. But my purpose is rather to argue that there was indeed patterned variation in changing pro-

[51] Bruce Robert is currently completing a dissertation at the University of Wisconsin, Madison, in which the theme of competitive price determination in dry Madras localities receives direct and complete attention.

ductive power relations under the Raj, and to indicate the promise
and challenge of comparative analysis in agrarian history. The
problems of comparative work are formidable; they are obvious in
the very complexity of South Asian agricultural geography. Perhaps
with such work in mind, Daniel and Alice Thorner two decades ago
divided India alone into 36 major agricultural regions (1962); and,
more systematically, R. L. Singh (1971) defined 67 regions in India,
each capable of further subdivision (see also J. Singh 1974; and
Spate and Learmonth 1967). The more variables one considers, the
more each locality begins to look unique, so that it becomes essential
to handle variables in clusters that together define types of localities
in bounded regions with specific historical characteristics. How many
types of regions and localities are there? The question has yet to be
addressed on a large scale, historically. But work on South India has
begun to lay foundations for the effort (Beck 1976; Bouton 1980;
Ludden 1978a, 1978b; Stein 1980; Washbrook 1976).

Studies of South India make it explicit that relevant variables have
distinct historical characteristics, which make a variety of time-
frames suitable for analysis, though what seems fixed in one frame
may well be changing in another. Long-term processes of change,
consuming many centuries, produced the agricultural landscape
itself, the distribution of caste groups, the technologies, and the
cultural and political geographies that modern studies would consider established features of regional definition. Political and market
networks, on the other hand, as well as production technologies,
would change rather rapidly in recent centuries, with more definite
effects on local relations of productive power. The relative significance of key variables would also change between periods, and,
perhaps, between regions; for example, that of religious institutions
in agrarian political economy. Moreover, scholars would certainly
assign explanatory importance to different variables, given diverging
theoretical or methodolgical orientations.

Though there can thus be no single blueprint for comparative
agrarian history, some principles are clear, as indicated by recent
work on South India and other parts of the subcontinent. First and
foremost, in my view, is the need for descriptive attention to the
social organization of production in particular agricultural milieus.
With all the data we have and all the arguments that rage concerning
agricultural development in South Asia, there is precious little on
the production process as day-to-day human interaction. Major

methodological traditions in agrarian history can therefore not be faulted alone for failing to produce very little work along these lines, but lack of it will hamper comparative efforts for some years to come. A closely related need is for an analytical vocabulary designed for comparative description, that is, one neither too localistic nor too tied to one theory or disciplinary paradigm. Many studies of agrarian South Asia either narrate particularistic detail so indiscriminately, or select relevant variables so formalistically, as to vitiate comparisons based on variable clusters. In short, comparative work seems by nature to be interdisciplinary, as illustrated by the disciplinary diversity of comparative studies to date, in anthropology (Mencher 1966), political science (Bouton 1980; Zagoria 1971), economics (Dasgupta 1975), and history (Bagchi 1976; Ludden 1978a; Stokes 1978; and Washbrook 1976).

Its basic features would seem to guarantee comparative work relatively low status among theoreticians and disciplinarians, but for scholars concerned with agrarian issues it holds great promise. Substantively, it would seem the only method by which to build a comprehensive understanding of living conditions, social relations, and development dilemmas in the South Asian countryside, where local diversity must be built into any valid understanding of 'the whole'. Methodologically, it provides a means to test a wide variety of propositions, and a logical bridge between established academic traditions. Comparative agrarian studies could thus comprise a common intellectual focus for the many scholars whose distance from one another leaves all in the dark more than they need to be.

BIBLIOGRAPHY

Journal Abbreviations
AS   *Asian Survey*
BCAS   *Bulletin of Concerned Asia Scholars*
BDS   *Bangladesh Development Studies*
BPP   *Bengal Past and Present*
CHJ   *Calcutta Historical Journal*
CIS(D)   *Contributions to Indian Sociology* (Delhi)
CSSH   *Comparative Studies in Society and History*
DUS   *Dacca University Studies*
EEH   *Explorations in Economic History*
EHR   *Economic History Review*

EJ	*The Economic Journal*
Enq	*Enquiry*
EPW	*Economic and Political Weekly*
HJE	*Hitotsubashi Journal of Economics*
IESHR	*Indian Economic and Social History Review*
IHC	Indian Historical Congress, Proceedings
IHRC	Indian Historical Records Commission, Proceedings
IHR	*Indian Historical Review*
JAS	*Journal of Asian Studies*
JEH	*Journal of Economic History*
J. Ind. H.	*Journal of Indian History*
J. Int. H.	*Journal of Interdisciplinary History*
JMU	*Journal of Madras University*
JPS	*Journal of Peasant Studies*
JSH	*Journal of Social History*
JSR	*Journal of Social Research* (Ranchi)
MAS	*Modern Asian Studies*
PHC	Punjab Historical Conference, Proceedings
PJR	*Punjab Journal of Research*
PP	*Past and Present*
PPP	*Punjab Past and Present*
PS	*Peasant Studies*
RC	*Race and Class*
Rev	*Review*
SA	*South Asia*
SAR	*South Asian Research*
SAR	*South Asia Review*
SEHR	*Scandinavian Economic History Review*
SIH	*Studies in History*
SS	*Social Scientist*

Abdullah, Abu Ahmed (1980), 'Landlord and Rich Peasant under Permanent Settlement', CHJ, 4, 2, January–June, 1–27, and 5, 1, July–December, 89–153.

Adas, Michael (1974), *The Burma Delta: Economic Development and Social Change on an Asian Rice Frontier, 1852–1941* (Madison).

—— (1977), 'Ryotwari in Lower Burma: The Establishment and Decline of a Peasant Proprietor System' in R. E. Frykenberg (ed.), *Land Tenure and Peasant in South Asia*, pp. 100–20.

Ahmad, Kamruddin (1970), *A Social History of Bengal* (Dacca).

Alavi, Hamsa (1975), 'India and the Colonial Mode of Production', EPW, 10, 33–5, August, Special Number, 1235–62.

Appadurai, Arjun and Carol A. Breckenridge (1976), 'The South Indian Temple: Authority, Honour, and Redistribution', CIS(D), December.

Arnold, David (1979a), 'Looting, Grain Riots, and Government Policy in South India, 1918', PP, 84, August, 111–45.

—— (1979b), 'Dacoity and Rural Crime in Madras, 1860–1940', JPS, 6, 2, January, 140–67.

Arnold, D., R. Jeffrey and J. Manor (1976), 'Caste Associations in South India: A Comparative Analysis', IESHR, 12, 3, July–September, 353–74.

Atchi Reddy, M. (1978), 'Official Data on Agricultural Wages in the Madras Presidency from 1873', IESHR, 15, 4, October–December, 451–66.

—— (1979), 'Wages Data from the Private Agricultural Accounts, Nellore District, 1893–1974', IESHR, 16, 3, July–September, 301–22.

Baden Powell, Henry (1892), Land Systems in British India (London), 2 vols.

Bagchi, Amiya K. (1972), Private Investment in India, 1900–1932 (Cambridge).

—— (1976), 'Reflections on Patterns of Regional Growth in India during British Rule', BPP, 95, 1 (# 180), January–June, 247–89.

—— (1978), 'Needed: A Political Economy of South India', SS, 7, 1–2, August–September, 95–102.

Bajaj, Jairus (1978), 'Capitalist Domination and the Small Peasantry: Deccan Districts in the Late Nineteenth Century' in Ashok Rudra et al., Studies on the Development of Capitalism in India, pp. 351–428.

Bajaj, S. K. (1972), 'British Policy Toward the Punjab Peasantry, With Special Reference to the Punjab Tenancy Act, 1866', PPP, 6, 1, April, 212–26.

Baker, Christopher John (1976a), 'Tamilnad Estates in the Twentieth Century', IESHR, 8, 1, January–March, 1–44.

—— (1976b), The Politics of South India, 1920–1937 (Cambridge).

—— (1978), 'Debt and Depression in Madras, 1929–1936' in Dewey and Hopkins (eds), The Imperial Impact, pp. 233–42.

—— (1979), 'Madras Headmen' in Chaudhuri and Dewey (eds), Economy and Society, pp. 26–52.

Ballhatchet, Kenneth (1957), Social Policy and Social Change in Western India, 1817–1832 (London).

Banaji, Jairus (1977), 'Small Peasantry and Capitalist Domination: Deccan Districts in the Late Nineteenth Century', EPW, 7, 33–34, August, Special Number, 1375–1404.

Bandopadhyay, Arun (1978), 'The Nature of Landownership in Tamil Nadu from 1820 to 1855', CHJ, 3, 1, July–December, 56–82.

Banerjee, Anil Chandra (1980), The Agrarian System of Bengal, Vol. 1: 1582–1793 (Delhi).

Banerjee, Himadri (1977), 'Agricultural Labourers of the Punjab during the Second Half of the Nineteenth Century', PPP, 11, 1, April, 96–116.

—— (1978a), 'Growth of Commercial Agriculture in the Punjab during the Second Half of the Nineteenth Century', PPP, 12, 1, April, 221–56.

—— (1978b), 'A Study of Some Aspects of the Effects of Transfers of Land on Agriculture in the Punjab during the Second Half of the Nineteenth Century', CHJ, 3, 1, July–December, 83–103.

—— (1979), 'Zamindar–Cultivator Relations and the Struggle over Rent in the Punjab (1849–1900)', PPP, 13, 1, April, 132–63.

—— (1980), Agrarian Society of the Punjab, 1849–1901 (Delhi).

Banerji, Tarashankar (1966), Internal Market of India, 1834–1900 (Calcutta).

Banga, Indu (1978), Agrarian System of the Sikhs: Late Eighteenth and Early Nineteenth Century (Delhi).

Barrier, Norman Gerald (1974a), 'The Punjab Disturbances of 1907: The

Response of the British Government in India to Agrarian Unrest', PPP, 8, 2, October, 444–77.

—— (1974b), 'Quantification in Punjab Social and Political History: Sources and Problems', PPP, 8, 1, April, 1–12.

—— (1979), 'The Formulation and Enactment of the Punjab Land Alienation Bill', PPP, 13, 1, April, 193–215.

Bayly, C. A. (1979), 'English-language Historiography on British Expansion in India and Indian Reactions since 1945' in P. C. Emmer and H. L. Wesseling (eds), *Reappraisals in Overseas History* (Leiden), pp. 21–54.

Beck, Brenda E. F. (1976), 'Centers and Boundaries of Regional Caste Systems: Toward a General Model' in Carol A. Smith (ed.), *Regional Analysis* (New York), pp. 255–88.

—— (ed.) (1979), *Perspectives on a Regional Culture: Essays about the Coimbatore Region of South India* (Delhi).

Bhaduri, Amit (1973), 'Agricultural Backwardness under Semi-Feudalism', EJ, March.

—— (1976), 'The Evolution of Land Relations in Eastern India under British Rule', IESHR, 13, 1, January–March, 45–58.

Bhattacharya, Durgaprasad and Rama Deb (Malakar) Roy (1977), 'Agricultural Wages in Bengal and Bihar, 1793–1972', SS, 6, 1, August, 65–73.

Bhutani, V. C. (1968), 'Lord Curzon's Agricultural Policy in India', PPP, 2, 2, October, 366–99.

Blyn, George (1966), *Agricultural Trends in India, 1891–1907: Output, Availability, and Productivity* (Philadelphia).

Bouton, Marshall (1980), 'Sources of Agrarian Radicalism: A Study of Tanjavur District, South India', dissertation, University of Chicago, forthcoming as a publication of Princeton University Press.

Breman, Jan (1974), *Patronage and Exploitation: Changing Agrarian Relations in South Gujerat, India* (Berkeley).

Broomfield, John H. (1966), 'The Regional Elites: A Theory of Modern Indian History' rpt. in Metcalf (ed.), *Modern India*, pp. 60–72.

—— (1976), 'Peasant Mobilization in Twentieth Century Bengal' in J. Spielberg and S. Whitefor (eds), *Forging Nations: A Comparative View of Rural Ferment and Revolt* (East Lansing), pp. 41–60.

Brown, Judith (1972), *Gandhi's Rise to Power: Indian Politics, 1915–1922* (Cambridge).

—— (1974), 'Gandhi and India's Peasants, 1917–1922', JPS, i, 4, July, 462–85.

Buchanan, D. H. (1934), *The Development of Capitalistic Enterprise in India* (New York).

Catanach, I. J. (1970), *Rural Credit in Western India, 1875–1930* (Berkeley).

Chandra, Bipan (1966), *The Rise and Growth of Economic Nationalism in India* (New Delhi).

—— (1979), *Nationalism and Colonialism in Modern India* (New Delhi).

Chandra, Satish (1976), 'Some Institutional Factors in Providing Capital Inputs for the Improvement and Expansion of Cultivation in Medieval India', IHR, 3, 1, July, 83–98.

Charlesworth, Neil, 1972, 'The Myth of the Deccan Riots', MAS, 6, 4, 401–21.

—— (1978), 'Rich Peasants and Poor Peasants in Late Nineteenth Century Maharashtra' in Dewey and Hopkins (eds), *The Imperial Impact*, pp. 97–113.

—— (1979), 'Trends in the Agricultural Performance of an Indian Province: The Bombay Presidency, 1900–1920' in Chaudhuri and Dewey (eds), *Economy and Society*, pp. 113–42.

—— (1980), 'The "Middle Peasant Thesis" and the Roots of Agrarian Agitation in India, 1914–1947', JPS, 7, 3, April, 259–80.

Chatterjee, S. P. (1949), *Bengal in Maps: A Geographical Analysis of Resource Distribution in West Bengal and Eastern Pakistan* (Bombay).

Chattopadhyaya, Haraprasad (1980), 'Madras Raiyats under the Raiyatwari Settlement—Their Treatment at the Hands of Revenue Collectors in the Pre-Mutiny Days—Possibilities of Peasants as a Revolutionary Force', CHJ, 4, 2, January–June, 43–62.

Chaudhuri, Binay Bhushan (1958), 'Agrarian Relationships in Bengal after the Permanent Settlement, 1793–1819', unpublished D.Phil. thesis, University of Calcutta, 1958.

—— (1964), *The Growth of Commercial Agriculture in Bengal* (Calcutta) (written under variant spelling: Benoy Chowdhury).

—— (1969a), 'Agricultural Production in Bengal, 1850–1900: Coexistence of Decline and Growth', BPP, 88, July–December, 152–206.

—— (1969b), 'Rural Credit Relations in Bengal', IESHR, 6, 3, September, 203–57.

—— (1970), 'Growth of Commercial Agriculture in Bengal', IESHR, 7, 1, 25–60, and 7, 2, 211–51.

—— (1972), 'Agrarian Movements in Bihar and Bengal, 1919–1939' in B. R. Nanda (ed.), *Socialism in India* (Delhi), pp. 190–229.

—— (1973), 'The Story of a Peasant Revolt in a Bengal District', BPP, 92, 2, July–December, 220–78.

—— (1975a), 'The Land Market in Eastern India, 1793–1940. I: The Movement of Land Prices, and II: The Changing Composition of Landed Society', IESHR, 12, 1, January–March, 1–42 and 12, 2, April–June, 133–67.

—— (1975b), 'The Process of Depeasantization in Bengal and Bihar, 1885–1947', IHR, 2, L, July, 105–65.

—— (1976a), 'Agricultural Growth in Bengal and Bihar, 1770–1860: Growth of Cultivation since the Famine of 1770', BPP, 95, 1, January–June, 290–340.

—— (1976b), 'The Agrarian Question in Bengal and the Government, 1850–1900', CHJ, 1, 1, July, 33–88.

—— (1977), 'The Movement of Rent in Eastern India', IHR, 3, 2, January, 308–90.

Chaudhuri, K. N. and Clive Dewey (eds) (1979), *Economy and Society: Essays in Indian Economic and Social History* (Delhi).

Cheng Siok-Hwa (1966), 'Land Tenure Problems in Burma, 1852–1940', *J. Royal Asiatic Society* (Malayan Branch), 38, July, 106–34.

Chicherov, A. I. (1971), *Indian Economic Development in the 16th–18th Centuries: Outline History of Crafts and Trade* (Moscow).

Choksy, R. D. (1945), *Economic History of the Bombay Deccan, 1818–1868* (Poona).

—— (1955), *Economic Life in the Bombay Deccan, 1818–1939* (Bombay).

Chowdry, Prem (1976), 'Rural Relations Prevailing in the Punjab at the Time of the So-Called "Golden Laws" Agrarian Legislation of the Late Thirties', PPP, 10, 2, October, 461–80.

Cohn, Bernard S. (1961), 'From Indian Status to British Contract', JEH, 21, 4, December, 613–28.

—— (1968), 'Notes on the History of the Study of Indian Society and Culture' in Milton Singer and Bernard S. Cohn (eds), *Structure and Change in Indian Society* (Chicago), pp. 3–29.

—— (1969), 'Structural Change in Indian Rural Society' in R. E. Frykenberg (ed.), *Land Control and Social Structure in Indian History* (Madison), pp. 53–122.

—— (1970), 'Society and Social Change under the Raj', SAR, 5, 4, October, 27–49.

—— (1971), 'Regions Subjective and Objective: Their Relation to the Study of Modern Indian History and Society' in T. R. Metcalf (ed.), *Modern India: An Interpretive Anthology*, pp. 33–59.

Cohn, Bernard S. and McKim Marriott (1958), 'Networks and Centers in the Integration of Indian Civilization', JSR, 1, 1, September, 1–9.

Cooper, Chester L. (1960), 'Moneylenders and the Economic Development of Lower Burma: An Exploratory Historical Study of the Role of the Indian Chettiyars', unpublished Ph.D. dissertation, American University.

Crawley, W. F. (1971), 'Kisan Sabhas and Agrarian Revolt in the United Provinces, 1920 to 1921', MAS, 5, 2, 95–109.

Crane, Robert I. (1963), 'Problems of Writing Indian History: The Case of Studies in Indian Nationalism' in S. Gopal, R. Thapar *et al.*, *Problems of Historical Writing in India* (New Delhi), pp. 35–49.

Darling, (Sir) Malcolm (1925), *The Punjab Peasant in Prosperity and Debt* (Delhi), 1977 rpt.

Das, Arvind ¡Narayan (1981), *Agrarian Unrest and Socio-economic Change in Bihar, 1930–1972* (Delhi).

Das, Arvind N. and V. Nilakant (eds) (1979), *Agrarian Relations in India* (Delhi).

Dasgupta, Biplab (1975), 'A Typology of Village Socio-economic Systems, from Indian Village Studies', EPW, August, 1395–1414.

Day, Lal Behari (1908), *The Bengal Peasant Life* (London), 1980 rpt.

Desai, A. R. (ed.) (1979), *Peasant Struggles in India* (Bombay).

Desai, Ashok V. (1978), 'Revenue Administration and Agricultural Statistics in Bombay Presidency', IESHR, 15, 2, April–June, 173–86.

Desai, M. B. (1948), *Rural Economy of Gujerat* (London).

Dewey, Clive (1972), 'Images of the Village Community: A Study in Anglo-Indian Thought', MAS, 6, 3, 291–328.

—— (1974), 'The Agricultural Statistics of the Punjab, 1867–1947', *Bulletin of Quantitative and Computer Methods in South Asian Studies*, 2, March, 3–14.

—— (1978), 'Patwari and Chaukidar: Subordinate Officials and the Reliability of India's Agricultural Statistics' in Dewey and Hopkins (eds), *The Imperial Impact*, pp. 280–315.

Dewey, Clive, and A. G. Hopkins (eds) (1978), *The Imperial Impact: Studies in the Economic History of Africa and India* (London).

Dhanagare, D. N. (1975a), *Agrarian Movements and Gandhian Politics* (Agra).

—— (1975b), 'Congress and Agrarian Agitations in Oudh, 1920-22 and 1930-32', SA, 5.

—— (1976), 'Peasant Protest and Politics: The Tebhaga Movement in Bengal, 1946-7', JPS, 3, 3, April, 360-78.

—— (1977), 'Agrarian Conflict, Religion and Politics: The Moplah Rebellions in Malabar in the Nineteenth and Early Twentieth Centuries', PP, 74, February, 112-41.

Dhar, Hiranmay (1973), 'Agricultural Servitude in Bengal Presidency around 1800', EPW, 8, 3, 28 July, 1349-57.

Dirks, Nicholas B. (1976), 'Political Authority and Structural Change in Early South Indian History', IESHR, 13, 2, April-June, 125-58.

Divekar, V. D. (1978), 'Survey of Material in Marathi on the Economic and Social History of India', IESHR, 15, 1-4, 81-118, 221-40, 375-408, 467-504.

Djurfeldt, Goran and Staffen Lindberg (1975), Behind Poverty: The Social Formation in a Tamil Village (London).

Dutt, Romesh Chandra (1874), Peasantry of Bengal (Calcutta).

—— (1901), The Economic History of India, 2 vols., 1960 edn.

Farmer, B. H. (1957), Pioneer Peasant Colonization in Ceylon (London).

—— (1974), Agricultural Colonization in India since Independence (London).

Fisher, Colin M. (1978), 'Planters and Peasants: The Ecological Context of Agrarian Unrest on the Indigo Plantations of North Bihar, 1820-1920' in Dewey and Hopkins (eds), The Imperial Impact, pp. 114-31.

Fox, Richard (1971), Kin, Clan, Raja and Rule (Berkeley).

—— (1976), 'Lineage Cells and Regional Definition in Complex Societies' in Carol A. Smith (ed.), Regional Analysis (New York), 2 vols., pp. 95-121.

—— (ed.) (1977), Realm and Region in Traditional India (Durham).

Frankel, Francine (1978), India's Political Economy, 1947-1977: The Gradual Revolution (Princeton).

Frykenberg, Robert Eric (1963), 'Traditional Processes of Power in South India: An Historical Analysis of Local Influence', IESHR, i, 2, October-December, 122-42.

—— (1965a), 'Elite Groups in South India: An Historical Analysis of Local Influence', JAS, February, 261-81.

—— (1965b), Guntur District, 1788-1848: A History of Local Influence and Central Authority in South India (London).

—— (ed.) (1969), Land Control and Social Structure in Indian History (Madison).

—— (ed.) (1977), Land Tenure and Peasant in South Asia (Delhi).

Fukazawa, H. (1974), 'Structure and Change of a "Sharehold Village" (Bhagdari or Narwadari) in Nineteenth Century British Gujerat', HJE, 14, 2, February.

Gallagher, John (1963), 'Imperialism and Nationalism in Modern Indian History' in S. Gopal, R. Thapar et al., Problems of Historical Writing in India, pp. 50-6.

—— (1973), 'Congress in Decline, 1930-1939' in Gallagher, Johnson and Seal (eds), Locality, Province, and Nation, pp. 269-325.

Gallagher, J., G. Johnson and A. Seal (eds) (1973), Locality, Province, and Nation: Essays on Indian Politics, 1870-1940 (Cambridge).

Ganguli, B. (1938), Trends of Agriculture and Population in the Ganges Valley (London).

Ghosal, H. R. (1966), *Economic Transition in Bengal Presidency, 1793–1833* (Calcutta).

Ghosh, Ambica Prasad (1980), *Development of Capitalist Relations in Agriculture: A Case Study of West Bengal, 1793–1971* (Delhi).

Gopal, S., R. Thapar *et al.* (1963), *Problems of Historical Writing in India*, Proceedings of the Seminar held at the India International Centre, New Delhi, 21–25 January.

Gordon, Stewart (1979), 'Recovery from Adversity in Eighteenth Century India: Rethinking "Villages", "Peasants", and Politics in Pre-Modern Kingdoms', PS, 8, 4, Fall, 61–80.

Goswamy, B. N. (1975), 'History at Pilgrim Centers: On Pattas Held by Families of Priests at Centers of Hindu Pilgrimage' in Gustafson and Jones (eds), *Sources on Punjab History*, pp. 339–73.

Gough, Kathleen (1971), 'Caste in a Tanjore Village' in E. R. Leach (ed.), *Aspects of Caste in South India, Ceylon, and Northwest Pakistan* (Cambridge), pp. 11–60.

—— (1976), 'Indian Peasant Uprisings', BCAS, 8, 3, July–September, 2–18.

—— (1978), 'Agrarian Relations in Southeast India, 1750–1976', Rev., 2, 1, Summer, 25–54.

—— (forthcoming), *Rural Society in Southeast India* (Cambridge).

Greenough, Paul R. (1977), 'Prosperity and Misery in Modern Bengal: The Bengal Famine of 1943–1944', unpublished Ph.D. dissertation, University of Chicago.

Guha, Amalendu (1966), 'Land Rights and Social Classes in Medieval Assam', IESHR, 3, 3, September, 217–39.

—— (1967), 'Colonization of Assam: Second Phase, 1840–1859', IESHR, 4, 4, December, 289–317.

—— (1977), *Planter Raj to Swaraj: Freedom Movement and Electoral Politics in Assam, 1826–1947* (New Delhi).

—— (1980), 'Assamese Agrarian Society in the Late Nineteenth Century: Roots, Structure, and Trends', IESHR, 17, January–March, 35–94.

Guha, Ranjit (1963), *A Rule of Property for Bengal* (Paris).

—— (1974), 'Neel-Darpan: The Image of a Peasant Revolt in a Liberal Mirror', JPS, 2, 1, October, 1–46.

Gunawardana, R. A. H. L. (1971), 'Irrigation and Hydraulic Society in Early Medieval Ceylon', PP, 53, 3–27.

—— (1979), *Robe and Plough: Monasticism and Economic Interest in Early Medieval Sri Lanka* (Tucson).

—— (1978), 'Social Function and Political Power: A Case Study of State Formation in Irrigation Society', IHR, 4, 1, January, 259–73.

Gupta, Ranjan Kumar (1977), 'Agricultural Development in a Bengal District: Birbhum, 1793–1852', IHR, 4, 1, July, 47–74.

—— (1979), 'Permanent Settlement in Birbhum: Impact on Landed Interests (1793–1856)', CHJ, 3, 2, January–June, 1–39.

Gupta, Sulekh Chandra (1959), 'Agrarian Background of the 1857 Rebellion in the Northwestern Provinces', Enq., 1.

—— (1960), 'Agrarian Structure in the United Provinces in the Late Eighteenth and Early Nineteenth Century' in Tapan Raychaudhuri (ed.), *Contributions to Indian Economic History* (Calcutta), Vol. I, pp. 21–45.

—— (1963), *Agrarian Relations and Early British Rule in India: A Case Study of the Ceded and Conquered Provinces, 1801–1833* (Bombay).

—— (1966), *India's Agrarian Structure: A Study in Evolution* (New Delhi).

Gustafson, W. Eric and Kenneth W. Jones (eds) (1975), *Sources on Punjab History* (Delhi).

Habib, Irfan (1960), 'Banking in Mughal India' in Tapan Raychaudhuri (ed.), *Contributions to Indian Economic History* (Calcutta), Vol. I, pp. 1–20.

—— (1962), 'An Examination of Wittfogel's Theory of "Oriental Despotism" ', Enq., Old Series, 6, 54–73.

—— (1963a), 'Aspects of Agrarian Relations and Economy in a Region of Uttar Pradesh during the Sixteenth Century', IESHR, 4, 3.

—— (1963b), *The Agrarian System of Mughal India* (Bombay).

—— (1964), 'Usury in Medieval India', CSSH, 6, 4, July, 393–419.

—— (1965), 'Distribution of Landed Property in Pre-British India', Enq., New Series, 2, 3, 21–80, rpt. in R. S. Sharma and Vivekanand Jha (eds), *Indian Society: Historical Probings in Honour of D. D. Kosambi* (New Delhi), pp. 264–316.

—— (1969), 'Potentialities of Capitalistic Development in the Economy of Mughal India', JEH, 29, 1, March, 32–78.

—— (1975), 'Colonialization of the Indian Economy, 1757–1900', SS, 3, 8, March, 23–53.

Hagen, J. R. and A. Yang (1976), 'Local Sources for the Study of Rural India: The "Village Notes" of Bihar', IESHR, 13, 75–86.

Harcourt, Max (1977), 'Kisan Populism and Revolution in Rural India: The 1942 Disturbances in Bihar and East United Provinces' in D. A. Low (ed.), *Congress and the Raj: Facets of the Indian Struggle, 1917–1947* (London), pp. 315–48.

Hardgrave, Robert L. (1969), *The Nadars of Tamilnadu* (Berkeley).

Hardiman, David (1977), 'The Crisis of the Lesser Patidars: Peasant Agitations in Kheda District, Gujerat, 1917–1934' in D. A. Low (ed.), *Congress and the Raj*, pp. 47–76.

—— (1981), *Peasant Nationalists of Gujerat: Kheda District, 1917–1934* (London).

Harnetty, Peter (1971), 'Cotton Exports and Indian Agriculture', EHR, Series 2, 24, 3, August.

—— (1976), 'A Curious Exercise in Political Economy: Some Implications of British Land Revenue Policy in the Central Provinces of India, 1861–c. 1900', SA, 6, 1976, 14–33.

—— (1977), 'Crop Trends in the Central Provinces of India, 1861–1921', MAS, 11, July.

Harriss, Barbara (1979), 'The Role of Agro-Commercial Capital in "Rural Development" in South India', SS, 7, 7, February, 42–56.

Hasan, Saiyid Nurul (1973), *Thoughts on Agrarian Relations in Mughal India* (New Delhi).

Hauser, Walter (1961), 'The Bihar Provincial Kisan Sabha, 1929–1942: A Study of an Indian Peasant Movement', unpublished Ph.D. dissertation, University of Chicago.

Hazelhurst, Leighton (1976), 'Ceremony and Social Structure in Nineteenth Century Punjab', EPW, 11, 35, 28 August, 1430–6.

Henningham, Stephen (1976), 'The Social Setting of the Champaran Satya-graha: The Challenge to an Alien Elite', IESHR, 13, 1, January–March, 59–73.

—— (1979), 'Agrarian Relations in North Bihar: Peasant Protest and the Darbhanga Raj, 1919–1920 (with an appendix on "The Darbhanga Raj General Department Records")', IESHR, 16, 1, January–March, 53–83.

Heston, Alan (1973), 'Official Yields Per Acre in India, 1886–1947: Some Questions of Interpretation', IESHR, 10, 4, December, 303–32.

—— (1978), 'A Further Critique of Historical Yields Per Acre in India', IESHR, 15, 2, April–June, 187–210.

Hjejle, Benedicte (1967), 'Slavery and Agricultural Bondage in South India in the Nineteenth Century', SEHR, 15, 1–2, 71–126.

Hobsbawm, E. J. *et al.* (1980), *Peasants in History: Essays in Honour of Daniel Thorner* (Delhi).

Hunter, Sir William Wilson (1877), *A Statistical Account of Bengal* (Delhi), 20 vols, rpt. 1976.

—— (1897), *Annals of Rural Bengal* (London).

Hurd, John (1975), 'Railways and the Expansion of Marketing in India, 1861–1921', EEH, 12, 3, July, 263–88.

Husain, Imtiaz (1967), *British Land Policy in North India, 1801–1833* (Calcutta).

Inglis, W. A. (1909), *Canals and Flood Banks of Bengal* (London).

Irschick, Eugene F. (1969), *Politics and Social Conflict in Tamilnad* (Berkeley).

—— (1975), 'Interpretations of Indian Political Development', JAS, 34, 2, February, 461–72.

Islam, M. Mufakharul (1978), *Bengal Agriculture, 1920–1946: A Quantitative Study* (Cambridge).

—— (1980), 'Problems of Agricultural Indebtedness in British India: Some Traditional Views Reconsidered', CHJ, 4, 2, January–June, 28–42.

Islam, Sirajul (1974), 'The Bengal Peasantry in Debt, 1904–1945', DUS, 22, pt. A, 49–64.

—— (1977), *Rural History of Bangladesh: A Source Study* (Dacca).

—— (1978), *Bangladesh District Records* (Dacca), Vol. I.

—— (1979), *The Permanent Settlement in Bengal: A Study of Its Operations, 1790–1819* (Dacca).

Jack, J. C. (1916), *Economic Life of a Bengal District* (London).

Jain, Puroshottam C. (1978), *A Socio-economic Exploration of Medieval India, from 800 to 1300 A.D.* (Delhi).

Jannuzi, F. Thomasson (1974), *Agrarian Crisis in India: The Case of Bihar* (New Delhi).

—— (1980), *The Agrarian Structure of Bangladesh: An Impediment to Development* (Boulder).

Jassal, Smita (1980), 'Agrarian Contradictions and Resistance in Faizabad District of Oudh (India), 1858–1970', JPS, 7, 3, April, 312–37.

Jeffrey, Robin (1976), *The Decline of Nayar Dominance: Society and Politics in Travancore, 1847–1908* (London).

Jena, Krishna Chandra (1968), *Land Revenue Administration in Orissa during the Nineteenth Century* (Delhi).

Jha, Jagdish Chandra (1964), *The Kol Insurrection of Chota-Nagpur* (Calcutta).

92   DAVID LUDDEN

—— (1968), *The Bhumji Revolt, 1832–3: Ganga Narain's Langama or Turmoil* (Delhi).

Jha, Jata Shankar (1966), *The History of the Darbhanga Raj* (Patna).

—— (1972), *Biography of an Indian Patriot: Maharaja Lakshmishwar Singh of Darbhanga* (Patna).

Karat, Prakash (1976), 'The Peasant Movement in Malabar, 1934–1940', SS, 5, 2, September, 30–44.

Keatinge, Gerald Francis (1921), *Agricultural Progress in Western India* (London).

Kessinger, Tom G. (1970), 'Historical Materials on Rural India', IESHR, 7, 4 September, 489–510.

—— (1974), *Vilyatpur 1848–1958: Social and Economic Change in a North Indian Village* (Berkeley).

—— (1975), 'Sources for the Social and Economic History of the Rural Punjab' in Gustafson and Jones (eds), *Sources on Punjab History*, pp. 9–44.

Khan, Akbar Ali (1979), 'Some Aspects of Peasant Behavior in Bengal, 1890–1914: A Neo-Classical Analysis', unpublished Ph.D. dissertation, Queens University (Canada).

Khan, Zahoor Ali (1978), 'Railways and the Creation of a National Market in Food Grains: A Study of Regional Price Levels', IESHR, 4, 2, January, 336–53.

Klein, Ira (1972), 'Malaria and Mortality in Bengal', IESHR, 9, 2, June.

—— (1973), 'Death in India, 1871–1921', JAS, 32, August, 639–60.

—— (1974), 'Population and Agriculture in North India, 1872–1921', MAS, 8, 2, April, 191–216.

Kling, Blair B. (1966), *The Blue Mutiny: The Indigo Disturbances in Bengal, 1859–1862* (Philadelphia).

Kolff, Dirk H. A. (1979), 'A Study of Land Transfers in Mau Tahsil, District Jhansi' in Chaudhuri and Dewey (eds), *Economy and Society*, pp. 53–85.

Kolliner, Andrew (1975), 'The Structure of Rural Credit in the Ceded Districts of the Madras Presidency with Particular Reference to Kurnool District, 1880–1930', unpublished M.A. thesis, University of Pennsylvania.

Kulkarni, A. R. (1976), 'Source Material for the Study of Village Communities in Maharashtra', IESHR, 8, 4, October–December, 513–25.

Kumar, Dharma (1963), 'Some Problems in Nineteenth Century Agrarian History' in S. Gopal, R. Thapar *et al.*, *Problems of Historical Writing in India*, pp. 82–7.

—— (1965), *Land and Caste in South India* (Cambridge).

—— (1974), 'Changes in Income Distribution and Poverty in India: A Review of the Literature', *World Development*, 2, 1, January, 31–41.

—— (1975), 'Landownership and Equality in Madras Presidency, 1853–4 to 1946–7', IESHR, 12, 3, July–September, 229–62.

Kumar, Ravinder (1968a), *Western India in the Nineteenth Century: A Study of the Social History of Maharashtra* (London).

—— (1968b), 'The Rise of the Rich Peasant in Western India' in D. A. Low (ed.), *Soundings in Modern South Asian History*, pp. 25–58.

Kumar, Shive (1980), *Peasantry and the Indian National Movement, 1919–1933* (Delhi).

Lakshmi, Champaka (1981), *Economic Condition of the Peasantry in the Deccan during the Nineteenth Century* (Delhi).

Landsberger, Henry A. (ed.) (1974), *Rural Protest: Peasant Movement and Social Change* (London).

Low, D. A. (ed.) (1968), *Soundings in Modern South Asian History* (Berkeley).

—— (ed.) (1977), *Congress and the Raj: Facets of the Indian Struggle, 1917–1947* (London).

Low, D. A., J. C. Iltis and M. D. Wainwright (eds) (1969), *Government Archives in South Asia: A Guide to National and State Archives in Ceylon, India, and Pakistan* (London).

Ludden, David E. (1978a), 'Agrarian Organization in Tinnevelly District, 800 to 1900 A.D.', unpublished Ph.D. dissertation, University of Pennsylvania.

—— (1978b), 'Ecological Zones and the Cultural Economy of Irrigation in Southern Tamilnadu', SA, I (NS), 1, March, 1–13.

—— (1978c), 'Who Really Ruled Madras Presidency?', IESHR, 15, 1, January–March.

—— (1979a), 'Dimensions of Agrarian Political Economy: Focus on Tamil Nadu, India', PS, 8, 4, Fall, 19–30.

—— (1979b), 'Patronage and Irrigation in Tamil Nadu: A Long-Term View', IESHR, 16, 3, July–September, 347–65.

Maddison, Angus (1971), *Class Structure and Economic Growth in India and Pakistan since the Moghuls* (New York).

Mahmood, A. B. M. (1962), 'The Land Revenue History of the Rajshahi Zamindar (1765–1793)', unpublished Ph.D. dissertation, School of Oriental and African Studies, London University.

Mann, Harold H. (1917–1921), *Land and Labour in a Deccan Village* (London), 2 vols.

—— (1967), 'A Deccan Village under the Peshwas' in Daniel Thorner (ed.), *The Social Framework of Agriculture* (Bombay), pp. 123–38.

McAlpin, Michelle B. (1974), 'Railroads, Prices and Peasant Rationality: India, 1860–1900', JEH, 34, 3, September, 662–84.

—— (1975a), 'Railroads, Cultivation Patterns, and Food-grain Availability: India, 1868–1900', IESHR, 12, 1, January–March, 43–60.

—— (1975b), 'The Effects of Expansion of Markets on Rural Income Distribution in Nineteenth Century India', EEH, 12, 3, July, 289–302.

Mehta, Shirin M. (1977), 'Social and Economic Background of the Bardoli Satyagraha, 1928', JIH, 55, 3, December, 159–66.

Mencher, Joan P. (1966), 'Kerala and Madras: A Comparative Study of Ecology and Social Structure', *Ethnology*, 5, 2, April, 135–71.

—— (1978), *Agriculture and Social Structure in Tamil Nadu* (Durham).

Menon, Saraswathi (1979), 'Responses to Class and Caste Oppression in Tanjavur District: 1940–1952,' SS, 7, 6–10, January–May, 14–31, 57–68, 52–64.

Metcalf, Thomas R. (1962), 'The Struggle over Land Tenure in India, 1860–1868', JAS, 21, 3, May.

—— (1964), *The Aftermath of Revolt* (Berkeley).

—— (1969a), 'From Raja to Landlord: The Oudh Talukdars, 1850–1870' in R. E. Frykenberg (ed.), *Land Control and Social Structure in Indian History*, pp. 123–42.

—— (1969b), 'Social Effects of British Land Policy in Oudh' in Frykenberg (ed.), *Land Control and Social Structure in Indian History*, pp. 143–62.

94   DAVID LUDDEN

—— (ed.) (1971), *Modern India: An Interpretive Anthology* (London).

—— (1979), *Land, Landlords, and the British Raj: Northern India in the Nineteenth Century* (Berkeley).

Mishra, Girish (1978), *Agrarian Problems of Permanent Settlement: A Case Study of Champaran* (Delhi).

Moffatt, Michael (1979), *An Untouchable Community in South India: Structure and Consensus* (Princeton).

Moore, Barrington (1967), *Social Origins of Dictatorship and Democracy: Lord and Peasant in the Making of the Modern World* (Boston).

Mitra, Dinabandhu (1958), *Nil Darpan* (Calcutta), 3rd Indian edn, containing the translated play and the story of the trial of its translator, Rev. James Long.

Moreland, W. H. (1929), 'The Indian Peasant in History', *Journal of the Royal Society of Arts*, 77, # 3988, 26 April, 605–13.

Murdie, R. F. (1931), *Cultivators' Debt in Agra District* (Allahabad).

Mukherjee, Aditya (1979) 'Agrarian Conditions in Assam, 1880–1890: A Case Study of Five Districts of the Brahmaputra Valley', IESHR, 16, 2, April–June, 207–32.

Mukherjee, Mukul (1980), 'Railways and Their Impact on Bengal's Economy, 1870–1920', IESHR, 17, 2, April–June, 191–210.

Mukherjee, Nilmani (1962), *The Ryotwari System in Madras, 1792–1827* (Calcutta).

—— (1975), *A Bengal Zamindar: Jaykrishna Mukherjee of Uttarpara and His Times, 1808–1888* (Calcutta).

Mukherjee, Ramkrishna (1957), *The Dynamics of Rural Society* (Berlin).

Mukerji, Karunamoy (1971), 'Land Transfers in Birbhum, 1928–1955: Some Implications of the Bengal Tenancy Act, 1855', IESHR, 8, 3, September, 241–63.

—— (1977), 'Rents and Forms of Tenancy in Birbhum since Permanent Settlement', IESHR, 14, 3, July–September, 363–76.

Mukherji, Saugata (1970), 'Trade in Rice and Jute in Bengal: Its Effects on Prices, Cultivation, and Consumption of the Two Crops in the Early Twentieth Century', unpublished dissertation, Jadavpur University.

Murton, Brian, J. (1973), 'Key People in the Countryside: Decision-Makers in Interior Tamilnadu in the Late Eighteenth Century', IESHR, 10, 2, June, 157–80.

—— (1975), 'Agrarian System Dynamics in Interior Tamilnadu before 1800 A.D.', *National Geographical Journal of India*, 21, 3–4, 151–65.

—— (1977), 'Land and Class: Cultural, Social, and Biophysical Integration in Interior Tamil Nadu in the Late Eighteenth Century' in R. E. Frykenberg (ed.), *Land Tenure and Peasants*, pp. 81–99.

Musgrave, Peter J. (1972), 'Landlords and Lords of the Land', MAS, 6, 3, 257–76.

—— (1978), 'Rural Credit and Rural Society in the United Provinces, 1860–1920' in Dewey and Hopkins (eds), *The Imperial Impact*, pp. 216–32.

—— (1979), 'Social Power and Social Change in the United Provinces, 1860–1920' in Chaudhuri and Dewey (eds), *Economy and Society*, pp. 3–25.

Nair, Kusum (1979), *In Defense of the Irrational Peasant: Indian Agriculture after the Green Revolution* (Chicago).

Nanda, B. R. (ed.) (1972), *Socialism in India* (Delhi).

Narain, Dharm (1965), *The Impact of Price Movements on Areas under Selected Crops in India, 1900–1939,* (Cambridge).

Neale, Walter C. (1962), *Economic Change in North India: Land Tenure and Reform in the United Provinces, 1800–1955* (New Haven).

—— (1969), 'Land is to Rule' in R. E. Frykenberg (ed.), *Land Control and Social Structure in Indian History,* pp. 3–15.

Nehru, S. S. (1932), *Caste and Credit in the Rural Area* (Calcutta).

Nicholas, Ralph (1968), 'Structures of Politics in the Villages of South Asia' in Singer and Cohn (eds), *Structure and Change in Indian Society,* pp. 243–84.

Omvedt, Gail (1973), 'Development of the Maharashtrian Class Structure, 1818–1931', EPW, 8, 31–33, August, 1417–32.

—— (1975), 'The Political Economy of Starvation: Bengal, 1943', RC, 17, 2, August, 111–39.

—— (1980), 'Migration in Colonial India: The Articulation of Feudalism and Capitalism by the Colonial State', JPS, 7, 2, January, 185–212.

Palit, Chittabrata (1975), *Tensions in Bengal Rural Society: Landlords, Planters, and Colonial Rule, 1830–1860* (Calcutta).

Pandey, Gyanendra (1977), 'A Rural Base for Congress: The United Provinces, 1920–1940' in D. A. Low (ed.), *Congress and the Raj,* pp. 199–224.

—— (1978), *The Ascendancy of the Congress in Uttar Pradesh, 1926–1934: A Study in Imperfect Mobilization* (New York).

—— (1980), 'A View of the Observable: A Positivist Understanding of Agrarian Society and Political Protest in Colonial India', JPS, 7, 3, April, 375–83.

Panikkar, K. N. (1977), 'Land Control, Ideology, and Reform: A Study of the Changes in Family Organization and Marriage System in Kerala', IHR, 4, 1, July, 30–47.

Pant, S. D. (1935), *The Social Economy of the Himalyas* (London).

Paustian, Paul (1930), *Canal Irrigation in the Punjab* (New York).

Perlin, Frank (1975), 'Cycles, Trends, and Academics among the Peasantry of Northwest India', JPS, 2, 3, April, 360–70.

—— (1978), 'Of White Whale and Countrymen in the Eighteenth Century Maratha Deccan: Extended Class Relations, Rights and the Problem of Rural Autonomy under the Old Regime', JPS, 5, 2, January, 172–237.

—— (1980), 'Precolonial South Asia and Western Penetration in the 17th–19th Centuries: A Problem of Epistemological Status', Rev., 4, 2, 267–306.

Ponniah, J. S. (1944), 'Production and Marketing of Raw Cotton in the Madras Presidency, with Special Reference to the Six Districts of Bellary, Kurnool, Coimbatore, Madurai, Ramnad, and Tinnevelly', unpublished D.Litt. dissertation, Madras University, 2 vols.

Pradhan, M. C. (1966), *The Political System of the Jats of North India* (Bombay).

Prasad, Pradhan H. (1976), 'Poverty and Bondage', EPW, 11, 31–3, August, Special Number, 1269–73.

—— (1979), 'Semi-Feudalism: The Basic Constraint of Indian Agriculture' in A. N. Das and V. Nilakant (eds), *Agrarian Relations in India,* pp. 33–49.

Premchand (1938), *Godan* (Allahabad).

Price, Pamela G. (1979), 'Resources and Rule in Zamindari South India, 1802–1903: Sivagangai and Ramnad as Little Kingdoms under the Raj', unpublished Ph.D. dissertation, University of Wisconsin.

96 DAVID LUDDEN

Qaisar, A. Jan (1974), 'The Role of Brokers in Medieval India', IHR, 1, 2, September, 220–46.

Rabitoy, Neil (1975), 'System vs. Expediency: The Reality of Land Revenue Administration in the Bombay Presidency, 1812–1820', MAS, 9, 4, 539–46.

Raj, Jagdish (1965), *The Mutiny and British Land Policy in North India, 1856–1868* (New York).

Rao, G. N. (1973), 'Changing Conditions and Growth of Agricultural Economy in the Krishna and Godavari Districts, 1840–1890', unpublished dissertation, Andhra University.

—— (1977), 'Agrarian Relations in Coastal Andhra under Early Colonial Rule', SS, 6, 1, August, 19–29.

Ray, Rajat K. (1973), 'The Crisis of Bengal Agriculture, 1870–1927: The Dynamics of Immobility', IESHR, 10, 3, September, 244–79.

—— (1977), 'Political Change in British India', IESHR, 14, 4, October–December, 493–518.

Ray, Rajat and Ratna (1973), 'The Dynamics of Continuity in Rural Bengal under British Imperium: A Study of Quasi-Stable Equilibrium in Under-developed Societies in a Changing World', IESHR, 10, 2, June, 103–29.

—— (1975), 'Zamindars and Jotedars: A Study of Rural Politics in Bengal', MAS 9, 1, 81–102.

Ray, Ratnalekha (1974), 'Land Transfer and Social Change under Permanent Settlement: A Study of Two Localities', IESHR, 11, 1, January–March, 1–46.

—— (1975), 'The Bengal Zamindars: Local Magnates and the State before Permanent Settlement', IESHR, 12, 3, July–September, 263–92.

—— (1979), *Change in Bengal Agrarian Society, 1760–1850* (Delhi).

Raychaudhuri, Tapan Kumar (ed.) (1960–1963), *Contributions to Indian Economic History* (Calcutta), 2 vols.

—— (1969), 'Permanent Settlement in Operation: Bakarganj District, East Bengal' in R. E. Frykenberg (ed.), *Land Control and Social Structure in Indian History*, pp. 163–74.

Richards, John F. (1981), 'Mughal State Finance and the Pre-modern World Economy', CSSH, 23, 2, April, 285–308.

Robb, Peter (1979), 'Hierarchy and Resources: Peasant Stratification in Late Nineteenth Century Bihar', MAS, 13, 1, February, 97–126.

Robert, Bruce L. (1979), 'Agricultural Credit Cooperatives in Madras, 1893–1937: Rural Development and Agrarian Politics in Pre-Independence India', IESHR, 16, 2, April–June, 163–85.

Rothermund, Dietmar (1976), 'The Land Revenue Problem in British India', BPP, 95, 1, January–June, 210–26.

—— (1977), 'A Survey of Rural Migration and Land Reclamation, 1885', JPS, 4, 3, April, 230–42.

—— (1978), *Government, Landlord, and Peasant in India: Agrarian Relations under British Rule, 1865–1935* (Wiesbaden).

Rudolph, Lloyd and H. Susanne (1967), *The Modernity of Tradition* (Chicago).

Rudolph, Susanne Hoeber (1971), 'The New Courage: An Essay on Gandhi's Psychology' in T. R. Melcalf (ed.), *Modern India*, pp. 240–56.

Rudra, Ashok, A. Majid, B. D. Talid *et al.* (1978), *Studies in the Development of Capitalism in India* (Lahore).

Sanyal, Hiteshranjan (1978), 'Congress Movements in the Villages of Eastern Midnapore, 1921–1931', *VIth European Conference on Modern South Asian Studies* (Paris).

Schoer, Karl (1977), 'Agrarian Relations and the Development of the Forces of Production', SS, 6, 3, October, 13–27.

Schwartzberg, Joseph (ed.) (1978), *Historical Atlas of South Asia* (Chicago).

Seal, Anil (1973), 'Imperialism and Nationalism in India', Introductory essay in Gallagher, Johnson and Seal (eds), *Locality, Province and Nation*.

Sen, Amartya K. (1976), 'Famines as Failures of Exchange Entitlements', EPW, Special Number, August, 1276–80.

—— (1981), *Poverty and Famine: An Essay on Entitlement and Deprivation* (London).

Sen, Sunil Kumar (1972), *Agrarian Struggle in Bengal, 1946–7* (New Delhi).

—— (1979), *Agrarian Relations in India, 1793–1947* (Delhi).

Sengupta, Kalyan Kumar (1970), 'The Agrarian League of Pabna', IESHR, 7, 2, June, 253–69.

—— (1971), 'Agrarian Disturbances in Nineteenth Century Bengal', IESHR, 8, 2, June, 192–212.

—— (1973), 'Agrarian Struggle in Bengal (1873–1885): Some Unknown Sources of Materials', IHRC, 44th Session, Goa.

—— (1974), *Pabna Disturbances and the Politics of Rents, 1873–1885* (New Delhi).

Sengupta, Nirmal (1980), 'The Indigenous Irrigation Organization of South Bihar', IESHR, 17, 2, April–June, 157–90.

Sharma, R. S. (ed.) (1971), *Land Revenue in India: Historical Studies* (Delhi).

Siddiqi, Asiya (1973), *Agrarian Change in a North Indian State: Uttar Pradesh, 1819–1833* (Delhi).

Siddiqi, Majid Hayat (1973), 'A Note on Some Sources for the Study of Peasant Movements', IHC, 1972 proceedings.

—— (1978), *Agrarian Unrest in North India: The United Provinces, 1918–1922* (Delhi).

Singer, Milton and Bernard S. Cohn (eds) (1968), *Structure and Change in Indian Society* (Chicago).

Singh, Dilbagh (1979), 'Tenants, Sharecroppers, and Agricultural Laborers in Eighteenth Century Rajasthan', SIH, i, i, January–June.

Singh, Jasbir (1974), *An Agricultural Atlas of India* (Varanasi).

Singh, Khushwant (1966), 'Taxation and Tenure of Agricultural Land in the Punjab between 1789 and 1849', PJR, Humanities, 1, 2, July, 131–61.

Singh, R. L. (1971), *India: A Regional Geography* (Varanasi).

Sinha, Narendra Krishna (1956–62), *The Economic History of Bengal from Plassey to Permanent Settlement* (Calcutta), 2 vols.

Sinha, Ram Narayan (1968), *Bihar Tenantry, 1783–1833* (Bombay).

Sivakumar, S. S. (1978), 'Transformation of the Agrarian Economy of Tondai-mandalam, 1760–1900', SS, 6, 10, May, 18–39.

Smith, Carol A. (ed.) (1976), *Regional Analysis* (New York), 2 vols.

Spate, O. H. K. and A. T. A. Learmonth (1972), *India, Pakistan, and Ceylon: The Regions* (London).

Spodek, Howard (1979), 'Pluralist Politics in British India: The Cambridge

Cluster of Historians of Modern India', *The American Historical Review*, 84, 3, June, 688–707.

Stein, Burton (1960), 'Economic Functions of the Medieval South Indian Temple', JAS, 19, 2, February, 163–76.

—— (1969), 'Integration of the Agrarian System of South India' in R. E. Frykenberg (ed.), *Land Control and Social Structure in Indian History*, pp. 175–216.

—— (ed.) (1975), *Essays on South India* (Honolulu).

—— (1980), *Peasant State and Society in Medieval South India* (Delhi).

Stokes, Eric (1959), *English Utilitarians and India* (London).

—— (1978), *The Peasant and the Raj* (Cambridge).

Stone, Ian (1979), 'Canal Irrigation and Agrarian Change: The Experience of the Ganges Canal Tract, Muzaffarnagar District (U.P.), 1840–1900' in Chaudhuri and Dewey (eds), *Economy and Society*, pp. 86–112.

Taniguchi, Shikichi (1978), 'The Permanent Settlement in Bengal and the Break-up of the Zamindari of Dinajpur', CHJ, 3, 1, July–December, 26–55.

Thapar, Romila (1976), 'The Scope and Significance of Regional History: Presidential Address', PHC, 10th, 11–23.

Thorner, Daniel and Alice (1962), *Land and Labour in India* (Bombay).

Trevaskis, H. K. (1928), *Land of the Five Rivers* (London).

Upadhyaya, Ashok K. (1980), 'Peasantization of Adivasis in Thana District', EPW, 15, 22, December 27th, A134–46.

van den Dungen, P. H. M. (1972), *The Punjab Tradition* (London).

Varghese, T. C. (1970), *Agrarian Change and Its Economic Consequences: Land Tenures in Kerala, 1850–1950* (Bombay).

Wadhwa, D. C. (1973), *Agrarian Legislation in India, 1793–1960* (Poona), Vol. I.

Washbrook, David A. (1973), 'Country Politics: Madras, 1880 to 1920', MAS, 7, 3, 475–531.

—— (1975), 'The Development of Caste Organization in South India: 1880–1925' in Washbrook and Baker (eds.), *South India: Political Institutions and Political Change*, pp. 295–315.

—— (1976), *The Emergence of Provincial Politics: The Madras Presidency, 1870–1920* (Cambridge).

—— (1978), 'Economic Development and Social Stratification in Rural Madras: The "Dry Region", 1878–1929' in Dewey and Hopkins (eds), *The Imperial Impact*, pp. 68–82.

Washbrook, David A. and Christopher J. Baker (eds) (1975), *South India: Political Institutions and Political Change* (Delhi).

Weisskopf, Thomas A. (1977), 'The Persistence of Poverty in India', BCAS, 9, 1, January–March, 28–44.

Whitcombe, Elizabeth (1972), *Agrarian Conditions in North India*, Vol. I: *The United Provinces under British Rule, 1860–1900* (Berkeley).

Wood, Conrad (1976a), 'The First Moplah Rebellion against British Rule in Malabar', MAS, 10, 4, 543–56.

—— (1976b), 'The Moplah Rebellions between 1800–2 and 1921–22', IESHR, 8, 1, January–March, 97–106.

—— (1978), 'Peasant Revolt: An Interpretation of Moplah Violence in the Nineteenth and Twentieth Centuries' in Dewey and Hopkins (eds), *The Imperial Impact*, pp. 132–51.

Yang, Anand (1976), 'Agrarian Reform and Peasant Dissidence: The Continuing Crisis in India', PS, 5, 9–14.

—— (1978), 'Between *Raj* and *Raiyat*: The Great Estate of Hathwa in the Nineteenth Century', unpublished paper presented at the Conference on Intermediate Political Linkages in South Asia, Berkeley.

—— (1979a), 'The Agrarian Origins of Crime: A Study of Riots in Saran District, India, 1886–1920', JSH, 13, 2, Winter, 289–306.

—— (1979b), 'Peasants on the Move: A Study of Internal Migration in India', JIH, 10, 1, Summer, 37–58.

—— (1979c), 'An Institutional Shelter: The Court of Wards in Late Nineteenth Century Bihar', MAS, 13, 2, 247–64.

Zagoria, Donald S. (1971), 'The Ecology of Peasant Communism in India', *American Political Science Review*, 65, 1, 144–60.

Rural Power Structure and Agricultural Productivity in Eastern India, 1757-1947

B. B. CHAUDHURI

The exact role of the structure of rural power[1] in the level of agricultural productivity is a controversial theme. A recent debate in Europe covers a wider ground: the role of the agrarian structure in the long-term changes in the pre-industrial economy of Europe[2] (R. Brenner 1976; *Past and Present*, February). While one school of historians seeks to relate the changes to the existing agrarian structure, a rival point of view tends to emphasize the role of demography and markets as being more decisive. In India the usual debate relates to a more specific theme: the implications of 'land reforms' in terms of improvement in agriculture. An influential opinion defends the reforms as a decisive step toward regeneration of agriculture. The Bengal Land Revenue Commission (1940),[3] for instance, argued on

[1] The phrase 'rural power' has been used in this essay in a restricted sense. It means here mainly the power derived from control over land, reinforced occasionally by control over rural credit. Other components of 'rural power', such as caste, have been considered to the extent that they bore on this specific kind of control.

[2] The debate has recently been reopened by R. Brenner (1976). For further contributions on the theme see *Past and Present* (February 1978; May 1978; June 1979).

[3] The Commission, appointed in November 1938, observed in its Report (1940): 'The Permanent Settlement has imposed on the Province an iron framework which has the effect of stifling the enterprise and initiative of all the classes concerned. . . . Whatever may have been the justification of the Permanent Settlement in 1793, it is no longer suited to the conditions of the present time . . . the zamindari system has developed so many defects that it has ceased to serve any national interest.' *The Report* (para 82, 96).

this score in favour of abolition of the 'Permanent Settlement', the foundation of the agrarian system of Bengal and Bihar since 1793. A similar argument, with reference to the agriculture of pre-Independence Bengal, stressed the 'need' for 'abolition of monopoly control of land by the landlords and the use of the surplus generated in agriculture for its modernization' (Islam 1978: 203). A typical counter-argument (Schultz 1964) denies that inequality in distribution of landholdings constitutes the chief barrier to agricultural growth in underdeveloped countries. The structure of all markets in such an agricultural set-up, it is argued, is nearly perfect and resource allocation efficient, and there is no surplus or unemployed labour in the disguised sense. The main prescription for agricultural growth, according to this view, is adoption by farmers of new technologies. A study[4] (Neale 1962: 4 and 156) on pre-Independence Uttar Pradesh, intended as a critique of the notion that land reforms could substantially contribute to agricultural growth, questions the basic premises of the proponents of land reforms. While admitting that 'organization of agriculture must contribute to development', he thus concludes: 'it does not follow that these areas are backward because there are landlords, or because the colonial powers pursued particular policies, nor does it follow that the abolition of landlords will remove the obstacles to development.'

This theme is examined here with reference to Eastern India during British rule, particularly the 'permanently-settled' regions—Bengal and Bihar.[5] Two methodological points need to be clarified. First,

[4] Neale thus indicated the roots of the retarded agricultural growth in India: 'The major force acting upon the societies of underdeveloped areas during the past century and a half has been the market capitalism. Enough western elements were introduced to disrupt the old society, but not enough to bring the rapid economic advance enjoyed by the West. The roots of poverty lie in the lack of capital, the social hierarchy of the village, and the lack of respect for the process of secular government' (p. 4). By way of refuting various interpretations of 'the stagnant level of welfare in U.P.' he argues: 'Analysis of most of these explanations shows that they do not get to the core of the problem: the incomplete meshing of markets, the lack of capital to provide alternative means of employment, and the persistence of an Indian social code totally at odds with the requirements of a market mechanism' (p. 156).

[5] The Permanent Settlement meant two things: the permanent fixation of the land revenue demand and the entrusting of its collection to the existing landed aristocracy, known as zamindars. Contrary to a widespread impression the composition of this aristocracy was only marginally affected by the new experiments of the Company's Government in Bengal in the sphere of land revenue administration between 1760 and 1793.

in view of the inadequacy of the available productivity data, particularly when it comes to the question of relating the varying levels of agricultural productivity to rural 'power', I intend to restrict this study mainly to the relationship, if any, between this 'power' and the changes in the size of cultivation. Expansion of acreage is admittedly a significant form of rural enterprise. On the other hand, the available data relating to acreage changes are generally more satisfactory.

This essay has three parts: an analysis of the main components of the rural power structure, and changes in this over time; an indication of the major trends in the agricultural production in our region; and an examination of the extent to which some of these trends could be related to the power structure.

I

As regards the rural agrarian structure we intend to concentrate mainly on the permanently-settled regions. Our notions about its nature have somewhat changed in the recent years. The old version primarily stressed the growth of 'landlord powers', powers of the group known as zamindars.[6] The 'settlement' of 1793 has been considered the most crucial factor in this. It 'determined the course of development of the economy of eastern India in general, and of the tenure relationships existing in land in particular for the next two centuries'[7] (Ghosh and Dutt 1977: Ch. 1). Two changes have been emphasized in this version. Uncertainties about the status of zamin-

---

[6] 'Zamindars' is used here to mean the section of the landed group from which the Government directly collected its revenue.

[7] How the Settlement determined the course of the economy has thus been explained: 'A system of money rent, the introduction of a currency and commercial practices were imposed on the country by a foreign power in its own interests. These institutions . . . were imported at a time when internal conditions did not make such a stage inevitable. To operate the system of money rent effectively feudal property rights were subjected to free sale and purchase. These steps forced open the closed feudal economy to the penetration of commerce and exchange in general. The feudal economy was geared to the market by the ruthless system of money revenue to the paid by a fixed date and the threat of sale to the highest bidder in case of default.' The resultant land sales 'led to a transformation of the customary relation between a tenant and his hereditary landlord into a contractual relation between a tenant and the owner of a piece of property. Zamindari properties were transformed into investments in real estate. The feudal barriers inherent in landlord economy following principles of birth were abolished' (pp. 8–9).

dars were now removed. The government would not treat them any longer as mere 'collectors' of revenue, allowing them to stay on or removing them altogether if it suited its purpose. The settlement of 1793 formally vested in them 'property rights in the soil'. The permanent fixation of land revenue was intended as a means toward stabilizing landed property. The formal 'property rights' were energetically enforced, with the purchasers of estates at the public auctions,[8] including urban groups, taking the lead in this, since they were keen on getting their money's worth. Secondly, the growth of landlord powers necessarily undermined peasants' rights, or left them utterly insecure. Rackrenting was an inevitable consequence. The evil was all the greater since the landlords seldom invested in agricultural improvement.

A slightly different version of the process of growth of landlord powers would stress the 'commercialization of subtenurial rights in land on an unprecedented scale'—the proliferation of intermediaries holding permanent leases of portions of zamindari estates, with the leaseholders agreeing to pay the zamindars considerably more than what they had been receiving.[9] The rent burden of peasants continued

[8] The government, while fixing the revenue demand forever, insisted on its collection with utmost rigour, penalizing defaults by auction sales of the defaulter's estate. Contrary to a widespread impression the urban groups could not dominate the land market, at least until about 1830. Chaudhuri, *Indian Economic and Social History Review* (April–June 1975).

[9] The typical arrangement under which zamindars granted away permanent leases (*patnis*) of portions of their estates was first tried by the Burdwan raj with two ends in view: getting rid, as far as possible, of the difficulties in collecting rent from all parts of a far-flung estate as punctually as the rigid collection by the government of a considerably increased revenue demand would necessitate; and the immediate pecuniary gains from the arrangement since the lessees had to pay considerably more than the old rental income from the portions leased out. A. Bhaduri in his paper, 'The evolution of land relations in Eastern India under British rule' (*Indian Economic and Social History Review*, Jan–March 1976) analysed the implications of the system for the rural economy. In the context of the ever-increasing claims from the proliferating intermediaries 'the peasants' consumption level had to be continually forced down to generate enough surplus'. Beyond a certain point the process resulted in increasing the peasant indebtedness, and the peasant, pressed for more cash, had to have recourse to distress sale of his crops. This 'forcible' involvement of the peasant in 'market relations through the mechanism of debt' was 'in essence . . . a forced process of buying and selling of paddy under the compulsion of debt'. A 'peculiar' exchange thus developed— exchange of paddy for paddy. As a result the normal exchange between agricultural and manufactured products 'got thwarted in the process; the mutual

to increase as a result since 'agricultural output in Bengal did not rise rapidly enough to absorb these increasing claims by the expanding class of rent-receiving intermediaries'.

Emphasis, however, has recently shifted from the supra-village zamindari power[10] to the power of a kind of village magnate as the dominant element in the rural agrarian structure. Two points of view have emerged in this regard. One, while admitting the growth of landlord powers after 1793 as a significant determinant of the rural agrarian structure, points to a distinct development over the years: the increasing domination over the rural economy by a new group of village-based landed magnates. It has been argued, with special reference to the first half of the twentieth century, that 'the basic conflict in Bengal has shifted from one of the old type zamindar–tenant to the modern type of kulak landlord and share-cropping labourer'[11] (Ghosh and Dutt 1977: 133). The second point of view, arguing from the premise that rural power primarily derived from 'control over land' and a close connection with the organization of agricultural production, would deny that zamindars had ever constituted a significant component of the rural power structure (Ray and Ray, MAS, 1975: 1; Ray 1980: Chs. 2, 3, 10). The arguments are the following. Unlike an English estate of the eighteenth century the estate of a Bengal zamindar was not a unit of production. The village constituted this unit, and a zamindar had little effective ownership of lands there, except the ones called *nijjot* and *nankar*.[12] Zamindari was merely a 'tribute-collecting structure over the village', an organization for the collection of land revenue and other dues of the State.

dependence between industry and agriculture from the demand side could not also develop to a corresponding extent.'

[10] An estate usually included a large number of villages, often widely scattered. Estates tended to be dismembered over the years in different ways, such as partitions and sales.

[11] A slightly different version, while agreeing with this formulation, tends to emphasize the role of the big *jotedars*. The zamindar, standing at the apex of the agrarian structure, was often an absentee, and 'among the residents the jotedars were at the top, held large blocks of land with full occupancy powers, rarely undertook any manual labour, and had their lands leased out or cultivated by agricultural workers . . . for about 100 years prior to the formal abolition of the zamindari system this class was slowly displacing the zamindars as the leading group in the countryside.' N. K. Chandra (1975), 'Agrarian Transition in India', *Frontier* (22 November–6 December).

[12] These were rent-free holdings, mostly petty. Except in certain districts, they constituted only a small portion of the cultivated area.

The real power in the village lay with the group,[13] called 'land-holding structure within the village', effectively controlling the lands there in diverse ways—a community of 'rich tenants' called *jotedars*[14] who, though formally tenants of a zamindar, 'were the real landlords in effective possession of land and labour within the village'.

'The backbone of the jotedar tenantry was made up of respectable agricultural castes', such as the Sadgops, Aguris and Kaivartas in West Bengal, and the Shaik Muslims in eastern Bengal.[15] The origins of the group have been traced to pre-British days and related to the 'considerably monetized commercial and revenue transactions' in Mughal Bengal. This 'facilitated concentration of wealth in the hands of a few men in village society', who controlled moneylending, moneychanging and grain-dealing in the village. Developments during early British rule helped them a great deal. Two are particularly noted: the new land revenue policy of the Company after 1760, and the famine (1769–70). The first, characterized by an abrupt increase in the land revenue demand and the temporary replacement of very many old zamindars by 'farmers of revenue', often aliens to the farmed villages, and consequently resulting in undermining the authority of the zamindars at the village level, came as a windfall to the ambitious village headmen (*mandals*) and the leading cultivators, particularly where the revenue farmers would not do without them in connection with rent collection. They gained mainly through frauds. They grabbed some of the best lands in the village, and their role in the distribution of the aggregate rent demand on the village enabled them to secure for themselves the best possible rates. The famine helped them in a different way. Their command over capital enabled them to take the lead in the wasteland reclamation, on which the zamindars, suddenly confronting a severe dislocation in the local agriculture caused by the extensive rural depopulation during the famine, were naturally keen. This gave them a firm control over the local economy. Their own holdings could now be enlarged, and the destitute survivors, peasants and labourers, could scarcely do without them. With the impoverished and battered zamindars slowly re-

[13] Control over land is here distinguished from control over collection of revenue.

[14] *Jote* simply means a rent-paying holding. However, the word *Jotedar* is usually used to denote a big holder.

[15] For the Sadgops: H. Sanyal (1981: pp. 45–7 and last chapter). For the Shaiks and the wider question of stratification in the Muslim society of Bengal: R. Ahmed (1981: Ch. 1).

covering their position, particularly after 1793, when new laws
greatly increased their powers in regard to rent collection and when
cultivation had been steadily increasing, the *jotedars* had obvious
constraints to face. The zamindars now felt that assertion of their
authority would be difficult without taming the 'overgrown ryots'.
Signs of antagonism between them thus appeared from time to time.
However, the relationship in general, it has been argued, was 'one of
collaboration rather than opposition'. Zamindars, when backed by
jotedars, succeeded more in the tricky business of increasing their
rental income through revising the rent rates. Offers of privileged
rent rates to the collaborators ensured their loyalty. The *jotedars* had
a crucial role, too, in the 'mechanics of rural control'. 'Any breakdown in the system of rural control was . . . local and partial, and
a consequence of breakdown of collaboration of owners of estates
and village leaders in particular estates. As a rule, the tensions in
rural society arising from the exploitation of small farmers, share-
croppers and agricultural labourers were kept in check by local
alliances between the estate and its superior tenants, which helped
in maintaining a remarkable quietude in the countryside during the
first half of the 19th century.'

The above view concludes that the domination of *jotedars* determined the rural agrarian structure: 'Over two centuries of British
rule the dominant character of the production relations within
Bengal villages was semi-feudal, marked by the small size of plots,
labour-intensive farming, and the master–serf type of relationship
between jotedars and bargadars (sharecroppers), reinforced by
usury' (Ray 1973: 121).

Two premises of the points of view noted above need to be examined: the marginality of the zamindars to the rural economy and
consequently to the rural power structure; and secondly, the domination of *jotedars* as the crucial determinant of this structure.

Zamindari was admittedly not a unit of production. This partly
followed from its composition, often a considerable number of
scattered villages. This had also much to do with the way it ori-
ginated. Most zamindars, having scarcely any role in the foundation
of village settlements, gradually established their authority over them,
often with the prior sanction of the State,[16] in regard to collection of
rent and other aspects of the administration.

[16] The State permitted it usually by way of rewarding exceptional services to
it by zamindars.

Zamindari not being a unit of production did not necessarily mean that zamindars had no role whatsoever in the rural economy. They did not decide how individual cultivators would organize their cultivation. However, they did control some aspects of the rural economy. A notable area of control was the reclamation of the village wasteland. The origins of some zamindaris were, indeed, an obligation to reclaim waste tracts. The way most zamindars exercised their authority in this regard determined the forms of their control over the rural society. They were rarely directly involved in the reclamation process, usually entrusting it to some resourceful local entrepreneurs, offering liberal terms of rent, and also providing in some cases part of the necessary finance.[17] Where zamindars did not carefully define the legal status of the reclaimers and their rent rates, conflicts recurred later when the land values tended to rise.

Zamindars' role in the economy of the settled villages of particular regions was significant too. In Bengal they traditionally looked after the maintenance of irrigation works and embankments. In parts of southern Bihar where agriculture mostly depended on large-scale irrigation, they initially paid for its construction, and usually maintained it. The villagers customarily provided the necessary labour free of cost where considerable repairs had to be done. Distribution of water was part of zamindars' responsibility too, particularly where the irrigation network included a large number of villages. Clashes over water commonly occurred where this authority became ineffective. Zamindars were, of course, amply rewarded for all they did. Half of the gross produce of the irrigated villages was normally their share.[18]

True that zamindars, despite such roles in the rural economy, seldom controlled the way that a substantial landowner, letting out his land to share-croppers, controlled their land and labour. The limited involvement of zamindars in the actual organization of cultivation partly explained some limitations of their powers. The internal organization of the village economy had its own necessities which determined the way part of the peasant surplus was distributed. For instance, a portion of the village produce was set apart, before zamindars received their share, for paying some village func-

[17] The *thikadars* of Bihar and the *jotedars, grantidars,* etc. of Bengal owed their origins to this process.

[18] From this gross produce a portion was set apart as payment to several 'village functionaries' before it was divided between cultivators and zamindars.

tionaries whose services the village community considered essential. The conditions on which a number of peasant groups held or cultivated lands were also largely determined independently of the zamindars' position in the village society. The founders of agricultural settlements, for instance, traditionally enjoyed special privileges, which continued to their descendants long after their original justification had disappeared. The privileges of some high-caste peasants in point of rent demand were due to considerations of caste. Zamindars during Mughal rule seldom ignored such customs and conventions. In fact it was their interest not to do so. Zamindari was a source of income and one of power too. It served a zamindar well that the peasants would be kept in a state of dependence. 'This way his income and prestige were assured.'

However, the notion that zamindari was not a unit of production need not be overstressed in connection with our analysis of the zamindar's control over the rural society. Direct land control alone, such as the one characterizing the share-cropping system, did not necessarily provide the crucial powers which determined the shape of the agrarian structure. Zamindars did exercise such power, even without possessing this control. In fact, even the 'collection of tribute', which has been distinguished from direct land control, involved enormous powers. The Mughal State, depending for the largest part of its income on land revenue, carefully upheld them. In fact the claim of the State to the income from land revenue was prior to any right of the village community or of the peasant society itself. The State, or its local representatives such as zamindars, therefore sought to thwart such actions of peasants, including desertions, as threatened the security of this income. The powers of zamindars were scarcely restricted to the ones derived from their role in the collection of tribute. The sources of such powers were far wider, such as the hereditary nature of zamindari property, the zamindar's participation in the local administration, particularly the maintenance of law and order, and his kinship and caste ties. In the long run, however, the powers of zamindars rested on the way they appropriated a sizeable part of the peasant surplus. The usual share of the dues collected by them on behalf of the State formed only a fraction of their rental income. A considerable portion of it was derived from occasional increases in the established rent rates, and particularly from numerous illegal or extra-legal cesses. A striking thing about the cesses was that a great many of them had no economic justification and were explicable mainly in terms of the wide social powers of zamindars.[19] The State rarely intervened to check such impositions. Peasants felt strongly over them, denouncing the zamindar's action as a 'lapse of natural justice'. However, they did not have much to do about it, except fleeing to the estates of rival zamindars in the neighbourhood. Right to an unspecified portion of the peasant surplus gave zamindars enormous powers. Enforcing it, presuming that peasants occasionally questioned it, evidently immensely widened them. Since sales of peasant holdings had not yet become an established legal practice, and were not indeed even worthwhile in the context of a limited market in these holdings, zamindars devised an efficient machinery of coercion[20] toward realization of contested claims and normally accumulating dues. Peasants tended thus to be subjected to an increasingly ramified subordinate authority, often not directly controlled by zamindars.

During early British rule the powers of zamindars suffered a temporary setback. This, however, often meant substitution of other authorities for that of zamindars. *Jotedars* were far from the main beneficiaries. This is inferable from the way the authority of zamindars tended to be undermined. The crucial factor was the land revenue policy of the new government. The government, keen on maximizing land revenue, and convinced that the old zamindars would seek to frustrate the aim, decided to take in strangers.[21] This substitution only marginally helped the government, while it inevitably weakened the authority of zamindars. The famine of 1769-70 greatly weakened the authority of zamindars by deranging their finances, since the government scarcely relented in enforcing their revenue demand despite the pervasive disaster inflicted by the famine. The perfidy of a section of the zamindari bureaucracy contributed to the breakdown of the control of zamindars. Not that this faithless-

---

[19] For instance, the cesses demanded on the exclusively private occasions in the zamindar's family, such as the birth of a son, the death of a close relative, the sacred-thread-wearing ceremony and various religious festivals.

[20] The coercions included distraint of crops, physical tortures of various kinds and imprisonment in the zamindar's private prison.

[21] The strangers, of course resourceful people, initially included persons closely connected with the European Revenue Collectors, or those whose ostensible official position the Collectors and other high officials used toward promoting their private interests. For the argument that 'farming of revenue collections decentralized zamindari management and shifted effective control over the land downward in the social hierarchy': J. R. McLane (1977) in R. E. Frykenberg (ed.).

ness was altogether a novel development. What was new was the
conditions in which their *amlahs* (subordinate officials) could now
manoeuvre and get away with their misdeeds. The plight of zamindars—the assault on their authority from different quarters and
their acute financial difficulties—came as a godsend to the scheming
amlahs. They cheated the zamindars and encouraged intrigues in
order to promote their selfish aims.[22] The occasional intervention by
the government in the management of estates, as a device toward
reorganization of their finances, and the temporary supersession of
the zamindars' control, also created conditions in which their authority, even when formally restored, continued to be an unstable
one. The intervention suddenly aggravated the internal power conflicts in the estates, causing frequent shifts in alliances and consequently eroding any unified control.[23] In some regions, such as
Rangpur, Dinajpur, and Maldah, the zamindars had to face a formidable rivalry from the company's commercial establishments looking after the production of cotton, silk goods and raw silk, particularly where the cotton weavers, silk producers, etc., were part-time
agriculturists too, and thus subject to the zamindar's authority. The
conflict between the two authorities arose when cultivators, aggrieved
over the rent question, looked to the commercial establishments for
protection, which usually readily provided it. It often happened that
the presence of the Commercial Residents made the cultivators
resent certain actions of zamindars which they would have otherwise
ignored.

Zamindars quickly recovered their lost position. Sales of defaulters' estates, ruthlessly enforced by the government for long, of
course ruined many an old zamindar after 1793. However, the
zamindari system as a whole tended to be stabilized. Purchases of
estates at the auction, initially not very attractive,[24] became increasingly worthwhile investments to moneyed people, both in point
of security and also of the level of returns on the money spent. This
was partly because the government, keen to make landed property
as attractive as possible, provided extraordinary powers to zamindars

[22] The *amlahs*, with their ill-gotten fortunes, succeeded in purchasing at the
public auction, at least initially, a considerable number of estates, particularly
in Rajshahi, Dinajpur, Birbhum and Nadia.
[23] In Dinajpur, for instance, the sweeping reforms initiated by the District
Collector Hatch resulted in severely restricting the authority of the Dinajpur raj.
[24] For reasons of this limited attractiveness of landed estates at the time:
B. B. Chaudhuri (1975a: part 1).

in relation to peasants, whenever they clamoured that without such powers their rental income would be insecure.[25] The government reasoned that the security of its revenue would be endangered unless this rental income was reasonably assured. Surprisingly, the findings of official enquiries into the alleged 'rent difficulties' of zamindars, particularly during the period 1794–8, seldom warranted the subjection of peasants to the new coercive powers of zamindars. The difficulties were often blamed on the treachery of a section of intermediaries, occasionally including affluent peasant groups, who had long ceased to cultivate their lands directly. The coercive laws (1799 and 1812), now indiscriminately applying to the peasantry in general, were all the worse, since, unlike before, a powerful State machinery upheld them.[26] To ensure that a purchaser at the public auction would get a property 'free of all encumbrances' the government also authorized him to annul, if he chose, all the commitments of his predecessor in regard to use of the resources of the estate—for instance, all tenures of intermediaries and even of peasants. The purchaser was free to revise the prevailing rent rates of peasants. The government seldom intervened, till about 1859, even where aware that these powers were being grossly abused, fearing that collection of rent, long associated with such abuses, would abruptly fall in their absence, thus imperilling the security of its revenue. In fact the government for long did not think increase of rent objectionable at all, and looked upon it as a 'natural phenomenon' in the context of the developing agricultural resources of the country, only preferring that the increase be kept within the legal limits.

Zamindars evidently widely used their new coercive powers, particularly some of them.[27] The implications of the process for peasant rights have been amply shown by the findings of occasional official enquiries. A rather startling one in 1828 was that peasants, particularly in the Bihar districts, were scarcely aware that they had any rights at all. What was worse, they seem to have been reconciled to

[25] The two dreadful pieces of legislation, which the peasants later recalled with horror, were Regulation VII of 1799 and Regulation V of 1812. In the peasant memory they were the symbols of unrestrained despotism of zamindars.

[26] Many of the powers now provided to zamindars were not altogether new. The novelty was the formal assurance to zamindars of unqualified help from the local police in enforcing their powers.

[27] For instance, the right of distraint, and the right to summon ryots to the zamindar's revenue establishment (*kachhari*) on the pretext of rent arrears. Such powers were enough for zamindars to terrorize the relatively obdurate peasants.

this position. It was their awareness of the enormous powers of
zamindars in the village that prompted the European indigo planters
to acquire such powers. They nearly universally admitted that the
decisive role of the powers in the enforcement of indigo cultivation,
with which the indigo growers had been consistently bitter on
account of its unremunerativeness, made them pay to zamindars
whatever price they demanded for leasing to the planters portions of
their estates. In Bihar the planters even succeeded, with the help of
these powers, in getting the necessary labour, apart from the one
connected with indigo cultivation, at a price considerably lower than
the usual market one.

The use of the coercive powers had initially much to do with the
pressure of revenue demand, which hit a great many of the old
zamindars, particularly those about whose resources the government had in different ways obtained a fairly accurate idea.[28] The
diminishing pressure of revenue over the years did not necessarily
result everywhere in any notable improvement in the zamindari
finances. Increased rental income was indeed a bad need even then
in very many cases in the context of the increasing cost of estate
management, the rising commodity prices, particularly in the second
half of the nineteenth century, and the growing number of dependents
on the given rental income. The use of the coercive powers therefore
continued, though, as noted later, zamindars had then many more
constraints to face than in the first half of the nineteenth century.

The correlation between acute financial pressure and use of the
new legal powers of zamindars need not be overstressed. The powers
were occasionally used just because they existed. The lead in this was
evidently taken mostly by newcomers: auction-purchasers; holders
of permanent leases (*patnis*) of portions of some old estates agreeing
generally to pay to the owners a considerably larger amount than
the existing rental income from the leased portions; 'speculators' in
land; and persons to whom zamindars, unable to cope with direct
management of estates, temporarily farmed out collection of rent,
thus transferring to them their authority over the villages. The third
group, usually uninterested in permanently retaining estates, and
keen on quickly making fortunes out of 'trading in land', i.e., purchasing estates merely to sell them out at a considerable margin of
profit, ceased to thrive once the land market became reasonably

[28] As a result, the revenue demand was fully adjusted to the known resources.
In general the relatively little-known estates often escaped with a light assessment.

stable. The first two groups, intent on making the best of their purchases, most methodically used the new powers. Assault on the old established rural groups, such as the rent-free holders and holders of lands at privileged rates, occurred oftener here than elsewhere. What prevented the last group from being as aggressive was its short tenures. It could as well consolidate its control over the rural community where the temporary leases were usually renewed. *Thikadars* of Bihar mostly belonged to this category. Their activities had worse consequences for peasants where they were the zamindars' creditors as they often were in Bihar. The zamindars were understandably unwilling to antagonize their benefactors by opposing their will.

Over the years the powers of zamindars increasingly came under constraints, and evidently declined in many areas. The intervention by the State in favour of peasants, in 1859, 1885 and later,[29] had initially a decisive role in the process, since the landlord powers considerably derived from legal sanctions, and were often upheld by extra-legal and illegal coercions, which the government had not for long seriously tried to stop. The first notable change in its attitude came in 1859. This was partially due to a conviction that making zamindars mend their ways was not any longer incompatible with the security of revenue. The government, however, scarcely intended to limit for ever the rent rates. The legitimacy of occasional rent increases was repeatedly upheld. Indeed, the government gradually refined the methods toward ensuring this. For instance, in 1859, rising agricultural prices were for the first time recognized as a valid ground for rent increase. Realizing that zamindars, in the absence of the kind of data acceptable to the law courts, often failed to establish the ground, the government, from 1885 on, annually provided a table of agricultural prices, asking the law courts to treat it as unquestionable evidence. After 1885, zamindars, baffled in their attempts to increase rent rates, could ask for the intervention of the government in this. On the condition that they would pay for the operations, collectorate personnel decided, on the basis of a careful local investigation, whether their plea was tenable, and, if it was found so, revised the rent rates. The government, while admitting the right of a zamindar to increase rent, was keen that the increase should not

[29] The famous Rent Act was passed in 1859 and the Bengal Tenancy Act in 1885. The latter Act was amended several times, most notably in 1928, 1938 and 1940.

be limitless.[30] Knowledge that zamindars had been pretty often grossly abusing some legal powers of theirs[31] led the government to abolish them altogether. The stricter watch that the local administration could now keep over zamindars, because of the considerable widening of the administrative network after 1855, forced many an erring zamindar to mend his ways. Setting of limits to rent increase often involved zamindars in protracted suits, where peasants contested their claims. Till about 1885 increase of rent on the ground of a rise in the agricultural prices was mostly negligible. Indeed, a law-abiding zamindar secured little increase except where cultivation had increased.

A far more crucial factor in the long run in the reduced powers of zamindars was the increasing consciousness of peasants about their rights, partly reflected in the growing strength of their combined resistance to arbitrary actions of zamindars. The resistance, though only partially successful, tended to sober the wayward zamindars. They had now to reckon with a probable recurrence of an organized opposition of peasants, and felt more diffident about easily imposing their will. They of course became far more cautious where the resistance was not confined to the aggrieved peasants alone. For instance, the Praja movement in parts of eastern and northern Bengal and primarily confined to the Mohamedans, eventually developed into a protest movement, having strong cultural and political overtones, of numerous sections of the community, largely against Hindu zamindars.[32] The teachings of the religious leaders, the Maulavis and the Ulemas, formed part of the ideology, particularly in rural areas. Influential members of the middle class, both urban and rural, pro-

---

[30] The limits applied only to a new legal category—'occupancy ryots'—defined as those who held land continually for a period of twelve years. The Bengal Tenancy Act of 1885 simplified the matter by providing that it would do if ryots held their lands in the same village during the 12-year period. An occupancy ryot's rent rate could be increased only on three grounds: where cultivation had increased; where agricultural prices had risen and where lands of a comparable quality paid a higher rate in the neighbourhood.

[31] For instance, the right to summon defaulting ryots to the zamindar's revenue establishment, and the right to imprison them on the ground that they had not paid their dues. Zamindars used such powers mostly in order to beat insubordination.

[32] For the Praja Movement: Jatindra Nath De (1977). The Praja movement, primarily an agrarian one, having even some radical programmes, gradually developed into a broad-based cultural and political movement, mostly in the Muslim-majority regions.

vided part of the leadership. Even share-croppers, having no direct tenurial ties with the dominant Hindu zamindars, joined the movement at times. The decline of the social powers of zamindars only reinforced the process of decline of their economic and legal powers. Their way of life increasingly appeared as oddly anachronistic. The way they derived their rental income and spent most of it made them look as unworthy parasites. Indeed, their complete elimination was regarded as a condition of economic regeneration of Bengal. The main reason for the gradual erosion of their social esteem was the appearance in the village of numerous new agencies of power—such as the more elaborate revenue and judicial machinery of the government; the new bureaucracy connected with the public irrigation system, which was a source of immense power and patronage; the rivalry of powerful and resourceful 'newcomers', mostly purchasers of estates at public and private sales, and substantial purchasers of peasant holdings; a growing educated middle class, including an articulate intelligentsia, bitterly critical of the old ways of zamindars; and the proliferating groups connected with the trade in rural products and with the provision of rural credit.

It would, however, be misleading to infer that this decline so much fortified his subordinate groups, previously either antagonistic or dependent, that it hamstrung the initiative of a zamindar in exercising whatever powers that he still possessed. A recent view of Professor Musgrave, with reference to the Oudh talukdars (1870–1920), may be examined in this connection (Musgrave 1972: no. 3). He seeks to amend the 'idea of an estate as an efficient and effective power structure, with power located at the summit and percolating through its hierarchy'. 'Far from being a tightly organized and closely structured social fact', he argues, 'the estate begins to look like a rather loose and vague clump of relationships, in part political rather than economic or social, or in a sense, like a super-connection, dependent on the cooperation of the lower levels'. The estate was thus an 'essentially diffuse organization, with no level, even the lowest, entirely lacking in power . . . the landlord . . . was dependent for his position in society, for his ability to collect rents on the consent of the important men within his estate', and he was 'powerless . . . when faced with the withdrawal of that consent'.

Such constraints need not be exaggerated. True that the apparatus of control at the zamindars' command could not dominate the complex relationships and distribution of power within the village.

However, all of such relationships did not necessarily decisively bear on the struggle for rent, since the determinants of such relationships and those of rent relationships were not identical. The limited extent of the direct exercise of their control by the zamindars over the whole community of peasants did not mean that this control was not effectively exercised at all. The agencies to which rent collection was sometimes trusted, mainly resourceful persons, could be as effective in this regard as any possible direct exercise of control by the zamindars. The success, for instance, of the Oudh talukdars in enforcing their rent demands is evident from the large increase in their rental income, the considerable scale of evictions of the ryots, and the non-occupancy status of the largest portion of the Oudh peasants.[33]

Musgrave himself made an important qualification: 'at all levels of society men found it useful within their local, political and social context to have good relationships with the estate, its bureaucracy and in particular the whole series of resources possessed by them which would be brought to bear in the struggles and rivalries of the little community. When a real power struggle developed, the summit was never entirely without resources, the landlord never at the mercy of the subordinates.' The landlord sought to frustrate his enemies by forming counter-alliances loyal to him. In Oudh, for instance, in order to baffle his recusant Rajput clansmen, he even preferred an alliance with the kurmis, though inferior to the Rajputs in point of ritual ranking, and occasionally introduced cultivators from elsewhere, presumably because of their direct dependence on him.

The notion of jotedari domination as the crucial determinant of the rural agrarian structure is now taken up for examination. Several questions need to be answered in this regard. Did all the groups included in the 'landholding structure' derive their powers from control over land, which might occasionally be reinforced by other activities of theirs, such as trade and moneylending? Was jotedari

---

[33] The literature on the question is abundant. The following works may be consulted: M. H. Siddiqi (1978: Ch. 1); G. Pandey (1978: 13–22). Thomas R. Metcalf, while agreeing with Musgrave that the landlord was 'hardly the lord of the land', concludes: 'Yet one cannot jump straightaway to the conclusion that the landlord had no way of enforcing his will upon the subordinate estate staff' (Metcalf 1979: 270). Also 'The Struggle with the Underproprietors', Ch. 3 of Jagdish Raj's *Economic Conflict in North India: A Study of Landlord–Tenant Relations in Oudh, 1870–1890*, contains enough evidence contrary to Musgrave's conclusion.

domination typical of the rural agrarian relations throughout Bengal and Bihar? Did the roots and forms of this domination remain unchanged throughout the colonial period? Presuming that the powers of *jotedars*, old and new, had increased, did this necessarily lead everywhere to the alleged shift of the rural conflict from the old zamindar–tenant type to the 'modern' one of 'kulak landlord and share-cropping labourer'?

All the groups included in the 'landholding structure'—affluent and leading cultivators belonging to the 'respectable agricultural castes' and the village headmen (*mandals*), both groups combining various economic activities, apart from cultivation—did not derive their position and powers in the village from an effective control over the village lands. The *mandal*, for instance, by virtue of his administrative position and his privileged landholdings, did sometimes exercise considerable control over a part of the rural community, particularly during the times when he could abuse his administrative position. However, two things are notable here. The source of his power and control was scarcely any control over the village lands. The holdings of *mandals* evidently constituted only a small part of the total village cultivation. A *mandal* also could not usually disturb the pre-existing distribution of the village lands. He could only manipulate the distribution of the lump assessment of the rental claimed by the zamindar. He and his favourites thus often gained at the cost of some other cultivators. Secondly, a distinct trend over the years was the declining position of the old *mandal* as a *mandal*. Their normal responsibilities could not ensure their control for ever. Ryots who had become affluent tended to replace them.

Some members of the rent-collecting bureaucracy of zamindars were probably rich peasants themselves. Their control over land was thus strengthened by their control over rent-collection too. However, there was no necessary connection between their landed status as such and their choice by zamindars as rent-collectors. Success in rent collection did necessitate some local powers which might or might not have derived from landed status.

The reclamation process after the famine (1769–70) strengthened the position of an enterprising and affluent section of the peasantry. The gains, however, were often temporary. The labour involved in the process was largely non-local migrant labour from the regions relatively less affected by the famine. So far as local power was concerned this constituted a source of weakness for the local entrepreneurs. The Birbhum raj, which took the lead in inducing non-resident cultivators to migrate to its estate, had later a tough time coping with them who, when pressed for payment of the raj dues or otherwise discontented, often fled to their original villages with most of their harvest.[34] A development further weakening the entrepreneurs was the resumption by the zamindars of the liberal terms of rent which first induced the migrant peasants to take up the reclamation. The government too agreed with the zamindar's position. In Birbhum, where the scale of the reclamation was the largest, the zamindar, facing an abrupt increase in the revenue demand (1786–87) and the continuing bitterness of the local resident peasants about the continuing discrimination against them in point of rent rates, was particularly keen that the resumption could be effectively carried out.

The real 'land-controlling group' in rural Bengal was the one connected with large-scale reclamation and variously known as *abadkar*, *hawaladar*, *grantidar* and *jotedar*. It was on them that zamindars, not having enough resources or the competence to organize the complicated reclamation work, relied for it.

The question whether jotedari domination was typical of the rural agrarian relations is far more crucial than that relating to the composition of the so-called 'landholding structure'. An affluent peasant group, usually substantial holders and combining agriculture with trade and moneylending, presumably existed. This, however, scarcely warrants the conclusion that it effectively controlled land throughout the village.

Such a domination is mainly true of the regions characterized by the existence of substantial landholders, owing their landed position largely to their role in the reclamation process, since concentration of landholdings seldom occurred in other ways. The roots of this domination somewhat varied from place to place. Some common features were as follows. The entrepreneurs trusted with waste reclamation by zamindars were evidently resourceful people, having enough capital to finance the initial reclamation and to sustain it through occasional aids, including credit to the actual cultivators. The conditions of their lease helped them a lot. The terms of rent were pretty liberal. Indeed, no rent was payable in some cases for the first two or three years. Rent progressively increased afterwards. The main source of their powers, after the cultivation had become reasonably stable, was their particular relations with the labour force

[34] For the nature of the raj's difficulties: B. B. Chaudhuri (1976: 299–302).

directly involved in the cultivation. The relations were of two broad types. In Purnea, as Colebrooke (1795) tells us, the cultivators were regarded as no better than agricultural labourers. In districts, such as Bakarganj, the entrepreneurs, once planning and financing the reclamation, gradually withdrew from the scene, seldom interfering with the way the subordinate holders managed their cultivation, though ever energetically enforcing their claim that rent revision was entirely their discretion. Complexities arose where they were also creditors to the cultivators. Debts accumulated, eventually blurring the dividing line between rental claims and interest charges. The usual non-interference of zamindars in such relations only reassured the entrepreneurs. The motives of zamindars in this varied. The Dinajpur zamindars feared, as Buchanan writes (Dinajpur Report), that an interference might even disrupt the continuing reclamation, since the entrepreneurs there sometimes reacted to it by leaving their estates altogether with their capital resources and dependents.

Paradoxically, a law designed to improve the landed status of peasants tended to fortify the entrepreneurs' control over the subordinate cultivators. A new idea introduced by Act X of 1859 was the special claim of a group of peasants, called 'occupancy ryots', i.e., the ryots having 'occupancy rights', to legal protection against arbitrary increase of rent. It was the conditions specified by the Act for the accrual of occupancy rights that helped the entrepreneurs. The crucial one was uninterrupted holding of land for a period of twelve years. It was immaterial whether a ryot directly cultivated his land or not. The entrepreneurs, successful in satisfying this condition, and thus regarded as occupancy ryots, gained in two ways: their legal protection against indiscriminate increase of rent by zamindars and the absence of any legal constraints on the revision of rent of the subordinate cultivators. The second gain proved in the long run more substantial in the context of the rising demand for land. Zamindars only partially succeeded in breaking the powers of the substantial landholders. Their success was considerable mainly in the tribal regions, where the tribal headmen, usually leading the tribal agricultural settlements, were often replaced by aliens of the zamindars' choice.

While it would thus be valid to argue that jotedari domination characterized the agrarian relations in the regions where a few resourceful persons organized large-scale reclamation, a qualification needs to be made in this regard. New cultivation everywhere did not necessarily result from reclamation of this kind. The latter occurred mainly where, for various reasons, the reclaimable waste was abundant and the scarcity of labour acute—for instance, in the districts like Rangpur, Dinajpur and Jalpaiguri, and the regions contiguous to the Sunderbans, such as Khulna–Jessore, Bakarganj and the 24-Parganas. The argument that 'respectable agricultural caste' constituted a component of the dominant 'landholding structure' may be examined in this connection. Agricultural castes such as the Sadgops did play a notable role in large-scale reclamation. This was not necessarily true of the other castes. The success of the Sadgops was largely due to specific circumstances (Sanyal 1981: 45–7). An offshoot of the pastoral Gop caste, they chose to concentrate on the laterite forest areas of south-west Bengal—Birbhum, Burdwan, Bankura and Midnapur—established a firm control over the best arable lands of the region, and created conditions for a stable agriculture. Considerable grain-trade and holding of key positions in the bureaucracies of the local zamindars helped them consolidate their powers.[35] The rise of the group, scarcely a recent phenomenon and traceable as far back as the middle of the sixteenth century, was largely due to the tenuous control of the Mughals over these remote forest tracts, and the usual political fluidity of the border areas, particularly Midnapur.

The point of view stressing the distinction between the 'tribute-collecting structure over the village' and the 'landholding structure within the village' tends to assume that jotedari domination during British rule had not much to do with the economic and institutional changes during that rule and was in fact traceable even before it. The sense in which the notion of jotedari domination during early British rule is a valid one has been noted above. However, this point of view seems to ignore the emergence of other types of jotedari domination during British rule, due to a considerable extent to the changes occurring then, and resulting in the increasing complexities of the rural agrarian structure. The differences between the earlier types and the new ones relate to the (1) origins of the dominant groups; (2) their

[35] Their economic strength and the growing consciousness of solidarity, partly resulting from their conversion to Gauriya Vaishnavism, led the Sadgops to seek a higher ritual status. This they eventually attained. Their separate identity as a Nabasak caste was recognized. While the parent group (Gop) was originally an *Ajalchal* caste (a group from which the Brahmins would not take water) the Sadgops, separated from the parent group, were recognized as a Jalchal group, taking of water from which did not pollute the Brahmins.

composition and the (3) relative degree of concentration of holdings.

In point of origins jotedari domination in some areas (such as Jalpaiguri, 24-Parganas, Khulna and Bakarganj) continued even later to derive from the traditional source—organization of large-scale waste reclamation. In fact the pace of reclamation even quickened then under the stimulus of rising agricultural prices. The motives of the entrepreneurs for securing a firmer control over the subordinate cultivators were all the stronger now because of the rising land values. The government, as owner of very many waste tracts, was far more determined than other zamindars in having a share in the affluence, and sought to adjust its rent demand on the powerful intermediaries to the actual appropriations by them from the cultivators. It met with a fierce opposition, and remained content with much less than it asked for. Typically the later jotedari domination had two main sources: the growing demand for land, mainly from petty holders in the context of the intensifying pressure on land, and an increasing loss of peasant lands, often as a result of distress sales. The groups from which the petty holders rented land were not necessarily composed of substantial holders. The main reason why they readily leased out portions of their holdings was the handsome rental income that this secured to them. This was possible because of the relative lightness of their own rent rates, while the petty holders, badly needing land, agreed to pay considerably higher rent rates. Of the reasons for the lightness of rent rates in several cases the two notable ones at the time were the success of the landholders concerned in preventing substantial increase of rent by zamindars, and the arrangement under which the zamindars themselves, either aware of the difficulties in increasing rent, or because of urgent financial needs, fixed the rent rates for ever, on the condition that they would initially be paid a substantial amount as compensation. Distress sales of peasant holdings, due, apart from urgent needs of a temporary kind, to accumulating rent arrears and debts, and evidently limited in number during early British rule, considerably increased over the years. The decisive factors in this from the purchaser's point of view were the increasing land values making acquisition of the holdings far more attractive than before and the availability of easier formal means of enforcing the realization of rent arrears and debts.

Of the two sources of the later jotedari domination the first is self-explanatory. The source here was the obvious control of the substantial landowner over the land rented from him by petty holders. Rent continued to be paid in cash till the rising agricultural prices, particularly since the 1890s, led the landowner to insist on produce rent. Sales of peasant holdings resulted in such a domination where the purchaser, instead of directly arranging their cultivation, leased them out either to their original owners or to other cultivators, usually on a share-cropping basis.[36] The landowner's motives in this were various. As far as income from the leased-out land was concerned, this arrangement was often found more suitable than direct cultivation. The motive here was stronger where the purchaser had neither any skill in agriculture nor taste for it. Indeed, non-involvement in direct cultivation generally ensured an improved social and ritual status. The purchased holdings were also sometimes too scattered for the purchaser to cultivate them efficiently.[37]

The origins of the later *jotedars* point to their complex composition. Even moderately well-off holders were attracted, as noted above, by the offers from petty holders to rent out portions of their lands. The relative smallness of the resources required for purchase of peasant holdings, generally tiny ones, apart from the rising land values, attracted even persons of modest means, provided they were free to purchase. Sales for rent arrears provided wider opportunities; sales for debt much less, since they largely occurred to the peasants' creditors.

The extreme heterogeneity of the composition of the later *jotedars* and the numerical strength of the *jotedars* of relatively modest resources implied that their control over land tended to be rather diffused over a wide area, while the early *jotedars* and some of the later ones, by virtue of their role in large-scale waste reclamation, controlled a large compact block.

This complexity in the composition of the later *jotedars* needs emphasis. The usual studies on them tend to ignore it, and concentrate on the type that prevailed in the areas where large-scale waste reclamation characterized new cultivation, such as Rangpur, Dinajpur, Jalpaiguri, and the sprawling Sunderbans. André Béteille, who questions the applicability of the category '*jotedars*' to the whole of Bengal, argues, by way of explaining it, that domination of *jotedars* and the pre-existing authority of zamindars were inversely

[36] For the reasons why direct cultivation was preferred sometimes: B. B. Chaudhuri (1975b: Sec. 10b, 153–4).

[37] Where moneylenders were the purchasers, their control over credit only reinforced the control that the leasing out of land normally provided.

related. *Jotedars*, according to him, dominated the rural society only where the powers of zamindars were either non-existent or feeble.[38]

The crucial question is one of choice of criteria by which to identify a *jotedar*. Béteille's criterion seems to be the largeness of the area of cultivation controlled by a *jotedar*. This control of course implies other kinds of control, such as the one over a section of agricultural labourers and dependent cultivators, where the *jotedar*, presumably unable to cultivate the entire area at his command by his family, had to hire labour or trust part of the cultivation to share-croppers or other 'undertenants'. Jotedari domination essentially derived from control over land of such a kind as led to control over village labour and dependent cultivators, often reinforced by control over credit supply. Two inferences seem legitimate here. Control over land need not have been of the kind that prevailed in the areas noted above. Even command over a much smaller area could provide it. Secondly, this control need not necessarily be related, as Béteille did, to particular kinds of 'land settlements', such as the ones of these areas, mainly designed to ensure reclamation of large blocks of waste as quickly as possible, at a minimum cost to the government, or in some cases, to the zamindars owning the wastes. Alienations of peasant holdings, in the way noted above, could as well give it to the new owners of the holdings. The main difference between a *jotedar* in Béteille's sense and the one in our sense relates to the size of the land controlled by him. However, a landholder would legitimately be called a *jotedar* where the criteria characterizing later *jotedars*, indicated above, applied to him. A larger landholding of course created a wider area of control.

We now examine the notion that the *jotedar*–share-cropper conflict tended to develop into the basic rural class conflict, overshadowing the old one between zamindars and peasants. The arguments in favour of it are first briefly summed up.[39] The foundation of the powers of *jotedars*, consisting of their control over 'most of the land in a given neighbourhood', was gradually strengthened by their success in appropriating the largest portion of the unearned incre-

[38] Béteille concludes: 'In fact wherever jemidars, pattanidars and the rest were firmly established, as in Burdwan, Birbhum and Bankura, those who were actually involved in cultivation through the use of either family or hired labour, occupied a fairly low position in the social hierarchy. It was in the areas outside the Permanent Settlement that large peasant proprietors, known as jotedars, really came into their own' (1974: Ch. 4, 131).

[39] A recent review of the arguments can be found in Alastair W. Orr: Ch. 7.

ment from the rising agricultural prices after 1860. Zamindars, in spite of their legal powers to claim a share, often failed in this, largely because of their inability to provide the kind of evidence that the law courts asked for. The expensiveness of law suits also sometimes deterred them from enforcing their legal claim. Furthermore, the law permitting increase of rent on ground of a rise in the agricultural prices applied only to a rise in the average local prices of staple food-crops, thus preventing zamindars from intercepting the profits from remunerative cash crops, such as jute. Moneylending and trading in agricultural commodities (which was not universal) contributed to consolidation of their powers. *Jotedars* thus became 'a force to be reckoned with politically' even by the late nineteenth century. 'Behind the tenancy legislation of 1859 and 1885 lurked the British fear that conflict between jotedars and zamindars might escalate to threaten British rule'.

We concentrate on two questions by way of examining this notion: how much of the cultivation was controlled by *jotedars*? Were they the only beneficiaries where the powers of zamindars declined? Statistical data relating to the first are usually fragmentary, and perhaps not wholly trustworthy. It would, however, be improper to reject them altogether. The size of the share-cropped area may be considered first. It was over such lands that *jotedars* or other land-owners directly and most effectively exercised their control. More-over, it was the share-cropping arrangement that landowners, including moneylenders and other purchasers of peasant holdings, invariably preferred, in the context of rising agricultural prices, where they chose to rent out their lands at all. Occasional official enquiries into the share-cropping system, probably the best possible source of information on the question, show that, except in some areas, the share-cropped area seldom constituted more than 20 to 25 per cent of the cultivation. This estimate scarcely applies to the whole of our period. The relevant data[40] come mostly from the 1930s, the period of the Great Depression, when the unprecedented strain on the peasants resulted in an abrupt increase in the rate at which they had been losing lands. The share-cropped area was presumably much smaller before. Another noticeable feature of the share-cropping system was its concentration in the regions inhabited by the tribals and the

[40] Those compiled by the Bengal Land Revenue Commission (1940: Vol. II, Appendix, Table No. VIII (f)), and by the officers in charge of the 'settlement' work being done at the time.

cultivators having the lowest caste ranking. At least the available data thus create a strong doubt about its typicality throughout Bengal. Data relating to the size of the area rented out by substantial owners on money rent are far less satisfactory. The officials, connected with cadastral surveys and revision, partly on their basis, of rent of 'occupancy ryots', occasionally estimated the area covered by this arrangement which, except in certain districts, such as Jessore, Khulna and the Sunderbans, barely exceeded 5 per cent of the cultivation.

The limited extent of the area of *jotedars'* control was partly the reason why the evident decline in the powers of zamindars did not benefit this group alone. The failure of zamindars in imposing an increase in the rent rates was as much beneficial to small holders as to the affluent ones. It would in fact be misleading to argue that Act X of 1859 and the Bengal Tenancy Act of 1885 were merely acts of recognition on the part of the government of the alleged 'political' weight of *jotedars*. Some of them did gain by the Acts. However, the government scarcely intended them as such. If they had any philosophy at all it was that the existence of a resourceful peasantry, which they thought could be ensured through restricting arbitrary rent increases by zamindars, would greatly contribute to the stability of peasant agriculture. The philosophy had not ever equated this peasant group with *jotedars*.

However, some aspects of the consolidation of jotedari domination, only marginally due to the decline of landlord powers noted above, did impinge on such powers, and occasionally severely hurt them. A notable one was connected with the increasing complexity of the peasants' economic relationships, particularly those with their creditors and with traders in agricultural commodities—also sometimes their creditors. For zamindars the crucial change resulting from the relationship was alienation of peasant holdings, called by the law 'transfers of occupany rights'. Zamindars evidently felt alarmed over the issue. The reason was not merely that they now lost their traditional right of choosing their tenants whenever a holding fell vacant. They feared that the old peasants, generally respectful of their authority, would be replaced by resourceful people, probably less amenable to their control—crafty moneylenders, affluent members of the middle class, usually critical of the ways of zamindars, and sometimes even hostile zamindars in the neighbourhood bent on ruining them. They therefore sought to frustrate the possible adversaries as far as possible. Initially they demanded a high price for formally approving of transfers—full payment of the outgoing peasant's rent arrears. They, naturally, inflated the rent claims. The battle then shifted to a new area. They unitedly opposed the plan of the government (1880–85) for legalizing transfers of occupancy rights. Their views prevailed. The government, retreating from its original position, asked the law courts to recognize transfers only where they had long been 'customary', forbidding them otherwise to approve of them. Much obviously depended on how the law courts defined the 'custom'. The resultant uncertainty tended to restrict such transfers. Zamindars, however, could not long have it all their own way. Peasants keen on selling their lands and the prospective purchasers soon learned the tricks of beating the zamindars, the usual one being hiding from them the fact of transfers as long as possible. Zamindars, realizing that they were losing the contest for power, sought to salvage as much as possible. They agreed to let go their control provided they were allowed to share in the purchase money, the amount varying from place to place. A law of 1928, while removing all constraints on transfers, formalized this claim. The share was now fixed at 20 per cent. Their defeat was complete in 1938, when they had to accept the transfers without any condition at all. Zamindars, keenly asserting for long their claim to choose the 'tenants', eventually failed to cope with their resourceful adversaries, with the intervention of the government in favour of the latter, helping to tilt the balance against them.

We now briefly indicate our conclusions on the debate, which we have surveyed above, relating to the rural agrarian structure of Bengal and Bihar. It would be misleading to underestimate the authority of a zamindar at the village level merely on the ground that his estate was not a unit of production. His non-involvement in the production process did not necessarily preclude his role in the rural economy as a whole. The role was a vital one, where large-scale waste reclamation had been taking place, and where the security of agricultural production over a wide area wholly depended on artificial irrigation and embankments. A zamindar's authority made itself far more widely felt where it derived from his role in the extraction and appropriation of the peasant surplus. Zamindars suffered a severe setback during early British rule. In a great many cases their old authority was considerably undermined. Their impoverishment was nearly universal. Better days came from about the time of the

Permanent Settlement. The ruthless auction sales of defaulters' estates ruined many a zamindar. These personal losses meant merely a change in the composition of the landed society, and only marginally affected the zamindari system consisting of certain specific economic and legal relationships. In fact the system tended to be stabilized. The government did its best to make landed property a worthwhile possession. Wide powers were provided to zamindars toward securing their rental income. It was generally reluctant to restrain the zamindars even where they greatly exceeded the powers. On the other hand, increasing cultivation, increasing stability of agricultural prices, with even a slow increase occurring in them during the first half of the nineteenth century in several regions, and a rising demand for land made landed property far more attractive than during the first bleak decade after the Permanent Settlement, which saw many a zamindar going to the wall.

The authority of zamindars somewhat declined in the second half of the nineteenth century and later, though the process was far from universal. Two things are notable in this regard. The decline was only partially due to any rival groups usurping the authority of zamindars. Secondly, *jotedars* only partially gained from the decline. The decline had various causes. The initial assault on the zamindar's authority came from the government itself. The legal powers which zamindars most abused were abolished. Though the abolition was far from immediately and universally effective, zamindars now could evidently far less freely misuse their powers and position. They had also now many more constraints to face in increasing rent. Combined peasant resistance, though occasionally led by an affluent peasant group, or by landed families hostile to the local zamindars, made the difficulties insuperable at times. The organization of agriculture itself constituted a severe constraint. New cultivation shrank to insignificance in very many regions. Cultivation of cash crops or the rising agricultural prices only partially benefited the zamindars. On the other hand, the rising commodity prices reduced the real rental income of zamindars. The continuing increase in the number of their dependents, more or less living off a nearly frozen income, made the finances of many a zamindar almost desperate. The old authority of zamindars could scarcely survive such changes. Growth of new ideas, emanating from various sources and critical of the old ways of life of zamindars, further sapped its foundation.

The role of rival groups in the decline of this authority occurred where they succeeded in establishing direct control over peasants, superseding those of zamindars. This resulted sometimes from the actions of zamindars themselves when, convinced of the increasing difficulties of estate management, they preferred to rent out portions of their estates at a permanently fixed rate. This often happened in spite of the zamindars; for instance, when purchasers of alienated peasant holdings let them out to the old owner cultivators on a crop-sharing basis, or when big holders, controlling a considerable block of cultivation and judicially establishing their occupancy status in it, deprived the zamindars of their old authority in the matter of regulation of the rent rates of the subordinate cultivators.

Where the authority of zamindars thus declined *jotedars* were far from the only or even the main beneficiaries. Zamindari *amlahs* often gained at their master's cost. The way zamindari accounts were usually kept enabled them to get away with their misdeeds. The decline of the zamindar's moral authority and his imperfect knowledge of the nature of distribution of peasant holdings also prevented him from knowing how moneylenders and others had been steadily replacing the old owner peasants, at least as long as an appearance was kept up that rent was being paid by the peasants themselves. Where the zamindar was baffled in different ways in his attempts to increase rent small holders gained as much as the big ones. *Jotedars* undoubtedly gained too. The gains, however, have been exaggerated. Zamindars persistently asserted their right to redefine from time to time their relations with *jotedars*, where they had not explicitly signed away their rights. Their success in this widely varied. The role of *jotedars* in the trade in agricultural produces, particularly rice and jute, has often been magnified. The available data relating to the marketing of these produces point to large-scale free market operations of petty producers. *Jotedars*, except in certain areas, controlled only a portion of this trade. In the case of jute it was the jute mill-owners who considerably controlled the buyers' market in this commodity, and *jotedars* constituted only one of the multiple links between the numerous jute-growers and the eventual market.

The control of *jotedars* at the village level, acquired whether at the cost of zamindars or not, has rather been overstressed. The notion seems to be amply refuted by the available data relating to the size of the share-cropped area or of the lands held by 'under-tenants'. It would be misleading too to concentrate wholly on the big *jotedars*, if the idea is to locate the area of domination and subordination in the rural agrarian relationships.

Obsession with the notion of 'land control' has thus prevented us from recognizing a significant fact of the rural agrarian structure: the numerical importance of small peasants controlling their own lands and making their own decisions in regard to cultivation. They did enter into various economic relationships in the course of production. These, however, did not necessarily amount or lead to 'land control' of the kind discussed above.

II

Lack of precise data prevents us from accurately quantifying the changes in the size of cultivation, particularly till the end of the nineteenth century. As regards the rest of our period our knowledge is somewhat better.[41]

It is, however, possible to indicate the broad trends and to identify the periods when the cultivation increased or declined, though we are unable to measure the magnitude of the change.

At the time the British took over (1757), the deep scars that the recurring Maratha raids (1742–52) left on the rural economy of several western Bengal districts, such as Midnapur, Burdwan and the 24-Parganas, had only partially healed. Reduced intensity of cultivation, mainly due to scarcity of labour, widely occurred. In fact, the landlords there, in the absence of a stable labour force normally provided by settled peasants, largely depended, contrary to usage, on hired labour for getting their lands cultivated. The process of decline resulting from the famine of 1769–70 was significantly different. The scale of the devastation was far wider. Excepting some eastern Bengal districts nearly the whole of Bengal suffered. The rural depopulation, mainly due to starvation deaths, was also unprecedented in the recent years. About one-third of Bengal's population died. Cultivation declined by as much. As noted later, several other developments retarded the process of recovery, and the rot could not be stemmed even by the late 1780s.

However protracted, the process of reclamation progressed nearly everywhere, with the slow demographic recovery playing a significant role in this.

[41] Several recent works have dealt with the question: Chaudhuri (1969); Chaudhuri (1976); Islam (1978: Chs. 2, 3, and 'Conclusions').

Most of the district collectors and judges replying to the elaborate queries circulated by the Governor-General Wellesley (1798–1805) agreed that cultivation had considerably increased since the Permanent Settlement. Later official reports, based on much better information, confirmed the continuity of this trend. Different regions, understandably, developed unevenly. In general, cultivation increased faster in the regions which, by the time of the Permanent Settlement, were relatively more backward in point of land use than where agricultural resources had been better exploited. The Collector of Tirhut, which suffered grievously from the famine, did not even as late as 1796 notice any signs of a breakthrough. However, by 1824 the size of the new cultivation was large enough to strike local observers. Wyatt, surveying the district in 1847, was agreeably surprised at the pace of the reclamation. The trend persisted. Alapur, one of the largest parganas in the district which in 1797 appeared to the Collector as a 'perpetual cause of great anxiety', developed by 1870 into one of the 'richest parts of the district'. Champaran, the most backward of the Bihar districts, except Purnea, had an equally impressive record of growth. In 1837 the Revenue Surveyor of the district pointed as a test case to what had happened in the Majhaua pargana, which formed the major part of the district: 'The pargana . . . at the time of the Permanent Settlement was chiefly waste; the northern parts were covered with forest which are now inhabited and under beautiful cultivation.'

The available statistics relating to Bengal proper, though much less satisfactory, amply testify to a similar increase in the cultivation. It seems to have been most rapid in the eastern Bengal districts. They had an initial advantage in that the famine of 1769–70 had only marginally affected them. The more or less assured water supply because of the greater water resources there accounted for the relative infrequencies of severe shortfalls in the agricultural production. The sizeable agricultural surplus that this ensured helped in sustaining the pace of reclamation. The size of new cultivation in the western districts of Bengal was much smaller. In the districts such as Midnapur and Bankura part of it was insecure too. In Midnapur the reclamation was mostly concentrated in the western parts where at the time of the Permanent Settlement labour was extremely scarce and cultivation, because of the rocky nature of the soil, was a far more difficult process than in the largely alluvial eastern parts. In the northern districts too the reclamation process was far from sustained. In 1871 the Dinajpur Collector Crawfurd, while noting the increase of rice cultivation there 'in the most marked manner' during the three previous decades, pointed to an element of instability in the agricultural organization: 'The ryots are fond of a change in the land they cultivate, and frequently relinquish one and take another holding.'

An abrupt and much more severe interruption in the reclamation process occurred in a large tract, mainly in central and western Bengal, in the second half of the nineteenth century. The primary cause was the recurring outbreaks of a deadly fever, indiscriminately described as malaria. The census data (1872–91) reveal the extent of the resultant devastation.[42] In Burdwan, Rangpur and Birbhum the descending spiral was not reversed in the course of two decades. The 6 per cent growth in Hugli was entirely due to the stream of immigration into the industrial belt of the district. The apparent puzzle of a growth during the decade 1872–81 even in Nadia and Jessore where the local officials repeatedly noted the virulence of the fever was admittedly due to the faulty enumeration in 1872. Murshidabad, Dinajpur and Rajshahi had for long a nearly stationary population. This contrasts sharply with the high rate of population growth where

---

[42] For the course of the fever and its effects on the rural economy: Chaudhuri (1969: 153–66). The relevant Census data have been summarized below:

Districts	Percentage of Variation	
	1881–91	1872–81
Burdwan	− 6.2	− 0.1
Birbhum	− 6.95	+ 0.6
Bankura	+ 7.55	+ 2.7
Midnapur	− 1.07	+ 4.4
Hugli	− 12.49	+ 6.0
Nadia	+ 11.31	− 1.1
Jessore	+ 8.66	− 6.1
Khulna	+ 3.15	+ 8.4
Murshidabad	+ 1.04	+ 1.9
Dinajpur	+ 0.82	+ 2.7
Rajshahi	+ 2.14	− 1.2
Rangpur	− 2.58	− 1.6
Bogra	+ 6.51	+ 11.2
Pabna	+ 8.26	+ 3.9

Source: *Bengal Census Report*, 1881, Vol. 2, Table No. 2; *Census of India*, 1891, Vol. 3, pp. 46–7.

the fever was absent or had only a limited hold—for instance in eastern Bengal. While in the malaria-stricken western and northern Bengal the percentage of growth in the decade 1881–91 was 4.1 and 3.4 respectively, in eastern Bengal it was 14.3. It was mostly a natural increase, with immigration having only a small role in this.

Agricultural decline was evident wherever the malaria epidemic had struck. The fever caused extensive rural depopulation and greatly devitalized the survivors. Observations such as the following on the reduction in the labour force are abundant in the local official reports: 'Families which were full of robust, working heads and could very well spare many of them from their own fields to work for others, can now scarcely supply labour adequate to cultivate their own lands.' A Hugli zamindar wrote in 1872 of the 'rare, perhaps hitherto unknown, spectacle of crops rotting in the fields or being destroyed by animals for the very want of labour and means necessary to reap and store them'. A Settlement Officer of Jessore wrote of the 'dearth of labour everywhere during the harvest season'.

Demand for land suddenly slumped as a result even in Burdwan, once a densely populated tract. There was 'little demand' for *bastu* lands (residential sites). Scarcity of labour led even the well-to-do peasants to relinquish portions of their holdings. In several villages here 'nearly a fourth of the good arable land has for several years remained uncultivated'. In Hugli, where once, because of the pressure of a teeming population on land, 'the residents had not even land enough to dry their parboiled paddy', one-fourth of the land was left uncultivated. During the 1880s 'many villages are relapsing into complete jungle' in western Pabna.

Cultivation had, however, been steadily increasing elsewhere, both in Bengal proper and Bihar. Part of it presumably occurred around settled villages. The largest portion was concentrated in remote regions. The necessary labour force was mainly immigrants from the relatively overcrowded regions, where, given the level of the existing technology, the intensity of cultivation had reached its limit. Consequently, population growth was most rapid in the new agricultural settlements.

The peasant migration was mostly confined within the boundaries of particular districts. In some, mostly the demographically decadent ones, the immigrant Santals constituted the labour force. The region where they were most active was the vast tract in northern Bengal, known as the *Barind*, covering the southern third of Dinajpur, the eastern half of Maldah, the western half of Bogura and the northern quarter of Rajshahi. The districts where immigrant tribal labour had a limited or no role at all in the reclamation process may be classified into three groups: malaria-affected districts having small pockets of growth; some districts, particularly of eastern Bengal, having a large population growth and at the same time a great scope for new cultivation; and the Bihar districts with a growing population but with a much smaller scope for reclamation.

Since the increase in the first was the smallest we concentrate on the other two. The scope for new cultivation was the largest in the second, provided in general by the extensive Sunderbans and the fertile alluvial lands constantly brought into existence by the active rivers there. Individual districts here had their own particular regions of growth. In Dacca and Mymensingh such a region was the thinly-populated Madhupur jungle, an elevated tract to the north of Dacca, with undulating surface and a soil of stiff clay. The lead in the reclamation here was taken by 'various mongoloid tribes'. The scene of reclamation in Faridpur was the vast marsh in the south, intersected by strips of highland along the banks of the numerous rivers that once flowed through the tract, and inhabited by a low-caste peasant community, the *Chandals*.

In many parts of Bihar, particularly Saran, Muzaffarpur and Darbhanga, where the density of purely agricultural population was the highest in the Bengal Presidency, scope for reclamation was nearly non-existent near the old villages. Hence the peasant migration to remote parts of the district, mainly northward, because of the concentration of the earlier settlements in the south. In Champaran, too, where the unhealthy climate had for long severely limited new cultivation, 'a wave of agricultural enterprise, starting from the southerly *thanas* [police stations], has flowed northwards', particularly during the last two decades of the nineteenth century. The organization of the reclamation here somewhat differed in that a tribal group, the Tharus, provided the labour and skill for reclaiming a difficult terrain.

Three distinct features of the reclamation process in Bihar, particularly in the districts noted above, were the smallness of the size of the new cultivation, the slower pace of reclamation in the second half of the nineteenth century than in the first, and the inferiority of the new lands to the old ones in the southern parts of the districts. Between 1845 and 1900 cultivation in Saran had increased by merely

2 per cent. In nearly the same period the percentage in Darbhanga was a little less than 5 and in Muzaffarpur 5. Even in Champaran where the percentage was much higher, 20 to 25, the pace of reclamation was much faster in the first half of the nineteenth century. The Settlement Officer of Champaran thus concluded: 'In Champaran, as in other districts, it was in the first half of the century that agricultural development advanced with extraordinary rapidity.' The inferiority of the lands in the north was not in point of fertility of the soil, measured in terms of yield of the principal crop—rice. It consisted in other things. The migration to the north was the movement of peasants from a region of multiple crops to one of a limited number of crops, from a region growing valuable cash crops to one of mainly 'subsistence agriculture with rice dominant', and from a region of more or less secure cultivation to one where the crop, mainly dependent on rainfall, frequently failed. The economy of the northern region thus became increasingly vulnerable to the least failure of crop, and tended to become a famine-prone zone, since in the event of failure of the winter rice the peasants had no spring crops of any value which could mitigate their resultant distress.

This trend in the Bihar districts became only pronounced during the first four decades of the twentieth century. Researches of Blyn and Islam show that the situation in Bengal proper was only slightly better. Islam's revision of the available statistical data scarcely contradicts Blyn's major conclusions; it merely shows that the inclusion of Bihar and Orissa in Blyn's 'Greater Bengal' considerably depressed the trend rates for Bengal proper. The major findings of Islam, relating to the period 1920–46, are as follows. 'There was hardly any improvement in yield at the aggregate level and only a marginal expansion of the acreage under cultivation.' The trends of the two crop groups, food crops and cash crops, considerably differed. In the case of the former the possible gains from a small expansion of acreage were neutralized by a corresponding decline in yield. 'The rate of expansion of the acreage under cash crops was even smaller, but the yield per acre increased considerably'.

III

How did the rural agrarian structure (analysed in Part I) affect the agricultural trends broadly indicated above (Part II)? Where the trends are not explicable in terms of the agrarian structure, what other variables can we identify?

Till about the end of the nineteenth century data relating to yield at the aggregate level are either non-existent or extremely unsatisfactory. The point for us to explain then is the variations in the acreage. By the time official reports started to provide somewhat more satisfactory productivity data the rate of expansion of acreage had nearly dwindled to insignificance. There is understandably a limit to the availability of arable land. But why did the yield per acre decline, particularly that of the most important crop of Bengal and Bihar—rice? Where deteriorating ecological conditions had not caused it, it was presumably due to inadequate investment in agriculture. The question for us to answer is why the case was so.

The first phase of the decline was due to the famine of 1769–70. Why did the famine occur at all? Had the existing agrarian structure anything to do with its occurrence, and with the later retarded pace of recovery of the economy from its effects?

As regards origins of famines a point of view, based on studies of some recent famines, questions the decisive role of the so-called food availability decline, and argues that even where famines were accompanied by such a decline, 'the causal mechanism precipitating starvation has to bring in many variables other than the general availability of food' (Sen 1981: Chs. 1, 5, 10). Famines, according to this view, result from 'failure of exchange entitlements'. Entitlement, i.e., right through ownership, may be of various kinds, such as trade-based entitlement, production-based entitlement and own-labour entitlement. What a person owned could be exchanged in a market economy for other commodities he needed, either through trading, or through production, or through a combination of both. Such commodities as he thus acquired could be called exchange entitlements. Famine conditions arose where the exchange entitlements failed. For instance, an agricultural labourer, with labour as his main or only entitlement, could face a situation where his employment sharply declined, or became extremely irregular or the wage rates considerably fell, while, on the other hand, the bundle of commodities (such as rice) which he got in exchange of his labour was much smaller in the context of the increased prices of rice. The food availability decline alone cannot explain why only some particular groups, such as agricultural labourers, mainly suffered while several others remained unaffected. This is not just a question of income either. What a person could earn depended on what he could sell and the selling price.

This view points to certain aspects of the agrarian structure as having a close bearing on the occurrence of famines. The stress here is not on the poor as an undifferentiated group, but on some sections of it.

The role of food availability decline in the famine of 1769–70 seems to have been a crucial one. True that only certain rural groups mostly suffered. However, the large number of starvation deaths (which, along with the emigration of the distressed, reduced the population by about one-third) remain unintelligible without the sudden upswing of food prices. A considerable shortfall in food production for two successive seasons, 1768 and 1769, initiated the spiral. The pressure on the supply intensified with the continuing withdrawal of food-grains from the local markets. The usual market mechanism, normally geared to export of grain, could not be suddenly suspended without seriously hurting the interests of grain-merchants. The inter-vention in the market by the Company's government itself, with its command over a large cash, as a large-scale purchaser of rice, mainly for the use of its army, inevitably worsened matters (Chaudhuri 1976: 295). The cornering of a considerable supply by the Company's servants privately involved in grain trade and their Indian agents (*gomasthas*) through setting up of local monopolies in grain con-tributed not a little to the process. A source of replenishment was nearly gone when, with the increasing signs that the next winter rice would largely fail, grain-merchants, normally making grain-advances to cultivators during the lean months of the year, altogether sus-pended them, fearing that in the event of this failure recovery would be improbable.

The existing agrarian structure had only a marginal role in the crisis that developed. The crucial role was that of the new political authority, which was external to this structure. Apart from the big shortfall in the food production the major factors in the sharply-reduced food availability were the indiscriminate rice-purchases by the government from a market already under severe pressure, its free-trade policy facilitating large-scale drain of foodgrains out of the famine-affected zones, and its complete failure to prevent the corner-ing of the local food-supplies.

It was starvation deaths that, notably, accounted for nearly the whole of the demographic loss. Even peasants of moderate resources died in large numbers. The decline in the cultivation, also estimated at one-third of the total cultivation, was evident everywhere. The Commissioners appointed in 1772 to investigate the real effects of the famine found the 'finest part of the province desolated by the famine'. The demographic recession, though not the only cause, was a significant one, the heaviest mortality having admittedly occurred amongst agricultural labourers, constituting, even then, a sizeable group.[43] The solution which the government conceived in the context of the acute labour scarcity, i.e., large-scale migration from the neighbourhood, was not forthcoming. The supply of agricultural capital steeply declined since the dislocation in agriculture ruined many a small peasant and impoverished the zamindars. The latter were now mostly unable to help the cultivators with advances, in grain or in cash, which they had been doing for long, during their times of difficulty.

The role of the traditional agrarian structure in retarding the recovery of the economy was a marginal one too, at least during the first two or three decades after the famine. Indeed, as noted later, the role of zamindars was a positive one in several regions. Initially the interruption of the process of recovery was caused by a rather unusual phenomenon: abundant harvests and a spell of falling grain prices for about three years after the famine. 'The extreme plenty and cheapness of grain', a commonplace of the contemporary official reports, was only partly due to 'bountiful harvests'. Two major factors in this were the undiminished revenue pressure despite the catastrophe, and the shrinkage of the internal market for food. The first forced peasants to sell more of their produce soon after the harvest than before. The reduced effective demand for food was thus explained by the government: '. . . the mortality was mostly among the workmen, manufacturers and people employed on the rivers . . . so that the number of the consumers who suffered in the calamity was greater in proportion than that of the cultivators of the grain'. Consequently, 'the present stagnation in the sale and currency of every kind of grain' was accompanied by 'the increase lately made in the price of manufactures'. The greatly reduced money circulation of the time, due mainly to silver scarcity[44]—a phenomenon originating prior to the famine and continuing, in varying degrees, till about the

[43] Recent researches have revealed that societies usually characterized as 'peasant societies' did include a considerable group of agricultural labourers. For a comparable situation in medieval England: Hilton (1975: Ch. 2).

[44] While on the one hand the usual inflow of silver into Bengal had been sharply reduced, mainly as a result of the abrupt decline at the time in Bengal's trade with the regions other than Europe, the demand for silver had then been steadily rising. In fact the second development seems to have been the decisive

end of the eighteenth century, did contribute to the process, though by itself it could not determine its course.

The falling prices reduced the peasant's income at a time when they needed it most. In fact the fall was so steep in some places, such as Purnea and Dinajpur, that peasants did not have even enough to pay their obligatory dues—rent and debt.

The disappearance of the brief spell of the slump in the grain prices could not by itself stimulate the economy. The policy of the government continued to depress it. Only a massive investment toward restoration of the lost cultivation could have nursed back the ailing economy to health. The government remained largely inactive. Its role was confined to encouragement of mulberry cultivation through liberalization of the rent rates on mulberry lands, and in this care was also taken to see that the usual rice lands were not converted into mulberry lands. The generosity in regard to mulberry growers was because of the need to increase the export of raw silk to London, and not designed to tone up the economy.

It was the revenue measures of the government that proved the greatest depressor in the rural economy for a considerable length of time. Even the pervasive disaster did not make the government relent in the matter of revenue collection. The government candidly admitted that its revenue income only marginally fell 'owing to its being kept up violently to its former standard'. One such violent method was *najai*, 'an assessment upon the actual inhabitants of every inferior division of the lands to make up for the loss sustained in the rents of their neighbours, who are either dead or have fled the country'.[45]

Indeed, the revenue policy resulted in largely undoing what zamindars, despite their financial stringency, intended to do toward an increase in cultivation, at least its stabilization. The two notable measures of theirs were liberal grants of rent-free lands, still mostly unreclaimed, as inducements to reclaimers, and encouraging migration of peasants from the neighbouring estates to theirs. The government, determined to bring all 'secreted' lands to light, sought to resume all rent-free grants, particularly after 1788, and to assess the reclaimed waste lands which peasants had clandestinely added to their original holdings. The large-scale reclamation on the basis of

---

factor in the acute silver scarcity of the period. Chaudhuri, 'Agricultural Prices in Bengal, 1757–1860' (unpublished).

[45] Knowing as they did that the tax had proved 'an intolerable burden' the government remorselessly enforced it. (Chaudhuri 1976: 298–9.)

migrant labour also came to be severely interrupted, particularly in Birbhum, one of the worst-affected zones. The Birbhum raj managed to lure peasants from the neighbourhood through offers of liberal rent rates. The process came nearly to a halt when in 1788 the district collector introduced a revised rent assessment. This threatened the privileges which the migrants had for long been enjoying. The Birbhum raj too hesitated to continue the generous terms of rent in the context of the persistent grumblings of the old resident peasants that the terms had amounted to a gross discrimination against them. The migrants, by then a force to reckon with in the local economy, unitedly resisted the changes. The district authority intervened with an armed force when the raj failed to cope with the rebellion.

How did the gradual increase of cultivation, evident nearly everywhere since about the 1790s,[46] occur? How did the existing agrarian structure bear upon the process?

The role of the demographic recovery in this is indisputable in view of the extensive rural depopulation which the famine had rather abruptly caused and of the unchanged techniques of agricultural production. Contemporaries were sure about the recovery, though not about the exact size of the growth. The testimony of Buchanan, who visited and carefully surveyed between 1808 and 1812 two of the districts worst hit by the famine, Dinajpur and Purnea, seems acceptable. He described the population of Dinajpur as 'enormous'. During the four decades preceding his survey the growth in Purnea was estimated by him at nearly 100 per cent. He was amazed by the 'immense population by which the country is overwhelmed'. Similar impressionistic evidence about a growing population elsewhere is abundant. Demographic gains alone did not ensure continuation of the reclamation process. What was decisive was the quality of the additional labour force and its availability for the process. Buchanan stressed the poor quality of the labour. The 'want of energy and activity of the people' of Dinajpur where 'the inhabitants are a puny and weak race' was attributed by him to the institution of early marriage, and partly to a recurring fever, which 'annually sweeps away immense numbers'. One of the reasons why despite an increase of about 33.3 per cent in the population during the four decades preceding his survey, 'the progress made in agriculture is miserably deficient' was that 'the natives are exceedingly unhealthy, and the children feeble . . .'. He similarly noted 'the great listlessness and

[46] See Part II of this essay.

want of energy among the people' of Purnea, and the 'uncommon indolence and want of skill' among the people of Bhagalpur. Buchanan also stressed how the prevailing credit relations limited the size of mobile labour so that despite an apparently large population enterprising farmers could not get enough labour. He thus explained the 'great difficulty' which 'a stranger finds in procuring porters' in Purnea, despite the fact that 'many more people live here as servants or hired labourers than even in Dinajpur': 'most of them are deeply involved in debt and their services are bound for many months in anticipation, so that they are no longer at liberty to engage themselves to a stranger'.[47]

That the increased cultivation did not result from the increased availability of labour alone is evident from two other circumstances: the natural growth of population was not enough to provide all the necessary labour, and the necessary finances for the reclamation process, where it was not confined to petty individual holdings of peasants, were only marginally provided by small peasants, where they were the immigrant labourers too.

Local labour was in several regions far inadequate for the reclamation there. The role of a substantial amount of migrant labour in the case of Birbhum has been noted above. Its source was not any population growth in the neighbourhood from which it migrated. It is likely that the migrants skilfully divided their time between their old cultivation and the new, and the incentive for this hard labour was obviously the nominal rent rates in the estates of the host zamindars.

This was not the kind of long-distance migration which in several parts of Bengal provided the largest part of the labour force engaged in new cultivation there. The long-distance movement did not start soon after the famine, and a large part of the immigrant labour was tribal and semi-aboriginal in nature. The large wastes to which the labour moved had not come into existence merely as a result of the famine, population there having been thin for long preceding the migration.

[47] The expansion of labour force in Assam, mainly through emigration from some neighbouring districts of eastern Bengal, provides a contrast in this regard. The remarkable increase of cultivation in Assam since about the beginning of the twentieth century was not due to this expansion alone. What was crucial was the skill of the immigrants as agriculturists, as reclaimers of waste lands and as growers of valuable cash crops, particularly jute.

The regeneration of agriculture in Midnapur and Bankura occurred mostly in this way, particularly in the western parganas where
cultivation had always been a difficult process, since the soil, being
of a rocky nature, could not retain much moisture. A tribal leader
called *mandal* usually led the new agricultural settlement. The fact
that the mandali system, connected with reclamation, prevailed only
where the tribal or semi-aboriginal tribes such as the Santals,
Bhumijs and Mahatos formed the bulk of the population, clearly
indicates the particular ethnic composition of the immigrant labour.
By the 1830s the mandali system had become an essential element
in the peasant economy of the jungly regions of Midnapur. The
officer supervising the revision of the revenue assessment in the region
in 1839 had to define carefully the position and rights of a *mandal*
in the land, since uncertainty about it had caused much bitterness
between him and the local zamindar. In Bankura too the 'Santals
and kindred aboriginal and semi-aboriginal races cleared the jungle'.

The immigrant labour responsible for the large-scale reclamation
in the northern parganas of Rangpur, such as Baikantpur, was
ethnically different; it was all Muslim. The Muslims, 'numerically of
no account' at the time of the Permanent Settlement, constituted by
the time of Buchanan's survey (1809) about 50 per cent of the total
population. The growth of new cultivation, mainly in the second half
of the nineteenth century, in the extensive Barind tract, covering
portions of Dinajpur, Maldah, Rajshahi and Bogura, was also due
to immigrant tribal labour, mostly Santals.

The financing of the new cultivation, where the local labour
formed a small part of the total labour force, is less clearly known.
However, we know enough for us to refute a widespread notion that
zamindars and the lesser landed groups had a negligible role in this.
They have been regarded as an entirely and universally parasitical
group, investing no part or little of their rental income in agriculture, and any improvement in it has been attributed to the enterprise of the small peasants.

This view seems simplistic and conceptually inadequate. The assumption that small peasants had enough to spare for financing any
new cultivation, involving some capital expenditure, is largely con-
tradicted by numerous contemporary reports describing the poverty
and destitution of the vast mass of the peasants. Dependence of a
considerable peasant community on moneylenders, grain-merchants
and rich farmers for loans toward their subsistence and financing of

cultivation was a commonplace of such reports. Half of the cultivation of Dinajpur, Buchanan tells us, depended on the loans provided by the substantial farmers and the grain-merchants.

As regards the zamindars, this view ignores the element of time and seems to assume that they were throughout a parasitical group. It also tends to take them as an undifferentiated group.

True that in the late nineteenth century and later the increasing demand for land and certain other developments more or less assured the zamindars of a certain level of rental income, mostly unearned. Things considerably differed earlier, particularly during the first three or four decades after the Settlement of 1793, when zamindars, confronted with a large revenue demand, while more than half of the arable land remained unexploited, were of course keen on increased cultivation. Some new zamindars, particularly auction-purchasers, showed greater enterprise in this. In Dinajpur, as Buchanan found, 'their lands are in general better cultivated'. His study of the post-1793 records of Jessore led the district collector Westmacott to a similar conclusion. The old zamindars, 'hampered on every side with debt', 'could do nothing for the benefit of their estates, having absolute no capital to work on. The new purchasers of the large zamindaris . . . for the most part men of business from Calcutta . . . had acquired the reputation of good managers of their estates . . . they extended the cultivation.'

The methods of zamindars in this varied from place to place. They had the sole control over the reclamation process where the waste lands had been included in their estates at the time of the Permanent Settlement. In several cases their involvement was a direct one. It was they who organized immigration of labour, provided the initial cost of new agricultural settlements, and sustained the efforts of the cultivators through liberal terms of rent. Another method, as in Dinajpur, was establishment by zamindars of numerous *hats* and markets through grants of rent-free lands for the purpose. In Birbhum immediately after the famine of 1769–70, in the extensive estate of Baikantpur in northern Rangpur after 1793, and in the vast jungle parganas of Midnapur and Bankura the new cultivation was secured mostly in this manner.[48] Understandably, zamindars left much of it to substantial entrepreneurs and the leases embodying the

[48] In the Barind, the vast unreclaimed tract in northern Bengal, the example of the manager of a government estate in Dinajpur in encouraging the migration of the Santals was later followed by the local zamindars.

arrangements in the southern and eastern parts of Bengal were variously called *granti, jote* and *howla.* As long as the latter could bargain from a position of strength zamindars were cautious not to antagonize them, since whenever they felt wronged they, as in Dinajpur, left with their men and resources for other estates in the neighbourhood, much to the prejudice of the zamindars' interests. The *mandals* of western Bankura and western Midnapur, though formally middlemen too, differed from the usual ones. They were persons of much lesser resources, and since they belonged mostly to the same clans or tribes as the common cultivators, their mutual relationship was considerably determined by their old social organization, persisting unimpaired in their new villages.

Even where the involvement of zamindars was not a direct one estate management was sometimes devised in such a way as to provide incentives in the matter of waste reclamation. In Dinajpur, as Buchanan found, an *ijaradar*, employed for collecting rent, 'takes for his reward the commission of from 4 per cent to 6 per cent and the whole profit that he can derive from the lands which are not rented'. It was thus the *ijaradar's* interest that the cultivation increased. The tenure, usually three to five years, was often renewed. In fact *ijaradars* and *thikadars* were continued for generations, particularly in Bihar. In view of the fact that 'the renters are in general perfectly conversant in country affairs' zamindars found it worthwhile to create such long-term leases.

While zamindars were thus not wholly parasitical and did have a role in the growth of cultivation it would be misleading to infer that the zamindari system as it worked throughout necessarily ensured this role. Presumably, their investment in agriculture was not altruistic at all. Perhaps it had not been so anywhere. They were interested in the new cultivation mainly as a source of increased rental income. Their interest declined where the new cultivation alone did not ensure the increase or where the increase was possible even without the increased cultivation.

In fact zamindars did not necessarily invest in agriculture even where they knew it would be worthwhile. The investment was merely one of the choices, and in the making of the right one foresight had an important role. Zamindars lacking this foresight might not choose to invest at all, and opt for short-sighted measures, which would only temporarily benefit them. Zamindars occasionally did prefer them, ignoring the probable long-term gains of an enduring nature from

other measures. For instance, they, lured by offers of an increased
rental income, entrusted estate-management to outsiders, usually on
short tenures, without caring to see that this could eventually cost
them dearly. Most complaints of exactions from cultivators came
from the estates thus controlled by outsiders, the extortions being
far worse where the latter were also the zamindars' creditors. The
existing law, providing to them a great deal of coercive powers,
enabled them to get away with their misdeeds. Sometimes zamindars
themselves preferred relying on such powers in order to achieve
their immediate aims. Notable developments in estate management
sometimes precluded or considerably reduced the probable investment by zamindars. Quite a common one was increasing dissensions
among shareholders of estates, with the rising market value of
landed properties. This prevented a consensus on matters relating
to investment, such as the one in irrigation which, usually covering a
number of villages, necessitated a unified control over the upkeep
of the irrigation network and over distribution of water. This
happened particularly in Bihar. Another development was leasing
out by zamindars of portions of their estates on a permanent tenure,
a measure first tried on a large scale by the Burdwan raj, and later
followed by other zamindars as well. The zamindars consequently
ceased to bother about what happened to the agriculture in the
alienated estates.

Investment in agriculture by zamindars had been declining over
the years for quite different reasons too. A typical one was that
zamindars, in the context of a declining land–man ratio and of the
increasing peasant demand for land owing partly to this and other
developments, could be sure of a certain level of rental income even
without this investment. The reluctance to invest was all the stronger
where they felt that the existing land laws did not provide for ample
rewards for their trouble. Improved agricultural productivity or increased security of cultivation resulting from the zamindar's investment did not constitute any of the three usual grounds of the
permissibility of rent increase.[49] It was, indeed, difficult to measure
the role of the specific inputs by the zamindar in the improvement
which might have resulted from other circumstances as well. Zamin-

[49] A zamindar could legally increase rent on three grounds: an increase in the
cultivation; an increase in the agricultural prices, and the prevalence in a neighbouring estate of higher rent rates for lands which, in point of quality, did not
differ at all from the lands belonging to the zamindar.

dars were nearly baffled in getting any rent increase where the peasants had learned the art of combined resistance.

The admittedly slower pace of reclamation in very many parts of Bengal and Bihar in the second half of the nineteenth century and later need not be blamed on the alleged want of enterprise among zamindars. The scope for new cultivation had been fast shrinking. Matters had become pretty desperate in most of the northern Bihar districts even by the 1890s. The census data show that the rate of population growth was by far the fastest where new lands were still available, the growth being presumably considerably due to immigrant labour. The ecology of such regions, however, did not make for a secure agriculture. A much larger investment was needed toward ensuring this security than in the older agricultural settlements. The trend was visible even in the eastern Bengal districts which for long had the most favourable land–man ratio.

On the other hand, while the scope for new cultivation was still a vast one in the extensive Sunderban forest, largely owned by the government, its pace was extremely slow. Reclamation here was a far more arduous process than elsewhere. The initial clearance of the maze of thick forests and luxuriant weeds required the presence of a far larger number of labourers than reclamation elsewhere usually did. Once cultivation had started it had to be continued without a break even for a year, since fallowing of the fertile soil there resulted in a rapid growth of weeds. Such a big and permanent human settlement was extremely difficult to sustain because of the scarcity of drinking water and the ravages of wild beasts. The conditions laid down by the government relating to sale or lease of waste land there had also much to do with the negligible growth rate. The revenue demand was sometimes too much for the entrepreneurs to think their efforts worthwhile at all. Far more galling to them was the rule by which they risked forfeiture of their lease unless a specified portion could be reclaimed within a certain time. What a local officer called the 'fetish of the *Sadar malguzar*', i.e., preference of the government for 'big capitalists' to direct settlement with cultivators and discrimination, in almost all important respects, against 'petty settlers', even where they were admitted, was also a reason why the cultivation there only haltingly increased.

The main arguments of the above section may now be summed up. The charge of parasitism against zamindars is only partially valid. They did invest when it suited them. Where their role was not a direct one they sometimes saw to it that the cultivation increased. This role, direct or indirect, tended to decline over the years even where there was enough scope for new cultivation. This was partly due to two developments relating to estate management: the increasing market value of estates occasionally causing bitter quarrels among the shareholders, and the conversion of the old zamindars into a purely rentier group where they preferred to lease out their estates on a permanent tenure. The investment by zamindars also diminished where they could be sure of a certain quantum of rental income even without much capital expenditure or enterprise of any other sort. Where the new cultivation occurred mostly near the old settled villages and where its scale was not very large, the necessary capital was now provided by a composite group—affluent peasants, exercising control over poor peasants and having enough means, on the other hand, of holding their own against their immediate landlords in the matter of rent, and even some enterprising middlemen who, as holders of permanent or short-term leases from zamindars, thought investment quite worthwhile.

The acreage expansion was not understandably limitless. However, the secular trend of declining agricultural productivity remains to be explained.

Historians have usually searched for supposedly universally valid explanations and tended to ignore the possible regional distinctiveness of the phenomenon. Such explanations are not wholly restricted to this question of productivity decline, and are intended to apply to the negligible pace of reclamation.

The major assumption in most of these explanations is the inadequacy of investment in agriculture. It would be in order to examine some of them.

The point of view relating this inadequacy to the alleged survival-mindedness of the Indian peasantry, i.e., preference for maintenance of position to an improvement in it, is not any longer acceptable to most historians. Peasants, indisputably, did respond to any reasonable opportunity of improving, or at least of stabilizing, their position. The reason for their usual caution in regard to 'innovations' was certainly not survival-mindedness, but their awareness that because of lack of systematic research and testing innovations often involved high risk. They paid dearly for any error of judgement. Any sudden fall in their usually low income, before their minimal subsistence had been assured, simply ruined the small peasants.

A different point of view[50] considers the landlords, not the peasantry, guilty of not making the requisite investment. This failure has been blamed on the limitation of the domestic market for agricultural products. The situation in England has been cited as a contrast. In England 'it was the Industrial Revolution which, through its impact on the produce market and the labour market, created favourable conditions for the landlords to make productive investment in agriculture'. In Bengal where the rate of industrialization remained insignificant growth of population was only 'increasing the pressure on the available land for cultivation'. The bearing of the limitation of the market demand on the size of investment in agriculture has thus been analysed: 'The inexpensive character of the market set* definite limits to the profitability of further capital inputs in agriculture, even in those cash crops which were produced for the world market. . . . The cash crops of Bengal, because of the limited market in the world, could not provide leading sectors in agricultural development on a sustained long-term basis. . . . Economic expansion therefore depended on the domestic market for agricultural and industrial products. However, in the absence of rapid industrialization, the urban market for agricultural products underwent virtually no expansion, the ratio between urban and rural population remaining practically unchanged. . . . The rural market for grain was constrained by the poverty of the majority of villagers' (Ray 1973: 277–8). Investment in agriculture, it is argued, was all the more unattractive to zamindars where transfer of their income to purchase of proprietary rights in land ensured to them a higher aggregate income, usually also a more stable one, since 'returns on capital invested in agricultural production tend to materialise slowly' and fluctuations in the price level and yield per acre were 'usually large' (Islam 1978: 189). This point of view is only partially valid. The alleged correlation between the narrowness of the domestic market for agricultural produce and the negligible investment by zamindars in agriculture is far from a necessary one. Agricultural prices can be taken as a measure of the size of the market.[51] The considerable increase in cultivation in the first six or seven decades of the nineteenth century occurred in the context of a

[50] For a recent version of this point of view: Islam (1978: 185–9); Ray (1973: 277–9).

[51] In the studies on the impact of the rising agricultural prices on the enclosure movement in England between 1760 and 1814 movement of agricultural prices

rather insignificant price rise. Cultivation increased as long as there was any scope for it, given the existing technological basis of agriculture. Indeed, even marginal lands, as noted above, were being taken up, in the context of the pressure of population, which constituted of course a stable source of demand in the domestic market. The secular rise in the agricultural prices since about the last quarter of the nineteenth century would normally have induced an increased investment in agriculture. The prices did not increase here as fast as in England between 1760 and 1814. However, the difference in the price level alone scarcely accounts for the insignificance of the investment by Bengal zamindars.

The emphasis on transfer of their income by zamindars to land purchases as being the invariably more sensible device for getting their money's worth, also seems misplaced. The implicit assumption here seems to be that where the zamindars did not choose to invest in agriculture they promptly went in for land purchases and that they went on making these purchases to an unlimited extent.

It seems to be of doubtful validity. A zamindar's choice in the matter of land purchases was a restricted one in view of the state of the land market at the time. Public auction sales of estates which once provided the largest opportunity to moneyed people to acquire landed properties gradually diminished to insignificance. Private sales of zamindari estates, intermediate tenures and 'occupancy' holdings did occasionally occur. However, the available data suggest that their market, unlike that of the zamindari estates sold at auction, was largely a localized one. Outsiders, even those of superior resources, could not quite compete with the local magnates. Possibly only a small portion of the savings of zamindars, if there were any, could be transferred to land-purchases under the circumstances.

Why the investment by zamindars in agriculture sharply declined over the years has been explained later. The view examined here contains, however, a valid argument, which is that zamindars, largely sure of a certain rental income from the existing landed properties, even without any investment by them in agriculture, altogether ceased to take any interest in agriculture.

Another explanation (Ray and Ray 1973) of the limited investment

---

has been taken as the main indicator of the changing level of demand for agricultural produce.

in agriculture points to a more complex conjunction of factors, with an emphasis on the role of 'dominant village groups', called *jotedars*. British rule and associated changes, it is argued, did create conditions favourable to expansion of productive forces in the agricultural sector of the economy. Why this potential growth did not occur constitutes the theme of this explanation.

The alleged conditions of growth have been attributed to considerable comercialization of agriculture, largely oriented to the needs of the London market. 'British capital carved out of a peasant economy a foreign export-import sector which profoundly altered the relationship between the rural and urban economies. Under this altered relationship the villages came to constitute a new market for British manufactures, and supplied the raw materials and food-grains which fed the commercial and industrial economy of Britain. . . . Such a radical realignment of resources in the economy as a whole, deriving from a more and more pronounced export-orientation and directional change in the flow of the agricultural surplus might have been expected to produce a profound impact on the agricultural production relations within the villages.'

This possibility did not materialize. The reason was 'a complex process by which the interests of the British export-import firms and the interests of the dominant village groups were brought to a nice readjustment and compatibility'. The adjustment did not necessarily result from the conscious actions of 'scheming individuals who knew exactly what they wanted'. The system as a whole within which they worked made it possible. 'Extraction of a greater surplus from agriculture and the marketing of commercial crops from agricultural producers for export' did not necessitate any 'great expansion of production [sic] forces through a realignment of production relations in the villages'. Cash crop cultivation could well expand 'within the framework of traditional agriculture, which was already equipped with a well-developed cash nexus, trading network and rural credit system'. Even this might have been a wholesome change. It was only partially so. Certain conditions under which the small peasants produced and sold their crops prevented them from gaining as much as they expected. The case of jute may be cited. The semi-monopsonistic European corporations could considerably determine which raw jute prices would eventually prevail. This 'structural weakness' of the jute market, i.e., the limited holding power of the jute growers and the strong combination of the jute buyers, 'slowed down the potential rate of domestic capital formation in the agriculture in Bengal'.

The validity of two central assumptions of the view seems questionable. It tends to exaggerate the size of the commercialized sector, and also the role of the 'dominant village groups' in the supply of the export commodities. The cash crop cultivation, despite its growth during British rule, still formed a small sector of the agrarian economy. Again, it was the small peasants themselves who, usually on their own, responded to the market stimulus, with the dominant village groups seldom decisively controlling their activities. If commercialization had not stimulated even the peasant economy of the regions where it had occurred, the alleged role of the dominant village groups had not much to do with it. The cultivation of jute may be taken as an illustration. The exceptional rapidity of its growth within a short period is evidence of the peasants' keenness on it, presumably because it paid them more than the usual food crops. Jute was attractive to its growers also because its cultivation did not normally necessitate dependence on other groups for their usual food requirements. The growers were cautious not to change over wholly to jute, devoting to it only a small part of their holdings. The reason why, on the other hand, the jute growers sometimes gained much less than they expected was largely unconnected with the activities of the dominant village groups. Such activities had hardly any role in the frequent fluctuations in the jute prices, which at times sorely disappointed the growers. Nor did they by any means constitute the chief factor in the limited holding power of the small peasants, a weakness fully exploited by the wily millowners. The smallness of the producers' usual surplus, to which this limited holding power was partly due, did not necessarily result from the activities of these village groups, as creditors, landowners or traders.

Our conclusions in regard to the two points of view noted above may now be summed up. The correlation between the size of the market for agricultural produce and the level of investment by zamindars was an uncertain and tenuous one. Cultivation pretty rapidly increased, with zamindars often having a notable role in this, even when the usual market demand, as distinguishable from the usual subsistence requirements of peasants, increased much more slowly. On the other hand, a secular rise in the agricultural prices indicating a pressure on the food supply did not necessarily induce a proportionately increased investment. The second interpretation is far less convincing. The size of the commercialized sector was so small that it could scarcely initiate a process capable of regenerating the economy. The explanation of how the activities of the 'dominant village groups' tended to frustrate even this limited possibility remains obscure.

The reasons why the active interest of zamindars in agricultural improvement, limited even before, further declined, and why agriculture tended to be depressed even where the zamindars were not to blame for it, lay elsewhere.

In general the active role of zamindars was throughout only of some specific kinds—a fact explicable in terms of the limited involvement of zamindars in the actual cultivation process. The general pattern of agriculture—distribution of the cultivated land, choice of crops and the general production process—was more or less given, largely determined by the ecological conditions in the context of the technological basis of agriculture at the time, and the historical development of the general production relations in agriculture. The active role of zamindars was normally restricted to restoration of the lost cultivation caused by exceptional natural calamities, and adoption of measures toward the security of the existing cultivation, such as irrigation, embankment and drainage. Several circumstances, apart from the sheer inability of zamindars to provide the required finances,[52] caused a considerable decline in this role. The scope for new cultivation shrank to insignificance in very many regions, inevitably reducing the usual role of zamindars in this. The major types of possible investment now were those which involved a large capital input, such as irrigation. How the increasingly strained relations among shareholders often prevented a consensus in this regard has been noted above. Zamindars had been facing other difficulties too. Some derived from the way the later acquisitions of landed properties—'estates', intermediate tenures and even holdings of occupancy ryots—mostly occurred. They were widely scattered, and

[52] Critics of 'parasitical' zamindars are not always right in presuming their resourcefulness. The estate-owners, predominantly small, had often not enough savings to spare. Most of the small zamindars in Bihar were evidently chronically indebted to the *thikadars*, to whom they had leased portions of their estates. In general the financial difficulties of zamindars were due to several reasons, such as the growing number of dependants on a more or less given income; the rising commodity prices often offsetting the occasional increases in the rental income and the increased frequency of divisions and partitions of estates which invariably resulted in a large increase in the aggregate cost of estate management.

costly irrigation works were not really worthwhile. A contrast with
the English situation is pertinent. The medieval open-field system
evidently inhibited the enterprise of improving landlords and farmers.
Its elimination through enclosures mostly preceded large-scale investments. The legally permissible rewards to zamindars in Bengal
and Bihar were sometimes uncertain, given the nature of their control
at the village level. Zamindars could normally scarcely disturb the
distribution of the cultivated land in the village and the pattern of
cropping in order to make their investments reasonably rewarding.
They had to be content with the prevailing rent rates which, however,
could be increased within certain limits. In fact their difficulties
in this had been increasing over the years and the conflict over rent
intensified. This tended adversely to affect the continuance of even
the old investment of zamindars, for instance, the one in the large-
scale irrigation in several southern districts of Bihar. Agriculture
there largely depended on such irrigation works, and the zamindars,
traditionally responsible for financing them, keeping them in proper
order, and supervising the distribution of water, received about half
of the produce that remained after obligatory payments to the usual
functionaries of the village community. The system evidently harmo-
niously worked until the agricultural prices tended to go up in the
late nineteenth century, particularly since the 1890s. The peasants, in
the context of the rising prices, were increasingly becoming keen on
a change over to cash rent, while zamindars systematically resisted
such efforts, and indeed, sought to convert, occasionally forcibly,
the prevailing cash rent into produce rent. The two attitudes became
nearly irreconcilable, and where the zamindars could not have their
way they utterly neglected their traditional obligations, and the
irrigation works naturally decayed there (Chaudhuri 1977: 329–35).[53]
Here also the English situation provides a contrast. The structure of
the landed property there was such as to ensure to the improving

---

[53] Where produce rent was not the issue zamindars sought to thwart the growth
of peasant rights as far as possible. They went to the extent of discouraging
investments by the relatively well-to-do peasants, such as those in tank-digging
and tree-planting, fearing that the peasant's position would thereby be consolidated. Such an attitude could at times even endanger the survival of peasants.
In several parts of Bihar, for instance, zamindars did succeed in creating an
impression that the so-called 'occupancy right' of peasants had no legal validity.
Fearing that the limited mortgageability of peasant holdings might as a result
render precarious the recovery of loans, moneylenders hesitated to lend at all to
peasants, even when they most needed it.

landlords their money's worth. The absence of a firmly entrenched small peasant property facilitated the landlord's initiative in England, while its presence in France discouraged the initiative. Indeed, the relative weakness of the enclosure movement in France was mostly due to this. In England the lead in the movement was taken by the landlords whose income from land only marginally derived from the rental income. Different was the case in France, and the small peasant property there tended to be consolidated and strengthened as a result of the Revolution of 1789.

While the limited control of zamindars over the village lands did constitute a constraint on their investment in agriculture, it would be a misleading inference that a complete control by itself would have ensured the required investment. The case of the share-cropping system may be cited here. The control of a *jotedar* over the share-cropped land was not subject to any restriction. Neither the law nor the custom prevented him from making use of the land in any way he chose. The government, once attempting to interfere with this custom and to improve the legal status of a share-cropper (*bargadar*), only brought a hornet's nest about its ears, and eventually yielded. This failure removed any uncertainty on the question, and formalized the *jotedar*'s domination over the *bargadar*. Conventionally, a *jotedar* only rarely replaced his old share-cropper by new. However, this was purely his discretion. This undisputed control scarcely made a *jotedar* any the keener on investment. Of the several factors in this, which varied from region to region, two are notable. The tenancy system normally ensured to him quite a high level of income. The share-cropper, merely for the use of the *jotedar*'s land, surrendered half of the gross produce. The *jotedar* did occasionally provide part of the other necessary inputs, such as seeds, ploughs, and cattle. This was mostly done not with an eye to increased output. Without this cultivation was not possible at all. However, his share of the gross produce proportionately increased.

The landowner's assurance on this count was enough to make him indifferent to any costly investment. Even where he was keen on it, he often had difficulties to face. A typical one was the scattered nature of the barga lands. The way such lands came into existence largely accounts for this. Except where a considerable landowner controlling a compact block of land preferred to rent it out to share-croppers, most barga lands originally belonged to small peasants who, somehow losing them, rented them from the new owners on a share-cropping basis. The barga holdings were usually also extremely small; the old owner peasant desperately sought to salvage as much of his holding as possible, surrendering only bits before he finally came to the wall. On the other hand, the lost lands did not all go to a single owner in the locality. A composite group gained, only a few of the beneficiaries having any real taste for agriculture or familiarity with the complexities of agricultural operations.

The share-cropping system has generally been regarded as a built-in depressor in Bengal's agriculture. The notion needs to be examined.

A qualification needs to be made at the outset. The system affected only about 20 to 25 per cent of the total cultivation, and was mostly concentrated in the regions having a predominantly tribal and aboriginal population. The decline in Bengal agriculture, where it happened at all, was therefore only partially due to the system.

Where the decline can be blamed on the system a pertinent point is to explain how it occurred. The usual explanation stressed the alleged insecurity of the barga tenure and the consequent slovenliness of the barga cultivation. The available evidence contradicts the impression. The barga tenure was a short one, but not necessarily an insecure one. The barga agreements, mostly informal, were nearly invariably renewed, unless where the landowners suspected that the *bargadars* were unitedly asserting claims and rights which the agreements had not at all provided for. This happened, for instance, during the countrywide controversy over the barga question in the 1920s. New hopes then led *bargadars* in some localities to defy their masters. The latter promptly reacted. Their insubordinate tenants were removed.

The landowners otherwise gained little from the frequent replacements of their old *bargadars*. Indeed, this could even make unviable the cultivation of the dwarf holding now separated from the surviving holdings of the owner-peasants. On the other hand, the barga rent was usually customarily fixed. Removal of the existing *bargadars* therefore scarcely helped the landowner. The impression that the barga cultivation was characteristically slovenly is not well-founded either. It makes sense to argue that the *bargadars* had no incentive in improving the barga cultivation, especially where they had to pay for the additional inputs. However, they need not necessarily have neglected it, particularly where their available resources, such as labour and cattle, would remain underemployed, with the loss of the barga land reducing the unit of cultivation. The neglect could be thus self-defeating.

The adverse effects of the barga resulted in other ways. They derived from the way the barga cultivation was organized, the heaviness of the barga rent and the general composition of the *bargadars*. Apart from the revenue collectors, the district 'settlement officers',[54] the Bengal Provincial Banking Enquiry Committee and the Bengal Land Revenue Commission (1940) investigated the question. An enquiry (1946–7), apparently far more carefully done than any before, had also a far wider coverage: all the districts, where the barga system prevailed to any significant extent, the districts being subdivided, for the purpose of investigation, into subdivisions.[55]

Rice throughout was the predominant crop grown under the share-cropping system. Once it was the only crop so grown. The system later covered some cash crops as well, such as jute, sugarcane and chilli.

Two features of the organization of cultivation of such cash crops are notable. The landowners themselves were often directly involved in their cultivation, or in the trade in them. This interest was quite different from the predominance of rent element in several forms of share-cropping arrangement. Secondly, the landowners, naturally keen that the cultivation was efficiently done, provided in very many cases the most important inputs, such as seeds and manuring, and where the cultivation was labour-intensive, involving a much greater expenditure than usual on account of labour, they adjusted the crop-sharing accordingly. In the Kushtia subdivision of Nadia, for instance, the *bargadars*, themselves organizing such works as the steeping of the jute plant in deep waters and the separation of the fibres from the barks, kept as much as 75 per cent of the crop.[56]

The share-cropping system in regard to rice had two major forms:

[54] 'Settlement' usually meant readjustment of rent rates on the basis of an official enquiry into such circumstances as the recent changes in the size of cultivation and the movement of agricultural prices.

[55] Confidential (unpublished) official enquiry (1947) into 'Relations between bargadars and their landlords: Tebhaga Movement'. The enquiry had a wide coverage, such as the local customs regarding various aspects of crop-sharing and the origins, organization and leadership of the *Tebhaga* movement, which aimed not at the abolition of the share-cropping system, but mainly at reducing the landlord's share from one-half to one-third of the produce.

[56] Ibid., Report from the Subdivisional Officer, Kushtia, 7 March 1947.

one more or less confined to a few regions, and the other far more extensive and rather typical.

The first prevailed mostly in some northern Bengal districts, such as Darjeeling, Jalpaiguri and some portions of Dinajpur, nearly all being the regions where large-scale land reclamation had occurred relatively recently. The landowners, usually the entrepreneurs in the reclamation, controlled a large area, and provided all the required inputs to the cultivators, consisting of a tiny portion of resident population, but mostly of immigrants. At the stage where the cultivation became tolerably secure the landowners gradually dissociated themselves from the direct supervision over the cultivation process, and left it to the cultivators, continuing, however, to provide the necessary inputs. In the Siliguri subdivision of Darjeeling the landowners normally bore the entire cost of production 'with a very few exceptions'.[57] The arrangement in the Jalpaiguri subdivision of Jalpaiguri has thus been described in a local report: 'a big jotedar who has hundreds of bighas of land is always anxious to find out *adhiyars* (share-croppers) for his own lands and keep them as long as possible, there being so much surplus land in the subdivision that there is always some rivalry amongst the jotedars to find out adhiyars . . . In such cases jotedars have to bear the entire burden of his adhiyars, both for cultivation as well as for their maintenance. Such adhiyars are given lands to build their homestead, are to be supplied with materials for construction and repairs of their huts, are given plough, cattle, manure and many other things by the jotedars. There are adhiyars whose jotedars have to pay even for the midwife in case of birth and for coffin in case of death in the adhiyar's family. This is probably the original and real type of adhiyars in this subdivision.'[58] In the Alipurduar subdivision of Jalpaiguri and in the Sudder subdivision of Dinajpur, the *bargadar's* dependence on the local *jotedar*, though not as complete, was crucial for sustaining the cultivation process, with the *jotedar* providing the costliest of the necessary inputs, ploughs and cattle.[59]

This dependence tended to perpetuate itself, primarily because the appropriations by *jotedars* hardly left much to *bargadars* to reduce it. Indeed, it had continued for so long that *bargadars* scarcely knew how much they had borrowed and how much of it they had repaid.

[57] Ibid., Report from the Subdivisional Officer, Siliguri, 8 March 1947.

[58] Ibid., Report from the Deputy Commissioner, Jalpaiguri, 11 March 1947.

[59] Ibid., Report from the Subdivisional Officer, Sadar, Dinajpur, 8 March 1947.

In fact, the *bargadars* themselves were not keen on severing their ties with their masters, fearing that this might even threaten their survival. The master ostensibly retained only half of the gross produce, 'but indirectly takes back almost the entire quantity on account of advances, interest etc. The process is repeated annually.'[60]

Considerably different was the typical share-cropping arrangement. The crucial difference was that the share-cropper here was not merely a labourer, but nearly universally an owner peasant, operating presumably a petty holding. His prior involvement in the cultivation process meant that he also had enough means to provide other inputs, such as cattle and ploughs. Occasionally he did borrow part of his working capital, but not necessarily from the landowner from whom he had rented land. Though leasing of land usually formed the basis of this kind of share-cropping, the landowner occasionally helped the *bargadar* with certain inputs, particularly the relatively costlier ones—seeds, manure, and canal water in the canal-irrigated tracts. It was seeds that were most commonly supplied. All these, however, were by way of loans, fully recovered, with interest charges, after the harvest.

Toward the cost of harvesting and thrashing too the landlord contributed little, except where the location of the cultivation was such as necessitated dependence on non-local labour (*pardeshis*). The exception prevailed where, for different reasons, the resident population near the cultivation was rather scanty, for instance, in the newly reclaimed tracts in the Sunderbans and in the new alluvial formation (*Chars*).[61] Thrashing, done either on the field or at the master's *khamar*, was also nearly everywhere the *bargadar's* responsibility. Its cost was understandably greater where the landlord's *khamar* (part of the demesne land, usually close to his residence) was pretty far off from the field. In fact the landlord, in order ostensibly to prevent pilferage of crops by his *bargadars*, but actually to control the division of the crop in the context of the growing bitterness between them, increasingly insisted on the division at his *khamar*.

However, merely for the use of the leased land, the *bargadar* surrendered half of the gross produce. A larger share was claimed where, because of the quality of the soil and of the easy availability of irrigation facilities, the *bargadar* spent less than usual.[62] On the other

[60] Ibid., Report from the Deputy Commissioner, Jalpaiguri, 11 March 1947.
[61] Ibid., Report from the Subdivisional Officer, Bagerhat, 7 March 1947.
[62] Ibid., Report from the Subdivisional Officer, Katwa, 8 March 1947.

hand, where the *barga* land was a fallow one, necessitating a greater quantity of labour and capital, the landlord was content with a reduced share.

The landlord claimed an excessive price for loans of seeds, manure and cattle. Twice the quantity of the seeds lent was recovered at the time of harvest, along with a specified quantity of straw. In fact 'repayment of seed was the first charge on the produce'.[63] In general, the cost of borrowing cattle and ploughs was pretty heavy. In the Khulna subdivision of Khulna the *bargadar's* share was only one-third of the produce where the landlord provided these inputs.[64] In the Alipurduar subdivision of Jalpaiguri one cow or bullock lent by the landlord used to cost the *bargadar* in 1946 about six maunds of paddy.

In point of burden of rent the share-cropper had in fact the worst lot. It was this heaviness of the rental demand, along with its variation according to the size of the gross produce, and not the net return, that precluded even short-term output-raising improvements. 'It is thus not irrational for a sharecropper to spread his efforts as widely as possible, either by renting more land if he can do so or by accepting wage employment to supplement his income, in lieu of intensifying cultivation on his present plot'.[65]

The survival of a *bargadar* despite the heaviness of his obligatory payments to his master is, however, explicable.

The *barga* holdings often formed only a small portion of the total holdings that small peasants mostly owned. In general the smaller the proportion of the *barga* lands to total holdings the stronger the peasant's position. Conversely, the greater the dependence of a *bargadar* on his *barga* land for his subsistence, the greater the chances of his losing the peasant status and of sinking into that of a pure labourer (*majdur*). The distinction was well understood in rural Bengal. The social ranking of a *majdur* was invariably an inferior one. The available data relating to the composition of *bargadar's* operational holdings, owned and leased, are much too inadequate for us to estimate the size of the group mostly operating *barga* lands and of the one mostly operating own lands. However, the dependence of marginal peasants on *barga* cultivation was evidently increasing.

A small peasant quite often leased lands on a *barga* tenancy also

[63] Ibid., Report from the Subdivisional Officer, Thakurgaon, 10 March 1947.
[64] Ibid., Report from the Subdivisional Officer, Khulna Sadar, 10 March 1947.
[65] Myrdal (1968: 1065–6).

because, without such lands, his available resources, such as labour, cattle and ploughs, remained underutilized. Whatever the size of his holdings, he had to keep ploughs and cattle, and the opportunity cost of his family labour was small too, so that the cultivation of the leased land did not necessarily proportionately increase the cost of cultivation.

Where such were the origins of the *barga* tenancy it probably had a positive role in the local economy. The role was all the more effective where the main motive of a landowner in leasing out portions of his holdings was his inability to cultivate them efficiently, particularly where they did not form a compact unit.

Conclusions

The point in discussing at some length the nature of the rural power structure is to indicate the wide area of disagreement among scholars on the question. We preferred to concentrate on the examination of a point of view which amounts to a drastic revision of the conventional notion about the evolution of the agrarian structure during British rule. This point of view locates the dominant rural power in a heterogeneous group called *jotedars*. According to one version, this was true of the pre-British times as well. Another version would regard it as a distinctive development during British rule.

Such a group did exist. The debatable point is whether it exercised as much control in rural Bengal and Bihar as a whole as this point of view suggests. A conclusion of this study is that the control has been exaggerated. The available data relating to the period 1930 to 1946, when the share-cropped area in Bengal proper was evidently the largest, show that this area constituted only 20–25 per cent of the total cultivation. This, again, was concentrated in certain areas where tribals and low-caste peasants formed the largest portion of the cultivating population. *Jotedars* did not control either rural credit or the rural trade, particularly the trade in the two most important agricultural produces, rice and jute. *Jotedars* were evidently the primary source of credit for most share-croppers. However, outside this special relationship they controlled only a segment of rural credit, a characteristic feature of which was plurality of control. Affluent peasants, including *jotedars*, succeeded in widening the area of their influence when the position of the established moneylenders was abruptly undermined by certain exceptional developments. This happened, for instance, during the depression of the 1930s.[66] A sudden slump in agricultural prices sharply reduced the ability of the peasants to repay. The widespread agitation against money-lenders and zamindars at the time encouraged a mood of repudiation of all dues, debt or rent. On the other hand, moneylenders, in the context of a pervasive trade depression, could not replenish the depleted loan capital from the usual urban sources.

An official enquiry in 1926 relating to rural trade in rice and jute contradicts an impression that *jotedars* largely controlled it.[67] The largest portion of the surplus rice found its way into the market through open market sales by individual peasants. The role of advance buying through advances to cultivators at the beginning of the agricultural season was then found inconsiderable. Borrowing, which most cultivators could seldom help, did not necessarily amount to advance buying. Loans, in cash or kind, were repaid with the usual interest charges. In cases of loans in paddy the charges were more or less customary. Where the local rice trade was a brisk one, and the prices of rice tended to go up, cultivators were understandably re-luctant to pledge their crop in advance to their creditors. Where advance buying prevailed it was far from controlled by the local *jotedars*. Interests connected with the rice trade tended to become increasingly heterogeneous. For instance, apart from the 'Marwaris and upcountry traders', the Murshidabad Collector wrote of the increasing role of the 'rice mills and their contractors'. The scale of advance buying was far larger in the case of jute. The role of *jotedars* and other landed magnates was not decisive here too. The dominant group was the one connected with the highly complex jute trade, far from vertically controlled. No local group, let alone *jotedars*, could control it, particularly during the period of a brisk trade in jute.

While the pervasiveness of jotedari domination over the rural economy is a questionable notion it would be wrong to argue that the powers of *jotedars* had not increased during British rule. The increase was evidently considerable. The development was not neces-sarily attributable to the non-existence or weakness of the zamindar's

[66] For the reasons: B. B. Chaudhuri (1975: Section 3d).

[67] The local reports sent to the Registrar of Cooperative Societies were published by the Government of Bengal in 1928 under the title *Marketing of Agricultural Produce in Bengal*. A detailed analysis of the structure of the trade in rice and jute, nearly wholly based on these reports, is to be found in Saugata Mukherji (*Colonial Framework for Agricultural Marketing in Eastern India: Rice and Jute in Bengal, 1900–1921: Trade, Production, Consumption and Prices*: Ch. 1).

authority. The point of view postulating an inverse relationship between the authority of zamindars and that of *jotedars* seems to have been heavily influenced by the evidence of domination of *jotedars* in newly reclaimed areas, where the zamindari system had not already entrenched itself. *Jotedars* did acquire increasing powers and control even in the spheres of zamindari influence. Indeed, for a considerable length of time, *jotedars* thrived as part of the overall estate management, particularly where zamindars were keen on wasteland reclamation. Conflict developed later; zamindars then sought to curb in various ways the powers of *jotedars*.

The point of view examined above tends to ignore the reality of the small peasant economy, in which small peasants, mostly owning holdings, planned cultivation on their own, with borrowed or own capital. In fact the particular organization of the economy, including the narrow market system in which the peasants were directly involved, constituted a constraint on the control by local landed magnates even over dependent peasants. That was why *jotedars*, acquiring peasant holdings, through foreclosures of mortgages or open purchases, often thought it pointless replacing the old cultivators and directly cultivating the holdings, and left undisturbed the planning of the cultivation.

Within this framework of the small peasant economy, the role of zamindars, including holders of leases of various grades, largely as extractors of peasant surplus, was a significant one. The struggle over rent continued in various forms, and as a whole zamindars succeeded more in Bihar than in many parts of Bengal.

Two conclusions emerge from our study. Control over the peasant economy did not necessarily wholly derive from control over land, and the functioning of the economy over the years is not intelligible in terms of concentration of this control of diverse origins in any single local economic group. Wider developments affecting the economy as a whole and the various rural classes and their interrelationships need to be identified. The autonomous role of the rural power structure in determining the shape of the economy should not be overstressed.

We need to be cautious in trying to relate the trends in agricultural production to this power structure, if only because we only imperfectly understand the trends during a considerable part of British rule. Whatever firm evidence we have about the changes in the size of cultivation and in productivity justifies this caution.

162   B. B. CHAUDHURI

Blyn points to a chief feature of the trends: 'widening of the crop-
land area rather than heightening acre productivity and slowdown
in acreage expansion despite accelerated growth in population'. This
was in fact true of 'a long-settled tradition-dominated country'.[68]
The reason is simple: 'expansion of acreage is often less dependent
on change in technology, and consequently appears as the more
likely means of increased output.' Inevitably, the greatest constraint
on the continuity of the expansion, under the existing technology,
was the shrinking scope for new cultivation. This explains why agriculture in Greater Punjab continued to be dynamic at the time expansion of cultivation in Bengal nearly reached its limit. While, at
the beginning of Blyn's period (the 1890s), Greater Bengal, the
wettest of his six 'Regions', had the densest population, Greater
Punjab, the dryest of the regions, had less than half of the population
density of Greater Bengal, and had just 'entered into a phase of being
colonized by settlers moving into areas newly irrigated by irrigation
canals'. Such lands, receiving little rain, mostly remained till then 'an
unutilized potential which was heavily exploited later'. In Greater
Bengal the scope for new cultivation gradually shrank to insignificance, eventually necessitating movement of peasants to marginal
lands.

One obvious reason for this was the technological barrier. A more
difficult question to answer is why this barrier could not be crossed.
This was partly an aspect of the limited knowledge of society at the
time of the means of taming the nature, particularly in the areas of
difficult terrains. This is not explicable solely in terms of the reluctance of some social groups to invest. The increasing cultivation
of marginal lands, which provides part of the clue to the 'crisis' in
the European economy in the fourteenth century, resulted precisely

[68] George Blyn (1966), *Agricultural Trends in India, 1891–1907* (University of
Pennsylvania Press, Philadelphia), p. 128. An important conclusion of Islam's
study of the problem of capital formation in Bengal agriculture (1920–46) is
as follows: 'In an under-developed agriculture most of the increase in capital
formation would be in such a form as would expand the productive acreage, and
if the scope for the extension of cultivation to new areas is limited such increase
would be achieved through an increase in the proportion of double cropped area'
(Islam 1978: Ch. 5, p. 156). Also see p. 202: 'The scope for obtaining increased
output from additional use of the traditional factors of production was limited
or negligible. . . . The basic problem was not the inadequacy of investment in
the traditional factors of production as such but the absence of technological
innovations.'

from such a technological barrier. The innovations in agricultural practices which contributed to the making of the Agricultural Revolution in England during the eighteenth century and later were rooted in the new scientific knowledge about crops and soils.

Even the existing knowledge was not, however, properly applied. The decisive factor in the agricultural growth in Greater Punjab was the massive investment by the government in irrigation. Investment in any form by the government was negligible in Bengal. It would be simplistic to conclude that the permanent fixation of land revenue in 1793 alone precluded it. The government did make landed groups pay for specific improvements it financed, such as irrigation. Investment by government was as insignificant even where the zamindari authority was non-existent. It was reluctant to invest where it was not pretty sure that the cost of investment could before long be realized with a sufficient margin of profit. Investment by zamindars too sharply declined over the years. Here also a simplistic notion needs to be examined. Contrary to a general impression the prospects of a more or less assured rental income alone did not account for the decline.

Part of the increased cultivation, particularly the one occurring around settled villages, was in fact largely due to the enterprise of the small peasants themselves, including the relatively resourceful ones. The decisive factor was the subsistence needs of a growing peasant population, with control by superior landed groups or the market system only marginally affecting the process. Things came to such a pass in several regions that peasants took up for cultivation lands which under easier circumstances they would not have done. This happened in very many parts of northern Bihar. The peasant migration from overcrowded Mymensingh and some neighbouring areas to the contiguous parts of the lower valley of Assam was, as regards motives, a similar phenomenon, the main point of difference here being that the host districts had abundant fertile lands to offer. The growth of jute cultivation in Assam, also due to the initiative of the migrants, was only partly attributable to market stimulus. That jute cultivation grew much faster in Assam during the first four decades of the twentieth century than in the Bengal districts where it had once been mostly confined is only partly explicable in terms of the jute prices (D. Narain 1965: 68).

Zamindars and *jotedars* did provide enterprise and finances in some cases. Zamindars, keen on increasing their rental income

through new cultivation, were naturally eager about it. Only a few
jotedars had a positive role in this—those initiating a large-scale
reclamation process and seeing it through difficult times. Even in
such cases their original role as entrepreneurs seldom continued for
long, and other resourceful people took over. The Sunderbans Commissioner related it partly to the lure of respectability associated with
pure landed status, which *jotedars* directly connected with supervision over the reclamation process did not command.

This specific role of *jotedars* need not be confused with the usual
role of the *jotedars* in general. They had little contribution to make to
growth of cultivation, though their control over land, acquired in
various ways, ensured to them a handsome rental income. In fact
except in certain regions, they had little role in the strengthening or
the stabilization of even the existing peasant production. Their
financial assistance to share-croppers, mostly in the form of loans,
and recoverable with high interest charges at the time of the harvest,
only tended to perpetuate the old basis of production. *Jotedars* continued the assistance since without it the share-cropping arrangement
could well break down. They were keen that the relationship continued, and this, as Bhaduri argued, was ensured by perpetuation of
debts and by persistence of a mode of cultivation which would
preclude any improvement in the material conditions of share-
croppers.[69]

The decline in productivity in Greater Bengal is not wholly
explicable either in terms of the rural power structure. The decline
was mainly true of the rice land. The productivity of the lands
diverted to cash crops in fact tended to increase. Since, however, rice
occupied by far the largest part of the cultivated area the decline, if
a real one, can be regarded as a characteristic of the peasant agriculture of the region.

[69] Bhaduri thus argues: 'Since the persistence of usury as an important mode
of exploitation depends largely on the *kishan's* having to borrow regularly for
consumption, the continuation of the system requires that the available balance
of paddy of the *kishan* must always fall short of his consumption requirement.
Consequently, technological improvements, which raise the productivity level
of the *kishan*, become undesirable to the landowner to the extent that they
increase the *kishan's* available balance of paddy in relation to his consumption
level so as to reduce his requirement for consumption loans. For it weakens the
system of semi-feudalism, where economic and political power of the landowner
is largely based on his being able to keep the *kishan* constantly indebted to him'
(1973: 135).

The decline, as both Blyn and Islam conclude, did not occur in Bengal proper and was confined to Bihar and Orissa. Blyn was not quite sure if the decline even there was a real one. He suspected that something was wrong with the official data.[70]

Bengal, however, seems to have been only slightly better off. The trend in the productivity per acre for all the crops there during the period 1920–46 was in fact near zero. It was perhaps a case of 'equilibrium at a low level of productivity'. A stable state seems to have been reached in agriculture, and no further decline in yield was likely to occur (Islam: 74–5).

No single explanation can be offered for this stagnation in Greater Bengal during the first four decades of the twentieth century. The origins of the process widely varied from region to region. Notably, the local variables were not all connected with the local power structure. Technological barrier had much to do with the process. For instance, population pressure necessitated peasant migration to regions in the northern Bihar districts where uncertain rainfall and negligible artificial irrigation prevented sustained cultivation of an intensive nature. In fact, as Blyn pointed out, 'rainfall trended sharply downward' in the period between 1911 and 1930, and he finds a correlation between the reduced rainfall and the declining productivity of the rice land during the period. In Bengal proper the declining productivity of lands in several districts, such as Murshidabad, Nadia and Jessore, was related to the eastward shift of the main flow of the Ganges into the sea, so that these regions 'were left with poorly-drained malaria-festering channels, and were deprived of the annual flood-distributed silts which tended to maintain soil fertility'. The moribund delta did appear long before the twentieth century. However, 'its effects, particularly on soil fertility, might have continued, ultimately reducing some lands to submarginal status'. It was a local development, since only about 5 per cent of the net cultivated area was affected by the process. The recurrence of malaria, to which the ecological deterioration in the region evidently contributed, had also a role in the agricultural decline, mainly because malaria sharply depleted the local labour force and greatly told on the efficiency of the survivors. It affected in fact a wider area.

[70] Blyn (p. 219) observes: 'There appears to be some justification for questioning the reliability of this portion of the data. These grounds are strengthened, though not conclusively, by an examination of the changes in standard yield per acre in Bengal and Bihar–Orissa.'

Some districts outside the moribund delta, such as Burdwan and Hugli, suffered far more than the ones mentioned above.

Another localized development, adversely affecting the productivity of rice lands, was diversion of the relatively more fertile lands from rice to more remunerative crops at the time, such as sugar cane. This was part of Blyn's explanation of the declining yield of rice land in Bihar in the 1930s. Sugar cane acreage rose there from about 300 thousand acres to over 400 thousand acres by 1933–34 and a peak of over 500 thousand acres by 1940–41. This abrupt increase of 66.6 per cent in a decade, while the size of cultivable land scarcely increased, occurred, presumably, mostly at the cost of rice. Its replacement by sugar cane on superior lands inevitably told on its productivity. The effects of the replacement should not be exaggerated. Even assuming that the whole of the increase by 1940–41 was at the cost of rice, it affected only 4 per cent of the total rice acreage (Blyn: 174–5).

Replacement of rice by jute in Bengal did not, however, have a similar consequence. Jute usually replaced only autumn rice, since winter rice, the most important one in Bengal, was alternative to jute only under favourable weather conditions. That even this limited replacement did not necessitate transfer of better land from autumn rice to jute is inferable from the fact that during the period 1920–46 the productivity of autumn rice did increase at the annual rate of 0.2 per cent, while that of jute increased only at a slightly higher rate—0.3 per cent.

The attempt made above to explain the evident stagnation in the agricultural economy of some particular regions of Greater Bengal in terms of developments largely unconnected with the rural power structure need not create an impression that we in any way ignore the possibility of a role of this structure in the stagnation. We merely intended to argue that the role was not necessarily invariably an autonomous one and that this role was mixed up with that of diverse developments on which the rural power structure only marginally impinged.

On the other hand, even the strong probability of a causal relationship between this structure and the general agricultural trends can often not be statistically verified. The share-cropping system may be cited as an instance. The conditions under which most share-croppers worked—an extortionate rent demand, its variability according to the size of the gross output, the perpetual indebtedness of share-croppers and the utter negligibility of the landowners' investment in agriculture—were probably incompatible with any improvement in agriculture. We can only guess what might have happened. Agriculture seems to have suffered most where the wretched share-croppers were obliged to replace bullocks, ploughs, etc., involving a cost which landowners did not often find worthwhile to provide. On the other hand, a share-cropper would not have normally neglected the barga cultivation, particularly where without it the subsistence of his family would have been precarious. However, we are not sure what exactly happened. One reason is that the share-cropped land was generally mixed up with the owner-peasant's land, and indeed, the same peasant family often combined the two types of cultivation.

Where declining productivity resulted from the decay of irrigation it is relevant to enquire whether this could be blamed on zamindars. Evidently very many zamindars neglected to take proper care of the old irrigation works and embankments. They were not wholly to blame for this during early British rule. The unimaginative revenue policy of the government, particularly its insistence on the collection of an exorbitant revenue demand irrespective of the state of the crops, often forced them to reduce their investment in these works. This happened particularly in Burdwan and Midnapur. The considerable decay in many regions of large tanks, once a major source of irrigation, was a different process. Tank-digging, on which zamindars had once lavishly spent, was not intended primarily as an economic measure. The motives were largely religious. This laudable activity inevitably declined with the weakening of the old religious sentiment over the years. This also happened where old zamindars had been replaced by new and where the territorial control of the surviving zamindars shrank as a result of dismemberment of their old estates through auction sales or distress sales of other kinds.

On the other hand, zamindars occasionally interfered with digging of new tanks (and with productive investments like plantation of trees) by substantial peasants. The reason was their fear that the legal position of the latter in the land would be strengthened thereby. Customarily tanks could not be dug without prior consent of zamindars, and they demanded a heavy price where they consented at all.

The decline of large-scale irrigation works (*ahars* and *pains*) in some parts of South Bihar had two distinct phases. Till about the end of the nineteenth century the decisive factor in this was the inability of zamindars to exercise an effective control over the complicated system of storage and distribution of water. Apart from the sheer incompetence of very many of them in estate-management, the main reason was incessant disputes among shareholders of joint estates. The background to the bickerings was the rising market value of estates, and the relations of estate-owners with cultivators over the rent question had not much to do with them. From about the end of the nineteenth century the struggle over produce rent was increasingly becoming the crucial factor in the decline of these irrigation works. While zamindars, in the context of rising agricultural prices, were keen on an extension and consolidation of the system of produce rent, cultivators were desperately seeking to convert produce rent into money rent. Where peasants succeeded, the frustrated zamindars tended to desert their old responsibility. On the other hand, peasants themselves did not often succeed in devising an alternative system of control over the irrigation works. They decayed as a result. Elsewhere too the intensifying struggle over rent had something to do with the declining investment of zamindars in agriculture, particularly since about the end of the nineteenth century. Acreage expansion had then reached its limit, and agricultural output could increase mainly through intensification of cultivation. Zamindars did not often feel enthusiastic about it. Unlike earlier, when wasteland was being reclaimed, zamindars now had to reckon with the established small peasant production. The legal position of of a considerable group of 'occupancy ryots' had by then become far stronger than before, so that adjustment of rent rates to the cost of the zamindar's investment was not always an easy process, despite a clear legal provision about it.[71]

[71] Washbrook has recently argued how in general British laws and institutions, in trying to safeguard petty peasant production, tended to inhibit investment of capital in agriculture. He argues: 'The attitude of the colonial state towards a hypothetical capitalist transformation of agriculture was notoriously ambiguous. . . . The legal and political environment which the raj was creating for the operation of market forces and the penetration of capital remained contradictory. While not undermining the relations of the market or preventing capital entirely from engaging petty commodity production, it limited the social possibilities of development, failed to provide capital with instruments to subordinate production and gave social groups resistant to the demands of the market much scope for manoeuvre. The clearest sign of the problem was the difficulty which large accumulations of capital, whether made during the mercantilist era in revenue and monopoly speculation or imported from outside, encountered in gaining access to, and control over, agricultural production. Adequate access and control, of course, meant having the ability to dispossess resident cultivators. Yet the biases of the law, the potential for prevarication contained in its processes and the lack of executive authority to enforce decrees if won, made dispossession, at

In cases such as these the way the rural power structure had impinged on agricultural production is identifiable. They were, however, not necessarily representative.

---

least by outsiders to the agrarian community, a parlous exercise. The cost of this impotence, from the perspective of capital, was to reduce the pressures of competition at work in the market and the possibility of investment in the means of production. If landlords could not charge competition rents, what forces drove peasants to increase production? If they could not repossess their tenants' lands, why should they invest in improving them?' (1981: 676–8).

REFERENCES

Ahmed, R. (1981), *The Bengali Muslims, 1871–1906: A Quest for Identity* (Delhi: Oxford University Press).

Béteille, André (1974), *Studies in the Agrarian Social Structure* (Delhi: Oxford University Press).

Bhaduri, Amit (1973), 'Agricultural Backwardness under Semi-Feudalism', *The Economic Journal*, March.

Brenner, Robert (1976), 'Agrarian Class Structure and Economic Development in Pre-Industrial Europe', *Past and Present*, February.

Buchanan, Francis (1951 Census of India Edition), *A Geographical, Statistical and Historical Description of the District of Dinajpore*. (Buchanan's survey of the district was carried out in 1808. Part of the Report was reproduced in the Census of India (1951), V1, Part IC.)

Chandra, N. K. (1975), 'Agrarian Transition in India', *Frontier*, 22 November–6 December.

Chaudhuri, B. B. (1969), 'Agricultural Production in Bengal, 1850–1900', *Bengal Past and Present*, July–December.

—— (1975a), 'Land Market in Eastern India, 1793–1940', *Indian Economic and Social History Review*, April–June.

—— (1975b), 'The Process of Depeasantization in Bengal and Bihar, 1885–1947', *The Indian Historical Review*, July.

—— (1976), 'Agricultural Growth in Bengal and Bihar, 1770–1860: Growth of Cultivation since the Famine of 1770', *Bengal Past and Present*, January–June.

—— (1977), 'Movement of Rent in Eastern India, 1793–1930', *The Indian Historical Review* 3: 2, January.

——'Agricultural Prices in Bengal and Bihar, 1757–1860' (unpublished).

Colebrook, H. T. (1795, 1st edn), *Remarks on the Husbandry and Internal Commerce of Bengal* (Calcutta).

Confidential (unpublished) Official Enquiry into 'Relations between Bargadars and Their Landlords—Tebhaga Movement' (1947).

De, Jatindra Nath (1977), 'History of the Krishak Praja Party of Bengal, 1919–1947: A Study of Changes of Class and Inter-community Relations in the Agrarian Sector of Bengal', unpublished Ph.D. thesis, University of Delhi.

Ghosh, A. and K. Dutt (1977), *Development of Capitalist Relations in Agriculture: A Case Study of West Bengal, 1793–1971* (New Delhi: People's Publishing House).

Frykenberg, R. E. (ed.) (1977), *Land Tenure and the Peasant in South Asia* (New Delhi: Orient Longman).

Hilton, R. H. (1975), *The English Peasantry in the Later Middle Ages* (Oxford: Clarendon Press).

Islam, M. M. (1978), *Bengal Agriculture, 1920–1946* (Cambridge: Cambridge University Press).

McLane, J. R. (1977), 'Revenue Farming and the Zamindari System in Eighteenth Century Bengal' in R. E. Frykenberg (ed.), *Land Tenure and the Peasant in South Asia* (New Delhi: Orient Longman).

Metcalf, T. R. (1979), *Land, Landlords, and the British Raj: Northern India in the Nineteenth Century* (Berkeley: University of California).

Musgrave, P. J. (1972), 'Landlords and Lords of the Land: Estate Management and Social Control in Uttar Pradesh, 1860–1920', *Modern Asian Studies* 6: 3.

Myrdal, G. (1968), *Asian Drama* (New York: Panthenon).

Narain, D. (1965), *Impact of Price Movements on the Areas under Selected Crops in India, 1900–1939* (Cambridge: Cambridge University Press).

Neale, Walter C. (1962), *Economic Change in Rural India: Land Tenure and Reform in Uttar Pradesh, 1800–1955* (New Haven: Yale University Press).

Orr, Alastair W. 'A Comparative Study of Agricultural Development in the Forth Valley (Scotland) and the Bengal Presidency, 1760–1840', Ph.D. dissertation in progress, Department of Economic History, University of Edinburgh.

Pandey, G. (1978), *The Ascendancy of the Congress in Uttar Pradesh, 1926–1934: A Study in Imperfect Mobilization* (Delhi: Oxford University Press).

Raj, Jagdish (1978), *Economic Conflict in North India: A Study of Landlord–Tenant Relations in Oudh, 1870–1890* (Bombay: Allied Publishers).

Ray, Rajat K. and Ratnalekha Ray (1973). 'The Dynamism of Continuity in Rural Bengal under the British Imperium . . .', *Indian Economic and Social History Review*, June.

—— (1975), 'Zamindars and Jotedars: A Study of Rural Politics of Bengal', *Modern Asian Studies* 9: 1.

Ray, Rajat K. (1973), 'The Crisis of Bengal Agriculture, 1870–1927', *Indian Economic and Social History Review*, September.

Ray, Ratnalekha (1980), *Change in the Bengali Agrarian Society* (Delhi: Manohar)

Report of the Bengal Land Revenue Commission (1940) (Calcutta: Government of Bengal).

Sanyal, H. (1981), *Social Mobility in Bengal* (Calcutta: Papyrus).

Schultz, T. W. (1964), *Transforming Traditional Agriculture* (New Haven: Yale University Press).

Sen, Amartya (1981), *Poverty and Famines* (Oxford: Clarendon Press).

Siddiqi, M. H. (1978), *Agrarian Unrest in North India: The United Provinces, 1918–1922* (New Delhi: Vikas).

Washbrook, David (1981), 'Law, State and Society in Colonial India' in C. Baker, G. Johnson and A. Seal (eds), *Power, Profit and Politics* (Cambridge: Cambridge University Press).

Power and Agrarian Relations: Some Concepts and Measurements*

MEGHNAD DESAI

I

This essay hopes to deal with one facet of the basic question concerning the inter-relationship of political power and the agrarian economy. I shall address the question as much from the point of view of clarifying concepts and definitions, constructing operationally viable measures of these concepts (e.g. power) and outlining fairly simple dynamic models which may help to study this inter-relationship of power and the agrarian economy.

The agrarian economy will be defined for the purpose of this essay as comprising landlords (zamindars), tenants, share-croppers and landless labourers. These four basic categories describe a variety of economic and social relationships around the two basic inputs of land and labour. There are other groups in the rural economy who may not be exclusively concerned with agriculture—moneylenders, for instance. These categories are, of course, abstractions. There is now a vast body of literature on South Asia which tells us about inter-regional as well as intra-regional variations in this classification

* This is a revised version of a paper which was presented in a first draft form to the SAPE Conference in November 1979, and some more drafts later to the SAPE Conference in December 1980. I am grateful to Hamza Alavi, Sukhamoy Chakravarty, David Ludden, Susanne and Lloyd Rudolph, Ashok Rudra, T. N. Srinivasan and Myron Weiner for their comments on earlier drafts. The LSE–ICERD Workshop in Economic Theory also heard a version of this paper and I am grateful to Ken Binmore and Tony Horsley for their encouraging comments. The usual caveat applies.

—a rich pattern of differentiation in the agrarian economy due to natural and environmental factors, historical and institutional backgrounds and more recent experience of commercialization, modernization, etc.[1] I am aware that this rich pattern implies that in any specific local agrarian situation, our categories will have to be modified or the model extended and revised. But for the time being, I intend to take this simple approach.

The economic activities of these people in the agrarian economy comprise production, consumption, exchange and accumulation. These activities are carried out against a background of non-agricultural activity in the rest of the (local) economy and there are also traditional and kinship networks besides economic exchange relationships which form the set of social relationships. These production, consumption, exchange and accumulation activities are not to be seen as static, once and for all outcomes. They allow the basic agrarian economy with its set of economic and social relationships to *reproduce* itself. Reproduction implies not only biological and physical survival but the renewal of the relationships such as landlord–share-cropper, landlord–landless labourer, etc. Reproduction means that from one production cycle to the next, the economy may change (output may grow, etc.) but its features retain a sufficient similarity to the earlier periods not to mark a sharp structural break.[2]

Against this general background what does it mean to say, for example, that the landlord has power over the share-cropper? Can we make the notion of economic and/or political power more precise and perhaps amenable to operational use in fieldwork?

---

[1] The other essays in this collection by Ludden, Herring, Rudolph and Rudolph, Rudra illustrate various historical, regional and local aspects of the agrarian economy. Reference should be made to the work of André Béteille on Tanjore (as an early example of a study bringing together the ecological, historical and economic aspects of the local economy to study power). A comprehensive annotated bibliography of all the village studies in South Asia as well as elsewhere has been made by the Institute of Development Studies in its Village Studies Programme. See Claire Lambert (ed.), *Village Studies: Data Analysis and Bibliography*, Bowker/IDS, 1976.

[2] Though formal definitions may often obscure rather than clarify, let us formalize reproduction as a mapping from the set of variables X_t comparing economic and social relationships in period t to X_{t+1}. If a mapping exists, then the system reproduces itself. A more restrictive definition would be to say that if a function F exists taking X_t into X_{t+1}, then the system is reproducing itself. X can then be defined quite generally. Further restrictions on F are required to account for stability, steady state growth or disequilibrium, etc.

First, let me define power. Power is the ability to do things to others which you do not expect they can do unto you. In its economic and political meaning, power involves *access* to resources, *control* over certain instruments and a social *relationship*. It involves *access* in the sense of outright ownership of resources with freedom to dispose of them as the owner wishes, or in so many cases access to institutions and agencies which may provide or withhold such resources. Resources may comprise land, water, credit, grain stocks, labour power, licences to sell certain inputs, etc. Access to resources in its turn provides a person with *control* over certain instruments whereby he can exert some control over other people's action. Control over amount of land to lease out, over the wage to be paid, over the rate of interest to be charged, over the timing and amount of water input, etc., are examples. The instruments enable the owner to control actions of others on the labour process, over the cropping pattern, over the rights to unionize, to strike, etc. But in the final analysis power is *a social relationship* between people mediated by their unequal access to resources, and consequently unequal control over instruments. Some forms of control involve all or nothing divisions of power—if one party has the power the other does not—if the employer has the right to hire and fire, the employee does not. But other levers of power may modify the overall relationship which may involve several instruments. Thus while the employer has the right to hire and fire, the employee may redress the balance by invoking the right to strike. This will modify the overall balance of power. Extraneous circumstances such as employment opportunities elsewhere or possibility of substituting labour by machinery will again modify the balance of power. It will be helpful therefore to define power in a continuous scale between 0 and 1 whereby one can have either a complete dichotomy or a fluctuating share.[3]

So far I have not separated economic from political power though many of the examples have been economic. There is, however, a central difficulty about speaking of power in the economic context which must be squarely faced. The most frequently used paradigm in economics—neo-classical general equilibrium theory—has been able to provide explanations of economic phenomenon and predic-

[3] My earlier formulations were in terms of an all or nothing, zero/one measure. It was only during the discussions at the SAPE conferences that I was persuaded to modify my view. I am especially grateful to Susanne and Lloyd Rudolph for pointing this out.

tions about likely outcomes of economic situations without any recourse to the concept of power. While institutionalist economists have demurred at this, by and large the challenge of general equilibrium theory must be faced if we are to demonstrate the necessity and usefulness of the concept of power. Various points can be made here.[4]

It frequently is the case in social sciences (but even in natural sciences on occasions) that two rival modes of explaining the same observable phenomenon coexist with no clear way of choosing between them. In the narrower context of econometrics this is known as underidentification whereby rival structural models lead to the same observable outcomes. More generally, the rival models may take a dramatically opposite view of the way societies function. The general equilibrium model is well known to be an ahistorical, by and large static, equilibrium formulation of economic relationships where the units are individual economic agents. Its competitive version is the most fully worked out and here all agents are price takers and no agent is quantity constrained on the demand or the supply side. If a complete set of markets exists in each of which the price-taking – quantity non-constraint assumptions are satisfied, the competitive model can generate explanations of many observed outcomes. This world exists outside and independent of any political context, and power, economic or political, has no role to play in it.[5]

Even within the general equilibrium paradigm, there has been dissatisfaction with the stringent assumptions required to obtain the equilibrium result. A variety of market imperfections has been explored in recent years to accommodate more complex aspects of the economic reality. Thus price rigidity, price distortion, quantity constraint and lack of a complete set of markets in face of uncertainty may all lead to outcomes different from the competitive one. But even here methodological individualism, exclusive concentration on economic relationships and a preference for an ahistorical equilibrium characterization remain the features of this new development. This has been especially the case in recent research on the relation-

---

[4] Much of this discussion owes a lot to the lively and searching criticism of T. N. Srinivasan of an earlier draft. While I have not met his criticisms, I have made my own assumptions more explicit.

[5] See Sukhamoy Chakravarty's essay in this collection. He also shows that Marx having taken over a Ricardian classical model, power has no role in Marx's *economic* scheme of value relations.

ship of landlord to share-cropper where a large body of results has been generated explaining the observed share-cropping arrangements in terms of economic theory. This model has been extended to take in the problem that often there are inter-related transactions in more than one market between the landlord and tenant. Thus a landlord may double as moneylender dispensing (grain) credit and land lease simultaneously, his 'power' in one market reinforcing his 'power' in another.

The essence of this extended competitive model seems to be that while the notion of power conveys compulsion, all its results are derived assuming *voluntary* optimizing behaviour on part of agents. The observed outcome is still the same as we shall look at below— share-croppers taking up contracts affording them little more than the wage they would earn as wage labourers.[6]

An alternate formulation of the same observed outcome is in game theoretic terms. This emphasizes the bargaining behaviour of landlords against share-croppers and explicitly deals with strategies employed by each side. In the game theoretic literature the landlord–share-cropper arrangement is explained not so much by uncertainty or incompleteness of markets but by presence of imperfect competition elements—asymmetry in size between participants for instance.[7]

I shall eschew the game theoretic approach as well as the approach of general equilibrium theory. Again, while I shall be explaining the same observed outcome, my approach derives more from the Marxian political economy tradition.[8] It is partly a matter of taste but I also think that a political economy approach leaves one free to endogenize many more aspects of a situation than the general

[6] The bibliography here is quite large. See, for a recent example, Braverman and Srinivasan (1979). They set up a model of individual utility maximizing behaviour in which the landlord faces an infinitely elastic supply of (share-cropping) tenants at a wage no better than what they would earn as labourers. The landlord has three instruments—plot size, output share and the rate of interest on grain loans. Avoiding any reference to power, they prove the existence of a share-cropping equilibrium. There are indeed many parallels in my argument with theirs but our approaches differ. See also the references under Bell and Bardhan in the bibliography.

[7] For a game theoretic treatment of the share-cropping problem, see Bell and Zusman (1976, 1978, 1979).

[8] I do not however make any formal use of the labour theory of value. Most of the argument below relies on a one good model where the explicit approach of a labour theory is unnecessary.

equilibrium approach. Thus it is not enough to assume that there is an infinitely elastic supply of labour/share-croppers at a given wage. The task is to explain how it comes about that such is the situation. Without attention to the history of the region and of the distribution of landed property, it would be hard to do anything but to take the situation as given. This does not mean that our argument will not be analytical but that we hope it will be qualitatively different from that of general equilibrium approach.

Even within the approach of political economy, there are contending schools. A major argument concerns the characterization of the mode of production prevalent in South Asia. Some scholars believe that it is the semi-feudal character of the mode of production which explains exploitative relations in a backward agriculture.[9] Others contend that the mode of production in Indian agriculture is capitalist. My own view is that given the uneven regional development of different parts of South Asia, a production of ecological and historical forces, it is incorrect to put a single label on the entire subcontinent. The increasingly dominant tendency in Indian agriculture at least is capitalistic though the contrast between the modern capitalism of Punjab/Haryana as against the backward nature of Bihar/Bengal agriculture is obvious. Indian agriculture, as indeed the whole economy, is a social formation characterized by multiple, overlapping modes of production but the dominant mode is the capitalist one. This said, when it comes to analysing local situations, sufficient attention has to be paid to the historical background before adopting a single view.

Thus I take a political economy approach, emphasizing market relationships but making the historical background explicit. The notion of reproduction imposes explicit dynamic requirements upon our modelling strategy. Since I also wish to derive an operational measure and link it with political power, I have to go beyond a single economic unit. The purpose is very much a methodological one of forging concepts. In the political economy approach especially, empirical measurements have in my view gone ahead of the theoretical formulation. The theory of agrarian relations is still very

---

[9] The semi-feudalism approach has been popularized by Bhaduri (1973, 1977). My own view that the mode of production in Indian agriculture is predominantly capitalist was presented in Desai (1970, 1975). I have benefited much from Ashok Rudra's comments on my earlier draft and his written work in this respect. See Bardhan and Rudra (1980a, 1980b) and Rudra's essay in this volume.

derivative of the pre-revolutionary Russian debates between Lenin and the Narodniks, of the researches of Chayanov and Kautsky. There is much, therefore, which can be done to build explicit analytical models using the notion of surplus and the struggle for the share of surplus.

A simple way to characterize the model outlined in Section II below is to say that surplus is a measure of power. It is in terms of maximal and actual shares in the economic surplus of the various groups—landlords, tenants, share-croppers and labourers—that we define and measure power. I set up the model in terms of a single landlord *vis-à-vis* tenants, share-croppers and landless labourers. But in setting up the determinants of the share of surplus, there needs to be a dynamic link between one period and the next to highlight the reproduction process. Some simple measures of power in terms of 'distance' are derived in the single period and the dynamic contexts. These measures which relate to a single landlord are then aggregated over all landlords to derive a measure of the *power structure*. No attempt is made in this essay to implement the measure empirically but I do make some remarks toward the end as to the ways this can be done.

Thus the political economy approach is used here as an alternative to the general equilibrium or game theoretic approaches. The emphasis will be on analytical, operational concepts and this inevitably means that the more qualitative, sociological-historical considerations which are usually given prominence in political economic writings will be ignored. My only defence in the face of that criticism is that it is in the analytical area that the political economy approach has been lacking. It also means that the approach can be compared with the usual paradigm.

II

In this section, I set up the basic model within which we can discuss some of the questions outlined above. The model is fairly abstract and only land and labour inputs will be discussed. There will be only one homogeneous output produced which will be called grain. I ignore here the problem of many outputs, relative prices of various crops and the relation of acreage under different crops to price fluctuations.

Following the example of the Circuits of capital in Marx's *Capital*

(Vol. 2), we set up an Exchange–Production–Exchange cycle. The Production cycle will be assumed to occupy two time periods—a slack season (period 1) when ploughing, weeding, planting operations take place, and a busy season (period 2) when harvesting takes place. The two periods need not be of equal length though nothing will hinge on their relative length. In the third period, no production takes place but contracts for the following production cycle are made in this period. This period also witnesses the division of output, payment of rent, repayment of loans. So schematically we have

Exchange $\rightarrow$ Production $\rightarrow$ Production $\rightarrow$ Exchange $\rightarrow$ Production
                        slack   busy   slack
       3   1   2   3   1

In the village economy, there are landowners, tenants and share-croppers as far as dealings in land are concerned. I recognize that often tenancy contracts are illegal or laws stipulate such tenurial conditions or rent that share-cropping entirely displaces tenancy arrangements. It still helps to think of all these three arrangements at once. Thus there may be own cultivation of land or leasing-in and leasing-out of land at an agreed rent or a share-cropping contract specifying share in output. We propose to begin with the case of one landowner, labelled zamindar, who cultivates some of his land and enters into tenancy and share-cropping contracts with others. The zamindar is thus endowed with land and implements as well as stocks of grain from previous harvests.

The tenant leases in land at an agreed rent, provides his own inputs and has control over the disposal of his output net of rent. He may borrow from the landlord but this is not essential to the tenancy contract. The tenant will thus be assumed to be endowed with implements and some grain stocks to sustain production over the two periods until output appears.

The share-cropper will be assumed to enter into a share-cropping contract, but as is now usual in the literature, we shall introduce in a later part the assumption that he has to borrow some grain from the zamindar to sustain himself over the production cycle. The zamindar stipulates the interest rate on the grain loan. The degree of the share-cropper's dependence on the zamindar will be measured by the proportion of the loan to his consumption requirements over the production cycle. These consumption requirements will be labelled

C_t for each period and are measured in grain units.

Apart from these three categories of dealers in land services, there are landless labourers. They work in agriculture during the production cycle at wage rates w_i for periods $i = 1$ and 2. In the exchange period, they work 'outside' agriculture at wage w_3. This outside wage is related to the overall economic conditions, e.g., in nearby urban area or in rural non-agricultural activity, etc. There is of course no full employment but I shall assume, for the sake of convenience, that enough wage income is generated to cover subsistence consumption. Also in this section, I shall assume that wages are paid in grain, even during the period 3.

We take now the case of one zamindar with tenancy contracts, share-cropping contracts and own cultivation/labour hiring contracts. The zamindar uses only hired labour but no household labour. The tenant will use household labour as well as hired labour. But the share-cropper will be assumed to use only household labour. All other inputs will be ignored for the time being. How does power impinge here?

In terms of our definition of power in the previous section, note that the different endowments of the different categories tell us about the *access* they have to resources. The zamindar has land and grain stocks, the tenant has grain stocks and the share-cropper may have grain stocks but not sufficient to sustain himself over the production cycle. One index of relative power would be the ratio of grain stocks at the beginning of the production cycle to the required subsistence consumption over the cycle. Thus if grain stocks are G_j for the j'th category of agent $G_j/(C_1 + C_2)_j$ is a measure of the j'th agent's power. Another element will be other opportunities available for earning subsistence (expected wage income in agriculture or outside agriculture in relation to subsistence requirements), as far as the tenant and share-cropper are concerned. For the landlord, a consideration is the availability of enough hired labour to be able to use all his land if no tenancy or share-cropping contracts can be made. But some of these things will depend on other elements in the village economy. So let us ignore them for the time being.

In terms of control, there are two main aspects in the production cycle—the commitment of labour input at various stages and the choice of cropping pattern. The zamindar has *no* control over the labour input of the tenant, *absolute* control over his own hired labour and *variable* control over the share-cropper. We shall see later what determines the degree of control over the share-cropper's labour input. (It is not only labour input but the entire 'labour process' which is at issue here. But I prefer the label labour input.) As far as control over cropping pattern is concerned, we delay any discussion till later since we have chosen a single crop economy here. But the graduation of low, variable and absolute control will also apply in the case of crop choice.

Net output will be labelled Y and will be taken to be function of land and labour inputs l_1, l_2 in each period. At this stage, we do not need to specify the production function specifically except to note that both l_1 and l_2 are needed to get output and that there is limited substitutability between them.

As a first approximation, we can treat labour input in the two periods in terms of the total. Differentiation by season will matter when we wish to look at wage determination.

Let us suppose that *the share-cropper* contracts to give the land-lord a portion α of the net output. His inputs are leased-in land L_s and his own labour l_s. To begin with we can leave the question of borrowing for consumption over the production cycle open. Then, there are two ways of defining the outcome of the operation that the share-cropper undergoes. His 'income' can be measured at that maximum level of consumption C'_s which will leave his previous grain stocks intact. So if he has started the production cycle with stocks G_s, then C'_s will leave $\Delta G_s = 0$. Thus

$$\Delta G_s = (1 - \alpha)\, Y_s\,(l_s, L_s) - C_s. \tag{1}$$

Then

$$k'_s \equiv C'_s / Y_s = (1 - \alpha). \tag{1a}$$

Alternatively one may compute the internal rate of return above costs. Thus the only variable input by definition is labour. Hence we write profits π as

$$\pi_s = (1 - \alpha)\, Y_s - (1 + \rho_s)\overline{W} l_s. \tag{2}$$

Here $\overline{W}$ is the subsistence wage earned by a landless labourer. Setting $\pi = 0$, we get the rate of return earned by the share-cropper ρ_s in terms of the share of wages in output.

$$\overline{\omega}_s = \overline{W} l_s / Y_s = (1 - \alpha)/(1 + \rho_s). \tag{2a}$$

Equations (1a) and (2a) define the income output ratio as

$$k'_s = (1 + \rho_s)\overline{\omega}_s. \tag{3}$$

Equation (3) defines in principle the advantage of the share-cropper over the landless labourer as being $\rho_s \bar{\omega}_s$, the extra income he has due to access to land. It is then straightforward to see that the zamindar's power *vis-à-vis* the share-cropper lies in his ability to fix α such that $\rho_s = 0$. A value of $\rho_s = 0$ would define maximum zamindar power. Then $C'_s = \overline{W}l_s$. This gives

$$\alpha' = (1 - \bar{\omega}_s).\qquad(4)$$

The advantage of (4) is that it defines the maximum share in terms purely of the land leasing relationship independently of transactions in other markets such as money (grain) lending.

The *tenant* starts with enough grain stocks to hire labour as well as feed his household. Let h be the proportion of hired labour and $(1 - h)$ family labour. Then parallel to equations (1) and (2) we have

$$\Delta G_t = Y_t(l_t, L_t) - R_t(L_t) - hWl_{ht} - (1 - h)C_t\qquad(5)$$

where l_t is all labour ($l_{ft} + l_{ht}$), R_t is rent paid on L_t land and Y_t is output.

$$k'_t = C'_t/Y_t = \frac{(1 - \gamma) - h\bar{\omega}_{ht}}{(1 - h)}\qquad(5a)$$

where $\gamma = R_t/Y_t$ and $\overline{W}L_{ht}/Y_t = \bar{\omega}_{ht}$.

$$\pi_t = Y_t - R_t - (1 + \rho_t)\overline{W}l_t\qquad(6)$$

$$\bar{\omega}_t = \frac{(1 - \gamma)}{(1 + \rho_t)}\qquad(6a)$$

then

$$k'_t = \frac{(1 + \rho_t)\bar{\omega}_t - h\bar{\omega}_{ht}}{(1 - h)}.\qquad(7)$$

If the zamindar is all powerful, he will be able to extract that rent which leaves the tenant only subsistence wage. That maximum rent γ' can be derived from (6a) as before

$$\gamma' = (1 - \bar{\omega}_t).\qquad(8)$$

Thus γ', α' are the maximum shares of net output extractable by a zamindar. If he can extract such shares, the zamindar is indifferent between own cultivation with hired labour, share-cropper leasing or

tenant renting. Just to keep our accounts complete, we can define
landlord's income and rate of return as

$$\Delta G_z = Y_z(l_z, L_z) - Wl_{hz} + \gamma Y_t + \alpha Y_s - C_z. \tag{9}$$

Then

$$k'_z = C'_z / Y_z = (1 - \bar{\omega}_{hz}) + \gamma Y_t / Y_z + \alpha Y_s / Y_z. \tag{9a}$$

The landlord's profits arise from own cultivation as well from leasing
land. So we get

$$\pi = Y_z - (1 + \rho_z)Wl_{hz} + \gamma Y_t + \alpha Y_s. \tag{10}$$

The internal rate is then

$$\rho_z = \frac{(1 - \bar{\omega}_z) + [1 - (1 + \rho_t)\bar{\omega}_t]\lambda_t + [1 - (1 + \rho_s)\bar{\omega}_s]\lambda_s}{\bar{\omega}_z} \tag{10a}$$

λ_t and λ_s are ratios Y_t / Y_z and Y_s / Y_z respectively and in (10a) we
have substituted for α and γ from equations (2a) and (6a). The most
powerful landlord will only allow $\rho_t = \rho_s = 0$ and hence $\bar{\omega}_t = \bar{\omega}_z = \bar{\omega}_s = \bar{\omega}$

$$\rho'_z = [(1 - \bar{\omega})(1 + \lambda_t + \lambda_s)]/\bar{\omega}. \tag{11}$$

There are thus two equivalent ways of looking at the economic
power of the zamindar *vis-à-vis* his 'clients'—tenant, share-cropper
and landless labourer. If the *actual* income of these clients defined as
maximum sustainable consumption does not exceed subsistence
consumption, then the landlord is most powerful. The distance
between actual consumption and subsistence consumption (equal to
subsistence wage) is thus one measure of the relative power of the
client *vis-à-vis* the zamindar. A second measure is the gap between
the rates of return earned by the different parties, i.e., the gap
between ρ_z and ρ_s, and ρ_z and ρ_t, etc.

Power measured as a distance is also relative to another party.
Thus the distance of the share-cropper from the zamindar is

$$d_{sz} = (\alpha' - \alpha) = (k'_s - \bar{\omega}_s). \tag{12}$$

When $d_{sz} = 0$, the share-cropper has zero power *vis-à-vis* the
zamindar.[10]

---

[10] The distance $\alpha' - \alpha$ may not be directly observable. There may, for example,
be historically established norms about shares, say, α^* The zamindar may be
compelled, say, by social pressures, to distinguish $(\alpha' - \alpha)$ as being $(\alpha' - \alpha^*) +$

$$d_{tz} = \frac{(\gamma' - \gamma)}{(1 - h)} (k'_t - \bar{\omega}_t). \qquad (13)$$

The distance of the landless labourer from his employers-tenant or zamindar is measured symmetrically by the gap between actual wage and subsistence wage.

$$d_{ht} = (\omega_{ht} - \bar{\omega}_{ht}) \qquad (14a)$$

$$d_{hz} = (\omega_{hz} - \bar{\omega}_{hz}). \qquad (14b)$$

We now can derive the total power of a tenant *vis-à-vis* the zamindar as well as the worker he hires as

$$d_t = \frac{d_{tz} - hd_{ht}}{(1 - h)}. \qquad (15)$$

Thus if the landless labourer can claw back some surplus from the tenant in shape of a higher wage this can only come from what the tenant has clawed back from the zamindar.

The other measure is in terms of the rates of return ρ_j. This of course cannot be applied to the landless labourer. But the ρ_j expressions can be derived setting $\bar{\omega}_j = \bar{\omega}$.

$$\rho_s = (1 - \alpha - \bar{\omega})/\bar{\omega} \qquad (16a)$$

$$\rho_t = (1 - \gamma - \bar{\omega})/\bar{\omega} \qquad (16b)$$

$$\rho_z = \frac{(1 - \bar{\omega})(1 + \lambda_t + \lambda_s) - \bar{\omega}(\rho_t \lambda_t + \rho_s \lambda_s)}{\bar{\omega}} \qquad (16c)$$

when $\rho_s = \rho_t = 0$, $\rho_z = \rho'_z$ as given in (11). Thus the antagonism of the power relationship is brought out clearly in these formulae. The zamindar has what the others do not have. This is not surprising since we have equated economic power with shares in net output.

$(\alpha^* - \alpha)$. If, however, economic circumstances persistently justify a share higher than the norm, the landlord may be able to extract an equivalent return in other services or the average norm may break down. Jan Breman's analysis of the Hali tenure with the Anavil zamindars of South Gujarat immediately comes to mind as an example of how norms can often be unprofitably binding on zamindars but which then can be done away with over time.

Another way of sustaining the norms would be for the zamindar to denote part of the surplus $(\alpha' - \alpha^*)$ he could claim to ritual expenditures—temple donations, etc. David Ludden's essay in this volume bears on this question.

The rates of return measures are all derived on assumption of subsistence wage and hence they are in some sense conditional upon a powerless group of landless labourers in case of ρ_t, ρ_z. Any deviation of ω_h from $\bar{\omega}_h$ will alter ρ_t and ρ_z.

Interlinked Markets and Measures of Power

Having established a baseline in the case of only land and labour contracts, we can now look at the complications caused by interlinked markets on measures of power. While interlinkage can spread across all input markets, attention has been focused in some recent work by Bhaduri on the tie-in between credit and land. Thus Bhaduri assumes that the share-cropper not only leases in land for payment of a share to the zamindar but that he also borrows from the landlord grain to tide him over the production cycle.[11] The share-cropper has some grain stocks but they only furnish a part of his consumption needs. He borrows a proportion σ of his consumption needs C_s. The zamindar charges a rate of interest ρ_{sz} on this. Then we can rewrite (1) as

$$\Delta G^s = (1 - \alpha) Y_s - (1 - \sigma) C_s - \sigma(1 + \rho_{sz}) C_s$$

$$= (1 - \alpha) Y_s - (1 + \sigma\rho_{sz}) C_s \qquad (17)$$

and

$$k''_s = (1 - \alpha)/(1 + \sigma\rho_{sz}) . \qquad (17a)$$

The presence of grain loan does not affect the internal rate of return ρ_s in any way. So we can see that in presence of a grain loan, the highest rate of interest a zamindar/lender can charge so as to leave $k''_s = \bar{\omega}_s$ is

$$\rho'_{sz} = \rho_{ss}/\sigma . \qquad (18)$$

We have labelled the internal rate of return ρ_{ss} to make it clear that the parties to this interest rate are the same. Equation (18) makes clear that when all grain is borrowed $\sigma = 1$, then the landlord can recoup the difference between α' and α by charging an interest rate equal to ρ_{ss}. In Bhaduri's model it is assumed that σ is equal to or even *above* one. This would then mean $\rho'_{sz} < \rho_{ss}$ since the maximum

---

[11] Bhaduri's description has been questioned on grounds of descriptive accuracy as to Bengal agrarian relations by Bardhan and Rudra (1980b). Srinivasan has questioned some restrictive assumptions of the Bhaduri model (Srinivasan 1979; Bhaduri 1979). My concern is to make my scheme comparable to his without delving into these issues.

a landlord can extract in share and loan repayment is total net output Y_s. An alternative way of seeing this is to write (18) as

$$(\rho'_{sz} - \rho_{ss}) = (1 - \sigma) \rho'_{sz} . \tag{18a}$$

Now α' represents the maximum the zamindar can extract by virtue of his ownership of land. The source of power behind α' is access to land which the landlord has and by assumption the share-cropper does not have. In (18), we then add a dimension of landlord power due to grain loaning activity—the source of power now being access to grain stocks. Thus even when there is no grain loan, i.e. $\sigma = 0$, the power measure we have proposed shows the relative power of the zamindar over the share-cropper. A new composite measure of power embodying these two sources then is

$$d''_{sz} = d_{sz}(L_s) + d'_{sz}(\sigma) . \tag{19}$$

Here $d_{sz}(L_s)$ indicates that the source of power is land ownership and $d'_{sz}(\sigma)$ that it is indebtedness of the share-cropper.

Since d'_{sz} arises from indebtedness, it is quite possible (but I do not know how likely in actual fact) that the share-cropper may choose a high C_s (i.e. $C_s \geq \overline{W}l_s$) and thus may put himself in the zamindar's thrall. This is then partly a behavioural matter. As we shall see below when we analyse uncertainty, a share-cropper may choose to be in debt as a way of generating a secure level of consumption. In such a case a measure of power would give a misleading impression since a share-cropper is choosing a high C_s which implies a high σ and in exchange for the entire output Y_s gets C_s. The result being a high C_s/Y_s ratio despite seemingly low power.[12]

The behavioural aspect alluded to above can be clarified by using (1a) and (17a). The reduction in consumption due to indebtedness is given by the difference between k'_s and k''_s. Call this μ_s, then

$$\mu_s = \sigma\rho_{sz}/(1 + \sigma\rho_{sz}) . \tag{20}$$

---

[12] To see this, let us go back to the measure of power suggested at the very outset—the ratio of grain stocks to subsistence consumption. We can then decompose this ratio $G_s/\overline{C}_s$ into four parts

$$G_s/\overline{C}_s = (G_s/C'_s) (C'_s/Y_s) (Y_s/C_s) (C_s/\overline{C}_s) \tag{21}$$

The first part G_s/C'_s is the 'wealth–income' ratio in terms of grain, C'_s/Y_s is the share in total output of the share-cropper, Y_s/C_s the actual consumption output ratio and $C_s/\overline{C}_s$ the relative affluence of the share-cropper *vis-à-vis* the landless labourer. These four components may move in different directions.

Now if ρ_{sz} were decided independently of σ then the share-cropper can minimize μ by choosing a high σ since $\partial\mu/\partial\sigma = \rho/(1 + \sigma\rho)^2$. So a zamindar (or any other lender) would make ρ_{sz} an increasing function of σ.

Dynamic Considerations

What we have obtained so far are simple measures of power on the assumption that net output is so disposed so as to leave grain stocks at their previous level. We improved them a bit by introducing rates of return of the different parties. We need now to discuss dynamic considerations of our measure. Some of them are implicit, i.e., reproduction of the share-cropper relationship by renewing the loan contract at the same level when $\Delta G_s = 0$. But output may grow and this means that proportions such as k'_s and $\overline{\omega}_s$, etc., will change over time. Before we do that let us examine the process whereby power is exercised.

Of the three aspects of power that we defined above, *access* to resources is measured by access to land and size of initial grain stocks. The landlord has land to lease out as well as stocks of grain to loan. The share-cropper has no land except what he can obtain from the landlord and he has limited stocks of grain ($= (1 - \sigma)C_s$). The tenant by assumption has enough grain stocks to hire labour and feed his family during the production cycle ($hC_{ht} + (1 - h)C_{ft}$). He needs to lease in land from the landlord.

The aspect of *control* only enters in the share-cropping contract for the landlord has no control over the labour process of the tenant. This control is exercised by the landlord because having given a loan of σC_s, he has no guarantee that the share-cropper will put in enough labour to be able to have output which can repay the loan. While our measures are in terms of proportions of output, total output is so far left indeterminate. Having secured enough grain to survive the production cycle, what incentive does the share-cropper have to put in labour, especially if his indebtedness is very high?

Having given σC_s as a loan and land L_s to the share-cropper, the landlord wishes to make sure that the labour input will be enough to ensure output which will at least repay his debt. Thus let $Y_s = Y_s(l_s, L_s)$. Then he wants

$$Y_s \geq \overline{Y}_s = \frac{(1 + \rho)\sigma C_s}{(1 - \alpha)}. \tag{22}$$

(I drop the subscript sz to the rate of interest since the context is clear.) But of course he will want higher output as well since he gets α of each additional unit. The control over the labour process is the way the landlord makes sure he recovers his investment. He will extract labour input from the share-cropper until he gets the same amount as if he was hiring labour at subsistence wage. Thus the minimum labour he wants is l'_s and of course the landlord expects that

$$Y_s(l'_s, L_s) \geq \overline{Y}_s \quad \text{where } l'_s = \sigma C_s / \overline{W} . \tag{23}$$

The share-cropper wishes at least to leave his grain stocks unchanged at the end of the production cycle. He wishes to have output which will give $\Delta G_s \geq 0$, so he wants

$$Y_s(l''_s, L_s) \geq \frac{(1 + \rho\sigma)C_s}{(1 - \alpha)} . \tag{24}$$

If the share-cropper finds at l''_s that the marginal product of labour is still positive, he will work more. This is because every additional unit of grain can be used to provide for future consumption. This will then reduce future indebtedness. This is what provides the linkage between current labour input, current output and future indebtedness. The share-cropper will maximize output since additional output can be used to reduce next period's indebtedness. (Of course it can also be used to increase consumption and the choice will depend as usual on intertemporal considerations involving ρ. We take it, however, that ρ is sufficiently high for him to maintain current consumption low and reduce debt.)

Let us then say that the share-cropper in the current period (labelled o) has borrowed $\sigma_o C_o$ at interest rate ρ_o. He then puts in enough labour so as to maximize output for the given size of land. Let this output be $\overline{Y}_o$. Then the surplus grain ΔG_s left over after repayment of loan can be expressed as proportion of subsistence consumption. (We omit the share-cropper subscripts unless it is likely to lead to confusion.)

$$\Delta G_s = \beta_1 \overline{C}_1 = (1 - \alpha)\overline{Y}_o - (1 + \rho_o\sigma_o)\overline{C}_o . \tag{25}$$

In equation (25) we label the exchange period which begins the new cycle 1 and the initial period 0. Now β_1 is the proportion of surplus to subsistence consumption. Ignoring once again any saving or dissaving in the exchange period, we can relate β_1 to σ_1 indebtedness in the new period since $\beta_1 = (1 - \sigma_1)$. Thus we get taking $\overline{C}_0 = \overline{C}_1$

$$\sigma_1 = 1 - (1 - \alpha)\overline{k}^{-1} + (1 + \rho_0\sigma_0). \qquad (26)$$

The simple dynamics of the share-cropper situation captured in (26) says that higher output will reduce the potential indebtedness of the share-cropper since at constant consumption level $\overline{C}$, more will be left over for storage and future use. This also shows the incentive the share-cropper has for maximizing expected output thereby putting in more labour than static profit maximization would predict. This is because every additional unit of output has to be valued in terms of its impact on future indebtedness.

The higher output from share-cropping sets up a problem for the landlord. Out of each additional unit he gets α but he loses $\rho_1\Delta\sigma_1$ of future loan interest from what remains with the share-cropper. His net gain depends on whether

$$\rho_1 \geq \alpha/(1 - \alpha). \qquad (27)$$

If ρ_1 is greater than $\alpha/(1 - \alpha)$ then the landlord's loss from future interest reduction will be greater than his gain of the extra α in output. If shares are typically equal, then this means that if interest rates are below 100 per cent the landlord will get more grain from extra output than he loses in future interest receipts. Of course extra output by increasing d_s makes the share-cropper relatively less dependent while giving the landlord larger grain resources. Thus the Bhaduri proposition that landlords have no interest in productivity gains depends on landlord monopoly of lending and some exceptionally high interest rates.

The share-cropping situation then consists of an interlinked relation involving land leased for a share of net output, a grain loan at a stipulated rate of interest and control over labour input. It will be reproduced from one period to the next as long as indebtedness is positive, i.e. $\sigma > 0$. But it will be reproduced in a modified form from one period to next if the relative distance changes. Otherwise it is reproduced exactly.[13]

In the absence of the indebtedness element, the only difference between share-cropping and tenancy relates to uncertainty since

---

[13] Note therefore that reproduction does not imply unchanging distance or any other comparative static equilibrium situation or even a steady state. It only requires that there be an outcome of period t which will lead to a renewal of the relationship in $t + 1$.

rent is fixed irrespective of final output and only the share is fixed in share-cropping. To reduce uncertainty and moral hazard, the land-lord undertakes supervision of labour input. We shall look into uncertainty a bit more in a later section. For the present we can end this section with a few concluding remarks.

The dynamics in the tenancy relationship also depend on the course of output. Since the tenant is assumed to hire labour, he cannot maximize output but with fixed rent, he would wish to maximize surplus above rent and wages. He may overutilize family labour but he will not use hired labour beyond the surplus maximiz-ing point. The higher the output the smaller would be γ'_1 and ω'_t. This will lead to obvious changes in d_t which need not be spelt out.

III

Measuring the Power Structure

In the previous section, I have proposed two simple measures of power. These measures take the form of distances and are in terms of consumption levels or wage levels. In *principle*, we can measure these distances. But measurement is only a step toward providing a theory so we must pursue the matter a bit further.

Our measure of power has two prongs. *First* we say that if the landlord who controls allocation of land and grain loans can so extract the surplus from land under various tenures that the other party to the contracts—share-cropping, tenancy, labour hire—are left only with subsistence consumption then we say that the landlord is most powerful. This implies in our terms that the relevant distances are zero. We state this condition as

$$d_{sz} = d_{tz} = d_{wz} = 0 . \tag{28}$$

What our d measure then represents is a world in which competi-tion among demanders of land for cultivation and for jobs enables the monopolist controller of land to extract maximum surplus. There is no coercion—no extra-economic compulsion needed to secure $d_{jz} = 0$ (for all j). There is implicit a lack of alternative opportunities and this needs to be spelt out.

The second prong of our measure is in terms of differences in rates of return. Thus in a neo-classical competitive theory, rates of return on different tenures and in different activities (moneylending/agriculture) will be equalized. From this point of view a situation of zero power would be $\rho_z = \rho_t = \rho_s$. We could further refine such measures by relating these ρ_j to riskless return in the economy as a whole.

The ρ_j measures therefore say that inequality in rates of return represents an ability on the part of one agent to secure a higher rate of return than another. These two measures tell two inter-related parts of the same story.

We now can look at *the structure of power* in terms of our measures. Notice that the condition $d_{jz} = 0$, $j = s, t, w$ already incorporates a world of one landlord and many competing tenants/share-croppers/labourers. But we can adopt a measure of a landlord's power over the set of share-croppers, tenants, workers contracting with him by looking at the distribution of d_{jz} for each category j for a single z.

An all-powerful landlord will again be able to have $d_{sz} = 0$ for all his share-croppers, $d_{tz} = 0$ for all his tenants and $d_{wz} = 0$ for all his workers. This immediately suggests that for a particular landlord one should be looking at the *mean* (in general the moments of the distribution) of d_{jz} for each category. Thus, take a landlord z with S_z share-croppers. Then

$$\bar{d}_{sz} = \frac{1}{S_z} \sum_{S=1}^{S_z} d_{sz}$$

is the mean distance of the landlord over all his share-croppers. Some share-croppers will be at $d_{sz} = 0$, others at $d_{sz} > 0$. The lower the mean the more powerful the landlord. Also for each landlord one can similarly define the mean distance over tenants $\bar{d}_{tz}$ and variance and mean distance over workers $\bar{d}_{wz}$ and variance.

The distribution of the d_{jz} singly or jointly then summarizes the power relation of a single landlord with all his 'clients'. The lower the mean and variance we conclude that the more powerful is the landlord. The higher moments of distance d_{jz} can also be similarly studied.

An extension of this idea to cover many landlords is straightforward. Within a given regional area, for each landlord one can *in principle* look at such distributions. Not all landlords will be equally powerful, *vis-à-vis*, say, share-croppers nor will a landlord be equally powerful against all clients.

How can one use the information in these distributions? Later on I wish to sketch a theory of the determinants of the mean/variance of these distributions in a way which will illuminate the data gathered in village studies. But before that, we can illustrate some uses of the distance distributions.

Take the case where in a particular region there are many landlords as well as many share-croppers, tenants and labourers. Now if the landlords were of roughly equal size in landholdings and were to *compete* with each other, the client groups could improve their positions, i.e., their d_{jz} would increase. This would lead to high mean of individual landlords distributions as well as high mean over all landlords. This would be the beneficial type of competition much expounded in economics textbooks.

If landlords were to collude, then share-croppers' conditions would be similar across landlords. The distributions would look similar and will have low means and low variances.

The *power structure* can then be defined as the degree of cohesion/ competition among landlords as well as the distance between land-lord and his clients and distances as between landlords. Landlords will be strong or weak relative to each other as well as relative to their clients. Thus a share-cropper working for a weak landlord may be better off than one working for a strong landlord, though share-croppers as a group may be quite badly off. If we could measure these distances for a village or a relevant size area, then looking at distributions singly and as a group will be a major step toward under-standing the power structure.

Notice that the data required for such measures are on outputs, wages, rent, consumption levels. These are not impossible to gather. What the discussion so far does is to show how to put such informa-tion in a systematic way to extract the power information.

IV

Reproduction of Social Relationships

A major problem confronting all theories of power in economic theory is that since we deal with voluntary contractual arrangements, it is hard to explain why any party would enter voluntarily into an exploitative arrangement. Having once entered such a contract, say by accident, why should anyone *renew* the contract or, in other words, why should such relationships be *reproduced*? This is the major stumbling block, for example, in economists' willingness to accept Marxian theory of exploitation. Marx himself tried to combine a world where at the phenomenal level voluntary exchange rules but structural class relations reproduce these arrangements which are unequal but not always perceived as such by the participants. To the economist, on the other hand, it is sufficient to show that it is in the interest of both parties to a contract to enter into it. The division of benefits of trade may be unequal but neither party can be worse off than they would be without the trade.

In the previous sections, I proposed a measure of power in terms of the difference between actual and subsistence consumption in the static case or in terms of the evolution of the unavoidable (in the sense that consumption is kept at subsistence) proportion of indebtedness over time. Neither of these measures involve any involuntary elements in behaviour. But we need to discuss in some more detail as to why share-croppers renew (reproduce) share-cropping arrangements.

Consider first the choices facing the share-cropper. To make matters easy assume that $\sigma \leq 1$ and $C_s = \overline{C}_s$. Thus at the beginning of any production cycle, he does not owe anything to the landlord and may have a small stock of grain. Typically this stock will be insufficient to feed him (and his household) over the production cycle, i.e. $0 \leq \beta < 1$. He has a choice between re-entering into a share-cropping contract and borrow $(\sigma - 1)\overline{C}_s$ at a high rate of interest or to work as a hired labourer. The choice is between a guaranteed level of consumption over the production cycle and perhaps no net surplus (or no addition to the stock of grain) and finding work at subsistence wage.

Now uncertainty is important here. First, the share-cropper cannot guarantee that he will find enough work at sufficient wage to provide subsistence since typically there is insufficient work in the slack season though 'full employment' in the busy season. So he has to compare the expected wage income as a hired labourer with guaranteed consumption at $\overline{C}_s$ but with unknown value for future indebtedness.

The value of future indebtedness σ_1 is unknown since output is unknown. By taking a loan he incurs a fixed repayment charge of $(1 + \rho_0)\sigma_0\overline{C}_s$ against an uncertain income $(1 - \alpha)\overline{Y}_{s,o}$. He knows the amount of land he will get and let us say that he is willing to put in enough labour to maximize *expected* output. The uncertainty in this case is due to weather and hence unrelated to any power consideration and hence to any variable controlled by the landlord. Let us say that θ is the random error with zero expectation and the production function for the year τ is,

$$Y_{s\tau} = Y_s(l_{s\tau}, L_{s\tau}) + \theta_\tau. \tag{29}$$

So his future indebtedness is, from equation (26),

$$\underset{\theta}{E}\, \sigma_1 = 2 + \rho_0\sigma_0 - \frac{(1-\alpha)}{C_s}\,\underset{\theta}{E}\, Y_{so} \tag{30}$$

where E is the expectations operator.

Compared with this, the expected wage income is a product of the wage rate and the amount of work available. The wage rate, one may take it, is impersonal or at best depending on village-wide conditions but the probability of finding work will depend not only on conditions such as weather which will affect sowings, harvesting, etc. (θ_τ), but also, for any share-cropper, it would depend on his personal relation with his landlord and the other landlords. If landlords competed with each other, then the probability of finding a job will be similar for share-croppers across landlords and the uncertainty will reduce purely to the natural factor. If landlords colluded (as members, say, of a *jati*) or were of unequal power but dependent on some particular landlord, then it will matter very much who the share-cropper worked for and the relation of his landlord to the power structure. Thus he may be denied employment by any other landlord in the area if they all collude or if his landlord is the most powerful amongst the landlords.

Now this personal element in the expected income will differ across different individuals, landlords, villages. But this is exactly what d_{jz} captures. We have to think of d_{jz} as consisting of systematic components (of which more below) and a random component. The relation of an individual share-cropper to the structure can be looked at as

$$(d_{sz} - \bar{d}_{.z}) - (\bar{\bar{d}}_{..} - \bar{d}_{.z}) = \eta_s \tag{31}$$

The first part is the relation of an individual share-cropper to the average share-cropper *vis-à-vis* his landlord and the second term is the mean distance over all landlords less the mean for his landlord and measures his landlord's power relative to other landlords. Thus η_s is the individual share-cropper's personal component which will enter into his chances of getting a job.

Thus his expected wage income will be

$$E(w_\tau l_{s\tau}) = (\bar{\bar{d}}_{wz} + \bar{w}) \underset{\theta_\tau \eta_s}{E} l_{s\tau}$$

E is again the expectations operator and the expectation is now over two random variables θ_τ, and η_s.

Thus at the beginning of each production cycle, a share-cropper has to compare the certainty of consumption $\bar{C}_s$ and future expected indebtedness $E\sigma_1$ against the expectation of wage income $E(wl)$. What makes a share-cropper reproduce the relationship is then the way he views his chances of alternative income given the power structure. Thus the weaker he is *vis-à-vis* his landlord (low d_{sz}), then not only will he pay high ρ_0 and perhaps ρ_1 but his expected wage income may also be low. Thus he is led to reproduce the share-cropping relationship 'voluntarily', but saying that does not imply that power relationships play no role in his decision.

If η_s captures the individual component in the power relationship, the systematic components $\bar{d}_{.z}$, $\bar{\bar{d}}_{..}$, $\bar{\bar{d}}_{wz}$ and $\bar{w}$ will be related to factors at the village and economy level. The sort of factors which enter here are well known. Thus availability of irrigation, extent of double cropping, concentration of land ownership, the ratio of cultivable land to active labour force, availability of non-agricultural employment in the area or within a proximate distance, existence of credit facilities, extent of unionization among workers, and of collusion among zamindars, the nature and enforcement of legislation concerning minimum wages, tenure arrangements, etc. To list such factors is easy, but as we all know it is the quantitative importance of these various factors which is difficult to obtain.

One way to implement the proposed measures and correlate them quantitatively with these factors would be to compute for each village on which we have data (e.g. in the village studies bibliography produced by IDS/(Sussex)) measures of power such as $\bar{d}$, $\bar{d}_{wz}$. Then we have to explain the within village variations in $\bar{d}$ measures and across village variations in $\bar{\bar{d}}$, using the information available on related factors. There will of course be tremendous inter-village variation but this is precisely what we want in order to be able to construct an explanatory equation for power. To some extent we can draw on work already done by Biplab Dasgupta and his associates on the village data using principal component analysis.

Another use of these measures is in designing future village studies. If the account presented here is useful then studies ought to be designed which can collect for as many individuals as possible the raw data which go into making up the distance measures. The moments of the distribution of these measures will give an indication of the *cohesiveness* of the power structure.

It is perhaps worth arguing that measures of mean and variance (and other moments) of, say, the power of zamindars as a group in a village will also throw light on the nature of political power. By and large, I have concentrated on the economic dimensions of power and even here taken a fairly abstract picture. But even here if the variance of power among the zamindars is low and the mean as well low, then the politics of such a village will be more dominated by zamindars than in a village with high mean and variance. Thus though the clients may be in a majority compared to the landlords by a simple head count, when weighted by their relative power, these two groups may show different strengths. Thus take a village of landlords and landless labourers. Suppose there are n landlords and N (much larger than n) labourers. Their power measure, however, is

$$P(z) = \sum_z \sum_h (1 - d_{hz})$$
$$P(h) = \sum_z \sum_h d_{hz}$$

$P(z)$ is the power of zamindars summed over all labourers working for each zamindar and then summed over all zamindars. $P(h)$, the power of hired labourers, is the remainder. When zamindars are all powerful, $d_{hz} = 0$ for all h and z; hence

$$P(z) = N, \quad P(h) = 0.$$

The measure

$$P(z) = n, \quad P(h) = N$$

i.e. the head count assumes $d_{hz} = 1$. Now $\bar{d}_{hz} = 0$ when $\bar{\omega}_{hz} = \omega_{hz}$ i.e. when workers' share of output is that given by subsistence. One can say $\bar{d}_{hz} = 1$ when workers get all output except for some share for landlords reflecting, say, competitive rates of return.

The head count measure can then be seen as one idealization of the power structure. The maximal measure $P(z) = N, \ P(h) = 0$ embodies the extreme feudal notion that dependents are completely controlled by their masters. There will of course be room for strategic coalition forming in different situations. Thus if one were to have village level basic democracy as the unit of election, then landlords in each village may be able to exert much power. Parliamentary election over a wider area will give political parties to mobilize those with low power but numbers on their side. By bringing in support from others outside a village, the hands of the powerless may be strengthened. Of course, zamindars may also use political networks to seek alliance with forces outside the village which will support the power structure. Actual outcomes are not predictable in general but one may be able to predict likely patterns if one knew more about the intra-village and inter-village variations in the distance measures.

V

Much of this essay has concentrated on devising concepts and measures of power by using and extending the simple Marxian notion of economic surplus as a source of power. I have deliberately kept to questions on which an operational measure of power could throw some light. Reproduction has been incorporated into the scheme and at various points I have illustrated how 'voluntary' reproduction of social relationship does not preclude the notion of power. There is much further work to be done in extending this measure to more realistic situations. Thus multiple cropping, technological change, institutional reform in land and credit distribution, political alliances —all these factors need to be thought out in terms of this scheme. I hope to have made a beginning which others may find of sufficient interest to follow.

REFERENCES

Bardhan, Pranab K. (1979), 'Agricultural Development and Land Tenancy in a Peasant Economy: A Theoretical and Empirical Analysis', *American Journal of Agricultural Economics*, February, pp. 48–57.
—— (1980), 'Interlocking Factor Markets and Agrarian Development: A Review of Issues', *Oxford Economic Papers*, March, Vol. 32, No. 1, pp. 82–98.
—— (n.d.), *Labour-tying in a Poor Agrarian Economy: A Theoretical and Empirical Analysis* (Berkeley: University of California).
Bardhan, Pranab K. and Ashok Rudra (1980a), 'Terms and Conditions of Sharecropping Contracts: An Analysis of Village Survey Data in India', *Journal of Development Studies*, April, Vol. 16, No. 3, pp. 287–302.
—— (1980b), 'Type of Labour Attachment in Agriculture: Results of a Survey in West Bengal, 1979', *Economic and Political Weekly*, 30 August, pp. 1477–84.

Bell, Clive (1976a), 'Production Conditions, Innovation and the Choice of Lease in Agriculture', *Sankhya*, Vol. 38, Series C, Pt. 4, pp. 165–90.

—— (1976b), *Some Tests of Alternative Theories of Sharecropping Using Evidence from North-East India* (Development Research Center: World Bank).

Bell, Clive and Pinhas Zusman (1976), 'A Bargaining Theoretic Approach to Cropsharing Contracts', *American Economic Review*, September, Vol. 66, pp. 578–88.

—— (1977), 'Sharecropping Equilibria with Diverse Tenants', *Économie Appliquée*, Vol. XXX, No. 3, pp. 391–412.

—— (1979), *New Approaches to the Theory of Rental Contracts in Agriculture* (Development Research Center: World Bank).

Bhaduri, Amit (1973), 'A Study in Agricultural Backwardness under Semi-Feudalism', *Economic Journal*, March, pp. 120–37.

—— (1977), 'On the Formation of Usurious Interest Rates in Backward Agriculture', *Cambridge Journal of Economics*, Vol. I, pp. 341–52.

—— (1979), 'A Rejoinder to Srinivasan's Comment', *Economic Journal*, June.

Braverman, Avishay and T. N. Srinivasan (1979), *Inter-related Credit and Tenancy Markets in Rural Economics of Developing Countries* (Development Research Center: World Bank).

Desai, Meghnad (1970), 'The Vortex in India', *New Left Review*, May–June.

—— (1975), 'India: Emerging Contradictions of Slow Capitalist Development' in R. Blackburn (ed.), *Explosion in a Subcontinent* (Penguin).

Lambert, Claire (1976), *Village Studies: Data Analysis and Bibliography* (Bowker/IDS).

Srinivasan, T. N. (1979), 'Agricultural Backwardness under Feudalism', *Economic Journal*, June.

—— (1980), 'Comment on Meghnad Desai's Paper' (SAPE, unpublished).

Economic Consequences of Local Power Configurations in Rural South Asia*

RONALD J. HERRING

Introduction: Political Economy, Exploitation and Growth

Political economy as a discipline necessarily involves analysis which integrates the relations among economic structures and forces, formal and informal political power, economic decision-making, and the role of the state. Analysis which focuses narrowly on any one of these dimensions is unlikely to explain adequately economic change in the villages. The purpose of this essay is to analyse the types of power, structural and conjunctural, narrowly political and narrowly economic, which are important in understanding observed differences in productivity and changes in these over time. Throughout, a central concern is to pose such empirical questions, and analytical distinctions, as would contribute both to future research and to a sharper understanding of relations between power and productivity. The final section concludes with a tentative answer to the general theoretical question of how local power structures impinge on levels of and changes in economic productivity and suggests that contradictory political imperatives produced by the existing relationship between local power, economic growth, and the rural class structures typical

* Revised version of a paper prepared for the SSRC/ICSSR Project I on South Asian Political Economy, presented in New Delhi, 14 December 1980. I am indebted to a number of people for comments on earlier drafts but would like to acknowledge especially the insightful comments of Susanne Rudolph, A. Vaidyanathan, and Meghnad Desai, and oral critiques by members of the Project I working group, particularly Ashok Rudra.

of the region profoundly influence the behaviour of any regime which seeks to retain national power.

These issues inevitably pose the question of relationships between exploitation and economic progress, relationships which are conceptually and empirically complex. A dominant theme in the policy and academic literature of South Asia is that concentrations of political-economic power (the fusion is explicit) in the villages simultaneously exploit the poor and depress economic growth potential. In one important school of Marxian thought, 'semi-feudal' configurations in rural South Asia block the transition to technically progressive capitalism (cf. Harriss 1980: 20–4, *passim*). Official policy documents of the region take similar positions; the Indian Planning Commission's Task Force on Agrarian Relations (India 1973: 7), for example, termed exploitative relations of land tenure 'insurmountable hurdles in the path of the spread of modern technology and improved agricultural practices' (cf. India 1976: pts. II, XV; Pakistan 1959).

The argument of this essay is that concentrated political-economic power at the local level does indeed permit reproduction of systems in which a very large share of the surplus of direct producers is extracted by dominant classes, but that the question of *deployment* of that surplus, particularly over time, is more critical for explaining change in productivity than is the mode of appropriation of surplus. Concentrations of power locally exert a powerful influence on the distribution of the costs and benefits of economic change, and on the distribution of income (and thus the structure of aggregate demand), but do not seem to constitute 'insurmountable hurdles' to change in production techniques at the farm level. The classes which determine the deployment of economic resources locally exhibit remarkable variability, flexibility and adaptability in economic decision-making quite inconsistent with static determinist models; structure is by no means unimportant, but it is not determinative.

A second theme concerns the boundaries of the arena within which forces relevant to local economic decisions operate. Economic decisions made locally cannot be understood outside the context of national public policy and national economic forces; the self-sufficient village republics are no longer with us, assuming they once were. Likewise, the distinction between economic decisions and political factors blurs on the ground; local economic decision-making inevitably has a political component, even if quite indirect: does one make tenancy contracts with or without the assumption that security of tenure legislation and rental limits are and will remain a dead letter? Does one assume it is necessary, possible, or desirable to attach economically dependent clients to insure local social and political power? What assumptions are made about the security of private property or land ceilings or price supports over time? How is risk assessed in the face of continuous changes in public policy, selective or *pro forma* enforcement of specific policies and the local mobilization of opposing classes?

Just as economic decision-making cannot be adequately analysed solely in economic terms, nor even in terms of purely *local* economic and political forces, local political power cannot be analysed without reference to the articulation of local structures with the national political economy, with local organs of the state, and the integration of state and society at the village level. For example, the power implied by control of the local credit cooperative is contingent, with varying degrees of real and potential contingency. Will the Registrar of Cooperatives make a serious attempt to uncover discrepancies in the books? Will the district-level Central Cooperative Bank demand enforcement of quotas for small farmer credit set by the Reserve Bank of India? Can the cooperative resist supra-local demands to clear overdues and pressures to refrain from funding chronic defaulters (who may well be locally powerful people)? Will answers to these questions change as political patrons of local figures lose power at higher levels in the system?

The evaluation of purely structural impacts on productivity suggests that structure must be conceptualized in terms broader than either the village or purely local economic structures. To illustrate the types of interactions I conclude to be important, it is useful to consider the case of paddy production in Palghat district of Kerala, where I conducted field research in 1979–80. Decisions about hiring and firing labourers have been largely removed from the landowner's control through the Kerala Agricultural Workers Act of 1974, mandating priority of employment and 'permanency' for labourers traditionally employed on the land; wages and hours are set as well. Enforcement of these regulations varies, however, depending on the real and perceived unity of the labourers locally and the strength and activity of the local branch of the labourers' union. The legislation itself represents the historical aggregation of movements of the rural poor through electoral victories and organization of the Communist

Party. The result of purely political forces in the labour market has been real wage increases relative to productivity in Kerala greater than in any other area of India, at least through the mid-1970s (Bardhan 1973; IJAE, 1974: 83 ff.)

The decision framework of local landowners is profoundly influenced by this political configuration and public policy in Palghat district. For example, wage rates vary significantly (up to 50 per cent) across farms and across labourers in the same village area. Casual labourers are paid more on some farms because they lack permanency rights in law. Farmers pay more to 'loyal' workers, and provide them with consumption loans (sometimes interest-free), as an investment in labour peace and security of the supply of labour power. The composition of the wage payment (the relative proportions of paddy and cash) fluctuates with prices and procurement policy (usually to the disadvantage of the labourers). Some large farmers align with the left in the belief that they will not be subjected to strikes or pressure to comply fully with labour legislation. Union activists differentiate among farmers in pressing cases of illegal labour transactions (employing outside labourers, paying less than the minimum wage, etc.) in an attempt to preserve the tenuous loyalty of middle peasants, and some large landowners, to the left.

The reaction of farmers to this situation is both economic and extra-economic, local and supra-local. Farmers feel they cannot profitably pay double the wage of neighbouring states unless the state government raises procurement prices and subsidizes non-labour input costs. These demands are expressed through farmer organizations or political parties across the ideological spectrum. The state government has been sympathetic, but is constrained by the federal power structure and the resource constraints it imposes, and in turn presses Delhi for *regional* minimum wages and higher paddy prices, as well as increased fiscal flexibility to subsidize the cost of rice to consumers and costs of production to landowners. Farmers simultaneously attempt to shift cropping patterns to crops with less labour input and high returns—sugar cane and coconut, for example—but are in law constrained by the Land Utilization Act, the relative enforcement of which depends on both purely local connections with officials and state decisions about the priority of enforcement. Farmer decisions about redeployment of resources, including labour-displacing mechanization, are influenced not only by economic forces in the local and supra-local environment, but also by the perceived possibility of evading enforcement of various laws, and the likely strength of protest from the labourers and their organizations.

The questions and dynamics sketched above suggest that the search for a genuine political economy paradigm must be more than a simple borrowing of concepts, literature, and insights across traditional academic boundaries. Optimally, such a paradigm would develop the same structural unity as the processes it seeks to explain: the allocation of scarce values in societies. Such processes are not either economic or political, but simultaneously economic and political, though of variable immediacy and dominance in terms of the narrowly political or economic factors which come into play. In all processes of allocation of scarce values, structural asymmetries appear in the power to influence the magnitude and character of purely situational inequalities. The decision (or reflexive non-decision) to maintain, reproduce, or alter such asymmetries of power is profoundly political (though often not the subject of narrowly-defined politics) and yet at the same time determines the operational rules and context within which narrowly economic decisions are made.

I. *Production, Surplus, and Productivity: Capitalist and 'Feudal' Agrarian Relations*

Because land is the centre of an agrarian system, and control of land has traditionally coincided with both political and economic power in agrarian societies, it is tempting to centre our investigation of power–productivity connections on land tenure system-efficiency questions. Indeed, this has been the thrust of the conventional policy wisdom in South Asia: there exist configurations of landholding—in particular skewed distributions of holdings and the existence of share tenancy as a social organization of production—which depress productivity in the short term and vitiate the prospects for investment, technical change and growth over time.[1] Land reforms were thus seen as necessary both to improve economic efficiency and to dissolve

---

[1] This assumption is so pervasive that only a representative review is justifiable; e.g., Myrdal (1968: Part II, Ch. 22, *passim*); India (1973); Thorner (1956); Jannuzi (1974); Kotovsky (1964); India (1976: *Report of the National Commission on Agriculture*, Part XV). On international acceptance of the paradigm, UNFAO (1979); Dorner (1972); Eckholm (1979); Berry and Cline (1979); World Bank (1974).

the local oligopolies of powerful landholders which stood in the way of genuine social and political democracy; the conventional wisdom concludes, somewhat ironically, that precisely because concentrations of economic power (primarily land) in the villages permit and sustain concentrations of political power, genuine land reforms (and other redistributive measures) are politically and administratively at best problematic, at worst impossible.[2]

It is widely and properly recognized that there is a great deal of truth in this scenario, which appears in both planning documents and scholarly treatments of South Asia. The argument of this essay is that the land-centred model requires significant qualification and elaboration. Most importantly, in a modernizing agrarian sector, land control becomes less determinative of both political and economic power. Moreover, the rationalization and technical progress characteristic of production in contemporary rural South Asia, heavily subsidized and influenced by the state, call into question the conventional land-centred focus. The integration of the village polity and economy into a national political economy profoundly influences local decision-making about the deployment of economic resources and calls attention to the articulation of local and national power structures—economic and political—and the crucial role of national public policy. That farmers recognize this logic is manifest in the emergence of powerful supra-local movements in contemporary India aimed at influencing public policies toward agriculture to the benefit of landowners (e.g., see Rudolph and Rudolph, 1980 and this volume).

In the dominant policy literature in South Asia, particularly for the first two decades of independence, the connection between concentrated rural economic power ('feudal' land systems), concentrated political power, and a traditional, inefficient, and stagnant organization of production was explicit and pervasive. The arguments for land reform were both political and economic, and the two were closely linked. On the narrowly economic side of the position, size of holding was presumed a dominant determinant of economic behaviour. In one of the most important formulations, reinforced by the Farm Management Studies in India in the early 1960s, the yield/holding-size relation became central, with large farms widely perceived to be inefficient.[3]

[2] For a powerful paradigmatic statement of the position, AICC, *Report of the Congress Agrarian Reforms Committee* (1949); also, India (1968).

[3] For a review of political and planning documents, Herring (1983: Ch. 9).

The size-of-holding/yield literature is both extensive and vigorous, and has been succinctly reviewed elsewhere.[4] From our perspective, the most important outcome would seem to be the growing evidence that the prevailing critique of large holdings fails to understand the (albeit incomplete) transition to capitalist agriculture: large holdings, representing a particular kind of concentration of economic power, cannot be assumed to be characterized by relatively low yields.[5] Though it is difficult to cull from the literature a summary conclusion, it seems appropriate to try. Large holdings in the traditional setting—defined by the overwhelming dominance of land, labour and farm-produced inputs in the production mix—may very well have exhibited lower yields per acre compared to small farms, reflecting primarily the Chayanovian intensification of labour on small farms (stressed by Kautsky and Lenin) and the concentration of large farms in many areas on inferior land. As modern production relations and technology penetrated South Asian agriculture, the small farms began to lose their traditional yield advantage because of inferior access to on-farm surplus, inexpensive credit, technical information, risk-taking margin and improved capital works (private tubewells, for example).[6]

For a classic statement of the inter-linkages and determinism in the paradigm, Pakistan (1959). An excellent discussion of the Indian literature is P. C. Joshi (1975); also, S. C. Jha (1971).

[4] The major points in the Indian debate are reviewed in Rudra and Sen (1980); on Sri Lanka, Peiris (1975); on Pakistan, Herring (1979).

[5] Important critiques of the dominant model are Rudra (1968a, 1968b); Saini (1969); Khusro (1973); Patnaik (1972); Dasgupta (1980); Rudra and Sen (1980). The same dominant assumptions concerning size of holding and yield in Sri Lanka have been refuted in Peiris (1975). On Pakistan, Khan (1975, 1977). For an overview, Herring (1983: Ch. 9).

[6] The many problems in the traditional paradigm's evidentiary support, stressed by Rudra (1968a, b) and others might suggest that the size–yield relation has always been bogus. However, empirical studies are virtually unanimous in finding greater intensity of labour inputs on small farms; with traditional technology, the paradigmatic relationship would thus almost certainly hold. Technical change produces new dynamics, as foreshadowed in Rudra's (1968b) finding that yields were not inversely but directly related to size of holding in the agronomically-advanced farm management study districts of Punjab. Herring and Chaudhry (1974) found that Farm Management Studies in Pakistan corroborated the Indian results on size of holding–yield relationships, but noted that a later study from an intensively developed pilot project produced quite smaller differences. More recent (1972) data from Pakistan show no consistent relationship between size and yield, and great variation across crops (Herring, 1983: Ch. 9). Khan (1975,

Simultaneously, as the average size of holding declined, and more families were forced to seek off-farm employment to meet new cash needs and high dependency ratios, relative productivity (yield) on the smallest farms was probably affected negatively by increasing involvement in off-farm work, particularly in peak seasons. Small farms which cannot offer the family a subsistence income must inevitably suffer as opportunities are sought off the farm. Such tiny farms also lack the ability to sustain important capital items economically (a plough team, for example) and suffer from the uncertainties of draft power rental markets during peak demand.[7] At the same time, the advantages of larger farmers in terms of larger on-farm surpluses, connections, and local political power, become decisive as new inputs come to dominate determination of yields. Labour intensification on small farms may for some time compensate for the technical advantages and economic strength of large farms, particularly for crops especially sensitive to careful cultural practices and management, but the high yields per acre are produced with appallingly low labour productivity, implying serious opportunity costs from the societal level and extreme poverty, perhaps 'self-exploitation' as in Chayanov (1966), at the individual level.[8] The superior 'efficiency' of small farms cannot be taken for granted, precisely because changing technological parameters and statist involvement in agriculture render the local economic and political power of larger farmers capable of being translated into productive opportunities which surpass those of farmers lacking political and economic power.

The second important critique of traditional landholding systems in terms of productivity is the supposed connection between share tenancy and efficiency. Share tenancy as a social organization of

---

1977) argues that the size–yield relation is especially weak for wheat (almost entirely HYV) in Pakistan's Punjab (the most advanced region). Berry and Cline (1979: 108–9, 114) report that the traditional yield advantage of small farmers in India has weakened. These results reinforce the thrust of Patnaik (1972; 1979), Harriss (1979), and Rudra and Sen (1980). For an analysis similar to that in the text, ICSSR (1980: 14).

[7] Diseconomies of small scale were given great importance in the *Report of the Congress Agrarian Reforms Committee* (AICC, 1949); also Kanel (1967); Berry and Cline (1979: 134); on Kerala, Herring (1983: Ch. 9); more generally, Khusro (1973). Predictably, the relationship varies with cropping pattern: Bharadwaj (1974); Khan (1977).

[8] For application of the Chayanovian model to India, Banaji (1976); a withering critique of Chayanov, which does not affect the text, is Patnaik (1979).

production (often termed 'feudal') has been pronounced inimical to high yields and technical progress. The critique of tenancy on efficiency grounds was articulated with the critique of concentration of land ownership, as large farms utilizing traditional technology tended to be operated through leasing arrangements of various kinds (though it was less frequently recognized that in fact leasing was widely prevalent among small owners as well).

Yet empirical support for the inefficiency argument, derived from the logic of Adam Smith and the marginalist economics of Alfred Marshall, is notably scarce; there is a great deal of evidence that share tenancy in at least some contexts in South Asia is compatible with technical change and relatively high yields.[9] The reason would again seem to involve Chayanovian labour intensification on small farms, as well as landlord power to choose diligent tenants and determine technical aspects of production and the power of at least some patron landlords to serve as brokers to obtain credit and other inputs for their client-tenants, in marked contrast to the difficulties

[9] For a discussion of 'Marshallian' and revisionist positions on share tenancy, Bell (1977). Studies which find no yield differences between share-cropped and owner-operated farms, or higher yields on share-cropped farms, include Chakravarty and Rudra (1973); Dwivedi and Rudra (1973); Newbery (1975, relying on Vyas); ARTI (1975); Chadha (1978); Herring (1978); Harriss (1979); Berry and Cline (1979: 115, 175). Bell (1977), in contrast to Dwivedi and Rudra (1973), found that tenants who also owned some land conformed more to neo-classical predictions, compared to pure *bataidars*. Bell's limited findings suggest that the existence of alternative economic opportunities is an important determinant of management practices on tenant farms. The existence of relatively high yields on tenanted farms does not mean that share tenancy is optimally efficient, but that landlord power along a number of dimensions and Chayanovian labour intensification (recognized by John Stuart Mill, who noted that share tenants under 'the whip of hunger' could be very productive) may result in relatively high levels of extraction of surplus from the land; there is no reason to believe that rentiers will be optimally efficient in choosing investment and consumption strategies from a social point of view (cf. India 1976: II, 43). There is evidence that in Pakistan productive investment per acre on tenanted land falls far below that on owner-operated land, despite the technical innovations of sections of the rentier class (Herring 1983: Ch. 9), suggesting that tenurial disincentives are more inimical to long-term 'efficiency' (cf. Bell in Chenery *et al.* 1974: 131). Empirical studies often mistakenly aggregate leases, at-will share tenancies, etc., and blur the distinction between 'capitalist tenancy' or 'reverse tenancy' and peasant tenancy (ICSSR, 2980: 22); indeed, tenancy is concentrated· in pockets in both the advanced and most backward states of India; in Pakistan, some of the largest farm operators take land on share leases (Herring 1979), illustrating again the interpenetration of modern and traditional social organizations.

of patronless small farmers in a context of scarcity and meagre farm surplus (Herring 1978). Once a system of production is conceptualized as a network of relations of power, it becomes obvious that the power of landlords *vis-à-vis* tenants and *vis-à-vis* sources of economic resources and political connections may create production possibilities on tenanted lands quite superior to those on the lands of patronless poor peasants; whether or not landlords will utilize such power to maximize production remains an empirical question, with answers heavily dependent on the perceived opportunity structures facing landlords locally and psychological variables about which we know very little: there is puzzling variation from farm to farm within similar opportunity and power structures, suggesting that objective functions of decision-makers cannot be assumed *a priori* but present difficult empirical and theoretical questions.

In the discussion thus far, I have accepted yield (output per acre) as an appropriate measure of productivity, as is conventional, but the analysis has suggested that other considerations are central to the evaluation of agrarian configurations. Two of these considerations are returns to factors of production other than land and the size and disposition of the economic surplus on the farm. The seemingly straightforward and scientific concept of productivity has created considerable confusion in the inquiries under discussion. Productivity of what? Productivity is a ratio—output of something per unit of something else. A core issue in the long intellectual and political debates over land reform has been the contention that certain agrarian structures are obstacles to increasing agricultural productivity. Not only is the empirical case tangled, as is well known, but, as is less frequently recognized, the notion of productivity itself is conceptually problematic. The conventional *economic* argument for land reform accepts productivity per unit of land (yield) as the appropriate criterion of efficiency and thus argues for the breakup of large estates in favour of small family farms (Dorner 1972; Berry and Cline 1979). But if we reverse the coin, and ask about productivity per unit of labour, exactly the same data which demonstrate the superiority ('efficiency') of small farms on economic grounds demonstrate the superiority of large farms.[10]

The size of holding and efficiency question is of course much more complicated than the two-factor static comparison presented here,

[10] Patnaik (1972) has buttressed this argument, made by Lenin (1938: Vol. XII), utilizing data from Indian large farms. Also, Patnaik (1979).

but the issue raised is central to any discussion of productivity. The relative 'efficiency' of large farms and small farms differs dramatically when we move from the criterion of yield to the criterion of labour productivity or to alternative criteria such as output per unit of foreign exchange consumed or non-renewable energy expended. There is thus inherent within any serious discussion of productivity a prior normative question of efficiency: which norms are appropriate?[11] This question assumes added significance because the traditional policy prescription—maximizing returns to the scarce factor of production, or land in this case—may divert attention from increasing the productivity of relatively abundant resources such as labour that are a potential source of capital formation which enhances the productivity of scarce land and water resources (through village-level infrastructure development, for example).[12] It is thus important to conceptualize productivity in broader terms than is frequently done, though to do so is admittedly to present complex analytical problems.

The conventional conceptualization of productivity also focuses attention only on those economic resources actually employed in production, whereas the evaluation of an agrarian system economically must include consideration of the potential production forgone by the underutilization of available resources. For example, extensive mechanization on fairly large holdings combined with biochemically advanced production technology may appear quite efficient in terms of productivity per acre and per labour hour and yet may contribute to the underutilization of the total work force locally available and thus forgo potential production and capital formation.[13] The tradi-

[11] There is no single measure of efficiency which is unexceptionable; it will not do to utilize output per unit of total cost, as there are significant, and unsettled, normative issues in cost accounting in peasant agriculture particularly because of the problematic treatment of imputed values of owned land and family labour. The Farm Management Studies in India utilize four measures of cost; farms which appear efficient by criteria including imputed values for non-purchased inputs appear relatively inefficient when only incurred costs are measured. Small farm 'efficiency' is significantly reduced when input–output ratios include calculation of imputed costs, but there are serious objections to imputing market values to family labour and 'rent' on peasant farms: Herring (1983: Ch. 9); Rudra and Sen (1980); C. T. Kurien (1980a); Shivakumar (1980).

[12] An important statement of the policy implication is ICSSR (1980: 49–60); for an intriguing speculative piece, Hewavitharana (1974).

[13] See Bartsch (1973); ICSSR (1980: 20); Binswanger (1978); C. H. H. Rao (1975); Herring and Kennedy (1979); Berry and Cline (1979: 138).

tional argument in favour of small farms has indeed been on employment grounds, but the characteristic labour intensity of the 'family labour farm' coexists with extremely low returns to the labour of small farmers and a marked inability to mobilize labour resources to improve the infrastructure of village agriculture. It is imperative that empirical investigations of the relationship between local power configurations and productivity define clearly and defend the norm of efficiency employed and, optimally, specify the productivity consequences in the broadest possible framework, including the social opportunity costs of underutilization of resources.

Finally, because of the extensive connections between local power holders and the local agencies of the state, and because of the different distributive implications of various developmental strategies/ideologies expressed by various regimes, the productivity (and opportunity costs) of resources—material, technical, financial, human —deployed by the state must be assessed in conjunction with analysis of local power structures. The examples which appear later—credit, irrigation water, extension information—raise these questions concretely.

A second dimension in conceptualizing productivity is static versus dynamic, or efficiency (in some sense) in the short term versus growth in the productivity of various resources over time. An especially useful theoretical framework is that of Paul Baran (1957): the critical question for understanding changes in productivity over time concerns the aggregate level and mode of utilization of the economic surplus. There has been great controversy over the concept of economic surplus, and Baran was frustratingly imprecise and inconsistent in his usage.[14] But the core notion is quite simple: after the necessary forces and means of production have been reproduced, how much remains and what is done with it? In a traditional peasant economy, the concept is readily operationalized: after the deductions from a given season's harvest for maintaining the human and animal labour power which makes production possible, after putting away produce for seed and working capital for the next crop, replacement, repair and depreciation of implements and productive infrastructure, how large a pile of grain is left? How the economic surplus is appropriated, and by whom, reflects the social organization of production, and thus the structure of power locally and nationally. After

[14] For critique and discussion, Barclay and Stengal (1976). On uses of the concept in peasant societies, Keyder (1975); Wolf (1966).

necessary expenditures for the reproduction of peasant society, *qua* peasant society, are incurred, what happens to the rest?

The question of level and utilization of the economic surplus is relevant from both the individual and aggregate perspectives. At the individual farm level, the various arguments against 'feudal', 'semi-feudal', or various extortionate production relations have been that the actual cultivator is deprived both of the necessary quantum of surplus resources and the incentive to invest whatever surplus there is by onerous rental (or other) exactions, and simultaneously produces with so little margin for error that risk-taking capacity is unnecessarily constrained. The individual cultivator thus lacks both ability and incentive to improve the production process.[15] At the aggregate level, the total available economic surplus is kept low by the relatively stagnant techniques of production and even that low level of surplus is utilized in ways which are not favourable to agricultural growth because of the social character and position in the production process of the appropriating elites—landlords, intermediaries, usurers, the state.[16]

Though there are cases which fit this model, and in such cases the productivity consequences are negative and severe, the more difficult empirical and theoretical questions concern the dynamics of change in such systems. Indeed, recent empirical work on European feudalism suggests that the common characterization in terms of economic stagnation requires serious revision (Anderson 1974a, b). For explaining change, it remains critical to ask of each agrarian system:

---

[15] For classic statements, Myrdal (1968: Vol. II, Ch. 22); Thorner (1956); for a succinct review of the mode of production argument and appropriate conclusion, ICSSR (1980); a broader review is Harriss (1980).

[16] It is possible to include behavioural proclivities of dominant classes in the *definition* of the mode of production, as powerfully argued by Genovese (1965). This inclusion is persuasive because economic power must be socially reproduced and legitimated, often necessitating clientelist distributive expenditures, lavish consumption, funding of collective rituals, and so on. Moreover, the internalized norms of elites reflect the dominant ideology of the society they rule. Yet so broad a conceptualization leaves change over time difficult to explain and tends toward tautology: if part of the definition of 'semi-feudal' production relations were to be disinclination of dominant classes to invest in land improvement or technical change, the absence of those activities would indeed be a direct function of the mode of production, but only via a circular definitional route. For examples of the frittering away of the agricultural surplus by pre-capitalist landed elites in South Asia, Metcalf (1979) and Wadhwa (1978); the National Commission on Agriculture (India 1976: II, 38) concludes rightly that the tendency is still evident.

how much surplus is generated? Who appropriates what share of the surplus? How is the appropriated surplus deployed? What incentive structure faces those who make the actual decisions about deployment of resources?

These questions are empirical and suggest that any *a priori* characterization of agrarian societies or structures as 'feudal' or 'capitalist' is unlikely to explain very much at all. The vigorous debate waged in India over mode of production in agriculture illustrates above all else the futility of cognitivist positing of universal typologies as explanatory devices.[17] As Marx himself emphasized, in the early stages of the growth of capitalism, capital operates through the existing social organization of production (the 'formal' subsumption of labour).[18] It is too often forgotten that bonded labour was an important form in the early industrial revolution in England or that slave labour was compatible with capitalist plantation enclaves in the colonial world (cf. Harriss 1980: 16). The point is that various traditional forms of labour process may be integrated into a dynamic capitalist agriculture just as free wage labour appeared in antiquity and throughout the feudal period in Europe (Anderson 1974a). Indeed, technical progress in agriculture may favour the strengthening or re-emergence of traditional forms; because of the higher level of working capital at risk, and the increased importance of a timely labour supply, landowners find it prudent to attach a secure labour force, whether through a credit–debt nexus or through letting out tiny share-cropping plots (e.g., Thorner 1967: 230–1).

Production in contemporary rural South Asia exhibits extensive evidence of interpenetration of social and technical organizations of production characteristic of modern capitalism with pre-capitalist relations of production;[19] the mode of surplus appropriation must

[17] Bhaduri's (1973) influential treatment is illustrative of problems in static determinist explanations for the absence of dynamism under 'semi-feudalism'. Bhaduri emphasizes inappropriately the threat to landlords of productivity increases, ignoring the empirically-verified possibility of rearranging modes of surplus extraction at a higher level of production (extortionate charges for tractor hire, tubewell water, etc.), and purely technical/agro-economic barriers to technical change (e.g., Nadkarni and Deshpande, 1979). Cf. Newbery (1975); Harriss (1980: 24; 1982).

[18] For discussion of this distinction in the Indian context, Mundle (1979: Ch. 4); Shah (1980); Harriss (1980: 5, 16, *passim*).

[19] Bardhan and Rudra (1978) demonstrate such interpenetration with survey

then be clearly distinguished from the deployment of the surplus. Surplus from rural labour may be appropriated through share-cropping, usury, unequal market exchanges, bonded or casual wage labour arrangements; the productivity implications are indeterminate, or at least not determined by the form of appropriation: there is evidence of both traditional and modern modes of appropriation being articulated with both productive and non-productive deployment of the surplus, largely dependent on the structure of opportunities locally.[20] Indeed, it is (at least theoretically) conceivable that extreme concentration and inequality of economic power (and the resulting dependence and inability of underclasses to raise their share of the total product), as manifest in usury, debt-bondage, or rack-renting, permit the extraction of so much surplus per unit of production as to facilitate high rates of investment and growth, should the appropriating classes be so inclined (or induced or compelled). In Marxian terms, high levels of extraction of absolute surplus value are not necessarily an obstacle to, and may be a facilitative or necessary condition for, technical change which eventually raises the level of relative surplus value extraction.

---

data from eastern India, supposedly the homeland of stagnant 'semi-feudalism'. Specifically, share-cropping and unpaid labour (*begar*) appear in conjunction with technically progressive agriculture and are not more prevalent in technically backward villages (cf. Chopra, 1982: 40–1). Share tenancy has been adapted to technical innovation through cost-sharing arrangements. The largest landowners in Pakistan, even in traditionally-regarded 'feudal' areas such as Sind, utilize modern technology in agriculture to the same extent as, or greater extent than, other categories of farmers (Herring 1979); compare Alavi (1976). Large owners who mechanize frequently do not evict all their tenants but reduce the size of holding below the prevailing level to assure an attached labour force (Alavi 1971; Herring and Kennedy 1979). Pakistani 'feudals' (large rentier landlords) have been extraordinarily active, even dominant, in modern institutional credit markets (see text). Attached and 'serf' labour was utilized to reclaim and develop the Kuttanad paddies in Kerala, historically a centre of dynamic capitalism (Pillai and Panikar 1965), and tenancy has long been associated with capitalist development in the state (Varghese 1970). For evidence of the interpenetration of forms suggested here in Africa and Latin America, Shah (1980); Harriss (1980).

[20] Mundle (1979: Ch. 5) argues that bonded labour in Palamau district, Bihar, simultaneously assures a labour supply during peak demand seasons and, most importantly, represents a higher rate of return on whatever investable surplus is available when compared to technically progressive alternatives which are beyond the *maliks'* resources. The same argument is made concerning usury in the 'semi-feudalist' school of thought, but there is nothing 'feudal' about maximizing return on investment.

In more concrete terms, the Pakistani *wadera* may use surplus extracted from generations of share tenants to purchase a tubewell and tractor or to buy into a local cinema, finance a political campaign, or increase his personal stock of surplus through commodity speculation or moneylending. His neighbouring *wadera*, employing wage labour rather than share tenants, faces exactly the same options. Their decision framework is determined more by the state's policies regarding input and output pricing, cost and terms of credit, taxation, and by the perceived necessity, advantages or possibility of attaching a local client network, as well as by locally-variable technical and agronomic problems in innovation, than by the mode of appropriation of surplus. Empirically, the large rentier landlords of Pakistan, the 'feudals' of planning documents and public rhetoric, have been among the major recipients of institutional credit and have, compared to all other agrarian classes, financed a higher percentage of their (heavily subsidized) on-farm investments—prominently including tractors, tubewells, and fertilizers—from modern institutional sources.[21]

The most serious objection to the line of analysis argued above is that social formations must be reproduced over time, necessitating diversion of the surplus into non-productive 'investments' in maintaining local power, ranging from consumption loans to collective social rituals to the hire of *goondas* or enforcers. This is a valid argument, expressed forcefully by Ashok Rudra (1980, and this volume). However, a number of such expenditures (usurious or interest-free consumption loans, gifts, food distribution at festivals) may usefully be considered functional requisites for the reproduction of labour power, bringing the consumption of direct producers up to a minimum, locally-defined, threshold. Certainly the large farmers of Palghat district, where I recently worked, understood that labourers in previous decades could not have survived in the absence of such payments. When wages were raised by union activities and by law, most of the farmers withdrew supplemental payments, loans, and gifts, except in the cases of especially loyal or destitute labourers.

---

[21] In a nation-wide sample survey of nearly 100,000 rural households, of the large rentiers (individually owning more than 50 acres each) who borrowed in agriculture, 36.5 per cent received institutional credit (compared to 1.0 per cent of the small tenants), and such sources supplied 61.5 per cent of the total credit needs of these borrowers (compared to 0.4 per cent in the case of small tenants). Pakistan (1974); my calculations.

These expenditures by dominant elites may indeed be investments in local social power (cf. Harriss 1982), but analytically are less a part of the surplus than a necessary part of the cost of reproducing labour power. As to other traditional non-productive expenditures, it would be interesting to know whether the percentage of surplus so consumed is as great as that consumed by anti-trust lawyers, industrial spies, plant security guards, public relations personnel, corporate philanthropy and the like under industrial capitalism. Every social system must be reproduced over time through expenditures which are not directly productive. There is a curious assumption in much of the literature that capitalism somehow marks the end of irrational or unproductive deployment of the economic surplus.

But the more fundamental problem is to explain changes in non-productive expenditures over time. Patron–client ties may become economically unattractive for local elites as the opportunity costs of capital rise with technical change and market development and new consumption possibilities appear. Likewise, with increasing state penetration and political integration, local elites may perceive that investment in supra-local politics is more conducive to protecting their interests than expenditure on local patronage functions, relying instead on economic dependence and desperation (and the local police) to maintain local power. Moreover, with greater politicization of subordinate classes, it may prove difficult to purchase loyalty and quiescence at any price, as dependents seek security through political action and pressure for policy implementation. When asked why he no longer maintained a large following in the village one aristocratic landowner in Palghat told me simply: 'Those days are past.'

The functionalist argument that social formations necessitate expenditures for their reproduction thus contains important insights into the disposition of the surplus at a given time, but provides no explanation for redeployment of the surplus and change over time. The work of Epstein (1962) illustrates how local resistance to innovation varies from village to village, and how technical change may prompt rearrangements of the social organization of production. Broader theory about the differential inertial resistance to change, and differential adaptation, can be produced only through patient aggregation of local studies; the South Asian region offers examples of a wide range of integration of new techniques with traditional social organizations of production, a range incompatible with prevalent deductivist notions of inevitable characteristic dynamics of generic structural configurations.

Capitalism in agriculture may thus not have the liberating effects, in either social or economic terms, that both supporters and detractors claim, nor the unambiguous or uniform political consequences frequently posited.[22] Moreover, there seems to be evidence that at least some configurations of concentrated economic power in pre-capitalist, traditional organizations of production, with concomitant control of subordinate classes bordering on the 'feudal' (i.e., control which is diffuse, multiplex, personalistic, sometimes extra-legal),[23] are amenable to the adoption of technical change in agriculture which increases productivity of both land and labour, particularly when the state subsidizes the process extensively and substantially. The extraordinary technical progress in rural West Pakistan in the 1960s, particularly in the irrigated tracts, illustrates the theoretical potentiality concretely.[24]

This final point raises a critical issue in the local power–productivity question: what does the state do with its share of the economic surplus? Since the state's share of the surplus in South Asian agriculture is typically small (at least directly) and subsidies to 'progressive farmers' rather large,[25] we are directed to look beyond the

[22] Much of the green-revolution-turns-red literature misunderstood both technical change in agriculture and the social process of agrarian radicalism. For relatively 'hard' statements characteristic of the genre, Cleaver (1973), Sharma (1973); for a muted and more complex statement, Frankel (1972). A useful review of the literature is Selnick (1978).

[23] For insightful views of the dynamics of economic dependency and its extra-economic consequences, Alavi (1971), Ahmad (1977).

[24] Though they disagree with each other, both Alavi (1976) and Burki (1976) document the process. On the subsidies involved, Kaneda (1969). For evidence that share tenants in Pakistan participate effectively in 'green revolution' technological innovation, Azam (1973); in South Asia more broadly, Herring (1983: Ch. 9; 1978) reports evidence of yields on tenanted farms equalling or surpassing those on owner-operated farms of a comparable size in some areas and on some crops. For a theoretical treatment of this outcome, Ghose and Saith (1976); Hsiao (1975).

[25] This point applies only to direct taxation and direct subsidies; a proper analysis would consider inter-sectoral terms of trade and credit flows, etc., presenting severe conceptual and technical problems. On the size and cooptation of irrigation and power subsidies and state losses in India, Minhas (1974: 120–3); India (1976: XII, 5, 9, 11–25). Even seemingly direct subsidies are difficult to evaluate in class-differentiated terms. For example, such programmes as Food for Work and Maharashtra's Employment Guarantee Scheme appear to sub-

agricultural sector, whatever its internal structure, and toward the broader political economy into which agriculture is integrated. How do local power structures articulate with the national political economy and national public policy?

Contrary to a great deal of received theory, there does not seem to be much evidence that traditional social organizations of production mandate agricultural stagnation. This does not mean that some structures of economic and political power locally are not immediate obstacles to productive investment, as will be explained later, but that at the farm level and the aggregate level the question of change over time is rooted in the size and disposition of the economic surplus in interaction with state policies toward agriculture and the resulting opportunity structure as perceived by those classes which command the lion's share of the surplus. These questions are then empirical and cannot be settled at the theoretical level. Moreover, evaluation of the economic consequences of local configurations of power— economic or political—should optimally move beyond traditional unidimensional standards such as yield, despite the fact that most of our existing literature and data base make such analysis problematic. A broader developmental perspective would focus on the forgone productivity of underutilized resources and take as a central question the productivity, and opportunity costs, of each unit of social surplus deployed by the state in agriculture. It is from this final question that we turn to discussion of the well-documented ability of locally-dominant elites to divert and coopt developmental resources.

II. *Economic and Political Power, Structural and Conjunctural*

Two kinds of economic power locally are of analytical importance. First, and decisive from the perspective of productivity, is the power to decide the deployment of economic resources in the production process, both in the short run and over time. Typically, such power

sidize the rural poor, and do so, but simultaneously create capital works which disproportionately benefit landowners and lower the social reproduction costs of labour by subsidizing the subsistence of local labourers who remain available to capital when needed, but are supported by the state when not needed. The need for more sophisticated inter-sectoral transfer analysis should not, however, obscure the intra-sectoral class-differentiated impact of macro-policy, a shortcoming in Dandekar's (1977) analysis.

is not evenly distributed, but is concentrated in patterns which vary widely across regions and ecological-tenurial systems. Command of the economic resources of a community may be said to constitute the definition of a dominant class, but it is important to emphasize that such classes in South Asian agriculture are complicated in their composition, characteristics and behavioural tendencies by nexuses and overlays with class-differentiated social groupings such as caste or faction.[26] The economic power of locally-dominant classes is not absolute, but is fundamentally and differentially affected by (*a*) state policies (minimum wage laws, tenancy legislation, land use restrictions, etc.); (*b*) the economic and political power of subordinate classes, which is in turn heavily influenced by demographic, organizational and resource-endowment variations regionally; (*c*) variable economic forces in the environment (prices of inputs and output, interest rates, access to credit, etc.) which are in turn profoundly affected by policies of (especially) the national state and the local political/administrative apparatus; (*d*) local norms of custom and legitimacy and their relative resistance to change (cf. Rudra 1980; Harriss 1982).

Power to make decisions about deployment of resources in production and their redeployment over time can be termed economic power; such power has both a structural component (property institutions and class configuration, or more broadly the mode of production) and a conjunctural component (state policies, shifts in macro-economic forces, collective action by opposition classes).

There is a second kind of economic power quite separable from the power to deploy resources: the power to extract economic surplus from production. Whatever the level of production, dominant classes vary in the mode of extraction of surplus and the share extracted from total production (cf. Desai 1980). To take the simplest example, landlords in Bangladesh and parts of Pakistan have sufficient economic power to appropriate more than one-half of the gross produce on share-cropped land whereas landlords in other parts of the subcontinent (Kerala, for example) have in recent times been able to obtain a much smaller share. Such differences also appear among individual landlords (the absentee versus Thorner's 'village oligarch' being one obvious example) according to a logic which does not seem to be entirely dependent on land productivity but has a great deal

[26] For a provocative collection of empirical and theoretical studies, see EPW (1979: XIV, 7–8); also Béteille (1974); Nair (1979).

218   RONALD J. HERRING

to do with demographic pressures, the caste composition of the
tenantry, levels of peasant organization, the norms of patron–client
systems and, of course, public policy.

Dominant economic classes thus vary significantly in their power
to extract and deploy economic surplus, and should be so differentiated in empirical investigations of power–productivity interactions.
But not all deployment of economic resources is determined by
access to a locally-generated surplus. Resources also flow from the
state (about one-third of all farm credit in India is now supplied
through heavily subsidized institutional channels) and other external
flows (professional income, emigrant remittances, etc.). Access to
state-supplied economic resources is heavily dependent on state
policy at the national level and the narrowly political power of
dominant economic classes locally as well as the structural articulation of those levels of power through specific institutions and their
operational rules.

The extent to which dominant economic classes are able to rule
locally is variable both over time and across variations in local political configurations of class and group mobilization, though it is by
now well established that such classes have both retained the lion's
share of local political power and have appropriated a disproportionate share of externally-supplied development resources, both
material and non-material, locally.[27] But it is increasingly obvious
that the direct translation of economic power into political power
is by no means automatic. Though making numbers count is certainly not as unproblematic as simplistic democratic theory would
suggest (e.g., Michie 1979), the mobilization of intermediate, backward, and even depressed classes to challenge the power of eco-
nomically-dominant classes is an important political phenomenon
across the subcontinent, though marked by great unevenness over
time and geography.[28] Among the various factors which retard such

[27] The phenomenon is by now so well established by official reports and
scholarly treatments that extensive documentation serves no purpose: e.g., ICSSR
(1980: 51, *passim*). For treatments with numerous examples, Rosenthal (1977),
Hale (1978). An insightful analysis of the dynamics in Pakistan is Gotsch (1971).
Béteille (1974) notes that progressive farmers have become 'ambidextrous', able
to manipulate both traditional and modern institutions to their advantage. Raj
Krishna (1979: 15–16) argues that misappropriation of the huge sums allocated
to rural development 'may aggravate rural inequality instead of alleviating it'.
For discussion of the phenomenon cross-culturally, UNRISD (1974).

[28] See, e.g., Blair (1980); Rudolph and Rudolph (1980); Rajendran (1974);
Saradamoni (1980).

challenges, local concentrations of economic power—and their expression in economic dependency and patron–client ties to subordinate classes—figure dominantly, as do factors such as those
Alavi (1973) terms 'primordial loyalties'.

The analytical distinction between political and economic power
should not obscure the fundamental point of political economy: the
power of some classes to appropriate the surplus directly produced
by other classes is constituted, guaranteed, enforced and modified
by the political power of the state—law, courts, police, and bureaucracy. Production (and distribution) take place in an institutional
framework of property relations and mechanisms to sustain those
property relations. It would be wrong to ignore the significant variations which are possible within a given political economy—police
have allowed labourers to harvest crops forcibly under left front
regimes in Kerala and West Bengal, for example—but every economic system, and its characteristic pattern of property and exchange
institutions, is produced by long-term political evolution and variable
expressions of state political power.

Though the notions of power sketched above are relatively simple
and commonly used, implicitly or explicitly, it seems that social
scientists have paid too little attention to problems of recognizing
and explicating power structures of agrarian systems. If power is the
demonstrated ability to command preferred outcomes, then the
fundamental manifestation of power in an agrarian system is ability
to appropriate and direct the utilization of the agricultural surplus
over time; all production relations are in this sense power relations.
But finer distinctions are obviously necessary: a landlord has power
over a tenant because he can deprive him of access to the means of
production; a moneylender's power is less decisive, and often must
be fortified by threats of violence, enforcers, or promises of further
loans or emergency assistance. The potential economic power of subordinate classes stems from the dependence of appropriating classes
on the supply of human labour for production, though exercising
that power requires concerted action which is typically contrary to
the short-term interests of individuals in obtaining some economic
security in the face of unequal bargaining power and widespread
insecurity. Where collective power of subordinate classes is exercised,
or even threatened, the decision frame of dominant classes is significantly altered.

In the analysis of public policy, both as it reflects and alters the
rural power structure, it is important to distinguish between struc-

tural power and instrumental-conjunctural power. Structural power includes the ability to benefit both disproportionately and in qualitatively different ways because of position in a system of property relations sanctioned by the legal system of the state and ultimately guaranteed by state power. That landlords in Pakistan are able to extract continuously between one-half and three-fourths of the gross product of share tenants is a manifestation of structural power. That state subsidies disproportionately flow to those who disproportionately control the agricultural means of production is a manifestation of structural power in conjunction with a particularistic set of state policies, which in turn are significantly influenced by the structural power of dominant classes nationally and locally.

Instrumental power is conjunctural; within a given structure of power, the particular combination of political forces varies over time and space, determined by quite particularistic variables. That one faction has taken control of the local cooperative society at the expense of another is a purely conjunctural phenomenon; that neither faction is headed by a landless labourer is indicative of the structural position of landless labourers, but is not determined by that structure. Indeed, the most important characteristic of conjunctural forces is their mutability; power is a relational and oppositional phenomenon, neither given *a priori* nor static. The process of acquiring, exercising, and maintaining power and privilege gives rise to challenges to the existing pattern, with consequent tension and change over time. While structures select, constrain, and shape forms and outcomes of political conflict, structure cannot be given the preponderant explanatory power characteristic of very 'hard' determinist positions.[29]

Political challenges to power structures, particularly where intense and prolonged, in turn have productivity consequences, most of which appear to be negative in both the long and short terms. Daniel Thorner (1967: 236) argued that the 'embittered, indeed poisoned, relations' between land and labour in Thanjavur hindered production. Labourers who collectively threaten the prerogatives of landed property quite naturally discourage landowners from further investment on the land (with the obvious exception of labour-substituting technical change). Class conflict results in crop losses and discourages

---

[29] A structuralist position which is sensitive to these problems, but distinctly determinist, is Gutelman (1974). Paige (1975) presents a 'hard' structural determinist model. For a useful discussion of modes of structural determination, similar to that of the text, Wright (1978).

labour-intensive investment by landowners. A configuration resembling the industrial pattern of intermittent lockouts and strikes has evolved in some sections of Kerala where the labourers are relatively well-organized, numerically superior, and connected to powerful political elites organizationally (Mencher 1978). My fieldwork in one of these areas in 1980 (Palghat district) uncovered a number of production-decreasing aspects of an ongoing intermittent class conflict as acknowledged by both labourers and owners: farmers leaving land fallow 'to teach the labourers a lesson', conversion of paddy lands (illegally) to less labour-intensive crops (primarily coconut), job-actions at critical harvest periods resulting in crop losses, reduction in quality of labour power to penalize farmers paying less than the minimum wage, etc. These class conflicts have become institutionalized, rather than resolved, as neither class possesses the political or economic power to win decisively, and because governing elites have an interest in promoting *ad hoc* compromises. A stalemated class conflict with negative productivity implications thus becomes one possible outcome in an agrarian system characterized by concentrated economic and political power which over time loses legitimacy and hegemony.[30]

Similar negative productivity consequences seem likely to flow from state policies designed to redress delegitimized aspects or consequences of concentrations of political-economic power. Perhaps the most frequent state response to agitations (or perceived threats of agitation) by agrarian underclasses for a larger and more secure share of the agricultural surplus has been land reforms. Land reforms then redirect the energies of landowners toward concealment and resistance rather than investment and accumulation, at least where the measures are serious rather than symbolic (cf. Sri Lanka 1975: 16–17; Berry and Cline 1979: 136). Indeed, an argument can be made that the brute power of capital, as described by Marx in the nineteenth century, is its great strength and redeeming value; capital shackled by restrictive regulations and denied the security and

---

[30] For an insightful treatment of how patrons lose legitimacy and patron–client networks break down, Scott and Kerkvliet (1973). For an argument complementary to that in the text, Joshi (1980). Alexander (1978: 47, 50) presents interview data from Kuttanad and Thanjavur which contradict the argument in the text: large farmers reported that class conflict was not a constraint on investment. Unless the farmers had in mind labour-displacing investment, Alexander's results puzzle me. The text is not merely a repetition of the lament of capital in opposing labour organization, but reflects the judgment of labourers as well.

stability necessary for long-range planning becomes anaemic and vacillating, losing its vitality while retaining much of its cruelty.

Class conflicts, whether as structural potential or seasonal reality, thus have important productivity consequences, and underline the importance of recognizing the difficulty of delineating power empirically in agrarian systems. Instrumental power tends to be issue-oriented, thus situational, or institutional, and thus observable: e.g., what classes or groups control the primary credit cooperative society? When their control is challenged, who wins? The more pervasive, and important, power imbalances are structural and not directly observable; some classes get what they want and need from the system simply because of their position in the economic structure, without having to make a fuss politically—large landowners can obtain large amounts of subsidized farm capital without active intervention because of the working rules of institutions which distribute boons. To receive comparable benefits, small owners or tenants must actively seek concessions or changes in the working rules. Too often these concessions are seen as evidence of the *power* of such groups, obscuring the fact that dominant classes obtain the same results without active politicking or pressure.

A second methodological and conceptual problem of structural power relations is the deference and quiescence of non-privileged groups. That agrarian underclasses frequently do not mobilize to press demands, or even step forward to accept legislated benefits, must be seen in the context of a structure of local power which (*a*) facilitates the victory of superior classes in both informal and formal-legal arenas should a challenge be mounted, thus making resistance or opposition potentially futile and irrational; (*b*) is multi-faceted and thus capable of depriving recalcitrants on one dimension what they gain on another.[31] Both aspects of structural power have been evident in the quiescence of tenants in tenure reform, and thus one of the causes of the failure of tenure reform in the region

[31] A currently important model in economic theory—'interlinkage of markets' —is another way of describing what anthropologists and rural sociologists have analysed in terms of the economic bases of patron–client networks and what Karl Polanyi (1944) meant by describing economic relations as 'embedded' in a broader and more complex network of social relations. The writings of Marx (1965) on pre-capitalist economic formations carry the same theme. For an insightful treatment of the structural power base of political dependence, Alavi (1971); on Rajasthan, Michie (1979); for south India, Harriss (1979); on Bengal, Harriss (1982). For a broader literature review, Bates (1977).

(Herring 1981; cf. Nair 1962). The central point is that the structure of power is not directly observable, in part because it would become observable only when challenged openly; potential challengers recognize very well that such challenges are likely to be futile or counter-productive because of well-known structural and conjunctural obstacles to effective opposition. Yet, narrowly-focused economic growth strategies which assume away the conflictual consequences of structural inequalities do so at risk of underestimating a significant productivity consideration.

III. *Productivity Consequences of Elite Domination*
of Public Resources

Power can be manifest in particularistic or class terms; if one large farmer obtains a loan for a tubewell at the expense of another because of kinship ties or political influence, there are no consequences for aggregate productivity unless, as is sometimes the case, boons secured on non-economic considerations are put to unproductive uses (there is a great deal of 'diversion' of state-subsidized credit).[32] But if the power distinctions and outcomes are systematically class-related, a different question arises. Do those, for example, who most *need* credit for productivity-increasing investment, short-term or long-term, find themselves denied access because of the superior power of larger farmers and locally powerful people?

Here the question of economic surplus is critical: poor peasants—share-croppers, very small holders—are unlikely to have the surplus farm income from current operations necessary to make significant developmental investments and indeed must often borrow simply to make ends meet and plant the next crop (e.g. Shivakumar 1980). For share-croppers this inadequacy directly relates to the exactions of landlords and thus the structural power of another class. For small owners, the inadequacy relates to the insufficient capital with which family labour is combined, a reflection of the skewed distribution of land and other assets. But whatever the causes, in those situations in which poor small farmers are denied credit needed to increase productivity in the long or short run, the net productivity consequences are negative *except* in those cases in which large owners

[32] My investigation of Agricultural Development Bank of Pakistan files and memos on chronic defaulters demonstrated a consistent pattern; for systematic studies, Bhat (1971); India (1965).

could not have afforded productivity-enhancing investment without the flow of institutional resources.

The productivity consequences of skewed credit distribution may extend beyond the moot point of whether investment on large farms or small farms is more desirable in narrow productivity terms. Resource insufficiency on small farms may at times be so severe as to cause disinvestment, as Mirza Shahjahan (1968) has demonstrated for Bangladesh. Moreover, there is evidence that, as one would expect, credit is a more serious constraint for small farmers than for large in adopting high-yielding varieties of wheat in Pakistan, leaving aside costlier items such as tubewells.[33] The fact that small farmers systematically pay higher interest rates on loans than do large farmers may indicate a higher marginal productivity of capital on small farms (which would be reasonable given relative labour intensity and yield differentials in some areas), but may as easily reflect the greater desperation of the poor and their narrow range of alternatives. These higher interest rates are directly related to inferior economic and political power, and thus greater dependence by weaker classes on non-institutional credit sources;[34] the result *may* be to depress investment on small farms by increasing costs above the likely return on investment, but alternatively may simply raise the average unit cost of production on small farms, aggravating the resource squeeze and enhancing the economic power of local classes with surplus resources.

[33] Punjab (1970), Tables 7 and 8. Whereas small farmers were more likely to cite lack of funds for not using fertilizer, large farmers were better able to finance fertilizer purchases from current income (Table 9) and, in addition, had easier access to institutional credit: 36.8 per cent of the farmers with more than 50 acres each utilized institutional credit, compared to 1.6 per cent of the 2.5–7.5 acre holders. Lowdermilk's (1972) study reinforces these conclusions. Similar credit constraints have been documented in Sri Lanka among small coconut producers (ARTI, 1977: 14–15).

[34] Herring (1977). For a convincing argument that official data understate interest rates paid by weaker agrarian classes, and evidence that high interest rates reflect greater dependence on non-institutional services, Kurup (1976). Ghatak (1975) found that interest rates paid in rural India were inversely proportional to income. The persistence of extremely high interest rates in rural Kerala (Kerala 1975) is noteworthy given the very extensive development of institutional credit in the State. On local elite domination of institutional credit flows, see Hale (1978), Ilaiah (1979), Desai (1979), Krishna (1979a), India (1978: 93), Reserve Bank of India (1969: Ch. 6, 7, pp. 173–6, 537), Pillai and Baks (1979: Ch. 15), Thorner (1968: 247), Harriss (1982).

The relative exclusion of the very bottom of the agrarian hierarchy from subsidized institutional credit in South Asia is well documented. Small farmers who own land have fared better, but have received far less credit relative to their needs and relative to their numbers than large farmers. But as I have argued elsewhere (Herring 1977), the explanation is only partly rooted in local power structures. Local elites in India have indeed tended to dominate primary credit societies (Thorner 1963) and maintain powerful links with official agencies which distribute *taccavi* loans; yet the skewed distribution patterns have persisted in areas where the rural poor are politically mobilized and represented.[35] Development strategies relying on market-determined distribution, social mythologies of 'progressive farmers' and 'hapless peasants', the internal dynamics of development bureaucracies, and planning ideologies of building on the best with trickle-down assumptions have all contributed to the skewed distribution of rural credit. Most importantly, despite two and a half decades of credit reform policies in India, allocation of institutional credit is still heavily dependent on and linked to value of assets owned, reproducing and reinforcing the existing skewed distribution of economic power.[36] Despite decades of land reforms and the presumed (ICSSR 1980: 37–41), though questionable, marginal decline in concentration of land ownership, the concentration of assets actually increased in rural India in the decade 1960–61 to 1970–71 (Pathak *et al.* 1977), significantly so in some regions (Kurien 1980a).

Raj Krishna (1979a: 15) has recently argued that 'deficiencies in

[35] Both Kerala and West Bengal have experienced a significant shift of political power in the direction of the rural poor relative to traditionally-dominant rural classes, yet redistribution of institutional credit to the weakest classes has proved difficult. In Kerala, though 'small farmers' (who constitute more than 92 per cent of all farmers by official criteria) have increased somewhat their share of credit from cooperatives over the past decade, the share of artisans and labourers (the largest rural class) has actually declined slightly (RBI, Annual: Author's calculations). On the inability of *bargadars* (share-croppers) to obtain credit in West Bengal, India (1973: 26); Harriss (1982).

[36] Jodha (1971), Shivamaggi (1977), Krishna (1979a). The latest data available to me on cooperatives, the institutions which have been under the longest pressure to break the 'asset-nexus' of rural credit, indicate minimal success and perhaps retrogression. In 1965–66, 28.2 per cent of all cooperative loans were secured by immovable property; in 1976–77, 45.2 per cent (RBI, Annual). Long-term loans and larger loans are particularly affected. But as I have argued elsewhere (Herring 1977), alternative criteria, such as sureties, have not guaranteed a reallocation of credit, even when adopted locally.

the credit system are proving to be the greatest obstacles to development' in rural India. Whether or not this is true, the evidence of credit constraints on productivity seems solid. But other critical inputs are also susceptible to diversion by economically and politically powerful individuals, groups, and classes. Much of what has been said about local power and unequal distribution of institutional credit applies to other developmental resources channelled through the political system, though the data sources and case studies of credit allow more extensive analysis. Locally powerful agriculturalists seem capable of diverting a larger share of irrigation water for their own use than is agronomically or technically justifiable, often to the detriment of less powerful farmers.[37] Likewise, extension personnel tend to cater to the needs and demands of locally powerful farmers, skewing the flow of technical information to the disadvantage of the powerless.[38]

It is no secret that criteria directly linked to the stated objectives of development schemes or economic rationality are not sufficient to determine the distribution of access and privilege in state-funded development programmes, unless such criteria are congruent with the local configuration of power and 'connections'. Economic and political power structures are neither monolithic, nor identical, nor permanent, but the tendency toward congruence is strong. The following summary of her fieldwork in Uttar Pradesh by Sylvia Hale (1978: 273) illustrates the mechanisms: 'Economic dominance as landowning elites can be readily converted into political influence as elected headmen and prominent faction leaders within the village councils. Those with political influence can in turn exploit the broker role for profit . . . Entrepreneurial skills and initiative count less than

[37] On India, Hart (1978: 2); Thorner (1962: 'The Weak and the Strong on the Sarda Canal'); Wade (1975); Reidinger (1974); India (1976: II, 45). On Pakistan, Lowdermilk et al. (1978: 19); Parker and Bromley (1978). On Sri Lanka, Harriss (1974) argues that in addition to economic-political power, physical force is important in influencing access to scarce water. For a review of the South Asian region which reinforces the text, Parker and Bromley (1978: 8–11; 15–16).

[38] This phenomenon emerges in many ethnographic accounts; on connections to productivity, Dasgupta (1980: Ch. V); Hale (1978); India (1976: Part XI); Minhas (1974: 106). The propensity of extension personnel to concentrate energies on wealthy farmers relates not only to local power situations but also to the working rules of the role: if success is measured in terms of acreage covered, it is rational to concentrate on the few farmers who have the most acres. Moreover, distribution of technical information is influenced by an underlying belief in the potential leadership role of the gentry as model progressive farmers.

political influence of kin and faction ties with these brokers in exploiting the development schemes. The political impotence of the lower strata effectively stifles their attempts to gain access to these schemes. Their economic advancement directly conflicts with the interests of elite brokers, and this conflict finds expression in the political opposition which meets the schemes designed to promote their development.'

Though several qualifications should be made, this model resonates with so much of the development experience in the region that it is worthwhile to consider its implications for productivity in agriculture. The qualifications are, first, that the lower strata are not so impotent as is frequently believed, though the *lowest* strata typically remain so even in the areas of significant class-based mobilization; secondly, the schemes 'designed' to uplift the underclass are not unambiguous in their intent or content and are not produced in a political vacuum, but rather incorporate political power considerations at higher levels (state and national) and development ideologies conditioned by genuine ignorance of local situations as well as by presumed imperatives of allocating scarce resources to those who can demonstrably put them to work, i.e., those who have secure control over appreciable economic assets (the example of 'credit-worthiness' as a distributive criterion is archetypal).

Supposing that this model of elite dominance resulting in diversion of development resources for the reproduction and reinforcement of concentrated economic and political power is accurate for a great many local configurations in South Asia (an assumption supported strongly in the literature), what are the implications for productivity? It seems entirely possible that the production consequences of such diversion could be neutral or positive. Precisely the same connections which facilitate the original diversion should facilitate the acquisition of complementary resources (further credit, scarce inputs, extension help, etc.) which would maximize the impact of the resources on production. Moreover, the economic security of such elites should permit risk-taking and supplemental investment from existing income to an extent unlikely in more marginal classes, just as superior education and modern skills in manipulating the environment (and, more speculatively, greater self-confidence to do so) enhance the prospects for success.

Concentrated political power in the hands of an aggressive entrepreneurial class, particularly when integrated into the supra-village

power structure, provides significant opportunities for breaking
through political–administrative bottlenecks which constitute obstacles to higher productivity (delayed sanctioning of loans, insufficient or untimely supply of fertilizer, inadequate electrical power
or fuel supplies, etc.), as illustrated by Maharashtra's sugarcane
sector (Hart and Herring 1977). It would be wrong to deny the
potential for dynamism inherent in concentrated power at the
village and supra-village level, but equally wrong to use this potential
to legitimate concentrated power. The fundamental flaw in the
laissez-faire position is that development is left to the whims of local
elites, who may opt for functional absenteeism as often as dynamism.
There is enormous variation in the role landlords play in the production process, for example, from relatively active (Kandy district,
Sri Lanka) to functionally absentee (Hambantota district, Sri Lanka;
Bangladesh) (ARTI 1975; World Bank 1979: 38). More importantly,
there is no reason to believe that the interests of locally-dominant
classes will coincide with socially-optimal policy, much less with the
interests of the rural poor. The *laissez-faire* policy stance forgoes
potential rationality in planning, effectively discounts alleviation of
poverty, denies democratic values of popular determination, and
offers no guarantee that the surplus extracted from subordinate
classes will be deployed optimally.

For the *laissez-faire* position *vis-à-vis* concentrated local power
and resource cooptation to be persuasive, it would have to be shown
that locally-dominant elites would be unable to make the investments
in question were it not for privileged access to public resources.
However, there is evidence that large farmers frequently have sufficient surplus to finance their own short-term and long-term investments; one dramatic example was the vigorous black market in
tractors in Pakistan in the early 1970s, when farmers were willing to
pay double the Agricultural Development Bank's tractor price
without any credit whatsoever (Herring and Kennedy 1979). Another
indication is the persistence of large farmers in the moneylending
trade, though of course a fraction of the funds loaned by large
farmers is recycled cooperative or public credit.[39] Secondly, it would
have to be shown that those deprived classes which do command

[39] Reserve Bank of India (1977: 40) data indicate that landlords increased their
share of rural lending from a negligible 1.1 per cent in 1961 to 8.6 per cent in 1972.
Given the significant decline in land under tenancy in that period (Sanyal 1972;
Laxminarayan and Tyagi 1977), these data suggest a more activist and inter-

productive resources are not severely constrained from improving their productivity by the shortage of resources caused by a skewed distribution in favour of locally-dominant economic and political elites. As argued in the case of credit earlier, such a case is difficult to make and indeed the obverse seems more consonant with evidence and logic.[40] It is now widely recognized that the purely technical divisibility of productivity-enhancing innovations is denied in practice by the social, economic, and political disabilities of depressed classes in taking full advantage of them, slowing the spread of technical change and skewing the benefits (Byres 1972; Minhas 1974: 106; Berry and Cline 1979: 114).

Two conclusions follow. First, even on narrow productivity grounds, it is difficult to sustain an argument that the elite-dominance/resource-diversion configuration is optimal; when the case is broadened to encompass developmental objectives in general (considerations of employment and effective demand, not to mention equity), the model seems even more flawed as a policy prescription, contrary to the various arguments for 'regulated capitalism' as opposed to redistribution of assets (cf. ICSSR, 1980: 46–7). Secondly, the point about complementarity of resources should not be dismissed; development resources spread thinly and flung willy-nilly at the rural poor in isolated components (cows without veterinary service, credit without extension, etc.) probably have minimal or negative productivity implications, particularly when the productivity and opportunity costs of the state's share of the economic surplus are considered.

Local concentrations of political power have further consequences in terms of the productivity of the state's share of economic surplus.

---

ventionist role of landlords in contrast to the traditional rentier. Agricultural moneylenders (primarily large farmers, presumably) decreased their share of lending from 47.0 per cent in 1961–62 to 23.1 per cent in 1971–72, but remained the largest source of non-institutional credit in rural India.

[40] The fact that the credit needs of marginal farmers are primarily for 'consumption', not 'investment', does not affect this argument, though it is an important explanation for the persistence of the skewed distribution. Reproduction of family labour power is as much an item of working capital as reproduction of bullock labour power and constitutes the first claim on resources. The conventional distinction is artificial, and indeed the predominance of consumption loans among small farmers is itself evidence of the severe resource constraints faced by the rural poor; the family must be fed and sheltered before it can consider buying a pumpset.

Not only may the state be effectively prevented from claiming its share of the surplus (note the high level of arrears of land revenue and cesses), but public resources become difficult to allocate efficiently, and also to recover. To illustrate the dynamics, and the costs, we may again consider agricultural credit, where state involvement has mushroomed over time.

The provision of credit to farmers at subsidized interest rates—indeed, at negative real interest rates whenever inflation rates are high—undoubtedly contributes to innovation, technical change (though sometimes prematurely and in socially questionable forms) and enhanced production in the aggregate. Despite well-known leakages, farmers who receive institutional credit do buy fertilizers, level the land, install tubewells, raise higher value crops, and so on. That large farmers obtain more (relative to needs, relative to acres cropped, and in aggregate terms), small farmers less, tenants and labourers virtually none, is in part a reflection of local power structures, in part a function of national ideologies of planning and the persistence of asset-linked lending policies. Differential local power is also manifest in the repayment process—governments and local institutions are unable to recover fully the subsidized loans, resulting in an even larger flow of surplus to those who are able to obtain such credit. The local organs of the state are collectively and selectively soft, and embedded in rural society, resulting in higher costs and lower returns per unit of state resources channelled through them.

Local power is demonstrably important in determining who has to repay loans, and who has the power to ignore the collectors. Some micro-studies, and my investigations of the Agricultural Development Bank of Pakistan, suggest that it is the locally powerful who can ignore default notices; the rural little people are sufficiently intimidated by the organs of both state and society to repay loans.[41]

---

[41] B. M. Desai (1979); Ames (1975), cf. Bell and Duloy in Chenery et al. (1974: 126). The latest available data (1976–77) on cooperative overdues (RBI, Annual) indicate a curious pattern. The lowest ratios of overdues to outstanding loan amounts, by a large margin, were among tenants (33.7 per cent), agricultural labourers (29.3 per cent), 'others' (artisans, etc.) (35.4 per cent)—arguably the weakest agrarian classes. The highest ratio of overdues to outstanding was found in the largest farmer category (holdings greater than eight hectares): 73.3 per cent. The second highest percentage (61.9) was among small farmers (less than one hectare) among whom I would guess a fairly high percentage of overdues and defaults could be genuinely attributed to distress.

But a comprehensive study by the Reserve Bank of India (1974) indicated that repayment delinquency was so pervasive a phenomenon that no class differences in propensity could be detected. However, the study failed to emphasize that despite the equal propensity across size categories to reject institutions' requests for loan repayment, the large farmers who represented 24 per cent of all delinquents accounted for 57 per cent of the overdues in absolute terms. The percentage of large farmers among delinquents was more than double their percentage of the farming population. Moreover, the report observed that defaulters were able to get onto management committees and received *taccavi* loans from state governments, despite their repayment records, reflecting considerable local political power. And, of course, the percentage of farmers who obtain coveted institutional loans, and thus have the *opportunity* to default, is still relatively small and reflective of the local power structure. Finally, I suspect, but cannot prove, that a higher percentage of the defaults by poor peasants were distress defaults, as opposed to wilful defaults, in comparison with wealthy farmers.[42]

Attempts by the state to recover a higher percentage of these flows have met with resistance at every level. At the local level, cooperatives juggle their books to obscure the overdues problem. At the state level in India, regimes sensitive to the farmers' lobby concede demands to write off or reschedule debts, a tendency viewed with grave misgivings and resisted by both the Reserve Bank of India and the central government (and, more recently, the World Bank); the recent conflicts between Maharashtra's government and the RBI and between the Government of Tamil Nadu and the Centre are illustrative. The productivity imperative, however, imposes severe constraints on any regime, state or national, which seeks to rationalize the rural credit system; to discipline defaulting individuals or local coops threatens not only an important electoral base but also the level of short- and long-term investments in agriculture with

---

[42] Reserve Bank of India (1974), data from pp. 44–48 and Ch. II, Section V. The *Report's* treatment of distress defaults was inadequate in that it considered only area-wide crop failures, failing to distinguish within distressed areas which kinds of farmers have access to water and other inputs in times of scarcity. One would expect that wealthier farmers would in general be less affected by climatic variations because of superior connections in the allocation of irrigation water and access to private wells and pumpsets and would have superior repayment capacity even in the event of crop failure because of larger surpluses and greater wealth.

potentially severe consequences for aggregate production.[43]

These patterns of default, and similar diversions, distortions and leakages of public resources, do have productivity implications in a special sense; the resources which disappear have opportunity costs and could be employed elsewhere. That share of the national economic surplus is then unavailable for productivity-increasing projects outside agriculture, within the agricultural sector generally, or for allocation to the oft-lamented 'weaker sectors' of the rural economy, upon which future productivity gains must be built.

IV. *The Productivity Imperative and Redistributive Policy*

Whatever the empirical case concerning power–productivity interactions—and I conclude that the connections are by no means so clear as the policy logic of development documents suggests—the *perceived* productivity consequences of skewed access to economic resources is an independent determinant of state policies designed to (or legitimated by stated intention to) reallocate stocks and flows of such resources in favour of disadvantaged classes, contrary to the wishes of local elites. That is, there is a production imperative in the logic of ruling a poor society; redistributive measures with productivity justifications occupy a central place in public policy formulation. That a great deal of such activity is only symbolic, with no intention of altering the existing structure, requires no elaboration. However, genuine equity concerns are almost certainly a partial explanation for those redistributive programmes which are serious, as are political concerns of preventing the counter-mobilization of the rural have-nots behind genuinely radical forces: both symbolic and real resources are deployed to retain the allegiance or quiescence of the rural poor.

Though the argument that concentrated political and economic power constrains economic progress is a prevalent justification presented by supra-local elites for redistributive policy, it is not at all clear that acceptance of the model is widely shared. Indeed, countervailing arguments linking inequalities to dynamism have been expressed throughout the region, more openly in some states

---

[43] The Reserve Bank of India (1969: 537) noted the connection between an accommodating stance on overdues and electoral politics. Institutional debt write-offs were a major election issue in Tamil Nadu in 1980 and a continuing source of friction among the farmer lobby, the state government, and Delhi.

(Pakistan) than others (India). That the policy logic of redistribution is not unexceptionable, and meets powerful political opposition, is of course one source of failure in redistribution. That the redistributive logic remains pervasive in official documents reflects in part the commitment of important intellectual sections to its premises, but more importantly its congruence with specifically political arguments that existing concentrations of power, and their consequences, threaten rural 'stability' and 'harmony', and thus both continued political hegemony and production.

National elites in the region are both able and compelled to take a broader view of the social consequences of rural inequalities than is possible in the ideologies of locally-dominant elites. The state is characterized by relative autonomy (Poulantzas 1968): autonomy because the narrow interests of locally-hegemonic classes may conflict with specific regime imperatives of retaining power in a multi-class society, necessitating periodic action against particular classes or class fractions in the interest of maintaining the fundamental structural power of dominant classes (control of the surplus on which the rest of society depends) and the instrumental power of dominant classes through aggregation of dependent and clientelist groups electorally or otherwise. State autonomy is particularly evident in the face of real or perceived crisis; ceiling reforms in Sri Lanka in 1972 and 1975 appropriated a very large share of the finest agricultural properties in the shadow of a rural insurrection, in marked contrast to such reforms in India and Pakistan (Herring 1983: Chs. 5, 8).

Redistributive initiatives, however genuine, are legislated with recognition of a major contention of social scientists: extreme concentrations of rural power, and their social consequences, constitute destabilizing social configurations.[44] Though the connection between inequality and exploitation on the one hand and violence or rebellion on the other is far more complex than is typically assumed, attenuated by factors such as social organization, dependency, ideology and fear of repression, that connection remains a primary explana-

---

[44] Stinchcombe (1961) provides an insightful analysis of the destabilizing and conflictual potential of share tenancy systems; a formal elaboration, with (problematic) cross-national data and analysis is Paige (1975). Zagoria's (1971) ecological analysis of the electoral base of communist support in India focuses on the extent of landlessness and tenancy. Cf. Russett (1964); Tanter and Midlarsky (1967).

tion for nominally redistributive policies under regimes which otherwise rest upon, work through, and reinforce locally-dominant rural elites. Redistributive policy is by definition contrary to the existing configuration of economic power, and often to the distribution of political power locally. Such policies are determined by a mix of productivity, equity, and political/electoral concerns, while legitimated primarily in terms of production and equity. Largely because of this complex and often contradictory mix of determinants, redistributive policies in the region have seldom been directed, even nominally, at uprooting rural power structures, but have focused instead on incorporating productivity imperatives into reformist schemes. Land reforms and credit reforms have been dominant examples.

Major efforts at the national level have been made throughout the region to reverse the skewed pattern of access to institutional credit, spurred both by the increasing electoral power of smaller farmers and by elite recognition that the great majority of farms in most of South Asia are small and that denial of credit to those producers could strangle or preclude the extension of agricultural dynamism. Reform strategies have been both aggregate and class-specific: attempts to channel more of the total credit available into agriculture, presumably freeing up rural credit markets, and class-directed programmes or quotas. The increased flow of resources has been extraordinary. In Pakistan, under Zulfikar Ali Bhutto's banking reforms and the Agricultural Credit Scheme of the National Bank of Pakistan in 1972, quotas were set by sector and farm size (though implementation was quite another matter).[45] Likewise, the Reserve Bank of India has set and progressively raised the quota of both aggregate rural sector and specifically small farm loans applicable to cooperative and commercial banking institutions, along with a 'differential interest rate scheme', new Rural Banks specifically

[45] One would predict minimal and partial implementation, given the local and national power structures and agricultural priorities. The power of medium and large farmers to pressure government to accelerate the pace of mechanization, for example, is a major obstacle to redistribution of rural credit. The latest figures available to me show that the major share of rural credit continues to be consumed by tractors; in 1975–76, the Agricultural Development Bank of Pakistan loaned 66.6 per cent of its record-setting outlay of Rs 53 crores for tractor purchase and another 9.6 per cent for tubewells. That does not leave much for the majority of Pakistan's farmers, who till less than the officially designated 'subsistence holding'. Data from *Pakistan Affairs*, 23 March 1977 (Washington, D.C.).

justified in terms of redressing the existing distribution of credit, grant subsidies and default insurance for small farmer loans. The goal is presently to increase the quota for 'small farmers' to 50 per cent of total farm credit. The Small Farmer Development Agency programme, beginning in 1970–71, professed the same objectives.

These efforts have met with limited success. An explicit aim of the Indian SFDA scheme was to identify potentially *viable* small farmers, recognizing that the problems of 'marginal farmers' and agricultural labourers were quite separate, more intractable, and should be allocated to a different agency (though the projects tend to fuse operationally). Some SFDA projects have shown real success, though coverage has been quite limited.[46] One would expect that differential success of small farmers in benefiting from the schemes would be heavily influenced by existing differentials in local mobilization and degrees of dependence as well as by the relative opposition and degree of unity within the dominant elite locally.

The extension of credit downward in the system, to less privileged groups, is a functional parallel to land reforms: the appropriate metaphor is that of a pyramid in which the state increasingly recognizes the demands and aspirations of progressively lower strata in the pyramid but never really touches the base, much less turns the pyramid upside down. To the extent that credit allocation policies remain asset-based, those who control the most assets will continue to be the most 'creditworthy' whereas those without assets of any significance will remain unlikely to acquire any, at least through institutional channels.

As in the case of land reforms, the shift of some credit resources to lower levels of the agrarian pyramid involves extension to agriculturalists more likely to attend to the land, better able and willing to identify with farming as a profession, and hence more likely to improve cultivation within the limits set by resource constraints. Presumably this process, like the 'abolition of intermediaries' in the areas of effective enforcement in India, also changes the local power structure, though primarily in favour of middle and rich peasant

[46] For summary and analysis, Raj Krishna (1979b); Minhas (1974: 114). A district study of the SFDA which confirms these views, and documents abuse (such as bogus claims to 'small farmer' status, etc.) is Kerala (1977). On the performance of commercial banks under the new reforms, Shetty (1979); India (1976: XII, 18). On credit reform measures in India generally, Ghosh (1976); India (1978); Shivamaggi (1977). On Ceylon, Tilakaratna (1963); Marga (1974); Sanderatne (1980).

classes, rather than marginal farmers and agricultural labourers. The task of recognizing and analysing such shifts in power structure in the context of public policy constitutes a continuing research priority.

But then the critical question remains: what does this marginal shift in the pyramid imply for those at the productive base? For the bottom of the pyramid to be touched by existing land or credit policies would require dramatic reconceptualization of the policies; for the base to be affected significantly by trickle-down processes would require as a necessary, but not sufficient condition, unprecedented dynamism in aggregate production.[47] The dominant policies in the region do not attempt to change this structure to enhance productivity, but rather assume that enhancing productivity will mitigate the more serious deprivations imposed by existing structures. Yet one conclusion of studies of local power configurations is that redistributive or developmental measures which are contrary to the interests of locally-dominant classes are likely to be coopted, distorted or vitiated in implementation (cf. Guhan 1980; Chenery et al. 1974: Chs. III, VI).

---

[47] The potential of trickle-down mechanisms to benefit 'weaker sectors' is widely disputed. Griffin (1979) demonstrates that there is little evidence that rapid growth has increased the flow of the trickle, and stresses that rapid growth may generate dynamics of immiseration and 'trickle-up' as well as trickle-down (cf. Rajaraman, 1975; Kurien, 1980b; UNRISD, 1974). Though frequently cited in support of the trickle-down thesis, Ahluwalia's (1978) analysis simply demonstrates that in good crop years in India, the incidence of rural poverty declines. Ahluwalia finds no evidence of a trend decline in the incidence of rural poverty even in the most dynamic states (p. 312) and the 'most disquieting' result is that 'evidence from Punjab and Haryana does not support the hypothesis that improved agricultural performance will help reduce the incidence of poverty' (p. 315). But as the ICSSR (1980) Working Group concludes (p. 35), we are on 'sandy soil' in assessing shifts in income distribution in India. The frequently-cited decline in the concentration of land ownership is (a) arguably more fictitious than real, reflecting intra-family divisions of property to evade land reforms (a phenomenon for which there is overwhelming evidence), (b) if real, more the result of public policy than growth, (c) more reflective of subdivision of existing holdings into slightly smaller holdings at each size stratum than of any dramatic redistribution of land from the top of the pyramid to the bottom. There has been no overall decline in the concentration of rural assets (Pathak et al. 1977). The absolute numbers of rural poor continue to increase in India, by about five million annually in Ahluwalia's (1978) estimate. On increasing concentration of land and immiseration in Bangladesh, see World Bank (1979: 37–8); Jannuzi and Peach (1980: Ch. 5); Huq (1976).

V. *Conclusion: Local Power, Productivity and Development*

If the position in earlier sections of this essay seems unduly sceptical about the obstacles to increasing productivity posed by existing local power configurations in South Asia, it is to add a needed corrective to the frequent assumption that breaking those power structures is sufficient (or even necessary) to generate growth. Without this corrective, it would be extremely difficult to explain the remarkable and extensive technical changes in South Asian agriculture, despite the persistence of traditional institutions (cf. Thorner 1967; 1968). It must be emphasized that labour-repressive and extremely exploitative social organizations of production, because the level of surplus extracted is a high percentage of gross output, are not necessarily inconsistent with high levels of investment, technical change, and growth, provided the surplus is so deployed.

This does not mean that the surplus will be deployed in economically progressive directions by local power elites, only that they have the power to do so, and under certain conditions have exhibited the inclination. The sources of differential inclinations are largely the province of psychology, and it remains easier to document variations in risk-taking proclivities across individuals (McClelland 1961; Broehl 1978) than to understand the reasons for individual and group difference and changes over time. Genovese (1965) has persuasively argued that the superstructural manifestations of a slave society in the American South included attitudes which constrained technical change and reorganization of agriculture; Neale (1977) has likewise argued that the land has been conceived more in terms of rulership than in terms of economic potential by landed elites in the Indic context. Though it seems obvious that such attitudes have inertial qualities, and are functionally related to the social organization of production and its characteristic norms of legitimacy and priorities, it remains difficult to explain differential responses to economic opportunities across individuals, farms, regions, and communities (cf. Nair 1979). What does seem clear is that new responses are powerfully influenced by changes in the economic environment, a major component of which is public policy and its variable expression at the local level as influenced by local power structures.

Having stressed that concentrated economic and political power locally is no absolute barrier to productivity-enhancing changes by dominant classes, it remains to consider some of the ways in which certain local configurations may depress economic potential. At the most basic level, there exists a level of exploitation of direct producers so severe that even simple reproduction of labour power becomes problematic, reducing labour productivity. Direct producers who supply major productive inputs but are deprived of surplus through high rates of extraction by non-producers lack the power to make large investments; when this incapacity is not remedied by contributions of non-producers, production inevitably suffers (e.g., rack-rented tenants-at-will of absentee rentiers). In regard to inputs which are in scarce supply locally, superior political-economic power of elites may divert resources (credit, irrigation water, extension information) away from non-elite producers most in need of them, depressing production potential. From a broader developmental perspective, agrarian configurations which produce or reproduce a large class of individuals at the subsistence margin depress aggregate demand which could otherwise stimulate local investment, employment, and production.

This essay has concentrated on economic decisions made by locally dominant classes, simply because by definition such classes decide the disposition and redeployment of the major portion of the economic surplus over time. If regimes at the national and sub-national level are unwilling to break those concentrations of power, there is a perceived political imperative to find means to coax or compel dominant classes to increase productivity. Modern national states have a variety of carrots and sticks—primarily carrots—to deploy in encouraging such utilization of the surplus; the mix of carrots and sticks itself has productivity consequences. Local power structures which maintain highly extractive mechanisms may thus contribute to the very narrow process of increasing productivity across a number of measures, at least in the short and medium terms, until such structures either generate tensions and conflicts which in turn have deleterious effects on productivity and growth (and eventually on local power structures) or, alternatively, create or leave untouched so large a class of impoverished rural have-nots[48] that

---

[48] Even from a narrow productivity perspective, extreme poverty may represent a negative factor by reducing labour productivity and diverting resources of poor households. For an empirical defence of the proposition advanced by Myrdal (1968) and others, that physical weakness and ill-health of the poorest agrarian classes significantly reduce labour productivity, see Ram and Schultz (1979).

broader economic development goals are frustrated by lack of broad-based effective demand in rural areas. Both of these possibilities are sufficiently compelling to argue against a development strategy which focuses narrowly on productivity and reinforces existing economic inequalities, despite persisting arguments to the contrary (e.g., Mellor 1976: 267 *et passim*).

But the state under regimes typical of the region is then caught in a political-economic bind—perhaps even a contradiction—which is evident in public policy throughout the region. It must simultaneously encourage rural haves to invest and accumulate and promise rural have-nots that redistribution and amelioration will take place. The juicy carrots of development policy are to reassure rural elites that their power and privilege are secure but must be justified by shouldering their entrepreneurial responsibilities; the sticks are to convince rural have-nots that the state will not let the economic power of the haves run roughshod over certain minimal social, economic and political rights. The state simultaneously has to face the growing recognition that its stick is (selectively) soft and the carrots are plucked from a common patch: both carrots and sticks are extremely expensive, diverting resources from alternative uses which have direct productivity pay-offs.

In sum, though we can identify obstacles to increasing productivity rooted in existing structures of concentrated local power, three points must be emphasized. First, the stronger case for alteration of rural power structures is broadly developmental and political and cannot be made easily on narrow productivity grounds. Second, it is not the local power structure which is entirely responsible for distortions in the flow of developmental resources and utilization of the economic surplus; the full explanation lies partially in the dynamics of bureaucratic behaviour, operative social mythologies, cultural conditioning and quiescence of disadvantaged groups, and, more decisively, in the dynamics of market forces and in national development strategies which accept these forces and their outcomes. The central dilemma of redistributive policy is that the mitigation of the consequences of local power concentrations in the absence of redistribution of the social bases of power generally fails, and simultaneously weakens the incentives to accumulation and dynamism if taken seriously by locally-dominant classes. Serious interference with the power and privileges (sometimes termed 'incentives') of dominant classes is contrary to the structural power of those classes most centrally in command of the agricultural surplus. Moreover, the possibility of existing South Asian regimes taking fundamentally radical measures which are contrary to the interests of the rural power structure is problematic at best. Indeed, the very existence of the state, distinguishable from the local power structure, is problematic in much of rural South Asia. The state, as it spreads from the centre, dissolves more and more into society until the distinctions are quite blurred at the local level. Where, then, are the levers for change that policy analysis assumes?

Finally, the preceding discussion has focused on productivity as dependent variable. It should be emphasized that some of the most important policy and intellectual questions involve reversing the causality: how do changes in productivity affect the local structure of power? The state throughout South Asia has increased its level and breadth of involvement in rural development, with ambiguous, but certainly not emancipatory, effects on subordinate classes. Developmental policy logic increasingly stresses devolution to democratic bodies and decentralization of implementation. Yet, in view of the fusion of economic and political power locally, it is not unreasonable to view the flow of state resources into developmental programmes and the encouragement of local bodies to administer these resources as mechanisms which potentially reinforce the dominance of local elites, putting more patronage resources in their hands, allowing more jobs to be allocated, more economic activity to occur, legitimizing their role as local patrons (for a discussion of the dynamics in Sri Lanka, Herring 1983: Ch. 3).

It is here that the central dilemmas of economic development, public policy, and participatory democracy come together. The absence of a consensual, legitimized collective authority structure at the village level is in part sustained and aggravated by acute inequalities in access to material resources, particularly as disadvantaged classes become politically aware and mobilized; the absence of such a structure is contrary to productivity objectives both in the macro-social sense of facilitating leakages of developmental resources and in the micro-economic sense of denying access to classes of direct producers who need such access. Development through existing patronage structures thus frequently has negative productivity consequences by the criterion of return per unit of state investment, but is the only strategy available to the caretaker state which is unwilling or unable to transform local power structures.

Meaningful participatory democracy—which is itself arguably a precondition for certain types of local development with low social cost—requires the devolution of power and resources to the local level. But such devolution and delegation typically advantage disproportionately incumbents of the existing local power structure and thwart attempts to generate genuine participation, redistribution, or community development. The Congress Agrarian Reforms Committee (1949) forcefully argued that there could be no vigorous community development without a radical levelling of the disparities in economic and political power in the village. Ironically, the all-but-unanimous conclusion of studies of land reforms—the most obvious tool to effect such a levelling—is that the reforms themselves cannot be made effective without vigorous local participation (e.g., India 1968). It is one thing to delineate the vicious circle, another to determine an effective point of entry; but it seems clear that developmental policy is unlikely to have the legitimating effects in terms of either equity or productivity unless it simultaneously addresses alteration of the bases of economic power in the villages, *despite* the empirical weaknesses of the narrowly economic determinist view of institutional obstacles to innovation.

REFERENCES

AICC   All-India Congress Committee
EPW   *Economic and Political Weekly* (Bombay)
IJAE   *Indian Journal of Agricultural Economics*
ARTI   Agrarian Research and Training Institute (Colombo)
ICSSR   Indian Council of Social Science Research

Ahluwalia, Montek S. (1977), 'Rural Poverty and Agricultural Performance in India', *Journal of Development Studies* 14: 3 (April).

Ahmad, Saghir (1977), *Class and Power in a Punjabi Village* (New York: Monthly Review Press).

Alavi, Hamza (1971), 'The Politics of Dependence: A Village in West Punjab', *South Asian Review* 4: 2 (January).

—— (1973), 'Peasant Classes and Primordial Loyalties', *The Journal of Peasant Studies* 1: 1.

—— (1976), 'The Rural Elite and Agricultural Development in Pakistan' in Robert Stevens, Hamza Alavi, Peter Bertocci (eds), *Rural Development in Bangladesh and Pakistan* (Honolulu: University of Hawaii Press).

Alexander, K. C. (1978), *Agricultural Labour Unions in Three South Indian States* (Hyderabad: National Institute of Rural Development).

AICC (1949), *Report of the Congress Agrarian Reforms Committee* (New Delhi).

Ames, Glen C. W. (1975), 'Who Benefits from Credit Programs and Who Repays? Large Farmers in Village-Level Cooperatives in Mysore State, India', *Land Tenure Center Newsletter* 47 (January–March).

Anderson, Perry (1974a), *Passages from Antiquity to Feudalism* (London: New Left Books).

—— (1974b), *Lineages of the Absolutist State* (London: New Left Books).

ARTI (1975), *The Agrarian Situation Relating to Paddy Cultivation in Five Selected Districts of Sri Lanka*, Part 6, Comparative Analysis (Colombo).

—— (1977), *Land Reform and the Development of Coconut Lands* (Colombo).

Azam, K. M. (1973), 'The Future of the Green Revolution in Pakistan: A Choice of Strategy', *International Journal of Agrarian Affairs* 5: 6 (March).

Banaji, Jairus (1976), 'Chayanov, Kautsky, Lenin: Considerations toward a Synthesis', EPW XI: 40 (2 October).

Baran, Paul (1957), *The Political Economy of Growth* (New York: Monthly Review Press).

Barclay, William J. and Mitchell Stengal (1975), 'Surplus and Surplus Value', *The Review of Radical Political Economics* 7: 4 (Winter).

Bardhan, Pranab (1973), 'Variations in Agricultural Wages,' EPW VIII: 17 (26 May).

Bardhan, Pranab and Ashok Rudra (1978), 'Interlinkage of Land, Labour, and Credit Relations', EPW XIII: Annual Number (February).

Bartsch, William H. (1973), 'Employment Effects of Alternative Technologies and Techniques—A Survey of Evidence' (Geneva: ILO).

—— (1977), *Employment and Technology Choice in Asian Agriculture* (New York: Praeger).

Bates, Robert H. (1977), 'People in Villages: Micro-Level Studies in Political Economy', California Institute of Technology Working Paper No. 195 (Pasadena).

Bell, Clive (1977), 'Alternative Theories of Sharecropping: Some Tests Using Evidence from Northeast India', *The Journal of Development Studies* 13: 4 (July).

Berry, R. Albert and William R. Cline (1979), *Agrarian Structure and Productivity in Developing Countries* (Baltimore: The Johns Hopkins University Press).

Béteille, André (1974), *Studies in Agrarian Social Structure* (Delhi: Oxford University Press).

Bhaduri, A. (1973), 'Agricultural Backwardness under Semi-Feudalism', *Economic Journal* LXXXIII.

Bharadwaj, Krishna (1974), *Production Conditions in Indian Agriculture* (London: Cambridge University Press).

Bhat, M. L. (1971), 'Diversion of Long-Term Agricultural Finance', EPW VI (9 October).

Binswanger, Hans P. (1978), 'The Economics of Tractors in South Asia', Agricultural Development Council (New York).

Blair, Harry W. (1980), 'Rising Kulaks and Backward Classes in Bihar', EPW 15: 2 (January 12).

Broehl, Jr., Wayne G. (1978), *The Village Entrepreneur: Change Agents in India's Rural Development* (Cambridge, Mass.: Harvard University Press).

Burki, Shahid Javed (1976), 'The Development of Pakistan's Agriculture' in

Stevens *et al.* (eds), *Rural Development in Bangladesh and Pakistan* (Honolulu: University of Hawaii Press).

Byres, T. J. (1972), 'The Dialectic of India's Green Revolution', *South Asian Review* 5: 2 (January).

Chadha, G. K. (1978), 'Farm Size and Productivity Revisited', EPW XIII: 39 (September).

Chakravarty, Aparajita and Ashok Rudra (1973), 'Economic Effects of Tenancy: Some Negative Results', EPW VIII: 28 (July 14).

Chayanov, A. V. (1966), *The Theory of Peasant Economy*, ed. Daniel Thorner, B. Kerblay, R. E. F. Smith (Homewood: R. D. Irwin).

Chenery, Hollis *et al.* (eds) (1974), *Redistribution with Growth* (Oxford: Oxford University Press).

Chopra, Suneet (1982), 'Bondage in Green Revolution Area', *Social Scientist* 10: 6 (March).

Clay, Edward J. (1975), 'Equity and Productivity Effects of a Package of Technical Innovations and Changes in Social Institututions: Tubewells, Tractors, High-Yielding Varieties', *Indian Journal of Agricultural Economics* 30: 4 (October–December).

Cleaver, Jr., Harry M. (1973), 'The Contradictions of the Green Revolution' in Charles K. Wilber (ed.), *The Political Economy of Development and Underdevelopment* (New York: Random House).

Dandekar, V. M. (1977), 'Nature of Class Conflict in Indian Society' (Bombay: Bhatka Foundation).

Dasgupta, Biplab (1980), *The New Agrarian Technology and India* (Delhi: Macmillan).

Desai, B. M. (1979), 'Delivery of Credit to the Rural Poor', *Kurukshetra* XXVIII: 3 (November).

Desai, Meghnad (1980), 'Political Power and Agricultural Productivity: Part I', Paper for the SSRC-ICSSR Conference on Power and Productivity, 14–20 December (Delhi).

Dorner, Peter (1972), *Land Reform and Economic Development* (London: Penguin).

Dwivedi, Harendranath and Ashok Rudra (1973), 'Economic Effects of Tenancy: Some Further Negative Results', EPW VIII: 29 (July 21).

EPW (1979), Special Issue on 'Caste and Class in India', Vol. XIV, Nos. 7–8.

Ekholm, Erik (1979), 'The Dispossessed of the Earth: Land Reform and Sustainable Development', Worldwatch Paper 30 (Washington, D.C.).

Epstein, T. S. (1962), *Economic Development and Social Change in South India* (Manchester: Manchester University Press).

Frankel, Francine R. (1972), *India's Green Revolution: Economic Gains and Political Costs* (Princeton: Princeton University Press).

Genovese, Eugene D. (1961), *The Political Economy of Slavery: Studies in the Economy and Society of the Slave South* (New York: Random House).

Ghatak, Subrata (1975), 'Rural Interest Rates in the Indian Economy', *Journal of Development Studies* 11: 3 (April).

Ghose, A. K. and Ashwant Saith (1976), 'Indebtedness, Tenancy, and the Adoption of New Technology in Semi-Feudal Agriculture', *World Development* 4: 4 (April).

Ghosh, Tushar Kanti (ed.) (1976), *Credit Institutions and Development* (Calcutta: *Amrita Bazar Patrika*).

Gotsch, Carl (1971), 'The Distributive Impact of Agricultural Growth: Low Income Farmers and the "System" ', Seminar on Small Farmer Development Strategies (Columbus, Ohio).

Gough, Kathleen (1980), 'Modes of Production in Southern India', EPW XV: Annual Number (February).

Government of India (1965), Programme Evaluation Organization, *Study of Utilization of Cooperative Loans* (New Delhi).

—— (1968), Department of Community Development, *Report of the Study Team on Involvement of Community Development Agency and Panchayati Raj Institutions in the Implementation of Basic Land Reform Measures* (New Delhi).

—— (1976), Ministry of Agriculture and Irrigation, *Report of the National Commission on Agriculture* (New Delhi).

—— (1978), 'Country Review, 1978: India', UNFAO Conference on Agrarian Reform and Rural Development (New Delhi).

Government of Kerala (1975), Planning Board, *Poverty, Rural Indebtedness, and Money Lending Practices* (Trivandrum).

—— (1977), *Small Farmers Development Agency, Cannanore: An Evaluation Study* (Trivandrum).

Government of Pakistan (1959), *Report of the Land Reforms Commission for West Pakistan* (Lahore).

—— (1974), Agricultural Census Organization, *Rural Credit Survey (Lahore) Unofficial preliminary report*.

Government of Punjab (Pakistan) (1970), Planning and Development Department, *Fertilizer and Mexican Wheat Survey* (Lahore).

Griffin, Keith with Ajit Kumar Ghose (1979), 'Growth and Impoverishment in the Rural Areas of Asia', *World Development* 7: 4–5 (April–May).

Guhan, S. (1980), 'Rural Poverty: Policy and Play-Acting', EPW XV: 47 (22 November).

Gutelman, Michel (1974), *Structures et Reformes Agraires: Instruments pour L'analyse* (Paris: Maspero).

Hale, Sylvia (1978), 'The Politics of Entrepreneurship in Indian Villages', *Development and Change* 9.

Harriss, John C. (1974), 'Problems of Water Management in Relation to Social Organization in Hambantota District', Circulated draft (Cambridge, U.K.).

—— (1979), 'Why Poor People Remain Poor in Rural South Asia', *Social Scientist* 8: 1 (August).

—— (1980), 'Contemporary Marxist Analysis of the Agrarian Question in India', Madras Institute of Development Studies Working Paper No. 14 (Madras: MIDS).

—— (1982), 'Making Out on Limited Resources: Or, What Happened to Semi-Feudalism in a Bengal District', CRESSIDA Working Paper (Calcutta).

Hart, Henry C. (1978), 'Anarchy, Paternalism, or Collective Responsibility under the Canals', Paper presented to Wisconsin Conference on South Asia, 3–4 November 1978 (Madison). Subsequently published in EPW.

Hart, Henry C. and Ronald J. Herring, 'Political Conditions of Land Reform:

Kerala and Maharashtra' in Robert E. Frykenberg (ed.), *Land Tenure and Peasant in South Asia* (Delhi: Orient Longman).

Herring, Ronald J. (1977), 'Land Tenure and Credit-Capital Tenure in Contemporary India' in R. E. Frykenberg (ed.), *Land Tenure and Peasant in South Asia* (Delhi: Orient Longman).

—— (1978), 'Share Tenancy and Economic Efficiency: The South Asian Case', *Peasant Studies* 7: 4.

—— (1979), 'Zulfikar Ali Bhutto and the "Eradication of Feudalism" in Pakistan', *Comparative Studies in Society and History* 21: 4 (October).

—— (1981), 'Embedded Production Relations and the Rationality of Tenant Quiescence in Tenure Reform', *The Journal of Peasant Studies* 8: 2 (January).

—— (1983), *Land to the Tiller: The Political Economy of Agrarian Reform in South Asia* (New Haven: Yale University Press; Delhi: Oxford University Press).

Herring, Ronald J. and Md. Ghaffar Chaudhry (1974), 'The 1972 Land Reforms in Pakistan and Their Economic Implications: A Preliminary Analysis', *Pakistan Development Review* 13: 3 (Fall).

Herring, Ronald J. and Charles R. Kennedy, Jr. (1979), 'The Political Economy of Farm Mechanization Policy: Tractors in Pakistan' in Raymond Hopkins *et al.* (eds.), *Food, Politics and Agricultural Development* (Boulder: Westview).

Hewavitharana, Buddhadasa (1974), 'Non-Monetized Capital Formation in Ceylon—A Marga', Marga Institute (Columbo).

Hsiao, J. C. (1975), 'The Theory of Share Tenancy Revisited', *Journal of Political Economy* 83: 5 (October).

Huq, M. Ameeral (ed.) (1976), *Exploitation and the Rural Poor: A Working Paper on the Rural Power Structure in Bangladesh* (Comilla: Bangladesh Academy for Rural Development).

IJAE (1974), 'Wages and Incomes of the Weaker Sectors in India', Conference Number 29: 3 (July–September).

Ilaiah, K. (1979), 'How "Grass-Roots" Plans Go Awry', *Kurukshetra* XXVIII: 3 (November).

ICSSR (1980), *Alternatives in Agricultural Development* (New Delhi: Allied).

Jannuzi, F. T. (1974), *Agrarian Crisis in India: The Case of Bihar* (Austin: University of Texas Press).

Jannuzi, F. T. and James T. Peach (1980), *The Agrarian Structure of Bangladesh: An Impediment to Development* (Boulder: Westview).

Jha, S. C. (1971), *A Critical Analysis of Indian Land Reforms Studies* (Bombay: Asian Studies).

Jodha, N. S. (1971), 'Land-Based Credit Policies and Investment Prospects for Small Farmers', EPW VI (September).

Joshi, P. C. (1975), *Land Reforms in India: Trends and Prospects* (Bombay: Allied).

—— (1980), 'Conflicting Pulls of Productivity and Employment', United Nations Institute for Training and Research (New Delhi).

Kaneda, Hiromitsu (1969), 'Economic Implications of the "Green Revolution" and the Strategy of Agricultural Development in West Pakistan', Pakistan Institute of Development Economics, Report No. 78 (Karachi).

Kanel, Don (1967), 'Size of Farm and Economic Development', *Indian Journal of Agricultural Economics* 22.

Keyder, Caglar (1975), 'Surplus', *The Journal of Peasant Studies* 2: 2 (January).

Khan, M. H. (1975), *The Economics of the Green Revolution in Pakistan* (New York: Praeger).

—— (1977), 'Land Productivity, Farm Size, and Returns to Scale in Pakistan Agriculture', *World Development* 5: 4.

Khusro, A. M. (1973), *The Economics of Farm Size and Land Reform in India* (Delhi: Macmillan).

Kotovsky, Grigory (1964), *Agrarian Reform in India*, transl. from the Russian by K. J. Lambkin (New Delhi: People's Publishing House).

Krishna, Raj (1979a), 'The Crucial Phase in Rural Development', *Kurukshetra* XXXVIII 3 (November).

—— (1979b), 'Small Farmer Development', EPW IX: 21 (May).

Kurien, C. T. (1980), 'Dynamics of Rural Transformation: A Case Study of Tamil Nadu', EPW XV: 5, 6, 7 (February).

Kurup, T. V. Narayana (1976), 'Price of Rural Credit: An Empirical Analysis of Kerala', EPW XI: 27 (July 3).

Laxminarayan, H. and S. S. Tyagi (1977), 'Tenancy: Extent and Inter-State Variations', EPW 12: 22 (May).

Lenin, V. I. (1938), 'New Data on the Laws of Development of Capitalism in Agriculture', *Selected Works*, Vol. XII (New York: International Publishers).

Lowdermilk, Max K. (1972), 'Diffusion of Dwarf Wheat Production Technology', Ph.D. dissertation (Ithaca: Cornell University).

Lowdermilk, Max, David Freeman, Alan Early and James Layton (1978), 'Farm Water Management: A Neglected Component of Irrigation Research and Development', Paper presented to Wisconsin Conference on South Asia, 3–4 November (Madison).

Marga Institute (1974), *The Co-operative System and Rural Credit in Sri Lanka* (Colombo).

Marx, Karl (1965), *Precapitalist Economic Formations*, transl. Jack Cohen, ed. Eric Hobsbawm (New York: International Publishers).

McClelland, David C. (1961), *The Achieving Society* (New York: D. Van Nostrand).

Mellor, John W. (1976), *The New Economics of Growth: A Strategy for India and the Developing World* (Ithaca: Cornell University Press).

Mencher, Joan P. (1978), 'Agrarian Relations in Two Rice Regions of Kerala', EPW XIII: Annual Number (February).

Metcalf, Thomas R. (1979), *Land, Landlords, and the British Raj: Northern India in the Nineteenth Century* (Berkeley: University of California Press).

Michie, Aruna Nayyar (1979), 'Agricultural Policy and Political Viability in Rural India', *Comparative Political Studies* 12: 3 (October).

Minhas, B. S. (1974), *Planning and the Poor* (New Delhi: S. Chand).

Mundle, Sudipto (1979), *Backwardness and Bondage: Agrarian Relations in a South Bihar District* (New Delhi: Indian Institute of Public Administration).

Myrdal, Gunnar (1968), *Asian Drama: An Inquiry into the Poverty of Nations* (New York: Random House).

Nadkarni, M. V. and R. S. Deshpande (1979), 'Under-Utilization of Land: Climatic or Institutional Factors', IJAE XXXIV: 2 (April–June).

Nair, Kusum (1962), *Blossoms in the Dust* (New York: Praeger).

—— (1979), *In Defense of the Irrational Peasant: Indian Agriculture after the Green Revolution* (Chicago: The University of Chicago Press).

Neale, Walter C. (1977), 'Land is To Rule' in Robert E. Frykenberg (ed.), *Land Control and Social Structure in Indian History* (Madison: University of Wisconsin Press).

Newbery, D. M. G. (1975), 'Tenurial Obstacles to Innovation', *The Journal of Development Studies* 11: 4 (July).

Paige, Jeffery (1975), *Agrarian Revolution: Social Movements and Export Agriculture in the Underdeveloped World* (New York: Free Press).

Parker, Donald E. and Daniel W. Bromley (1978), 'Institutional Aspects of Farmer Water Management: Empirical Evidence from Pakistan' (Washington, D.C.: Agency for International Development).

Pathak, R. P., K. R. Ganapathy and Y. U. K. Sarma (1977), 'Shifts in Pattern of Asset Holdings of Rural Households, 1961–62 to 1971–72', EPW VII: Special Number (August).

Patnaik, Utsa (1979), 'Economics of Farm Size and Farm Scale', EPW VII: Special Number (August).

—— (1979), 'Neo-Populism and Marxism: The Chayanovian View of the Agrarian Question and Its Fundamental Fallacy', *The Journal of Peasant Studies* 6: 4 (July).

Peiris, G. H. (1975), 'The Current Land Reforms and Peasant Agriculture in Sri Lanka', *South Asia*, No. 5 (December).

Pillai, S. Devadas and C. Baks (eds.) (1979), *Winners and Losers: Styles of Development in an Indian Region* (Bombay: Popular Prakashan).

Pillai, V. R. and P. G. K. Panikar (1965), *Land Reclamation in Kerala* (Bombay: Asia).

Polanyi, Karl (1944), *The Great Transformation* (New York: Farrar and Rinehart).

Poulantzas, Nicos (1968), *Pouvoir Politique et Classes Sociales* (Paris: Maspero).

Raj, K. N. (1975), 'Agricultural Development and Distribution of Land Holdings', *Indian Journal of Agricultural Economics* 30: 1 (January–March).

Rajaraman, Indira (1975), 'Poverty, Inequality and Economic Growth: Rural Punjab, 1960/61–1970/71', *The Journal of Development Studies* 11: 4 (July).

Rajendran, G. (1974), *The Ezhava Community and Kerala Politics* (Trivandum: Kerala Academy of Political Science).

Ram, Rati and Theodore W. Schultz (1979), 'Life Span, Health, Savings, and Productivity', *Economic Development and Cultural Change* 27 (April).

Rao, C. H. Hanumantha (1975), *Technological Change and Distribution of Gains in Indian Agriculture* (Delhi: Macmillan).

Reidinger, Richard B. (1974), 'Institutional Rationing of Canal Water in Northern India: Conflict between Traditional Patterns and Modern Needs', *Economic Development and Cultural Change* 23 (October).

Republic of Sri Lanka (1975), Central Bank of Ceylon, *Annual Report 974* (Colombo).

Reserve Bank of India (Annual), *Statistical Statements Relating to the Cooperative Movement in India, Part I, Credit Societies* (Bombay).

—— (1969), *Report of the All-India Rural Credit Review Committee* (Bombay).

—— (1974), Rural Credit Department, *Report of the Study Team on Overdues of Cooperative Credit Institutions.*

—— (1977), *Indebtedness of Rural Households and Availability of Institutional Finance, All India Rural Debt and Investment Survey* (Bombay).

Rosenthal, Donald R. (1977), *The Expansive Elite: District Politics and State Policy-Making in India* (Berkeley: University of California Press).

Rudolph, Susanne Hoeber and Lloyd I. Rudolph (1980), 'Determinants and Varieties of Agrarian Mobilization', Paper presented to SSRC-ICSSR Conference on Power and Productivity, 14–16 December (New Delhi).

Rudra, Ashok (1968a), 'Farm Size and Yield Per Acre', EPW III: 26–28 (July).

—— (1968b), 'More on Returns to Scale in Indian Agriculture', EPW III: 43 (26 October).

—— (1980), 'Local Power and Farm Level Decision Making', Paper presented to SSRC-ICSSR Conference on Power and Productivity (New Delhi: 14–16 December).

Rudra, Ashok and Amartya Sen (1980), 'Farm Size and Labour Use: Analysis and Policy', EPW XV: Annual Number (February).

Russett, Bruce (1964), 'Inequality and Instability: The Relation of Land Tenure to Politics', *World Politics* XVI: 3 (April).

Saini, G. R. (1969), 'Farm Size, Productivity, and Returns to Scale', EPW IV: 26 (June 28).

Sanderatne, Nimal (1980) 'Institutionalizing Small Farm Credit: Performance and Problems in Sri Lanka', *Staff Studies* (Colombo: Central Bank of Ceylon).

Samarasinghe, S. W. R. de A. (ed.) (1976), *Agriculture in the Peasant Sector of Sri Lanka* (Peradeniya: Ceylon Studies Seminar).

Sanyal, S. K. (1972), 'Has There Been a Decline in Agricultural Tenancy?', EPW VII: 19 (May).

Saradamoni, K. (1980), *Emergence of a Slave Caste: Pulayas of Kerala* (New Delhi: People's Publishing House).

Scott, James C. and Benedict J. Kerkvliet (1973), 'How Traditional Rural Patrons Lose Legitimacy', *Cultures et Développement* (Summer).

Selnick, Irwin (1978), 'Agrarian Radicalism and the Green Revolution in India 1965–1977: A Bibliographic Essay and Annotated Bibliography', unpublished essay (New York).

Sen Gupta, N. (1977), 'Further on the Mode of Production in Agriculture', EPW 12: 26 (June).

Shah, Mihir (1980), 'On the Development of Capitalism in Agriculture', Centre for Development Studies, Working Paper No. 107 (Trivandrum).

Shahjahan, Mirza (1968), *Agricultural Credit in East Pakistan* (Dacca: Dacca University).

Sharma, Hari P. (1973), 'The Green Revolution in India: Prelude to a Red One?" in Kathleen Gough and Hari P. Sharma (eds.), *Imperialism and Revolution in South Asia* (New York: Monthly Review Press).

Shetty, S. L. (1979), 'Performance of Commercial Banks since Nationalization of Major Banks in 1969', National Institute of Bank Management (Bombay), reprinted from EPW 13: 31–33 (August 1978).

Shivakumar, S. S. (1980), ' "Efficient" Small Farm, Demographic Differentiation, and "Iron Chest" Accounting System: Some Aspects of Peasantist Economics', EPW XV: 13 (March 29).

Shivamaggi, H. B. (1977), 'Case Studies of a Few Agricultural Families Belonging to the Weaker Sections in India', *Reserve Bank Staff Occasional Papers* 2: 2 (Bombay).

Stinchcombe, Arthur L. (1961), 'Agricultural Enterprise and Rural Class Relations', *American Journal of Sociology* 67 (September).

Tanter, Raymond and Manus Midlarsky (1967), 'A Theory of Revolution', *Journal of Conflict Resolution* XI: 3 (September).

Thorner, Daniel (1956), *The Agrarian Prospect in India* (Delhi: Delhi School of Economics, University Press).

—— (1963), *Agricultural Cooperatives in India* (Bombay: Asia).

—— (1967), 'Capitalist Stirrings in Rural India: Tour Notes', *The Statesman* (Calcutta) (1–4 November). Reprinted in Thorner (1980).

—— (1968), 'The Emergence of Capitalist Agriculture in India', Paper for Conference of European Scholars on South Asia, Cambridge. Reprinted in Thorner (1980).

—— (1980), The *Shaping of Modern India* (New Delhi: Allied).

Thorner, Daniel and Alice (1962), *Land and Labour in India* (Bombay: Asia).

Tilakaratna, W. M. (1963) *Agricultural Credit in a Developing Economy* (Colombo: Central Bank of Ceylon).

United Nations Food and Agriculture Organization (1979), 'Declaration of Principles and Programme of Action', World Conference on Agrarian Reform and Rural Development (Rome).

United Nations Research Institute for Social Development (1974), 'Research Notes' (June).

Varghese, T. C. (1970), *Agrarian Change and Economic Consequences* (Bombay: Allied).

Wade, Robert (1975), 'Administration and Distribution of Irrigation Benefits', EPW 10 (November).

Wadhwa, D. C. (1978), 'Zamindars in Debt' in R. Rothermund and D. C. Wadhwa (eds.), *Zamindars, Mines and Peasants* (Delhi: Manohar).

Wolf, Eric (1966), *Peasants* (Englewood Cliffs: Prentice-Hall).

World Bank (1974), *Land Reforms* (Washington, D.C.).

—— (1979), *Bangladesh: Current Trends and Development Issues* (Washington, D.C.).

Wright, Eric Olin (1978), *Class, Crisis, and the State* (London: New Left Books).

Zagoria, Donald S. (1971), 'The Ecology of Peasant Communism in India', *The American Political Science Review* 65.

Local Power and Farm-level Decision-making

ASHOK RUDRA

Introduction

We shall at the very outset define what we mean by the terms 'local' and 'power'. By a locality we mean the smallest social unit (above that of the family) in which power in the sense we shall define it may be observed and therefore postulated to operate. We shall be concerned with rural localities and we shall postulate (once again on the basis of empirical observations) that the locality in rural areas coincides with the village.[1]

By power we mean a social phenomenon given rise to by such institutional factors as class divisions, caste hierarchy, distribution

[1] In India there are various definitions of the village. Villages as defined for the purposes of the census may not be the same as villages recognized by the revenue authorities. The revenue villages are territorial units which include cultivated fields, fallow and uncultivable areas as well as such land as are devoted to residential purposes. For our purpose, we mean by a village a cluster of homesteads in close proximity to each other and usually separated from each other by open spaces. Such a village constitutes a social unit and it is this unit we call a locality. In the real world, however, there are exceptions. In some parts of India (e.g. Kerala) one cannot distinguish any clusters of homesteads: they are found to be scattered over the countryside in a continuous stretch. In other areas it may happen that a village consists exclusively of upper caste landowning families and in such a case one can usually discover a nearby settlement of labourers, poor tenants, etc., possibly with a different census or revenue identification. In such a case these two settlements are to be taken together as constituting the smallest social unit. In certain other cases a very large census or revenue village may have several quarters or wards not all of which may constitute a single social unit. That is to say, there may be different localities each consisting of one or more of the quarters or wards.

of wealth and income, occupational patterns, etc., and such ideological forces as customs, traditions, taboos, etc., affecting the process of decision-making by economic agents. This concept of power excludes the concept of economic power. It includes political power in so far as it is born out of the local social structure and applied by local agents but excludes state power as applied by the representatives of the state to the local community. The reason for excluding economic power is that it is already taken care of in some fashion or other in the received theories of economics. By 'economic power' of an individual we mean the command over and the access to resources which an agent can acquire by virtue of his possession of wealth or his entitlement to income, the power being proportionate in some way to the importance of his wealth or income. From a theoretical point of view differences in such power from agent to agent does not pose any problems in economics; as is well known, in the latter discipline analysis always starts by according different quantities of what are called 'endowments' to different agents. Exclusion of state power from our consideration is motivated by the following reasons. In so far as state power is concerned with the implementation of policies of the government it is once again taken care of in received theories. Farm-level responses in principle belong to the two domains of economic theory which go by the names of Public Finance and Welfare Economics.

It is true that there are many public policies affecting the rural sector in Indian economy which have not been adequately treated in the literature. Thus, such an important package of measures like the levy on foodgrains, support prices and procurement prices, restrictions on movement of grains between districts and zones, etc., have not yet been subjected to thoroughgoing analysis. Farm-level responses to such measures are therefore not fully understood and their macro-economic repercussions not fully evaluated. On the other hand, how power structure in India as a whole or in a region as a whole gives rise to unequal distribution of public resources like credit, inputs for agriculture, etc., among private operators is a subject that has been amply studied and there cannot be too many obscure corners in that area.

All the same, in this essay our concern is not with issues which are in principle taken care of in received theories but are neglected in practice. Our focus is on issues which are left out of the ambit of received theories even in principle. It is for this reason that we are leaving out economic power altogether. We also exclude from the concept of local power the administrative power exercised by local-level administrative and police officials in so far as they act to implement state policies, because this particular role is nothing other than the concrete expression of state power which we have already decided to exclude. On the other hand, we include the power of such local-level officials when it is not used to implement state policies but is exercised independently of them. Even though this power is derived by the persons concerned from the offices held by them it does not constitute a part of state power. An example would make clear the distinction. A police official, when he acts to enforce a levy on a cultivator, is applying state power. But when he lifts vegetables from a cultivator's field he is merely acting as a bully and is applying local-level power.

Model of a Self-contained Village Society

We present in this section a model of a village society showing the functioning of social power at the local level. Like all models this model also differs from reality in matters of detail. But like all valid models in science it is suggested by empirical observations and constitutes an idealization of those observations. In later sections, we shall present some data based on some case studies which will illustrate the degree to which the model approximates reality.

A village society is composed of two parts. One part consists of those who possess little or no means of production and who live by exchanging their labour power against money or items of food in the capacity of agricultural labourers or tenants. These people, whom we shall simply call labourers, constitute the majority among the villagers. The other part consists of a minority of property owners who derive income by appropriating a surplus out of the use values produced by labourers. Among the property owners there is usually a handful of big landowners who effectively dominate the village society.

The village society functions with three kinds of local power. The first is exercised by the minority consisting of property owners over the majority consisting of labourers. The second is exercised by labourers over the property owners. The third consists of certain ideological forces of customs, traditions, taboos, etc., and applies to all sections of the population including property owners and labourers. All these three powers affect the economic decisions of the affected parties in such a manner as to make them depart from the principles of profit maximization in the case of property owners and of utility maximization in the case of labourers. Of these three kinds of power, the last, consisting of ideological forces, is part and parcel of a culture and tradition which operates at much higher levels than the village. Some of them are of regional dimensions and some even of countrywide dimensions. The intensity with which they work, however, differs from village to village. The two other kinds of power, however, are entirely village specific. They are the products of a phenomenon of isolation and self-sufficiency of the society which is a peculiarity of the Indian village society.

Each village society is self-contained and isolated from the other in so far as production relations are concerned. That is to say, persons who enter into relations with each other around acts of production in agriculture belong to the same village society. Conversely, persons belonging to different village societies, even of adjacent villages, do not enter into such relations. In concrete terms, the majority of villagers who are fully or partly wage labourers or fully or partly tenants are forced by conditions, which we shall analyse, to restrict their transactions either as sellers of labour power or lease holders of land or borrowers of money to employers, landlords and agricultural moneylenders respectively, all of whom are residents of the same village. The employers, landlords and agricultural moneylenders in their turn are also obliged to restrict their transactions to only those who are residents of the same village.

For a member of the property-owning minority, labourers belonging to the village constitute a reserve of labour specifically meant for himself and his property-owning neighbours. He knows the labourers individually and has continuing long-term association with some of them. Even among those whom he might employ casually but not regularly there are some on whom he can depend when he requires labour urgently. For a labourer belonging to the village the farms of the property-owning minority constitute a reserved terrain for his exclusive exploitation. The property-owning people, in fact, constitute the sole source for all the assistance that he requires in money, in kind, as well as in moral terms to survive in his precarious existence. He would starve to death should he lose his moorings in the village society.

This gives rise to a patron–client type of relationship between the majority of labourers and the minority of property owners, a relationship of mutual though necessarily unequal dependence.[2] This relationship is not confined only to such economic exchanges as can be quantified, priced and contracted. It extends much beyond them and pervades the entire social life of the village community. As such the dependence of labourers on employers is not restricted only to the labour processes in which they participate but covers all aspects of their life process.

The basis of such exchanges is *personal knowledge* between individual employers and individual labourers. It is this personal knowledge that makes unnecessary any collaterals of the usual kind for loans, which in any case labourers cannot provide. It is the physical existence of the labourers with the potential of labour power always at the disposal of the village society which acts as a collateral. Such personal knowledge is a privilege of people who are close neighbours, whereas it is not practical between people who live far apart from each other. It is for this reason that the labourers and employers

[2] Some economic theorists trained in the Walrasian tradition and therefore living in a world of beatific equalities among all economic agents fail to understand the concept of a relation of 'unequal' mutual dependence between two parties. While it is not possible for us here to enter into the philosophical aspects of the concepts of equal and unequal which seem to plague these theorists, we may briefly state the particular concrete expressions of inequality that we have in mind. An employer of labour in a village has many options if village labourers should refuse to work for him. He may bring in labourers from distant areas, though that is admittedly not possible in all areas and in all seasons. He may forgo cultivation for one season, which will not make him starve. His current consumption requirements are met by withdrawals from stocks of food items which he has got from previous harvests. This apart, he has various other sources of income. The rich farmer typically puts his eggs in several baskets. It is typical of him to have made some investments in such side occupations as fishery, animal husbandry, poultry, retail trade and, in the case of bigger farmers, various service businesses with their centres of operation in nearby towns. They also have savings in the form of money, gold, utensils, etc. The agricultural labourer and the poor tenant are, however, solely dependent on work on the employer's or landlord's fields for their livelihood. They usually do not have any stock of food items at home nor do they have any savings in money or gold. On the contrary, they are typically indebted to their employers and their landlords. Some of them do have some subsidiary occupations but that is usually not enough to make them survive through a season without employment on the employer's or landlord's farm.

It is thus seen that our concept of unequal dependence is based on the unequal power of causing damage to the other party by withdrawing co-operation in the production process.

entering into production relations belong to the same village.

As an illustration of the patron–client relationship extending well beyond exchanges which can be quantified, priced and contracted, the following typical explanations provided by two interviewees are significant:

'I may require a labourer to come and help me in the middle of the night, for example, if it has rained and the living quarters and the paddy godown have got flooded. There are no rates for such work to be done at such an hour. Such a service cannot be purchased.'

'I am a poor man and I do not even have enough to eat every day. I may require urgently some money for a funeral in the family. To whom shall I go?'

It may be noted that the villages are not isolated from the rest of the world in every aspect of their social and economic life, as they are conceived to be in the theory of the Asiatic Mode of Production. As a matter of fact, relations given rise to by the distribution of goods as well as flow of money capital are not restricted to the interior of the village society. On the contrary such exchanges typically connect persons belonging to one village with persons and institutions in nearby urban centres and (to a much lesser extent) with persons in other villages. In concrete terms, the marketable surplus of products are sold to merchants and their agents who typically are non-residents of the village. The surplus value realized by the property owners in the form of money capital is largely invested in various productive and unproductive fields outside the village. On the other hand, capital from the rest of the economy enters the village in significant amounts in the form of government investments in development projects as well as working capital loans advanced by commercial banks and other lending institutions to the property owners. Also the professional moneylenders (as distinguished from the agricultural moneylenders) do not operate in a single village but over a large number of them in an entire neighbourhood.

The phenomenon of unequal mutual dependence of property owners and labourers includes some kind of collusion among the property owners and some amount of collective understanding or action by the labourers. It may take extreme forms like strikes by workers or of all employers following the leadership of the single most important employer in the village in the settling of the wage rate. On the other hand, it may take loose forms like mere consultations. In either case the phenomenon we are talking about is a social one, in the sense that it represents certain conditions which all parties have to respect. Contracts entered into by individual property owners and labourers have to be such as to be within the boundaries of these conditions. When we use the expression 'village society' as an actor, what we really mean is the acceptance by all individuals of this commonly accepted boundary.

The phenomenon of absentee landlordism does not constitute any departure from the ideal of self-containment enshrined in the model. The absentee landlord fully belongs to the village society even though he is normally not a resident of the village. Likewise seasonal in-migration of labourers does not in any way constitute an imperfection in self-sufficiency. As a matter of fact, the need for in-migration of labourers is made more acute by the isolation of neighbouring villages from each other and that isolation is further reinforced by the in-migration itself in a process which will be elaborated below.

We have completed presenting our model of the self-sufficient isolated village society. In the following sections we shall describe how the local power of the village society with its three dimensions affect farm-level decision-making. We shall consider in particular decisions involved in the transactions between employers and labourers, tenants and landlords and borrowers and agricultural moneylenders. We are deliberately avoiding the terms 'labour market', 'lease market' and 'credit market' as in our judgement the usual properties of such markets assumed in economic theory are prevented by the village society from operating on the transactions referred to above.

Employer–Employee Relations

The local power generated by the self-contained village society affects the economic behaviour of employers and wage labourers in the following fashion:

(*a*) Cultivators as well as labourers fail to maximize their income as a result of voluntarily refraining from all or certain kinds of manual operations.

(*b*) Labourers cannot maximize their income by working for employers paying the highest wages in an area which is within the reach of labourers.

(*c*) Employers cannot maximize their profit by employing labourers at the lowest wages available in an area from where labourers can reach the village.

(*d*) Better labourers cannot earn more than their inferior colleagues in the same village as a function of their higher productivity.

(*e*) Employers cannot lower their costs by paying lower wages to labourers with lower productivity.

The first constraint affecting members of labouring as well as self-employed cultivating families arises from the operation of the power represented by the ideological forces.[3] The next two constraints, i.e. (*b*) and (*c*), on the employers and employees arise from their restricting labour recruitment and search for work opportunity to the inside of the village society. The results, (*d*) and (*e*), are given rise to by there being at any time in a village a uniform wage rate for all male casual labourers for the same operation, which varies drastically from village to village.[4]

The model that we have outlined postulates total isolation and self-containment of each village, which of course is an idealization that goes with any model-making. The reality, however, is never so streamlined. There are indeed many villages from where no labourers

---

[3] See Table 1. The data presented in this as well as in subsequent tables to illustrate some of the points made in the text of the essay are based on some investigations that were carried out by me in two clusters of adjacent villages, both in the proximity of Santiniketan, where this essay was written. These investigations were part of a research project which was supported by the International Labour Organization. Many other findings of the project may be found in the working paper entitled 'Extra-economic Constraints on Agricultural Labour' published by ARTEP (Asian Regional Team for Employment Promotion), ILO, Bangkok, and also in the forthcoming paper 'Labour Mobility and the Boundaries of the Village Moral Economy' by Bardhan and Rudra. One of the subjects of the investigations was to find out the extent of non-participation in manual labour by such members of agricultural households of different categories who might be demographically regarded as suitable for being members of the labour force. Table 1 presents figures relating to such non-participation, separately for different categories of agricultural households, and also separately for male and female labourers.

[4] Table 3 presents the wage rates, prevailing in the period mid-October to mid-November 1980, in a number of pairs of villages which are adjacent to each other being mostly separated by a distance of less than 2 km and only in some cases by a maximum distance of 3 km. One may notice that even in such close proximity village wage rates may differ not only in value but also in the composition of the wage basket. Table 2 presents a frequency distribution of different wage rates prevalent in the dense cluster of 39 villages in the Illambazar area where we carried out one of our case studies. Table 4 presents some pairwise comparisons of seasonal wage rise in neighbouring villages.

go out for work to any other place and to which no labourers come from any other place. But there are other villages from where some labourers do go out for work to other places and likewise villages to which labourers come for work from other villages.[5] However, unless one is talking of such special villages which constitute nodes for out-migration the proportion of labourers going to work in places outside their own village is usually quite small. In the case studies that have been the basis of our information the proportion of labourers going to other places of work constitutes less than 10 per cent; whereas the proportion of employers hiring labourers from other villages was simply zero, indicating a very low incidence in the population.

The investigations which have yielded the data presented in the tables also provide explanations for the different restrictions under consideration as articulated by villagers themselves in response to appropriate questions. As to the reasons for non-participation in manual labour, social status is explicitly stated to be the most important explanation applicable to both male and female members of the cultivating families. In our case studies of the non-participating male members nearly 80 per cent gave either social status or being out of habit as the explanation. This particular explanation gets combined with a related one which may be worded as 'religious taboo' when it comes to female members. It is interesting that this factor affects participation in manual labour not only of the female members of cultivating families but even of those of labouring families. The importance of the cultural factor in this particular respect is reflected in the important differences in the two areas in which our case studies were carried out. One area was Muslim-dominated where the female participation rate even among labouring families was much lower than in the other Hindu-dominated area. Also, the reason most commonly given in the Muslim-dominated area amounted to religious taboo, which was much less important in the explanations provided by the respondents in the Hindu-dominated area.

Among the reasons for labourers and employers in neighbouring

[5] Table 5 presents a classification of the 39 villages in one of the clusters according to the nature of their relations with their neighbouring villages in terms of the movement of labour among them. Table 6 presents a frequency distribution of the same villages over a number of villages in the same cluster with which they have any relation of labour movement.

villages not being workwise related, the following are the most important:

(*a*) As labourers do not go out to other villages for work employers reciprocate by not employing labourers from other villages, lest village labourers be not available during busy periods.

(*b*) Labourers do not allow labourers from the neighbouring villages to come in.

(*c*) There is an understanding among labourers of adjacent villages that they would not enter into each other's territories.

(*d*) Labourers do not go to other villages for fear of losing the benefits of consumption loans and other help from village employers.

In comparison with the reasons cited above, such practical difficulties as labourers having to travel some distance from their residence to their place of work, the consequent reduction of the working time available, etc., were found to be much less important. Also, the number of cases where a labourer could not work in some other village because of his having already taken some consumption loan from employers of his own village was not very large. In other words, it is not so much the fact of being already committed to some village employer or employers that is of decisive importance: what is so is the condition that the labourer has to keep himself in readiness for any call on his services by any village employer.

The villagewise wage variation suggests that the factors affecting the process of wage determination are at least partially village specific. As a matter of fact, the differences are not only in the value of the wage basket. There are differences in all the dimensions of the phenomenon of wages—the composition of the wage basket, sex discriminations, seasonal fluctuations, once for all wage rises, etc. As to different wages for male and female labourers, it happens that the villages we investigated constitute some kind of exceptions, in that in most of them there is no difference between the wage rates for male and female labourers. This egalitarian treatment might, however, be quite illusory. It might be merely reflecting the fact that for most of the operations employment of female labourers is not at all customary. On the other hand, a few specific operations, like transplanting of paddy, might be given exclusively to female labourers. If these conditions happen to be true, comparison between male and female wage rates is simply not possible. However, our present interest is villagewise variation. From that point of view it is noteworthy that in two out of a cluster of 39 contiguous villages female wages were reported to be lower than male wages and in one higher. Whether female labourers are really paid different wages or whether male and female labourers are non-competitive is a different issue; what is significant in either case is the fact that these villages in a dense-cluster fall out of line with the rest of the villages.

If there was any kind of mobility of labour between neighbouring villages it could not have happened that there would be seasonal wage-rise affecting some of them whereas some others would be left untouched. But this is precisely what may be observed among a number of neighbouring villages.[6] Yet another related point is the sharp differences that may be observed in the amount of seasonal rise even between villages which are separated by a distance of no more than a kilometre or two.[7]

The way the process of wage-formation seems to take place independently in each village is illustrated by the varying histories of changes in the wage-level in the neighbouring villages investigated in our case studies. In the 39 villages constituting a dense-cluster in which we carried out one of our case studies wage-rise took place in each one of them sometime during the last two years. But the processes differed. It would appear that labourers in these villages have not developed any organized contacts among themselves and have not acquired any consciousness of their common interests. They could not obviously conceive of any collective action in all the villages taken together. Not only that, even labourers belonging to the same village do not reveal any capability of acting in a collective fashion. Even in the villages where there were strikes they were precipitate actions without any collective bargaining; that is to say, they were in the nature of wild-cat strikes typical of undeveloped working-class consciousness.[8]

---

[6] See Table 4.   [7] Ibid.

[8] In the Illambazar cluster there were strikes in only nine of the villages. In six of them there were negotiations before the event whereas in three of them the strike was precipitated without any attempts by the two parties at any negotiated settlements. In the remaining thirty villages the process of wage rise not only did not involve any strike, but in most of them there was not even any collective bargaining or negotiations. In nine of them the wage rise was effected by one big landowner acting unilaterally and announcing a rise for his labourers, the remaining employers being obliged to follow his leadership. In nine other villages the initial step was taken by such a single big employer, but the final settlement came only after other big employers of the village had deliberated over the matter in a collective manner. In the remaining twelve cases there was no leadership role

We shall now try to see the consequences for economic theory of the conditions of labour supply and the nature of relations between labourers and employers that we have described. We have said that one can hardly think in terms of a labour market for the analytic treatment of this phenomenon. By a 'market' we mean an institution in which purchasers and sellers exchange a commodity at a standard price and with full freedom. That is to say, there are no restrictions on who can sell the product and who can purchase it. Anybody who is ready to pay the price is free to purchase it. Anybody who is ready to receive that price is free to sell it. Conversely, somebody who is not ready to sell a commodity for a price or to pay the price for that commodity cannot be coerced to do so. As is well known, such a market is treated analytically in economic theory in terms of demand and supply functions, and it is also well known that most of the important results of economic theory are derived by postulating perfect competition.

There is a host of difficulties in applying this framework to the exchange of labour against wages in our model of the village society. First, the condition of the same price for the same commodity does not apply. Labourers with the same productive qualities receive different prices for being located in different villages. This may happen even within the same village if one is considering not casual labourers but other kinds of labourers like farm servants and semi-attached labourers.[9] On the other hand, labourers with different productive

---

played by any single important employer; all the important employers of the village put their heads together and came to some agreement.

The obvious inference is that there was general discontent which was expressed in the form of murmurings and not in the form of any collective demands. Labourers expressed their dissatisfactions separately and individually to their respective employers. The employers being more conscious of their own class interests pre-empted the labourers getting together and acting collectively. This is an aspect of the patron–client relationship preventing the formation of a class out of agricultural labourers.

[9] We have discussed in this essay only casual labourers working on daily wages. There are, however, various other categories of labourers in Indian agriculture. One such important category is made up of those who are called farm servants. They usually work on an annual contract basis for a single employer. Quite often the same servant may work for a given employer over several years through renewals of the contract at the end of each year. While casual and attached labourers dominate among agricultural labourers, there is a rich variety of labour contracts that fall somewhere in between the two polar cases of daily contracts and annual contracts. They are intermediate not merely in contract duration but

qualities receive the same wages for no other reason than belonging to the same village society.[10] Secondly, the freedom of purchasers and sellers is also not respected. A particular labourer may not be free to work for just any employer if he has been called upon by a particular employer to work for him. This may happen even when there are no contractual obligations between them. It is a part of the patron–client relationship between them that they should render such preferential treatment to each other. Not only the supply and demand for labour might be thus dependent on the persons involved; even the prices offered and taken might be personalized. A labourer may work for a lower wage for a particular employer. Sometimes it may be the other way round and an employer may voluntarily offer higher wages to a labourer with long-standing loyalty toward him.

In such a world one can hardly think in terms of a supply schedule for individual labourers according to which he would supply different quantities of labour at different wage rates. That does not seem to be the way labourers look at wages. At a given time they would either accept a certain wage rate or they would not, and in doing this they do not act individually but collectively. On the other hand, they have

---

also in the degree of attachment to the employer. They are characterized by having some continuous association with some employer with the understanding to work for him on a priority basis whenever the employer would require his services, while retaining the freedom of working for other employers at other times. This guarantee of labour supply is often based on the allotment of a piece of land by the employer to the labourer who cultivates it with the employer's bullock and plough and gets a share of the product. An ancient debt could also be a basis, but this has lost its importance in present-day India. Much more important is a current loan taken on condition of its being repaid through labour whenever the employer would require labour. Some lump sum payment does also sometimes act as a basis for such a guarantee. But semi-attachment relation may occur without any such concrete basis. (See Bardhan and Rudra, 1980a, 1980b and 1981.)

[10] Different labourers with different productive qualities receiving the same wages may prompt some theorists to look for explanations in the cost of information. The argument would be that the trouble of finding out differential productive qualities of different workers and fixing differential wages would exceed the resultant gains. This, however, is not very convincing. The labourers of the village are all personally known to the employers of the village. Their qualities as labourers are established facts of village social life. There is therefore no question of wages being settled through fresh bargaining every time a labourer is employed casually. It should also be kept in mind that uniform wages prevail not only during busy periods but also during lean periods when the cost may be zero.

no consultations over the matter with labourers of other villages, even neighbouring ones.

It is clear therefore that such tools of analysis as the aggregate supply function and the aggregate demand function cannot be applied to labourers and employers respectively aggregated over the different villages or within individual villages. As the wage rate for the same operation and at the same time varies from village to village, one cannot establish any correspondence between prices, aggregate demands and aggregate supplies. This difficulty does not affect aggregation within the same village but, as we have mentioned before, the number of agents being very small, there cannot be any competitive model in which these aggregate demands and supplies can be treated as functions of price.

A die-hard theorist may make a formulation of the following kind: the market for labour is segmented, each village constituting a segment. One wonders, however, what might be the analytical use of working with such a concept of a segmented market. While the number of segments could run into hundreds and thousands in the economy as a whole, the numbers of labourers and employers in each segment would be such that neither the results of perfect competition nor those of monopolistic competition would be applicable to them. As is well known, the former requires the number of competitors to be infinite in rigorous theory and extremely large for all practical purposes. On the other hand, the numbers involved are too large for the application of any of the analytic tools of imperfect competition. There are no kinds of theoretical models of competition, perfect or imperfect, which can be applied to a 'market' consisting of, say, fifty or a hundred sellers and, say, ten or twenty employers, which may include two or three 'dominant' ones.

We have been talking in terms of the applicability or otherwise of the standard assumptions and analytic tools of neo-classical theory. We shall now discuss some consequences of this model of the village society for Marxian political economy. According to the latter, the crucial criterion for a mode of production being regarded as capitalist is that labour in it must have become a commodity, free of all extra-economic constraints. It is quite clear that labour in the village society is far from being free in that sense. The territorial limits to the activities of labourers and employers as well as non-participation of potential members of the labour force in certain kinds of manual operations are not dictated by any economic rationality. They are not imposed by any juridical forces either; they are enforced by custom working through the village society.

Yet another theoretical consequence of the inter-village and intra-village heterogeneity and segmentation of the labourers is that the concept of class, in the Marxian sense of class-for-itself, cannot be applied to the labourers in Indian agriculture. The common economic positions occupied by the individual members of the agricultural labourers in the total economic structure and the subsidiary nature of the contradictions of interests among them as compared with the dominant contradiction of interests between them and their employers do make these labourers constitute what Marx called a class-in-itself. For a class-in-itself to develop into a class-for-itself it is necessary that the members of the class-in-itself become conscious of their common economic interests, the subsidiary nature of the contradictions among them and the primary importance of their contradictions with their employers and get organized so as to struggle to further their own class interests. We have seen before that labourers in different villages are isolated from each other to a large extent by their own volition. Labourers of one village would fight with those of the next village should they trespass into their village. The labourers thus identify themselves more with the employers of their own village than with the labourers of the next village.

If the analytical tools of aggregate demand and supply functions be not applicable nor class struggle on a countrywide scale provide any clue to the process of wage determination, one has to look at new directions for theoretically understanding how wages for casual labourers come to be very largely uniform within each village while differing drastically in different villages in the same neighbourhood. In tackling a new problem whether only to twist and turn and manipulate existing analytical tools or to recognize that a new paradigm is called for is something that cannot be answered with the help of any kind of logic or models; for the judgement involved here concerns the functional and aesthetic qualities of models and the question belongs to the domain of meta-science. Our own view is that a totally new paradigm is indeed called for to make possible satisfactory model-building to explain the processes of demand and supply of labour and wage formation in Indian villages.

In our view the process has to be understood in terms of the countervailing power of the labourers exercised over the property owners. It is probably native wisdom of the labouring people that it would prove dangerous for them should they permit the employers to pay different amounts to different labourers, depending on their assessment of skill, capacity to work, etc., of individual labourers. They probably legitimately fear that if this were permitted the wage rate could be driven down to zero. They also know that different wages offered to different labourers would cause disunity and dis-affection among them. Even when labourers are not organized in unions they have a sense of community and an understanding of collective self-interest which is an integral part of the ethos of the village society.

Landlord–Tenant Relations

We shall now see how economic decision-making by landlords who get their land cultivated by tenants on a share-cropping basis is affected by the three kinds of power exercised by the village society. We shall not consider fixed rent tenancy which happens to be of extremely rare occurrence in the villages we studied. We shall also keep out of our purview the emerging phenomenon of rich tenants leasing in land from poor landowners. Our concern will be the classic phenomenon of big landowners dealing with poor tenants.

Just as most labourers and employers dealing with each other belong to the same village society, with of course some marginal exceptions, landlords and tenants entering into relations with each other through land lease also mostly belong to the same village society. Just as the wage rate for daily labourers is uniform within a village but may vary widely even among neighbouring villages, the set of product and cost shares ruling in one village may also vary considerably among neighbouring villages. In one village there may be a single share (say 50:50) for the main crop and no cost shares whatsoever. In the very next village there may again be only a single share, that for the main crop, but that may be different (say 60:40, meaning 60 per cent for the owner and 40 per cent for the tenant). And in the third village within a radius of five miles there may be three alternative sets as given in the table on p. 266.

It may be mentioned that economic theory has not yet managed to grapple satisfactorily with even much simpler patterns of share-cropping tenancy even though it has received attention from neo-classical theorists at least from the time of Marshall. Most models of

Sets	Ordinary Paddy	HYV Paddy	Seed	Fertilizer
A	50 : 50	—	0 : 100	— *
B		40 : 60	40 : 60	40 : 60
C	50 : 50	50 : 50	50 : 50	50 : 50

* No application.

tenancy take the rental share as an exogenously determined parameter. They also make the simplification of retaining only a single
share, that of the main crop, ignoring all cost shares. The few models
that do treat the rental share as an endogenous variable usually end
up with the share depending on the endowments of the landlord and
the tenant, which would mean that the share would be different for
each landlord–tenant pair. If one has at all generalized for many
tenants, that has been done by assuming identical tenants—a most
unrealistic assumption. Of late, there have been several attempts at
developing models that would explain the uniformity of the rental
share operating in different lease transactions, irrespective of the
different endowments of the different pairs of landlords and tenants
—a most intriguing and as yet unresolved problem. Even if these
attempts would soon bear fruit, they would not answer why the
rental shares are uniform within the same village but drastically
different among nearby villages.

We submit that such within-village uniformity and inter-village
variations cannot be compatible with any kind of individual maximizing behaviour as is assumed in economic theoretical models. We
suggest that this variability can be explained only in terms of the
different villages being isolated, self-contained worlds as far as the
functioning of the lease markets is concerned. The different sets of
proportions represent different balances of local power as between
the minority of landlords and the majority of tenants as well as the
resultant consensus among both the parties regarding what is 'fair',
'just', etc. The fact that certain rational fractions numerically dominate over others shows that the implicit economic calculations that
underlie the village society consensus, while differing from village
to village, are neither arbitrary nor irrational.

We shall now turn to certain other aspects of the patron–client
relationship as obtaining between the landlords and the tenants. For

the poor tenant the landlord is often the only source of consumption loans on which his dependence is not much less than that of the landless labourer. The landlord is quite often a willing lender (though, it is important to emphasize, *not all landlords are so*), given the fact that it is to the *landlord's* interest that the tenant manages to survive and retain his physical capacity to work; given also the fact that the crop share to which the tenant is entitled acts as a collateral. The landlord has a second protection against the risk of default in the power that he enjoys to evict the tenant. The owner is dependent on the tenant not only for the satisfactory completion of farm work during the current season: the poor tenant also sometimes acts as a labourer for him. However, exploitation in the form of unpaid or underpaid labour services would seem to be, at least in eastern India, much less important than some people's preconceptions about it. The interest of the landlord in such a relation does not lie so much in saving money on wages as in his getting an assured supply of labour; and that too not for the usual operations but to meet sudden emergencies.[11]

The landlord is also the most important source of production loans for the tenant. It is again important to emphasize that not all owners provide such loans. The poor tenant has got no access to any institutional credit. Left to himself he can barely arrange for any purchased inputs, which means that he may not go in for improved methods of cultivation. Low yields adversely affect not only the interest of the tenant but equally that of the owner. It is in the owner's interest to increase productivity on the tenant's farm, which he tries to

[11] Quite a lot of information about relations between landlords and tenants were collected by me in collaboration with P. K. Bardhan through an extensive survey carried out in different districts of West Bengal and some of the other eastern states. Some of the data are presented in Bardhan and Rudra (1978a, 1978b). It was found that consumption loan giving by landlords to tenants prevailed in 51 per cent of the cases of tenancy surveyed in West Bengal whereas the practice was absent in the remaining 49 per cent of the cases. It was also found that in 28 per cent of the cases such consumption loan was interest-free whereas in the remaining 23 per cent of the cases interest was not only charged but the rates involved were extraordinarily high. As to rendering of unpaid or underpaid labour services by the tenant, the incidence seems to have become of very low quantitative significance. Thus, it was found that only 5 per cent of the tenants investigated rendered unpaid services to their landlords. Another 5 per cent rendered services for which they were paid but at lower than the market wage rate. A larger proportion, 18 per cent of tenant respondents, reported working for their landlords at times, but they received full wages for their services.

achieve in two ways. First, he goes in for cost sharing in selected items requiring money expenditure, like HYV seeds, chemical fertilizers, etc. Secondly, he advances the tenant's share of these items of cost. In practice, the owner often himself procures from the market these items and for that he takes advantage, whenever he can, of his access to institutional credit. This production loan to the tenant is secured against default in the same way as consumption loan is secured. After the harvest a quantity of grain equivalent in value to the loan advanced by the landlord (plus interest, where there is interest) is deducted from the tenant's share of the harvest.[12]

A characteristic feature of this lease market in many parts of India is that there are no documents in which the terms and conditions of the contract are written down. As such it is more appropriate to talk of oral agreements rather than contracts. All the same the terms and conditions are quite clearly understood on either side. Cases of disputes arising out of any differences between the two parties about the terms in the course of the tenure are rare and exceptional. The village society as a whole acts as a guarantor of the terms and conditions being observed by both sides.

The patron–client relationship between landlords and tenants in many areas is so strong as to have been able to successfully resist its being transformed into a legally recognized institution. As is well known, in many parts of India there is a large amount of concealed tenancy, and this continues to remain so even when attempts are made to bring the matter to the surface by registering the tenants, as is being done in West Bengal under Operation Barga. Concealment of a tenancy arrangement can never be done without active collusion by the tenant: he has to declare himself either as cultivating his own land or as working as a labourer for the landlord. It is this collusion that explains the failure of the Operation Barga to register more than a fraction of the tenants in West Bengal to this day.

The reason why the tenants have in so many cases on their own abstained from registration is expressed by themselves in some such words as: 'No, we have not registered ourselves. We have done no such *adharma* [i.e. wrongful or sinful action]. Why should we take

---

[12] The survey referred to in note 11 above yielded the following information. Landlords making production advances to tenants featured in 44 per cent of the cases, and in 21 per cent among them these advances were interest-free. On the other hand, in the remaining 56 per cent of the cases production loans were not available to tenants from landlords even against high interest.

away land from those to whom it belongs? After all they have been good to us since our father's time. If we should act traitorously now, to whom shall we turn when we require any assistance?' This takes us to the very heart of the patron–client relationship.

Sellers and Buyers of Paddy

We have said earlier that the phenomenon of self-containment of the village society giving rise to local power is much weaker with respect to the exchange of product than with respect to the relations given rise to by land, labour and credit. That is because, firstly, the market for agricultural products is largely a non-rural phenomenon, market transactions in such products within a village being minimal. Secondly, the majority of villagers are not sellers of products. Either they do not produce at all or they produce for self-consumption. As a result, the product market is largely a phenomenon of the regional level, involving the village only in the relatively bigger-sized farmers. Power in this market is very much the power exercised by rice millers, traders, etc., who do not belong to the village society.

However, though the majority of producers in a village have only a relatively small surplus for the market, even that little bit subjects them to local power because of the fragmented nature of the product market in which they have to sell. The most important aspect of marketing of products by poor farmers lies in that a large portion of their products can reach any traders only after passing through the channel of local-level rich farmers. This flow of products from small farmers to rich farmers takes the form of payments of rent by share-croppers, repayment of loans by tenants and other poor peasants as well as direct purchases by rich farmers from poor peasants made immediately after the harvest.[13]

The compulsion of the poor peasant to sell immediately after the harvest arises from a lack of storing facilities as well as a lack of holding capacity. Further, he is unable to avail himself of the many trading channels, sometimes offering better prices than are available

[13] The survey referred to above in note 11 also yielded information about marketing channels for paddy operating in the West Bengal villages and the conditions confronting different categories of sellers. It was found that in as many as 45 per cent of the villages rich farmers constituted one of the trading channels for the poor farmers and in about 20 per cent of them they constituted the most important channel for that category. The other important locally available channel was constituted of small traders.

in nearby market centres and rice-mills, for lack of his own means of transport. The product market is thus divided into two parts: one part consists of dealers in nearby market centres—rice-mills, *hats* (periodic markets), wholesale traders, etc.—and the other part consists of village-level traders—retailers, agents of market centre traders, agents of rice-mills, itinerant merchants and, of course, the big farmers. Smaller farmers' dealings in product are confined within this village-level market. In so far as they deal with the big farmers they are subject to the local power wielded by them.[14]

Small farmers come under the power of big farmers in the product market through a second mechanism. This has to do with a second compartmentation of the product market which is given rise to by the time factor. Schematically one can think in terms of two markets for any crop between two successive harvesting periods. The first market lasts over the first harvest period and the immediate post-harvest period. The second prevails over the period preceding the next harvest period. The sellers in the first market are poor peasants; the purchasers in this market are professional traders and rich farmers. In the second market the sellers are rich farmers and the purchasers are professional traders as well as poor peasants who were sellers in the first market. The entry into these two markets is far from 'free'. The poor peasant is not free to enter as seller in the second market which is the preserve of the rich farmers who save up their marketable surplus from the previous harvest to take advantage of the high prices prevailing during the next pre-harvest season.

Borrowers and Lenders

The village society provides the following alternative sources of credit to all but a few of the most affluent members of the society (the latter have access to outside and institutional sources): (*a*) professional moneylenders; (*b*) big farmers; (*c*) grain traders;

---

[14] The different trading channels do not offer the same prices nor does the same channel offer the same price to all the different parties selling to them. Thus, it was found in the survey we have been referring to that big farmers typically offered lower prices than other trading channels, in principle open to all sellers. On the other hand, they typically sold grains, whether produced in their own farms or purchased from their poor neighbours, to rice-mills as well as wholesalers in nearby market towns. The rice-mills and market wholesalers typically offered higher prices to these important clients.

and (*d*) retail shops. Of these it is the big farmers and retail shops that constitute the principal source for majority of labourers and poor peasants, including tenants. Professional moneylenders are beyond the access of poor people because of the latter's inability to provide any security: as these people live at the very border of subsistence, the moneylender cannot enrich himself by impoverishing them any further. Professional moneylenders seem to be declining in importance at least in some parts of India, presumably because of their clients, consisting principally of better-off farmers, having increasing access to institutional credit. Professional moneylenders of the traditional variety do not belong to the village society as they normally carry on their activities in a whole cluster of villages. The same is true of itinerant moneylenders (e.g. Kabuliwallahs). We shall not treat these moneylenders as holders of local power.[15] Likewise we shall also exclude grain traders from our discussion because the capital that is advanced to small cultivators against commitment of future delivery of crops belongs to traders who operate at a level much above the local level. The village traders who might actually distribute the advances are mere agents of these bigger outside traders. As such the power exercised by this trading capital is not a part of local power. The number of small cultivators who are subject to this external power is much smaller than those who are subject to the power of the rich farmers. It is to this latter category and the retail traders that we shall restrict our discussion.

The loans taken from retail shops usually consist of small amounts and they carry an interest rate which is computed in money terms and on a monthly basis—between 10 to 15 per cent per month is quite common. This particular transaction between retail shops and their customers is not of much interest from the point of view of local power. From that point of view it is the big farmer acting as moneylender which is of supreme importance. The loans given by rich farmers are largely in the form of grains and the interest on such loans, when taken, is also in the form of grains. The practice is for a loan of one maund (1 maund = about 42 kg) to be repaid after

[15] Professional moneylenders were found to reside in only 30 per cent of the villages covered by the survey. On the other hand, 96 per cent of the villages reported the existence of agricultural moneylenders, that is, rich farmers indulging in lending of money or grains in a systematic manner as a side occupation. It is, however, understandable that the beneficiaries of these indigenous lending institutions should be confined mostly to the better-off farmers, and the poorer people who live by their labour should be left out of their reach.

the harvest with an interest of 1/4 maund, 1/2 maund or even one full maund, irrespective of the time duration between the taking of the loan and its repayment. This credit institution, dealing with a different clientele than the retail shops, is itself divided into a number of fragments.[16]

Thus, to take care of the consumption needs of poor tenants there is a special credit institution where the lenders are the landlords and the borrowers the respective tenants. A poor tenant's access is restricted to his own landlord or landlords; the landlord restricts his loan-giving operations to his own tenants. Some landlords do indulge in loan giving to parties other than their own tenants, but they are considerably fewer in number than those who give loans only to their tenants.[17]

A similar institution operates to meet the consumption needs of farm servants. Here the security is the unpaid labour provided by the servant for which he receives his wages at the end of the year. As a matter of fact, the farm servant's consumption loan is just a form of wage payment in instalments. Just as in the case of tenants, most employers of farm servants keep their loan-giving activities strictly restricted to their own servants whereas the latter are denied access to all other sources of credit. The proportion of employers who give loans to parties other than their own farm servants is much smaller than those who give loans to their own farm servants.[18]

Another specialized credit institution is the one where the borrowers are casual or unattached labourers and the lenders rich

[16] For more information about indigenous lending institutions and practices see Rudra (1975, 1982).

[17] We have seen in notes 11 and 12 that the proportion of tenants who received consumption loans and production advances from the landlords were 51 per cent and 44 per cent respectively. The proportion of landlords who gave loans to parties other than their own tenants was, however, found to be only 38 per cent. It is only these 38 per cent among the landlords who may be properly regarded as agricultural moneylenders. Those who lend only to their own tenants do not in our judgement qualify to be treated as agricultural moneylenders.

[18] The proportion of farm servants who reported receiving consumption loans from their employers was found to be 61 per cent, among whom 53 per cent paid no interest on those loans. It may, however, be borne in mind that in the case of a farm servant a consumption loan can hardly be distinguished from an instalment payment of his legitimate earnings by way of wages as they become due over the course of the year. As in the case of the landlords vis-à-vis tenants the proportion of employers who indulge in lending to parties other than their own farm servants was found to be less, e.g. 45 per cent.

farmers who give consumption loans in the lean seasons to these labourers against commitment of future labour. Here again the loan transaction is restricted on the one side to such labourers who have no employment during the lean seasons and on the other to such rich farmers who might require an assured supply of labour in the busy seasons.[19]

A characteristic feature of this fragmented credit institution is that extraordinarily high rates of interest prevail side by side with zero rate of interest. We have cited above the exorbitant interests (which would amount to between 100 to 200 per cent if reckoned on an annual basis) that are commonly charged on grain loans. When the transaction is in money and the interest is reckoned on an annual basis the rate is usually around 50 per cent. But side by side with borrowers paying such high interest there are many others who may regularly or on occasions get totally interest-free loans.

Some economists find it difficult to believe that the phenomenon of interest-free loans can exist at all. Their faith in their theoretical conceptions about the Economic Man maximizing money income is so strong that they would deny the existence of the phenomenon even though it has been widely encountered not only by us but also in surveys conducted by official agencies like the Reserve Bank of India. According to them, whoever lends must be doing so to maximize his money income and therefore cannot be giving loans at lower than the market rate of interest. Also, a grain loan of one maund taken before the harvest and repaid in one maund after the harvest would involve a negative interest because of the difference in prices before and after the harvest and this must be nonsensical.

The trouble lies, in our opinion, with the assumption of the rich farmer being a money income maximizer operating in a static economy with well-defined opportunity costs expressed in money. We think that this is a very inappropriate model for the big farmer. The model we would suggest for the big or rich farmer is one of a maximizer of social power which requires him to be, among other

---

[19] 68 per cent of the casual labourers investigated reported taking loans against commitment of labour, and of them 60 per cent were bound by the condition of working under less than the market wage rate that would rule at the time of repayment of the loan. However, none of these labourers getting semi-attached to some employers in this fashion reported having any other kind of servile obligations toward those employers.

things, a maximizer of wealth in real terms and a minimizer of risks arising from social frictions. For such an agent it is perfectly comprehensible that he should give loans without interest on certain occasions and to certain parties: by that means he ensures the personal loyalty of labourers and tenants with whom he has direct dealings as well as of his poor neighbours in general.

Our model big farmer is prone to judge his economic well-being and measure his social power in real terms by such yardsticks as the amount of grain in his stock, the number and items of capital goods in his possession, the number of labourers in his employ, the number of poor people at his beck and call, etc. For many of his resources like his unsold stock of product, cattle or his homestead, his economic calculations do not involve any opportunity costs. He seems to clearly prefer storing value in unsold stocks of goods to having bank accounts. He evaluates his monetary transactions in terms of grain equivalents rather than the other way round.

Even while these rich farmers operate their farm economics on non-monetary principles, they are linked with the world of money beyond the village level by means of various links. Much money flows from outside into their hands from banks and co-operatives as well as from the product market, which provides them with working capital for the credit operations. The poor villagers are, however, cut off from this external world of money precisely by these rich farmers acting as a buffer. They are cut off not only from the outer world of money but are also insulated from the credit markets operating in other villages even in the neighbourhood. In the absence of security in the form of land or gold with which the professional moneylender works, personal knowledge of the poor borrower is of paramount importance to the agricultural moneylender. Personal knowledge may extend beyond the rich farmer's own tenants or labourers to other poor persons living in the village. But it can hardly extend beyond the boundary of the village society.

This damming up of the village credit system with its fragmentations gives rise to local-level power enjoyed by the minority of rich farmers which is the most important cornerstone of the entire structure of local-level power. This power is not merely an aggregation of the economic power of individual rich farmers; it is a social phenomenon arising out of their optimizing their positions in respect of a host of economic as well as non-economic variables.

TABLE 1

Non-Participation of Family Members in Manual Labour in Cultivation

Category of Families	Number of Families with Non-participating Members			
	Illambazar		Sian	
	Male	Female	Male	Female
1. Cultivators				
a. with machines	5	21	8	9
	(22.7)	(95.5)	(88.9)	(100.0)
b. with farm servants	11	44	17	27
	(24.4)	(100.0)	(63.0)	(100.0)
c. others	10	191	8	20
	(9.8)	(99.0)	(28.6)	(71.4)
2. Poor peasants	47	18	0	1
	(100.0)	(38.3)		(50.0)
3. Kishans	0	4	0	1
		(12.9)		(50.0)
4. Labourers	5	88	0	20
	(2.6)	(48.9)		(15.5)

ASHOK RUDRA

TABLE 2

*Frequency Distribution of Villages according
to Daily Wage Rate: Illambazar
(mid-October – mid-November 1980)*

Daily Wage Rate	No. of Villages
Cash only	
Rs 4.00	4
Rs 5.00	10
Rs 6.00	6
Rs 8.00	1
Cash and kind	
Rs 2.00 + 1.5 kg rice	5
Rs 3.00 + 1.5 kg rice	22
Rs 3.50 + 1.5 kg rice	1
Rs 4.00 + 1.5 kg rice	2
Rs 6.00 + 1 meal	1
	52

Note: The total frequency is more than the number of villages surveyed, namely 39, because of many villages having more than one wage rate.

Local Power and Farm-level Decision-making 277

TABLE 3

*Inter-Village Wage Variations—Pairwise
Comparison: Illambazar
(mid-October to mid-November 1980)*

Name of the Village	Wage Rates	Distance between the Villages (km)
Bagalbati	Rs 4.00	1.0
Baruipur	Rs 5.00	
Nabagram	Rs 4.00	1.5
Beloa	Rs 6.00	
Nabagram	Rs 4.00	2.0
Balithala	Rs 6.00	
Nohana	Rs 5.00	1.0
Dangapara	Rs 3.00 + rice	
Khadimpukur	Rs 3.00 + rice	3.0
Bagalbati	Rs 4.00	
Sahapur	Rs 3.00 + rice	1.5
Chotochak	Rs 8.00	
Dumrud	Rs 3.00 + rice	1.5
Chotochak	Rs 8.00	
Jaipur	Rs 5.00	2.5
Chunpalasi	Rs 3.00 + rice	
Jaipur	Rs 5.00	2.0
Jalalnagar	Rs 3.00 + rice	
Bagalbati	Rs 4.00	2.0
Nanasole	Rs 6.00	
Ghurisa	Rs 6.00	3.0
Chotochak	Rs 8.00	
Nohana	Rs 5.00	2.5
Dumrud	Rs 3.00 + rice	

The quantity of rice in each case in the Illambazar cluster is 1.5 kg.

TABLE 4

Some Examples of Different Seasonal Wage
Rises in Adjacent Villages

Adjacent Villages	Distance between the Villages	Amount of Wage Rise (in Rs)
Illambazar		
1 Jaipur	1.0	Rs 2.00
Sabazpur		Rs 1.00
2 Jaipur	1.0	Rs 2.00
Murundi		Rs 4.00
3 Beloa	1.5	Rs 2.50
Nabagram		Rs 1.00
4 Bagalbati	1.0	Rs 2.00
Baruipur		Rs 1.00
Sian		
5 Dakhinpara	0	Rs 2.00
Shahajapur		Rs 1.00
6 Pihipara	0	Rs 1.50
Baidyanathpur		Rs 1.00
7 Muluk	1.5	Rs 2.00
Sukhbazar		Rs 1.00

TABLE 5

Labour Movements among Villages—Illambazar Cluster

From where labourers	Number of Villages	To which labourers	Number of Villages
do not go to any other village or distant place	8	do not come from any other village or distant place	12
go to some adjacent villages	22	come from some adjacent villages	20
go to some non-adjacent villages	19	come from some non-adjacent villages	18
go to distant places	10	come from distant places	2
go only to some adjacent villages	6	come only from some adjacent villages	9
go to all the adjacent villages	5	come from all the adjacent villages	4
go to some of both adjacent and non-adjacent villages	13	come from some of both adjacent and non-adjacent villages	11
go only to distant areas	3	come only from distant areas	0
go to some non-adjacent villages but not to any adjacent ones	6	come from some non-adjacent villages but not from adjacent ones	7

TABLE 6

*Number of Villages with which a Village has
Connections of Labour Movement:
Illambazar Cluster*

Number of Villages	Frequency of Villages	
	To which labourers go	From which labourers come
0	11*	12
1	9	7
2	5	7
3	4	4
4	4	7
5	4	2
6	1	–
7	1	–
Total frequency	39	39

* There are three villages from where labourers go to distant areas but not to neighbouring villages.

REFERENCES

Bardhan, P. and A. Rudra (1978a), 'Terms and Conditions of Share-cropping Contracts: An Analysis of Village Survey Data in India', *Journal of Development Studies*, Vol. 16, April.

—— (1978b), 'Interlinkage of Land, Labour and Credit Relations: An Analysis of Village Survey Data in East India', *Economic and Political Weekly*, Vol. 13, February.

—— (1980a), 'Types of Labour Attachment in Agriculture: Results of a Survey in West Bengal 1979', *Economic and Political Weekly*, Vol. 15, August.

—— (1980b), 'Labour Employment and Wages in Agriculture: Results of a Survey in West Bengal Villages in 1979', *Economic and Political Weekly*, November.

—— (1981), 'Terms and Conditions of Labour Contracts in Agriculture: Results of a Survey in West Bengal 1979', *Oxford Bulletin of Statistics*.

Rudra, A. (1982a), *Indian Agricultural Economics: Myths and Realities* (New Delhi: Allied).

—— (1982b), 'Extra-economic Constraints on Labour in Agriculture', Working Paper published by Asian Regional Team for Employment Promotion, ILO, Bangkok.

Determinants and Varieties of Agrarian Mobilization

LLOYD I. RUDOLPH
SUSANNE HOEBER RUDOLPH

Mobilization is a form of purposeful public and collective action. It is a way of creating and using political power. Those who engage in mobilizations intend to influence policy choice and implementation, asymmetrical bargaining situations or electoral choice. Mobilization is designed to generate bargaining advantages or political power on behalf of actors who believe themselves disadvantaged by established institutions and rules. If politics is the art of the possible, it is also the art of articulating and establishing the realm of the possible.[1] Mobilization can affect both domains, the struggle for power and the bargaining over interests which marks the domain of the possible, and the defining and establishment of world views and collective goods that shape new possibilities.[2]

[1] For theories of power and collective behaviour, see Olson (1965), Moe (1980) and Smelser (1962). Suzanne Berger (1981) in her otherwise admirable introduction argues that 'as individuals or groups *seek* [our emphasis] to maintain or improve their position relative to others, they locate themselves with references to . . . clusters of social, economic and political resources, which are unevenly distributed across society . . . The principal means of improving one's lot . . . is to exploit those resources of which one has the most or to which one has the easiest access.' She recognizes that pluralist forms of representation exclude those with 'too few resources to reach the organizational threshold . . .'

Our analysis of mobilization does not *assume* that 'individuals or groups seek to maintain or improve their position relative to others' nor take as given (i.e., an initial condition) that those with 'too few resources' are excluded because they cannot reach 'the organizational threshold'. We stress the critical importance of mobilization because it is a means to generate political resources and to use them to affect the outcome of political competition and bargaining.

[2] In this essay we are concerned with intended and organized mobilization, not

Mobilization can affect both competitive and revolutionary politics. Our interest in mobilization arises from efforts to explain redistributional and growth-oriented social change in the context of competitive politics. It arises also from a related historical problematic, the non-self-executing nature of public choices that mandate social change. Laws and policies that mandate social change are not sufficient to bring it about. In the absence of normative and political pressure in the form of mobilization from below by its intended beneficiaries, social change is not likely to occur.

This volume addresses the relationship between agrarian power and agrarian productivity. Mobilization as a form of political power may or may not enhance productivity because productivity may not be among the goals of those who mobilize. We will show that for the most disadvantaged the primary or initial goal is physical and economic security that yields enhanced personal liberty. Greater wealth based on productivity, i.e., greater access to and use of productive assets and/or human capital, may be a goal and a consequence of successful mobilization. Historical circumstances, ideological orientation, and policy choice and techniques may yield goals and consequences that, at least in the medium term, result in the attainment of forms of physical and economic security that constrain rather than enhance productivity. Ronald Herring (1980, 39) has shown that in Kerala the consequences of mobilization that made tenant owners and agricultural workers economically secure has been to lower productivity.

In this essay, we attend to mobilization in rural India. Who can be mobilized, and for what objectives? We are concerned with the entire spectrum of rural society, although we deal more with mobilizations from below than from above. Our concepts distinguish a variety of (social) actors but we leave open the question of whether cultural, social or economic determinants predominate in their formation and the goals they pursue. We find that empirical investigations of context and problematic reveal more about the degree to which a particular actor exhibits a distinct orientation than do *a priori* theories. We have not adopted the alternative conceptual

---

'functional' mobilization conceived of as an 'input' of a 'system' nor spontaneous mobilization. Spontaneous mobilizations would include accounts by Rudé (1959, 1964) on revolutionary mobs and radical crowds; Hobsbawm (1959) on social banditry; Rudolph (1959) on American colonial mobs; Wolf (1959) on peasant risings in Latin America, and Fanon on violence as value and therapy.

strategy of collapsing the variety of groups determined by economic, social and cultural forces into one hegemonic category (e.g., class, status order or cultural community and their subsets) because we find that strategy loses more than it gains in explanatory power.

Our conceptual categories for social actors identify four agrarian economic classes: (1) agricultural labourers, (2) small holders, (3) bullock capitalists, and (4) large landholders. They also identify four status orders: (1) scheduled castes and tribes, (2) backward classes, (3) middle castes, and (4) upper 'twiceborn' castes. Cultural communities, a third type of social actor based on language and confessional (religious) affinities (other than the *dharmic* order or ritual rank), will not be systematically analysed. Anyone who has tried to establish a taxonomy of social actors or their sub-sets (e.g., classes, status orders or cultural communities) will recognize the problematic and contingent nature of the attempt (Oldenburg 1981). That a five-acre holding is small in the Rajasthan desert and large in the irrigated rice lands of Tamil Nadu illustrates some of the difficulties involved. One justification for using such categories is that they capture rough 'common sense' distinctions that figure in the minds of principal actors engaged in mobilization efforts, e.g., parties and politicians who try to attract the attention of social groups with putative common interests or identities. A second justification is that it allows observers with theoretical orientations to identify and order commonalities and incongruences that can arise among classes, status orders and cultural communities within rural society as a result of modes and relations of production and exchange, principles of stratification and cultural differences.

The objective interests of these categories are not easily differentiated and distinguished. Do landless labourers and tenants have common or conflicting interests? In the context of objective economic forces, both tenants and labourers are poor and dependent, yet tenants sometimes employ labourers and command significantly more resources. How do the diverse and often self-contradictory interests of small and marginal farmers, many of whom are simultaneously cultivators, renters and wage labourers, affect their responses to the ideologies or policies advocated by political actors engaged in mobilization efforts? Under what circumstances do untouchables who are wage labourers respond to class or status appeals? André Béteille (1972, 137), focusing especially on the sharply hierarchical Southern social landscape, notes that hierarchically ranked castes (status orders) are isomorphic but agrarian economic classes are not. They are apt to overlap. In the less precipitous caste hierarchy of the North, castes that are exclusive in ritual or marriage contexts often recognize shared economic, status or community objectives. What happens when class and status categories are congruent, e.g., when an economic class parallels a status order such as can be the case with respect to 'backward classes' or scheduled castes that are tenants and wage labourers respectively? What difference does the overlap make for prospects of mobilization? Are congruent or summed objective inequalities more amenable to translation into motives for action than are dispersed inequalities? How should the objective interest of economic classes, status orders and cultural communities be counted when the same people, albeit in different contexts, 'belong' simultaneously to all three analytic categories?

The objectives which such social groups have pursued in recent times include: (1) transformations of the agrarian economy and/or society that modify or eliminate established property rights and the *dharmic* norms of ritual rank; (2) redistribution of land, income and status that do not overtly challenge established property and/or *dharmic* norms and relationships; (3) market advantage and profit for a wide but disputed range of cultivators; and (4) defence of landed and commercial vested interests threatened by redistributional or transformational politics and policies. This variety of objectives and the conflict among them suggests the range of appeals proffered by political actors engaged in mobilization efforts. The first objective, transformation of the agrarian economy and society, may involve replacing extant property and production relations based on private ownership and cultivation with collective arrangements, and replacing ritually based caste stratification and *dharmic* social norms with a political order based on equal citizenship and a social order that provides more equality of opportunity, wealth, power and status. The defeat in 1959 of the Nehru-initiated joint cooperative farming resolution at Congress' annual meeting and the turn of the Indian communist parties to multi-class electoral and mobilization strategies have virtually eliminated party interest in agricultural production based on collectives. There are few signs of its revival. While such objectives continue to surface in India, they do so marginally, with even extreme left movements such as those of the CPI-ML adopting strategies (land grab) that emphasize the interests of the individual cultivator. In the absence of revolutionary transformation, collectivist strategies for agriculture lack political viability. They are incompatible with the multi-class policy constraints imposed by class pluralism and fragmentation on the conduct of competitive politics in India's parliamentary and federal system. Caste hierarchies have been weakened or displaced by competitive politics as the larger middle and lower castes have used their numerical advantage to capture power and redistribute resources. The effect of democratic politics based in part on horizontal mobilizations of lower castes has been to render stratification based on ritual rank less relevant for political power and social interaction (Rudolph and Rudolph 1967, 1969).

Redistributing land and income covers a wide gamut of possibilities, from ceilings and land redistribution through tenancy reform and demands for administrative regularization (e.g., records of rights) that can reduce exploitation. These objectives attract the attention of small owners and tenants more than they do landless agricultural labourers. Redistributional policies are related to the interests of landless agricultural labourers when they address higher wages, more working days, better working conditions, job security (including protection from outside labour willing to work at lower wages), and procedural safeguards—vested bargaining rights, secure contracts, trade union recognition. Land redistribution in recent years has become objectively and politically more difficult. Given India's man–land ratio and agrarian class distribution, politically feasible ceilings followed by land redistribution can make only a marginal contribution to the overall condition of the landless poor (Minhas 1974). Left parties favouring redistribution have learned that success may be failure, that redistribution may, as in Kerala, translate tenants into petty landlords whose bourgeois consciousness and interests lead them to vote for non-left parties that *inter alia* refuse to support and sometimes oppose the interests of agricultural wage workers. On the other hand, land redistribution and rights have remained an effective slogan among democratic socialist and populist parties who appeal to small holders and tenants. The agrarian politics of the late Devraj Urs, Karpoori Thakur and Sharad Pawar in Karnataka, Bihar and Maharashtra were based on such an approach. Parties seeking support among less participant, have-not constituencies near the bottom of the rural pyramid against parties based on support from arrivée, satisfied or vested economic classes are likely to keep the land redistribution strategy alive.

The pursuit of market advantage and profit can involve the interests of all agricultural producers, owner-cultivators, tenants, and agricultural workers. Their collective interests are affected by advantageous terms of trade with industrial producers. Even agricultural labourers have an objective interest in a favourable relationship between the price of inputs and the price of agricultural commodities because their employment prospects (number of working days per year) and the possibility of better wages depend on it. The terms of trade between agricultural and industrial products and the differential distribution of government investment and services were key elements in Charan Singh's (1978) critique of the Nehru-inspired industrial strategy.[3] Whether disingenuous or sincere, leaders of the agrarian mobilizations that erupted in the early eighties in Maharashtra, Gujarat, Tamil Nadu, Karnataka and other states to secure higher prices for agricultural commodities took care to address the interests of agricultural labourers and to relate them to the goals of the various agitations.

Overt defence of landlord or capitalist farmers' vested interests by rural mobilizations is as rare as mobilizations to realize systemic agrarian transformation. Under the favourable conditions created by the British raj, landlords until Independence formed associations to defend their interests against state efforts to help tenants and debtors and to block demands by agricultural workers.[4] After 1947, efforts to represent landlord interests via political mobilizations quickly faded from view. The Nehru government's anti-landlord stance and its abolition of intermediaries (zamindars, *jagirdars*) dominated policy. Organizations such as the Thanjavur Paddy Producers Association, organized to defend landowners against labour organizations, are a relatively rare phenomenon. Such associations have been delegitimized by Congress' dominant egalitarian and redistributionist (socialist) public philosophy and by the conventional consensus in Indian politics on socialist objectives. During the 1960s, the conservative Swatantra Party spoke for landed property interests. Since then, rural notables have retained and exercised considerable power but do so privately or covertly. Notables rely on social networks of kin that give them access to state bureaucracies

[3] See our discussion below of the new agrarianism, p. 328 ff, for a more detailed account of these agrarian mobilizations.
[4] Consult Chapter 7, 'Congress and the Landlord Interests' in McLane (1977) and Metcalfe (1965).

(including police) and on their continued substantial presence in state legislatures and cabinets to protect and promote their interests.

In the sections that follow we examine at various levels of analysis the determinants and varieties of agrarian mobilization. Mobilization occurs in the micro-context of the village or region; it occurs at the state level; it is evoked by the actions of national movements and parties. Mobilization at these various levels may be linked or continuous, but sometimes is not. In Part I we identify and justify a number of objective determinants (causes). In Part II we explore how and why in varying local contexts they have or have not been translated into subjective determinants (reasons) and collective action (mobilization). In Part III we shift the focus to nationally aggregated categories, agrarian economic classes and status groups. Again, we examine how and why agrarian mobilization does or does not occur. In Part IV, we examine national party strategies.

I. Causes and Reasons:[5] Objective Determinants of Agrarian Mobilization

The poverty of most rural Indians, both small holders and agricultural workers, is attested to by estimates that place over 40 per cent below variously devised poverty lines.[6] The pervasiveness of poverty suggests that the poor have ample reasons to protest their condition and to mobilize to change it. Yet the literature on agrarian radicalism in particular and on political mobilization in general makes it plain that the conditions leading to protest or mobilization are obscure and complex. Apparently desperate objective conditions do not always translate into sufficient reasons to engage in political action aimed at rectifying the micro- or macro-causes of poverty.

By causes we refer to objective determinants that social scientists as observers use to explain, predict or prescribe social action. Objective determinants, however, are distant and necessary, not proximate and sufficient conditions for social action, including mobilization. By reasons we refer to meaning and intention, the purposes, goals and values that inspire and orient actors and the calculations that they make about risks and costs in relation to the

[5] For a discussion of causes and reasons in social action, see Toulmin (1972), Vol. 1.

[6] For a sceptical review of the nutritional calory counts that form the largest component of poverty estimates, see Eberstadt (1979).

probabilities and benefits of success attending proposed remedial measures. Reasons supply proximate and sufficient conditions for mobilization. What are the causes and the contexts that provide reasons enough to fuel mobilization?

Among the objective determinants that limit the choices and help define the objective interests of actors we count technology; historical conjunctures; ecological circumstances; agrarian structure and relationships; government policy (seen as an 'input'); caste and community bonds; and family and affinal relations. None of these determinants are self-evident to actors or self-executing with respect to mobilization. Whether mobilization results depends on how well leaders translate them, singly or in combination, into reasons (subjective determinants) and create consciousness and organization. It depends too on how those to whom appeals are directed at whatever level calculate the risks and costs of action and the probabilities and consequences of 'success'.

(1) Technology has figured as a *deus ex machina* for the creation of human values and the organization of society among social prophets across the political spectrum. It has been understood as the initiating agent for creating new relations of production. We see it as a powerful and independent force but not as the ultimate arbiter of the human condition. In recent years Gandhi's formulation, that man can be the master rather than the slave of the machine, has been revived in Indian and non-Indian thinking. Technology has come to be viewed as controllable, able to serve rather than define human purposes (Winner 1977).

The connection between technology viewed as an objective determinant and mobilization is in any case lagged and mediated rather than direct. A good deal of the early literature about the consequences of the green revolution (a shorthand term for accelerated technological change in agriculture) took for granted or argued that there was an automatic, direct and predictable relationship between rapid and marked technological change and political consciousness and action (Ladejinsky 1969; Frankel 1971; Griffin 1974). Its architects held out the prospect that the green revolution would make the country self-sufficient in food. Those interested in its political consequences expected and soon thought they found that it polarized agrarian classes by exacerbating and accelerating the unequal distribution of income and wealth. By speeding the monetization and commercialization of agricultural labour, it would hasten the demise of dependent and sentimental ties based on that variable mix of coercion, obligations and duties that linked masters to servants and patrons to clients.

A steadily accumulating literature casts doubt on the initial anticipation of an automatic connection between improved technology and political consciousness and action. The green revolution was not a uniform thing. Its impact was enormously variable over time, by region, by crop, and by organization of the productive process. It had technological and administrative phases. The effectiveness and consequences of new technology in agriculture were as much a result of ecological circumstances and social contexts as of the availability of new inputs. The new technology's success and consequences are determined by an increasingly complex set of factors. These include historical conjunctures such as OPEC's new-found capacity to manipulate the supply and price of oil (and thus the availability of chemical fertilizer and other agriculturally relevant imports purchased with foreign exchange). They also include the feedback effects on ideological interpretations of scholarship about the causes and consequences of the green revolution.

The ambiguous and variable effects of technological upgrading in agriculture were strikingly illustrated in an early, pre-green revolution study by Scarlett Epstein (1962: 182–3). She examined the effect of newly installed regional irrigation in two contrasting Mysore villages. The numerous small landowners in Wangala benefited directly from the irrigation. One consequence of the new-found prosperity that followed was to reinforce the traditional social structure. Prosperity slowed outmigration and strengthened hereditary economic and ritual relations between patrons and clients. The neighbouring village of Dalena did not receive irrigation. Its agricultural production remained stagnant but many inhabitants responded to the increased opportunities irrigation brought to the area. In Dalena unlike Wangala, traditional social relations, notably patron–client relations, did decay, but the result was not class polarization. As agricultural labour sought and found work outside the village, its potential for mobilization eroded (Epstein 1962: 309; Breman 1974b).

The debate about present and potential productivity of various size holdings also illustrates ambiguities about the determinative power of technology. If one assumes that increases in production are desirable in the face of population growth and of commitments to reduce poverty and to satisfy minimum (basic) needs, diverse possibilities ensue. In so far as new agricultural technologies are proved to be scale neutral or to promote higher productivity on small units, they justify efforts to enforce or even lower ceilings in order to redistribute land.[7] On the other hand, in so far as the new technologies prove more productive on large holdings, they can be used to justify capitalist agriculture or collectivization.

(2) Historical conjunctures such as the circumstances attendant on victory or defeat in war, ecological catastrophe, or disastrous inflation create new opportunities for action and change the odds for failure and success among established adversaries. Thus it is unlikely that the Russian or Chinese revolutions would have succeeded at the time and in the manner they did without state disintegration and military defeat (Skocpol 1979). Land reform in Japan, Taiwan and South Korea would have been much less likely in the absence of external intervention and pressure. Few theories would have predicted American occupation under the aegis of Douglas MacArthur as the agent of agrarian reform. The rise in Middle East oil prices in the early seventies significantly slowed the pace of the green revolution when fertilizer consumption stagnated in the face of steep price increases.

(3) Ecology too is an important objective determinant because it is associated with crop variety and social stratification that together help to structure agrarian relations (Zagoria 1971, 1972). The effects of ecology on agrarian relations can be conceptualized and applied at a macro-regional level, as David Ludden shows in an essay in this volume, on a micro-level, as Scarlett Epstein shows in her two neighbouring but ecologically differentiated Mysore villages, or at an intermediate (district) level as Marshall Bouton shows through a zonal ecological disaggregation of Thanjavur district of Tamil Nadu (1980). At the all-India (macro) level, ecological circumstances are associated with important differences between wheat and rice cultivation and parallel regional caste profiles.

The wheat agriculture of Northern India and the rice agriculture of Southern and Eastern India can be distinguished globally in terms of the type of labour used. Northern wheat cultivation features family farms that rely more on family than on wage labour while Southern and Eastern features irrigated rice cultivation that utilizes more wage

---

[7] However, Herring elsewhere in this volume shows that problems of access to technology due to the difficulties of securing credit can neutralize the advantage labour-intensive small farms may have in employing the new inputs.

than family labour. Northern low caste agricultural labourers are in a less favourable position for mobilization than agricultural labourers in the South because comparatively fewer work for the same employer or depend on the same patron. In the South if not the East, because relations to employers and/or patrons are more concentrated and collective and structured by caste hierarchy than in the North, objective conditions for mobilization are more favourable. Stokes' (1978) detailed study of late nineteenth-century conditions shows that in some areas of Northwest India—Punjab, Delhi and its wheat-growing hinterland—the prototypical self-cultivating family farms of middle agrarian castes usually employed few agricultural labourers or service castes. As a consequence, landless castes were separated rather than concentrated by the conditions of production.[8] Even where, in the North, non-cultivating Brahman and Rajput families relied on labourers or share-croppers, vertical relations among *jajmans* and *kamins* tended to override horizontal solidarities and proved more powerful and durable than in the South. There rice cultivation on irrigated land often concentrated low caste wage labourers in the employ of non-cultivating high caste owners. Thus some Southern if not Eastern conditions of labour were—and are—more favourable to mobilizations based on variable and contingent mixtures of class and caste.

(4) The distribution and nature of rights in land is a critical objective determinant for collective action. Although their rights vary enormously, those who control land include owners and a variety of tenants, including share-croppers. Tenants may be relatively secure or insecure; they may control enough or too little land to warrant economic risk or political risk. Such variations establish thresholds of receptivity to mobilization appeals because they affect calculations about risk, benefits and ulterior consequences. Like tenants, those with no rights in land, whose only source of income is wage labour, are not a homogeneous group. The scale, organization and relations of agricultural production and the availability, regularity, kind and remuneration of non-agricultural wage labour profoundly affect its mobilization potential. So too does the parallel existence of extra-

---

[8] Stokes focused on North Indian examples in Delhi territory and Punjab, suggesting the relative scarcity of untouchable families in villages. This circumstance changes as one moves East, away from Jat *bhaiachara* tenures toward Rajput and Bhumia and Brahmin villages in which untouchable agricultural labour was more heavily used.

economic bonds and interests such as those provided by status orders
and cultural communities.

Social theories vary with respect to the importance of economic
classes that arise from rights in land, and with respect to mobilization (Wolf 1969; Alavi 1973b; Stokes 1978; Habib 1963). For
example, a significant body of literature on peasant protest in
nineteenth-century India identifies 'middle peasants' as the most
militant agrarian economic class.[9] It was a time when commercial
agriculture was in its infancy and social dependency was more important than economic in determining the nature of agrarian relations. A century later, scholars of Indian society more concerned
with the capitalist features of commercial agriculture tend to identify
insecure tenants or wage labourers, particularly those without land,
as most prone to militancy. The difficulty is that such propensities for
mobilization are assumed or deduced from theoretically derived
objective interests. Actors may not identify with the categories to
which particular theories assign them. If they do, they may not
respond to the associated rationales or accept the contextual risks
required for collective action. Times change. Mobilization is located
in changing historical circumstances. Having rid themselves of the
raj and benefited from zamindari abolition and the green revolution,
yesterday's middle peasants may be today's bullock capitalists (see
below, pp. 315 ff) in the double sense of having an etiological connection to middle peasants and being the most mobilizable agrarian
class. Assuming that rights in land and the economic classes that
result from them do constitute objective determinants of mobilization, their translation into subjective determinants that lead to
collective action is affected, as are other determinants, by intervening
variables and mediating circumstances.

(5) Government policy in the form of legislation, advisory boards,
programme implementation, district and local administration, etc.,
shapes mobilization as much as mobilization shapes government
policy orientation and choice. This is why we conceptualize government policy as an objective determinant or cause. New policies
impinge on objective interests and established policies often take on
new meanings under changed historical circumstances (as the re-

---

[9] For a sceptical review of the literature on the middle peasant, see 'The
Return of the Middle Peasant' in Stokes (1978). For an account that construes
seventeenth and eighteenth century revolts against the Mughal power as a variant
of middle peasant uprising, see Habib (1963).

gistration of 'foreigners' did in Assam in the late 1970s) or under new modes of administration. Like other objective determinants, government policy may induce or trigger mobilization by helping leaders to create consciousness and organization. Robert Stern (1970) has shown how the Gold Control Order (later Act) led hitherto unorganized *shroffs* and goldsmiths to form interest groups to articulate and defend their interests. The revised policy orientation of an established government advisory board, the Agricultural Prices Commission, combined with changing prices of agricultural inputs, fluctuating export possibilities and fluctuating production levels of cash crops, created objective conditions for a new form of agrarian mobilization, the farmer movements for remunerative prices that erupted in 1980–81. Producers of agricultural commodities affected by the price support policies of the Agricultural Prices Commission as adopted or modified by the Government of India responded at the state level, where price support policies were applied and their organizations could use agitational tactics with maximum effect.

(6) Caste (a status order) and cultural community constitute other objective determinants of agrarian mobilization (Alavi 1973a). Like the *mélange* of race and class that characterized black consciousness and action in America, the *mélange* in India of caste or community on the one hand and class on the other has plagued scholars of India seeking theories to explain social reality and politicians seeking guides for action. As in the case of the bullock capitalists and backward classes whom we shall discuss, status order and economic class may merge in ways that make them indistinguishable except contextually. Religious community (e.g., Muslims in Bengal) too often overlaps with economic class. Communities (of language, religion) or status orders (particularly untouchables or tribals whose inferiority is legitimated by *dharmic* values) can be the vehicles for capturing the consciousness and orienting the action of wage workers and poor cultivators because they speak for what is familiar, comprehensive and relevant.

Identifying objective determinants is itself an artifice for shaping consciousness and orienting action. Knowledge about which objective determinants exist is often controversial. What men make of their circumstances depends on what they see, believe, and value. Successful ideologies, leadership and strategies interpret circumstances in ways that simultaneously speak to and shape the times. The calling of a politician, unlike that of a scholar, does not feature argument about the nature of social reality and its connection to history and action. With some few exceptions, praxis, not theory, is their medium. Whether they use tacit, ideological or scientific knowledge, they must identify the realm of the possible to practise the art of the possible, take positions on the nature and saliency of causes, and translate causes into reasons and action.

Liberal and socialist rationalists such as Jawaharlal Nehru de-recognized religious communities and caste groups as objective determinants because they express superstitions or 'feudal' relations[10] that science and capitalism have (or ought to have) superseded. They assumed that only wage labour and poverty are objective determinants and used them to try to fashion the class consciousness and organization required for political action. In the 1937 U.P. election, Jawaharlal Nehru, on the assumption that economic class was a more powerful determinant than religious community, thought that poor Muslims would vote for land reform rather than for Muslim political rights. He proved more wrong than right.

Sometimes rationalist or progressive politicians accept status groups or religious communities as 'real' and legitimate objective determinants because they recognize that they are inextricably intertwined with economic class. E. M. S. Namboodiripad (1952, 1957, 1981) found that for a time caste was the vanguard of class, by which he meant that poor, landless untouchable Iravas achieved consciousness, organization and brotherhood via a familiar and accessible medium, caste.[11] Muslim interests and votes are valued by secularists who decry appeals to Hindu interests and votes because Muslims are a poor, backward and discriminated against minority. Namboodiripad as well as Indira Gandhi (who claims to be a friend of Harijans and Muslims as well as of the poor) accept the reality and legitimacy of status orders and confessional communities when they shape their appeal to untouchables and Muslims in ethnic and communal as well as class and interest group terms.

(7) Kinship and affinal patterns used to explain the differential capacity among cultivators to cooperate economically can also help to explain their differential capacity to cooperate politically. Thomas

---

[10] We use the term 'feudal' here as articulate actors at the time did. For difficulties associated with using this much abused term see Rudra (1981).

[11] For a critical assessment of Nehru's views, see Azad (1959) and Boulware (1960). For a perspective that regards caste as a mystification or non-phenomenon, see *Economic and Political Weekly*, Annual Number (1979).

Rosin's systematic survey (1978) of the economically adaptive functions of joint families in a Jodhpur village suggests the outlines of such an argument (see also Kolenda 1978). Economic adaptiveness in these villages requires cooperative patterns among at least four families of lineage-linked cultivators to sustain self-sufficient two crop cultivation.[12] Rosin attributes successful adaptation to agricultural production by some castes to factors such as size of resident family and elaboration and intensification of affinity (through sibling and cousin set marriages, by repetition of alliances with families previously allied by marriage, etc.). By these criteria, cultivating and herding castes—Jats, Gujars—possessed the necessary means for cooperation, while castes ranked at the top and bottom of the local hierarchy—Rajputs and artisans and service castes—did not. Jat and Gujar families typically have seven or eight resident family members,[13] Rajput and low castes five (Rosin 1978: 489). Rosin found that the local village Rajputs, putatively related to the former dominant landlords (*jagirdars*), and often their agents in the villages 'have neither the joint family structure' nor the 'requisite affinal network' to cultivate cooperatively. Near the other end of the caste hierarchy, weavers' small average family size and high frequency of nuclear or fragmented families limited economic cooperation. Rosin also reports that labourers 'have a preferred pattern of nuclear families and rarely engage in cooperative effort among themselves. They continue to cultivate not the land but the social landscape, developing dyadic ties with elite families whom they serve as bodyguards, henchmen or bagmen in intrigue' (Rosin 1978: 490).

Brij Raj Chauhan's account (1967: 126–7) of farming castes in Udaipur also supports the view that certain kinds of kinship patterns foster political as well as economic cooperation while others do not. The exogamy of patrilineal Rajput clans, more often landlords than farmers, extended marriage networks outward over considerable distances. However useful kinship relations at a distance were for purposes of feudal domination, Rajput landlords lack today the local kinship and affinal resources needed for cultivation and elec-

[12] Kolenda does not relate her findings to economic adaptation, as Rosin does, except in the narrower sense of noting that sibling and collateral set marriages save ceremonial expenses over the life cycle.

[13] Kolenda (1978: 243) does not compare castes with respect to joint and nuclear family patterns, but shows more than half of the Jat families in her village as joint or supplemented nuclear.

toral influence. By contrast, the more localized marriage networks of farming and herding castes such as Jats, Gujars, Gadris and Dhakars sustained kinship resources for farm production and political participation.[14] Rajat Ray's account (1978) of the exemplary Bijolia Satyagraha in Udaipur in the 1930s identifies local kinship and affinal relations as a necessary condition for peasant rebellion: 'this very factor enabled them [local castes, particularly the Dhakars] to put forward, whenever necessary, strong local combinations comprising several villages of the neighborhood' (216). Without the support of dense lineage and affinal ties, Ray doubts that the Dhakars would have risked resisting the power of local landlords and Udaipur state.

Some family literature suggests that affinal patterns, rather than exercising an independent influence on economic and political activity, are themselves dependent on economic or social circumstances. The poor cannot afford joint families or to develop and therefore utilize kinship resources. Affinal, kinship and lineage solidarities at the top and bottom of the social hierarchy are 'thin' because vertical ties linking masters to servants and patrons to clients displace or replace family and lineage connections. Greater prevalence of joint families among the relatively prosperous is the consequence rather than the cause of economic prosperity. Regardless of whether kinship resources are chicken or egg in such causal relationships, once they are invested in, kinship resources become an important means for the conduct of economic and political activity, including mobilization. Poor economic classes and status orders have families and kin but are disadvantaged economically and politically because they lack kinship resources.

Agrarian mobilization varies by system level as well as by unit of analysis. Even though based on regional or local studies, some accounts of mobilization speak of India as one analytic unit. Others assume that because of India's ecological and cultural diversity explanations of agrarian mobilization must be contextualized. The

---

[14] Sisson (1969, 1972: Ch. 4) shows how Jat *kisan sabhas* were able to play a prominent role in participation and competitive politics in Rajasthan's Congress Party because the caste's elites could draw on higher levels of cohesion and organization than other castes in Rajasthan. Pradhan, in his study of North Indian Jats (1966), contrasted the Jat situation with that of Rajputs in a manner parallel to Rosin's: 'On account of the lack of kinship proximity and local contiguity, cooperation and kinship obligations within Rajput lineages are loose and ill-defined' (240–1).

sharp contrasts we found among accounts of mobilization in Gujarat, Bihar, Bengal and Tamil Nadu, etc., make clear that some explanations of mobilization at the national level must be multi-causal and aggregative. On the other hand, it would be a mistake to assume that explanation of agrarian mobilization is fully constrained by regional variations. Some determinants are national. The wide areal response to agricultural prices and price policy in 1980–81, and, more broadly, Ronald Herring's explanatory use in this volume of the national environment for state agricultural policy makes clear that policy determinants that affect similarly placed agricultural producers can be national. At the same time, Herring recognizes that most agricultural producers are not similarly placed. National policy determinants (not only for prices and inputs but also for land reforms, bonded labour, credit, etc.) become common stimulants and constraints that elicit specific responses at state and local levels. Clearly, efforts to explain agrarian mobilization must recognize the differential existence, salience and mix of national, regional and local environments.

We have arrayed a series of determinants that appear relevant to the explanation of agrarian mobilization and examined their explanatory utility and scope. Whatever the nature and scope of objective determinants, they are not self-realizing or self-executing. Among the many possible historical outcomes enabled by the variety and complexity of causes, only some in fact become history. In the next two sections, we examine how a variety of local and regional conditions affect the likelihood of leaders translating objective into subjective determinants, and how national policies for agriculture have shaped the mobilization of agrarian classes and status orders.

II. *Objective Determinants and Leadership in Context*

Translating objective determinants into subjective is the work of political leadership. By leadership we refer to specially motivated, endowed and skilled individuals with ideas and means for collective action. The challenge to leadership is structured by the intersection and mutual reinforcement of determinants. Such interaction, and what leadership makes of them, is most easily observed in local and regional contexts. We will look at two sets of micro-studies, one focusing on Tamil Nadu, and reporting the determinants of growing consciousness and action, the other focusing on diverse locations in the North, and reporting the correlates of passivity and apolitical withdrawal.

A series of studies in Tamil Nadu by Bouton (1980), Mencher (1978), Alexander (1975a, 1975b) and Béteille (1972) focus on the contrast between high mobilization and low mobilization areas within the region. The effect of technology is interwoven with and modified by ecological condition (e.g., irrigated versus unirrigated, type of soil); the distribution and nature of rights in land (e.g., self-employed cultivators or tenants, landless labourers employed by large landowners); historical conjunctures, e.g., rises in the price of essential consumer commodities; and active and credible leadership. These analyses also take into account that the green revolution affected Southern rice cultivation less than Northern wheat cultivation.

Thanjavur district has been the focus for several of these investigations. It presents a microcosm in which considerable variation and contrast can be studied in a limited area. Variations in the asymmetry of land rights, ecological conditions, and degrees of polarization tend to co-vary systematically between *talukas* that coincide roughly with the Old Delta and the New Delta area. Béteille, Bouton, and Alexander have specified these variations and Bouton subjected them to statistical analyses that related objective determinants in five ecological zones to political behaviour and outcomes. In the wet double-cropped paddy lands of the Eastern and Northern Old Delta, large concentrations of agricultural labourers work for a few large landowners who do not personally cultivate. This area overlaps with *talukas* whose percentage of agricultural labour in the work force reaches 50 to 70 per cent while the proportion of untouchables among them reaches 60–80 per cent (Béteille 1972: 144–5). Caste (status order) and economic class overlap with a rare degree of congruence. Concentrations of wage labour approximate industrial conditions. This is the area of Thanjavur where agrarian radicalism and conflict has been most evident.

By contrast, agrarian radicalism and conflict were absent or muted in the New Delta area of the Western and Southern portions of the district. Unlike its Eastern and Northern zones, the upland and dry cultivation of the West and South featured family operated holdings and higher levels of self-employed labour. The proportion of untouchables among the smaller percentage of agricultural labourers was lower too. Inequality in the New Delta was less pronounced than in the Old Delta because caste asymmetries were less severe and less congruent with class asymmetries. Family operated small holdings separate from each other both the poor cultivators who work the holdings and the attached labourers they employ. Mencher's findings (1978: 197) in Chingleput District of Tamil Nadu,[15] where small holdings operated by tenants or owners on the basis of their own labour were the norm, confirm that conditions like those found in the New Delta area separate cultivators more.[16] Under such circumstances mobilization in the form of agrarian radicalism becomes less likely because objective determinants are less susceptible to translation into reasons for action.

The Thanjavur case bears on our central question, how are objective determinants transformed into subjective, how do causes become reasons that induce risk-averse poor cultivators and labourers to act politically? As most of these observers point out, the structural condition just described characterized Thanjavur's Old Delta for many years before conflict erupted. 'It is impossible', Béteille observes, 'to give a general sociological answer to the question as to why human beings who live under conditions of extreme inequality at a certain time begin to find these conditions intolerable at another time' (1972: 140). Additional objective conditions introduced by the new technology of the green revolution may well have undone a shaky equilibrium and created new opportunities for leadership. As pointed out above, its effects were defracted in many different ways by the prism of varying land and production relations. In the context of small holdings, such as those in the New Delta or in adjoining districts, the new technology did not affect objective determinants in ways that changed consciousness or enhanced conflict. Small operators used new inputs as much per unit as medium and large operators (Harrison 1972; Mutiah 1971), and the uneven gains to large and small operators documented in other contexts were not marked.[17] On the other hand, in the two Old Delta zones of Thanjavur which

[15] Small 1 to 2 acre farmers tended to oppose the demands of agricultural trade unions.

[16] Gough (1960), who argues that agricultural workers can be the vanguard of rural mobilization, bases her case especially on the experience of the Old Delta.

[17] Harrison (1972) shows that small operations (under 3.8) used new technology and inputs as much per unit operated as medium and large. Mutiah (1971) found that holders under 5 acres accounted for 39 per cent of the cultivated area but 42 per cent of the HYV area.

Bouton isolates as highly polarized, the initial use of new inputs led to commercialization, increased demand for labour, enhanced wage demands by labour, resistance by landlords, and the import of outside labour. These technologically induced changes led to class-based conflicts between the Paddy Producers' Organization on the one hand and Kisan Sabhas on the other. An historical conjuncture, the poor monsoons of 1965 and 1966, coincided with the introduction of new technology (Bouton 1980). The monsoons led to price rises and demands for higher wages by agricultural workers even before the effects of the new technology began to be felt. The struggle reached national attention and affected political and scholarly thinking when, at Kizhavenmani in 1969, 44 labourers and members of their families who were resisting the importation of lower cost labour were confined in a hut and burned to death.

The subjective use in Thanjavur in the late sixties of a set of mutually reinforcing objective determinants for collective action depended on leadership; so too did the decline of agrarian radicalism and class conflict in the 1970s. Political leadership in Thanjavur has a long but variable history. The Communist Party became active in the district from the 1940s (Baliga 1957). The possibility of mobilization in the 1950s and 1960s depended not only on the presence of known and trusted cadres and on propitious objective determinants (a destabilized equilibrium) but also on whether party strategy called for initiatives on the part of cadres and on what kind of initiatives. Leadership initiatives and objectives have varied. The CPI successes in the 1952 and 1957 parliamentary elections led the party to favour electoral over agitational methods in the struggle for power. After the party split in 1964, competition for local bases of support between the CPI and CPI-M radicalized both as they sought to find and exploit situations suitable for agitations. This competitive period coincided with the beginning of the green revolution and was associated with party-influenced favourable wage settlements in 1969 and 1972. The abandonment in the early seventies by both communist parties of a strategy that identified wage labourers as the critical class in rural society was associated with a return by local cadres to electoral and parliamentary rather than agitational and conflictual tactics (Sharma 1973; Sen Gupta 1972). In line with this strategic choice, the parties appealed to a wide range of producer classes by pressing for easy availability of credit and low input and high commodity prices. Their strategy and demands abandoned primary reliance on agricultural workers, who now became only one of the producing classes meant to benefit from a prosperous agricultural sector.

However one treats objective and subjective determinants in explanations of mobilization or its absence in Tamil Nadu, micro-studies there have the satisfactory quality on occasion of having something to explain. Objective determinants were translated by leaders into subjective determinants (reasons) that led risk-averse labourers and tenants to act. Accounts by Breman in Gujarat (1974a), Gent in U.P. (1979) and Juergensmeyer in Punjab (1979) on the other hand remind us to eschew the assumption that objective determinants are self-realizing or self-executing, that causes automatically become reasons. Each depicts landless status groups—tribal Halpatis in Gujarat, Harijans in U.P. and Punjab—unwilling to act cooperatively or collectively. Why should this be so?

In these studies the most apparent objective determinant is poverty. Poverty can take the form of declining real incomes associated with immiseration or of a growing but maldistributed GNP associated with rising expectations and relative deprivation. While both are important preconditions for mobilization they are less important than the normative and structural conditions that make for insecurity and risk aversion. Poverty can be an objective determinant under the diffuse but summed inequalities of traditional ('feudal') relations or under the emergent market—particularly labour market—conditions of capitalist relations of production. Poverty exists under both of these generalized, abstract forms but its structural causes and consequences vary with the ways each form affects insecurity and risk aversion.

The poor perceive insecurity as more pervasive and impersonal under capitalist-tending market conditions and their associated state manifestation, a nominal government of laws that in fact is biased in its administration of justice and welfare. Under traditional domination the legitimizing ideologies and power asymmetries of local hierarchies sustained interdependence within relatively stable local social equilibria. They sanctioned rights and obligations as well as duties and dependencies by linking putatively non-antagonistic strata in harmonious social orders. Under the objective (structural and normative) conditions of a declining traditional domination, master–servant, patron–client and ritually ranked caste relations are subject to decay and displacement by an impersonal labour market and discriminatory state administration of order, justice and development programmes.

In the studies analysed below, traditional social equilibria have been badly eroded. However, the poor—whether Halpatis in Gujarat or untouchable labourers in U.P. or Punjab—lack the resources (organization, kinship, or political) to overcome market and state-induced insecurities or to take the risks needed for collective action. Nor have the potential triggering effects of new agricultural technology that improved the mobilization circumstances of the poor in Thanjavur district affected the circumstances of these Northern poor. Particularly in Thanjavur's Old Delta, leaders found it possible to translate causes into reasons because technological change reinforced the positive circumstances of its socio-economic configuration. The contrast between local socio-economic configurations in the Gujarat, U.P. and Punjab studies with the configuration in the Old Delta reveals that different mixes of apparently similar objective conditions may inhibit rather than facilitate mobilization.

Almost all of the findings of these studies identify objective conditions unfavourable to mobilization: the low numerical ratios between landlords and labour inhibit collective action; work patterns do not aggregate cultivators or labourers; where vertical bonds such as master–servant and patron–client relations persist, they isolate and constrain workers, and where they are in decay they have not been succeeded by horizontal solidarities of class or caste; alternative work outside agriculture fragments potential local solidarities, as does the increasing orientation to the world outside the village; families tend to be nuclear, and unable to create or benefit from kinship resources in production or politics.

The importance of numbers as an objective condition favourable to mobilization, i.e., the preponderance of hired agricultural labour over cultivators using their own and family labour, is highlighted in the Old Delta of Thanjavur by the 50 to 70 per cent proportions agricultural workers constitute of the work force. Even within Thanjavur, such proportions are extreme. The ratios of self-employed cultivators to hired agricultural labourers vary with ecological, crop and stratification differences by macro-region and within micro-region. At the macro-level, rice areas use hired agricultural workers more than do wheat areas. In the rice-growing areas of Tamil Nadu, West Bengal and Kerala, the ratio of family to hired labour is approximately even or favours wage workers, 1:1, 1:1 and 1:2

(Government of India, Directorate of Economics and Statistics 1975: Table 2.1a); the ratio in the wheat-growing areas of Punjab, U.P., and Haryana, by contrast, favours family labour over hired workers by 2:1, 3:1 and 4:1 respectively. These macro-contrasts by region and crop mask important internal variations. Within rice-growing states such as Andhra and Tamil Nadu particular districts such as West Godavari and Coimbatore/Salem show a preponderance of cultivator's own labour over hired labour. Even within districts such as Thanjavur where hired labour predominates over family labour, there are localities in which family labour is more frequently used than hired labour. Such variations are not trivial. They lie at the heart of the political question. Collective action arises in the first instance in local contexts. The variations just cited in ratios of family to hired labour differentially favour or constrain the possibility of mobilization.

If we turn to village micro-studies that focus on local configurations, those done in North and central India often report agricultural labour forces in which hired workers do *not* outnumber self-employed cultivators. In Orenstein's 'Gaon' in Maharashtra (1965), some 600 persons belong to the cultivating castes. Most of them are self-cultivators of small plots. They employ 117 Mahars and 112 Mangs, untouchable castes available for field labour (1965: 28). In Breman's Chikhligam in Gujarat the concentration of workers was greater; 125 landowning Anavil Brahmans could employ 200 Dubla labourers; in his Gandevigam 225 Anavil Brahmans could employ 429 Dublas (1974b: 95 and 155). In practice, however, the mode of cultivation limited concentrations of hired labour. One Anavil Brahman might employ 1 or 2 Dublas, and that on a seasonal basis. Mayer's central Indian village contained about 300 substantial (14 to 20 acres) cultivators in a village of 900 but numerous service castes with small holdings limited the use of hired workers (1960: 80). Only 24 persons regularly served as agricultural labour. In the U.P. village studied by Pradhan, Shoron, Jat cultivators outnumbered Chamar field workers in the three pattis of the village by 170 : 97, 110 : 72 and 98 : 67 (1966 : 26).

These ratios suggest that the decisive numerical advantage of agricultural workers in the Old Delta is exceptional, i.e., it is not approximated in the large number of villages where large landholders are absent or scarce and self-cultivation on small plots is preponderant. Indeed, the all-India proportion for agricultural workers, about 24 per cent (Sinha 1982), many of whom are simultaneously small holders, confirms the statistical unlikelihood in most localities of numerical parity, much less preponderance.

These figures take on additional significance for constraints on mobilization when one examines the pattern of employment. Agricultural workers in the above villages are not concentrated; they are scattered across the social landscape. One or two or three labourers are attached by dyadic ties to a cultivator, although the word 'attached' conveys a durability of relations that is no longer characteristic. Most farm land in a given village is self-cultivated by its holders. Even more prosperous peasants, controlling what in India passes for a 'large' holding—20 to 30 acres—often employ only a few labourers and those seasonally, at the time of high intensity cultivation and harvesting. Where such patron–client relations persist, their vertical pull counters the potential for horizontal solidarities.

More often, however, such relationships decay. Scarlett Epstein in 1962, Orenstein in 1961, Breman in 1963 reported the decay of patron–client relations in their respective areas in Mysore, Maharashtra and Gujarat. Such decay (incipient social disequilibrium) is often taken as a precondition for the emergence of horizontal, possibly class, ties. Barrington Moore's argument about commercial agricultural (1966) and Francine Frankel's argument (1971) about the green revolution turn on this assumption: that the consequences of enhanced market relations and improved technology will dissolve dependent but affective patron–client ties in the icy water of commercialization, impersonality, and relative deprivation and thus prepare the ground for protest, mobilization and class conflict. As we suggested above, Epstein found that commercial agricultural and improved technology may intensify rather than dissolve traditional ritual and agrarian relations. While Orenstein suggests that the horizontal ties of regional caste associations or egalitarian religious movements (Ambedkar's Buddhism) were beginning to affect village consciousness and action (1965: 257), Epstein and Breman paint a picture of insecurity whose correlates were apathy or anomie. 'The process of "depatronization" has left the agricultural labourers in a condition of isolation', Breman writes (1974b: 227). It seems likely that in many local contexts normlessness and apathy will replace decaying vertical ties.

The possibility of apathy or anomie among the poor in local settings can be reinforced by the growth of alternate forms of employment outside the village, district or state that further fragment the labour force. Typical are the Dublas who left Gujarat villages to work as brickmakers in Bombay part of the year and the contract labourers who left a Mysore village part of the year to work on earthworks in the region. They remained part of village society, if an increasingly ephemeral part. Of the 95 Dubla working men in Breman's Chikhligam (1974b: 219), 38 remained agricultural workers in Chikhligam, while 52 went to the Bombay brickyards much of the year. Formerly they shared a potential interest as clients of adjoining patrons. Now they are fragmented into a variety of types of employment; 'as sharecroppers, servants, casual labourers, and gang labourers, they have no parallel interests' (256).

Given such inhospitable conditions, it is not surprising that in the Breman, Gent and Juergensmeyer studies, leaders are unable to transform apparent objective interests into subjective interests that create group consciousness and inspire action. Breman describes Halpati passivity, amoral individualism and fatalism. Gent and Juergensmeyer provide similar accounts of Harijans. When the 'culture of poverty' literature[18] argued that destitution and discrimination cause anomie, social disorganization and selfishness, critics noted that the analysis failed to take into account the extent to which such responses were rational adaptations. Failure to mobilize may be rational in contexts where the margin to take political and economic risk is absent or minimal. Without the security associated with traditional dependent relations, some economic margin in terms of control of productive assets or labour market bargaining power seems to be required. Labourers who lack not only assets or income but also a sense of self-worth and efficacy are unlikely to believe they can influence their fate by taking the risks associated with collective action. This is a threshold that precedes by some distance mobilization based on immiseration or rising expectations and relative deprivation. Juergensmeyer's comparison (1979, 1981) of levels of ideological or religious commitment and organizational affiliations of three different Harijan communities differentiates two that have such a margin from one that does not.

What did leadership make of the conditions found in the Breman, Gent and Juergensmeyer studies? When objective determinants are

---

[18] For a review of this literature and powerful arguments that discredit it, on the grounds that Oscar Lewis *et al.* mistake adaptive behaviour for culture, see Charles Valentine (1968).

weaker and less congruent with each other than in the Thanjavur Old Delta context, leadership has less to work with. In the three studies at issue, leadership was absent or could not translate the conditions making for impoverishment and insecurity into reasons for action. Breman finds that the class collaborative ideology of the Gandhian Sarvodaya workers engaged in organizing the Halpatis and the cooptive effects of government subsidies to Halpati schools pre-empted the possibility of conflictual mobilization. Gent reports that his one year effort (over three crops) to build a self-sustaining production cooperative collapsed with his departure. In 'Bimla', one of the three Harijan communities Juergensmeyer studied, there were no signs of leadership. Yet leadership of the 'right kind' remains a critical mediating determinant of mobilization because it is more likely than any other to translate objective into subjective interests that result in action.

Gandhian Sarvodaya workers and left party leaders of poor status groups are outsiders whose high caste backgrounds, considerable education, vested career interests or ideological orientations are alien to those they profess to serve and benefit. Are they or can they be the right kind of leaders? For example, Sarvodaya leaders in Gujarat were known as 'service workers', volunteers in the well established Gandhian style. They sought to 'uplift' the lower orders by exposing them to a Sanskritic equivalent of the 'Protestant ethic' or Methodist virtue, urging their benighted and depraved members to be self-disciplined, to abjure drink, to join in communal singing (*bajan mandlis*), and to become educated. As E. P. Thompson and earlier students of the history of the working class in England have pointed out, in saving the souls of England's lower orders, Methodism also helped to create a compliant and disciplined work force. Breman sees the less successful efforts of Sarvodaya service workers among the Halpatis in a similar light.

When Halpati Seva Sangh leaders begin to be recruited from among the Halpatis themselves another dimension of finding the right kind of leaders arises. Halpati Seva Sangh leaders are coopted. They join the rank of masters. They don terylene, accept the rules and style of government officials and observe conventions designed to keep poor Halpatis in their place. Some believe that untouchable leaders are more prone than other group leaders to use office for personal gain. This difficulty has been recognized and faced by an untouchable mobilization movement in Tamil Nadu. Its training programme includes ethical instruction for future *panches* (village headmen) designed to arm them against the self-serving temptations of office.[19]

Indigenous leadership is often subject to cooptation and self-aggrandizement. Those raised up adopt the ideology and interests of their former masters and answer the call of individual rather than collective interest. Personal desire for mobility and respectability overcomes earlier commitments to the collective needs of 'their' community.

Non-indigenous leadership is problematic too. Its social provenance and ideas are alien and it patronizes those it serves out of a spirit of *noblesse oblige*. Upper caste/upper class leadership of poor and oppressed groups can symbolize their inferiority. It was recognition of this meaning and its rejection that led to the expulsion in 1963 of white leaders óf the civil rights movement in America's South and to the parallel appearance of black consciousness in politics (black nationalism); in language (black 'English'); physical appearance ('black is beautiful', Afros) and style (African ornaments such as dashikis); society (separatism in college dormitories and canteens); and economics (black business for black customers; affirmative action). Juergensmeyer's account of village 'Bimla' in Punjab, where one-fourth of the population is Harijan living under conditions of extreme social asymmetry, poverty and oppression, describes the Harijans as without a cultural identity or symbolic life of their own. In the other two villages Juergensmeyer studied, where Harijans were somewhat better placed with respect to property and income, they had established identities and self-respect by transvaluing the negative identity provided by the larger society into a positive one via involvement in Dalit and Ad Dharm cultural and sectarian movements (1981). It is possible that the poorer Harijans of 'Bimla' do not respond to class consciousness and mobilization by upper caste/ class leadership not because they are poor and miserable but because it would merely mean replacing one appropriation of their identity and interests by upper caste landlords with another upper caste appropriation. Do those below the threshold for mobilizations based on rising expectations and relative deprivation need to recognize themselves in symbolically separate terms? Must they have symbols that speak to their own experience and that transvalue their op-

[19] Fatimah Natesan, social worker with Rural Community Development Movement in Tamil Nadu, personal communication.

pressors' negative perceptions of them (what Erikson 1969: 135, 174 refers to as affirming a negative identity)[20] in ways that give meaning and dignity to what they know of themselves and their history, before they can acquire the self and social esteem required for collective social action.

Recent work on the Dalit movement in Maharashtra and elsewhere by Ravinder Khare, Eleanor Zelliot (1977), Gail Omvedt (1976), V. M. Sirsikar (1970) and Mark Juergensmeyer (1982) seems to converge on the importance and value of symbolic separatism and indigenous leadership. The authors differ, however, on the orientation and role of cultural and political elites, the relationship of cultural identity to class consciousness, and consensual, conflictual and separatist modes of political representation and social action. These studies indicate that symbolic separatism is often a condition for self and social esteem and mobilization. Short of revolution or political separation, ultimately cultural or symbolic separatism requires recognition from the larger society to confirm its validity and establish its legitimacy. The successful efforts to place Dr B. R. Ambedkar's statue in the great hall of Parliament with the other founders of the Indian state; the unsuccessful efforts to establish a Mahar regiment and to include the name of Dr Ambedkar in the name of Marathawada University; the backlash against untouchable conversions to Islam; even the continuing debate about reservations for scheduled castes and tribes, illustrate the hazards and problematics of mobilizations designed to validate and legitimize cultural separatism.

We are not arguing that cultural separatism is necessary for or the preferred mode of mobilizing poor and oppressed status orders and cultural communities. Accounts of successful mobilizations over the past 30 years by local communist leaders in two zones of Thanjavur district of poor Harijans make clear that under the right contextual

---

[20] Juergensmeyer (1982), for example, found that 'from the point of view of . . . lower caste people in Ferozepur and Ludhiana, there are only the rich and the poor, the exploited and the exploiters. The upper castes, however, have a different view of the situation perceiving social divisions in caste rather than functions of economic class' (18). Yet, as the title of his book, *Religion as Social Vision*, indicates, Juergensmeyer found the path of first recourse for untouchable liberation to be not class but religious identity. In order to disengage themselves from Hindu customs and forms of social control, untouchables formulated and chose 'some workable religious community from the variety of models available' (6).

conditions class rather than status order or community consciousness can be the predominant element for solidarity and action. We say predominant because local communist class mobilizations recognized and worked with Harijan consciousness and social organization. Similarly, the symbolic separatism of mobilizable status orders and communities often incorporates and expresses class dimensions. Regardless of whether class, status order or cultural community is ascendant in particular contexts, conflict accompanies mobilization. It is in this sense that caste and communal conflict is like class conflict; all three reflect the successful efforts of social formations (i.e., ideologically conscious and organized classes, status orders and communities) to translate objective into subjective interests.

So far we have stressed local context in our discussion of mobilization and leadership. Locality joins ecology with specific social structures, property relations and forms of labour. Local contexts vary enormously and have remained remarkably isolated from each other. The great variety and isolation of local conditions makes the agrarian sector more resistant than the industrial to the common consciousness and organization that large-scale mobilizations require. Such considerations led Marx to despair (in Western Europe if not in Tsarist Russia) of peasants becoming a class capable of representing itself in political struggles. Peasants' homologous condition rendered them as unorganizable as potatoes in a sack.

But was Marx right in believing that peasants living in isolated localities and working separately from each other were immune from large-scale mobilizations? The physical and economic risks of mobilization for insecure and dependent poor cultivators and labourers in India often makes apathy a rational political strategy. Broadening the arena of conflict and bargaining to state or national levels can reduce risk by socializing it. Such higher level mobilizations can reduce risk and enhance bargaining advantages at the micro-level by altering the social 'terms of trade' between subject and dominant groups. Higher level collective action may change norms and expectations, add the weight of numbers, recruit class, elite or interest group allies and attract political and organizational resources. In the next section we shift the focus from village and locality to agrarian classes and status orders. These analytic categories allow us to examine the prospects for state and national mobilizations that incorporate or transcend locality.

III. *Subjective Interests of Agrarian Classes and Status Orders*

Our analysis of determinants and varieties of agrarian mobilization involves the conceptual and empirical identification of agrarian classes and status orders and accounts of their likely subjective interests and political strategies. We prefer staying closer to actors' perceptions, motives and self-definitions than to theoretically derived structural or historical forces and their putative necessary or logical consequences.

We distinguish four agrarian classes, agricultural labourers, small holders, bullock capitalists and large landowners, and four status orders: scheduled castes and tribes, backward classes, middle castes, and upper (twice-born) castes. In this section we focus on the characteristics and likely subjective interests of bullock capitalists, backward classes, labourers, and small holders. The categories are both empirical, i.e., based on the size distribution of operational holdings (see Table I) and ideal-typical, i.e., based on global qualitative or non-quantified characteristics. We follow Weber's heuristic injunction to select the dominant (stereotypical) qualities that, for the purposes of the investigator, yield knowledge about actors' orientation for social action.[21] We recognize that those within particular categories do not wholly or uniformly share the ideal-typical or non-quantified characteristics attributed to each. We rely on tendencies and prevalences, not isomorphic uniformities. For example, relations of production in the four quantitative categories are affected by variable mixes of labour and capital-intensive production techniques and of family and hired labour. The degree to which each is present is uncertain or unknown at macro-statistical levels. Yet we know from micro-studies, proxy-measures, and inferences from other aggregate data that cultivators in the bullock capitalist category, for example, are more likely than are large landowners to rely on family than on hired labour and are more likely than small holders to possess the quality of human capital needed to complement the improved physical capital and inputs of green revolution agricultural technology.

---

[21] We depart from Weber by distinguishing for analytic and explanatory purposes objective and subjective determinants and interests (causes and reasons). Weber's conjoined use of material and ideal interests to explain social action led him to neglect the transition process from causes to reasons that we consider vital in explaining mobilization. See our discussion of Weber's methodology in 'Authority and Power' (Rudolph 1979).

TABLE 1

*Changes in Size of Holdings of Agricultural Households
1954–55 to 1971–72*

Size of Operational Household Holding (acres)	1954–55		1971–72	
	Households (per cent)	Area Controlled (per cent)	Households (per cent)	Area Controlled (per cent)
1. Landless				
0*	28	—	27	—
2. Small Holders				
.01– 0.99	14 ⎫ 28%	1 ⎫ 5%	15 ⎫ 33%	2 ⎫ 10%
1.00– 2.49	14 ⎭	4 ⎭	18 ⎭	8 ⎭
3. Bullock Capitalists				
2.50– 4.99	15 ⎫	10 ⎫	16 ⎫	15 ⎫
5.00– 7.49	9 ⎪ 35%	10 ⎪ 42%	9 ⎪ 34%	13 ⎪ 51%
7.50– 9.99	5 ⎬	9 ⎬	4 ⎬	9 ⎬
10.00–14.99	6 ⎭	13 ⎭	5 ⎭	14 ⎭
4. Large Landowners				
15.00 and above	9	53	6	39
All sizes	100	100	100	100

All percents are rounded.

Source: S. K. Sanyal, 'Trends in Rural Unemployment in India: Two Comments', Part 2, Table 3, *Economic and Political Weekly*, Vol. 12, No. 5, 29 January 1977, pp. 245–8.

*The figures in this should not be read as giving the households of agricultural workers, who have increased, and can be found in both category 1 and 2.

We do not make any *a priori* assumptions about necessary antagonisms or a principal contradiction among the four agrarian classes and status orders. Indeed, our reading of their prior record of cooperation and conflict; of their present and future subjective interests; and of the play of contextual and party differences on their political orientations leads us to expect that all permutations and combinations are possible, even those deemed unlikely in terms of deduction or inferences from hypothesized objective interests.

The figures in Table 1 give some sense for the magnitudes of each class. Note that they are categories showing operational holding, which is a concept that conveys the amount of land *controlled* by a household as cultivators, not its legal relationship to the holding.

Thus 'small holders' may include both tenants and owners. The categories in the table and our four agrarian classes do not overlap perfectly. Thus agricultural labourers may be found in category 1, landless, in category 2, small holder and even in category 3, bullock capitalist, because many small holders and some bullock capitalists supplement their incomes by agricultural labour. We draw the boundaries for the bullock capitalist class at 2.5 and 14.9 acres because within this range independent, self-employed agricultural producers can be productive and prosperous. Holdings within this range are large enough for agricultural producers to take advantage of new technology and credit institutions, to use their own human, physical and financial capital and to benefit from the quality and 'surplus' of their own labour. Again, the category is not homogeneous. Caste conventions often inhibit 10 acre Rajputs, Bhumiars and Brahmans in the East Gangetic plains from cultivating, while 20 acre Jats in Western U.P. often put their hand to the plough. We have designated producers at 15 acres and above large landowners because at that scale they are, figuratively, more often 'tractor' than 'bullock' capitalists. Large landowners are more prone than are bullock capitalists to use capital rather than labour-intensive production techniques; to rely on less committed and skilled wage and/or attached labour or on insecure tenants; and as a consequence to be more involved in capitalist and/or feudal (master–servant; patron–client) relations of production.

Our agricultural labour category designates households with little or no land (owned or leased-in) who rely for their income on wages and/or payment in kind. This category too is not without complexities that can affect the formation of subjective interests and political orientation. Agricultural labour can take a variety of forms, e.g., attached and casual; organized, contract and unorganized; protected or unprotected by enforceable minimum wage legislation. Agricultural labourers can have variable access to non-agricultural labour markets and productive or service activities and thus alternative sources of additional income.

Most small holders (1.01 to 2.49 acres) lack sufficient land (via ownership or leasing in) and capital (including creditworthiness) to benefit as cultivators from new technology and their own labour.[22]

[22] The question whether the new technology of the green revolution is scale neutral or to what size it is was preceded by discussion among economists of the proposition that there is an inverse relationship between farm size and yield. The

Most operate holdings below the level required to support a pair of bullocks or to afford the rental of tractor and lack the means to benefit from easily divisible (seeds, fertilizer) much less lumpy (e.g. tube-well) improved inputs. Most rely on wage labour as well as cultivation as a source of income, some to supplement earnings from cultivation, others, particularly those who lease out their land, as a primary source of income. Because of the ambiguity of their objective circumstances, the subjective interests of small holders are more varied, unstable and difficult to anticipate than the subjective interests of the other three agricultural classes.

The proportion of small holder households (category 2) and of agricultural labourers (who are found in categories 1 and 2) increased between 1954–55 and 1970–71 while proportions of households in categories 3 and 4 decreased. Table 1 does not reflect the change in the proportion of agricultural labourers because landless households (category 1), which decreased slightly, are not congruent with agricultural labourers, who increased. (This problem will be dealt with at greater length below.) Agricultural labourers and small holders, the two poorest and most disadvantaged classes of the agricultural sector, together constitute a majority of rural households and share certain characteristics. The political significance of this numerical majority will depend on the plausibility and efficacy of the objective grounds used to distinguish them and the related likelihood of their behaviour being oriented by distinct subjective determinants. For example, can small holders whose incomes arise from agricultural labour as well as cultivation be distinguished in objective or sub-

---

larger farms were thought to produce less per unit of land than smaller farms. The statistical evidence mounted at the time—before the green revolution inputs became available and before the oil price rises of 1973 and 1979 reduced the cost advantages of larger-scale 'mechanized' agriculture—already tended to support the negative relationship between size and productivity per unit of land. Two articles by Sen (1962, 1964) sparked the debate; Khusro (1974), Rudra (1968), Bhattacharya (1972), Bharadwaj (1974) made important contributions to the issue of size and productivity. Biplab Das Gupta (1977) reviewed the evidence through 1973, before the oil price rises in 1973 and 1979.

His arguments favouring the relative efficiency of size have been seriously undercut by the rise in operating costs subsequent to 1973. Nor does he attend to the effects of the quality and commitment of labour, a consideration that favours the efficiency of operating units whose scale is commensurate with higher quality family labour. Finally, he does not consider the long-run benefits from relying on the renewal resources associated with bullock power, or the depletable and high cost resources associated with mechanized farming.

jective terms from landless agricultural labourers? Are the classes depicted in Table 1 becoming more homogeneous or more heterogeneous? In either case, are the subjective interests that orient their respective political action becoming more conflictual or cooperative (K. Bardhan 1977)?

The increase shown in Table 1 in the proportion of small holder households and in the proportion of land under their control is less disputed than the size of the increase in the proportion of agricultural labourers. Some scholars of India's agricultural economy accept the figures in the 1961 and 1971 census which show a 10 per cent increase in the proportion of agricultural labourers, from 15 per cent in 1961 to 25 per cent in 1971 (K. Bardhan 1977: I, A-37). Some of these scholars anticipated significant political consequences. Other scholars, working with NSS data, question both figures on the ground that change in census definitions accounted for part of the shift in proportions. Visaria, for example, finds that the porportion of agricultural labourers in 1961 was between 19 and 20 per cent rather than the 15 per cent given in the 1961 census, that the proportion in 1971 was 22 rather than 25 per cent, and that, as a consequence, the increase over the decade was approximately three rather than 10 per cent. The 1981 census, when there was no change in census definitions, supports the sceptics by showing a small decline in the proportion of agricultural workers (Visaria and Sanyal 1977).

The dispute over the amount of increase in the proportion of agricultural workers arises out of the ambiguous and changing nature of those we have included in the bottom two classes. Our categories, like most used in the social sciences, are not isomorphic. Those included in a particular category may share a 'family resemblance' with those included in other categories, particularly among those included in adjacent categories in the same universe of discourse. As a result, differences among investigators over the properties and size of particular categories are bound to arise. Those responsible for the 1971 census operations attempted to refine the distinction between cultivators and workers by counting as agricultural workers agricultural producers whose principal source of income was wages and counting as cultivators agricultural producers whose principal source of income was cultivation. Enumerators' instructions were revised accordingly. Critics argue that the one consequence of changing enumerators' instructions was to make the 1961 and 1971 figures for agricultural workers non-comparable (Vasaria and Sanyal 1977).

BULLOCK CAPITALISTS

We anticipate that over the next decade bullock capitalists and backward classes (an overlapping status category to be discussed below) will be at the centre of political events and constellations of power. Wide agrarian support in North India for the Janata Party in 1977 and for its erstwhile components in 1980 (Rudolph and Rudolph 1981) and agrarian mobilizations since 1980 favouring higher commodity prices depended on bullock capitalist size holders. Brass (1980, 1981) shows that in Uttar Pradesh middle castes of peasants in the 1977–80 elections were the core of Janata and Lok Dal support.[23] In these cases, party and interest group leaders translated the objective determinant of government policies for input costs and commodity prices into subjective determinants of mobilization.

We use the term 'bullock capitalists' heuristically to suggest a congery of qualities that other linguistic usages do not evoke. Bullock capitalists are self-employed and funded producers. Their holdings are large enough to support a pair of bullocks and use of the new inputs associated with the 'green revolution'. Their costs of production tend to be more efficient than those of small holders or large landowners. At the same time, their assets are not large enough to enable them to engage in capital-intensive agricultural production based on extensive use of machinery or to require them to rely wholly or mainly on wage or tenant labour. We use the term 'bullock' more figuratively than literally. Bullock capitalists may use tractors or other lumpy forms of physical capital on their modest size holdings typically by renting such items in or out. The important point is that they are cultivators of moderate means who own or control the physical capital involved in farm production and they and members of their family provide the complementary and differentiated human capital to operate and manage it.

We prefer the term 'bullock capitalists' to 'middle peasants' because of the mix of capitalist, pre-industrial and non-capitalist features that characterizes their economic circumstances. The con-

[23] For the size categories that provided the support base for Janata and its components, see Brass (1980, 1981). Brass shows bi-modal support for Congress, among 30 acre and above and 1 acre and below cultivators, while the support for Charan Singh led parties that joined and left Janata was more from among 2 to 15 acre holders.

cept 'peasant' does not convey this mix because it relies too much on pre-capitalist economic circumstances. Some large landowners share this mix too but the scale of their operational holdings and other assets, their reliance on hired or tenant labour or their greater use of capital-intensive production techniques distinguish them from bullock capitalists. Bullock capitalists operate family farms as family firms; the family broadly defined is the primary if not the exclusive source of capital, management and labour. Bullock capitalists produce enough for the market to be oriented to and constrained by it but not so much that consumption of their own products or non-monetized exchanges of goods or services have ceased to matter. Factor costs, of seeds, fertilizers, water, capital, and, to an extent, labour, like product prices, are powerfully but not wholly determined by market forces. They are also selectively and variably modified by state policy interventions such as subsidies for inputs and services, preferential taxation and support prices. They operate typically between 2.5 and 15 acres, may lease in an appreciable proportion, sometimes employ but do not depend on attached or casual wage labour, and, at the margin of the category, themselves work for wages. Bullock capitalists employ new techniques and inputs when conditions and costs justify doing so. While they use and pay for capital and participate in markets, they are 'non-capitalist' producers because, being self-employed owners of capital, their relations of production are undifferentiated and non-antagonistic.[24] Charan Singh, the principal spokesman for bullock capitalist ideology and interests (Singh 1978), has specifically and consistently opposed 'mechanization', a code word for capital-intensive farming based more on machinery such as tractors and hired labour than on draft animals and family labour. He did so by *inter alia* supporting high central government taxes on tractors to encourage labour-intensive farming.[25]

[24] Rudra more or less excludes bullock capitalists from his analysis of relevant categories in the rural landscape precisely because their relations with other classes are non-antagonistic. See Rudra (1978) where he explains why he treats them and many small holders as 'not constituting any class'.

[25] 'Mechanization or further mechanization of the economy has, therefore, to be discouraged. . . .' See also Charan Singh's discussion of arguments for non-mechanized farming (or farming by manual and animal labour) (Singh 1978: 116, 119–21). On the other hand, the Devi Lal Janata government in Haryana abolished that state's tax on tractors indicating that Devi Lal's erstwhile BLD dominated government was more concerned to serve the interests of large land-

Most important for consciousness and politics, the economic circumstances of bullock capitalists unite the interests of capital, management and labour. Bullock capitalists own or control the means of production they use, manage the productive unit and themselves provide most if not all the labour. If there is exploitation involved in their relations of production, it is self-exploitation, e.g., they benefit from the 'surplus value' of their labour. Put another way, bullock capitalists are the direct beneficiaries of differentiated and upgraded forms of human and physical capital. They apply high quality, intense and committed labour to the tasks, tools and techniques of cultivation, management and entrepreneurship.[26] The late Daniel Thorner used actors' language to distinguish three agrarian classes, *maliks* (bosses), *kisans* (cultivators), and *mazdurs* (workers). In so far as bullock capitalists are managers and entrepreneurs as well as cultivators and workers, they combine all three terms.

---

owners engaged in capital-intensive agriculture than to follow his leader's ideological injunctions and mobilization strategy.

[26] See, for the concept of self-exploitation by family firms in the market sector and household economy, Galbraith (1973); for circumstances and calculations of agricultural producers under traditional and modernizing technological circumstances see Schultz (1964). We prefer Galbraith's formulation of self-exploitation to Chayanov (1966) because Galbraith, unlike Chayanov, not only posits but also estimates prices for labour costs in family firms and households that make calculations about their value and purchase possible. Schultz (1981) convincingly argues that human time increases in value as human capital improves and complements physical capital's improved productivity. Chayanov, by contrast, held that there was no valid way to estimate in money the value of family members' work. He treats family labour on peasant holdings as drudgery. In positing a family 'labour-consumer balance', Chayanov argues that increases in output are weighed against the irksomeness of extra work. Self-exploitation occurs because the quality of peasant labour is undifferentiated and static and its productive value constant. Schultz (1964) shows that without improved inputs Chayanov's assumptions about self-exploitation hold, i.e., that it is rational for traditional agricultural producers not to work more when there is little return for additional labour. Schultz shows that when the state of the art changes, i.e., when improved inputs and physical capital become available, they require, and in India have elicited, complementary improvements in human capital. The 'new breed' of farmers in low income countries such as India '. . . have learned how to use land, labour, and capital efficiently in response to production opportunities associated with agricultural modernization. . . .' Their entrepreneurial ability 'to perceive, interpret and respond to new events in the context of risk is an important part of the human capital of these countries' (1981 : 25–6). Schultz links improvements in human capital to mobilization by observing that the human agent '. . . by virtue of his personal human capital . . . seeks political support to protect the

At the time of zamindari abolition, the objective and perceived interests of an emergent bullock capitalist class clashed with those of feudal landlords.[27] Bullock capitalists as well as large landowners fell heir to the land surrendered by zamindars. In the absence of serious administrative and legislative efforts to enforce or further lower ceilings on landholdings, bullock capitalists' objective interests with respect to landholding are not now likely to place them in antagonistic relationships with other agrarian classes. Under such circumstances, they are in a position to make alliances up or down in defence of agrarian sector interests. But bullock capitalists overlap with a status order, 'backward classes', castes just above the untouchables who seek to distinguish themselves socially as well as economically from untouchable landless labourers and marginal cultivators. The backward classes and scheduled castes (untouchables) compete in the policy arena too, not least for jobs and educational reservations in what both sides usually take to be a zero sum game. This compounding of economic and status policy differences makes conflict more likely than would class differences alone.

Bullock capitalists are not *kulaks*. *Kulak* carries with it the specific historical baggage of nineteenth and twentieth century Russian usage. Before the revolution it referred to an agrarian class of prosperous non-cultivating middlemen. This usage is not appropriate for India's independent farmers. More recently *kulak* acquired a more contemporary meaning from Stalin's usage, an enemy class that required elimination. It can be used today for certain normative or polemical purposes, as Walter Neale showed when he observed: '*Kulak* is the product of a conjugation: "you *talk* to farmers, you *shout* at peasants, you *shoot kulaks*", and in each case the appellation

---

value of that capital. . . . The legal rights of labour are enlarged and in the process some of the rights of property are curtailed. The legal rights of tenants are also enhanced' (1981: 60, 76). Chayanov's depiction of peasant labour as static and undifferentiated drudgery and of increased production and thus consumption requiring self-exploitation proved to be not only reductionist but also ahistorical in the face of new agricultural technology and labour's improved quality, differentiation and productivity. That peasant and household labour need not be mere drudgery becomes more evident when farm and household work began to benefit from electricity and mechanization.

[27] Merle Fainsod's remarkable study of collectivization (1958) not only provides vivid detail for the process but also makes clear how difficult it was to distinguish *kulaks* from other peasants and the remarkable lineage, affinal and economic interdependence among rich, middle and poor peasants.

justifies the action.'[28] The Indian backlash against rural demands often finds it convenient to use *kulak* in this pejorative manner. For social scientific purposes, there are problems about employing the term to designate heterogeneous groups, especially to elide the distinction between owner cultivators and non-cultivating owners.

It may be worth quoting Merriam Webster's Unabridged to clarify the issue:

> *Kulak* Russian, literally fist, of turkic origin, akin to Turk *kol*, arm. 1. A prosperous or wealthy peasant farmer in 19th century Russia often associated with gaining profit from renting land, usury, or acting as a middleman in the sale of the products of other farmers. 2. A farmer characterized by Communists as having excessive wealth, usually by possession of more than a minimal amount of property and by ability to hire labourers or sometimes merely by unwillingness to join a collective farm and as a result denounced as an oppressor of less fortunate farmers and subjected to severe penalties (as heavy fines and confiscation of property) (a large proportion of the kulaks of the twenties were liquidated).

Our definition of bullock capitalists as an agrarian class distinguishes them from *kulak*-like Indian farmers (large landowners) on the one hand and marginal farmers or landless agricultural workers on the other. Because they are neither capitalists or workers nor exploiters or exploited, they pose a problem for liberals as well as Marxists in political target making or coalition building. If bullock capitalists are on the whole self-exploiters, what is the justification for making them a class enemy or class ally? Their 'categorical invisibility' in agrarian class theory is due precisely to their anomalous standing.

Bullock capitalists are advantageously placed by their objective circumstances to become the hegemonic agrarian class. As of 1971–72 they were probably more numerous and controlled more land than the other three agrarian classes. Large landowners as a statistical category lost ground to bullock capitalists between 1954–55 and 1971–72 in terms of households and area controlled, a change that was punctuated by the 1977 election when Congress' rout by the Janata Party made bullock capitalists rather than large landowners the senior partners in many state governments and for the first time placed them in an advantageous position at the centre. Table 1, which specifies operational holdings by size groups, shows bullock

[28] Personal communication.

capitalists as 35 per cent of agricultural households, operating about half the cultivated land. Though these proportions suggest a higher level of concreteness than is warranted, we use them because the heuristic category, bullock capitalists, has its nearest empirical referent in the size class from 2.5 to 15. Anomalies arise because similar size does not invariably capture similar qualities. We have already mentioned that East Gangetic high caste landholders do not self-cultivate. Some of the 2.5–15 acre holdings are spurious, parts of larger landholdings disguised by legal fictions as smaller in order to evade, at least for a time, land ceilings legislation. On the other hand, some small holders and some large landowners no doubt qualify as bullock capitalists in their uses of physical capital and family labour. Ronald Herring (1982) and Utsa Patnaik in different contexts have seriously challenged the congruence of size categories with qualitative production relations.[29] In the absence of relevant macro-data about qualitative aspects of size holdings we have used the 35 per cent of households in the size class 2.5 to 15 acres to approximate the magnitude of the bullock capitalist agrarian class.

Small holders may collaborate politically with bullock capitalists if they can be led to believe in the Indian equivalent of America's Horatio Alger myth about mobility in industrial society. It held that with pluck and luck poor boys can become if not a millionaire like Andrew Carnegie at least successful members of America's vast middle class, a myth which mixed enough fact with its fiction to inhibit the growth among America's poor of class consciousness and antagonistic class relations. The bullock capitalist myth holds that small holders and even some of the landless can cross the poverty line to become independent farmers if properly designed and implemented ceilings and tenancy legislation makes land accessible and the productivity gains of new agricultural technology are made available through state investment in infrastructure, accessible institutional credit, cheap inputs, high support prices, and favourable terms of trade with the industrial sector. In so far as small holders accept India's mobility myth, bullock capitalists can lead a coalition that encompasses much of the 80 per cent of India's society that constitute its agricultural sector and rural society. From this position of strength, bullock capitalists can bargain effectively with the components of the organized economy and mostly urban society: organ-

[29] We are very much indebted to Herring for an extended critique of our attempt to suggest a size category for bullock capitalists.

ized white and blue collar workers, private and state industrial and financial capitalists, state bureaucrats, professionals, small business classes and the 'parasitical intelligentsia'.[30]

Our analysis of bullock capitalists has proceeded at an all-India level. Yet we recognize that what is true for India may not be true for South, West, East, and North India, much less for particular states, districts and indeed villages. All-India generalizations may miss differences that can prove decisive for national historical outcomes. As a result, bullock capitalists may remain more dominant in Northern, Western and upper Southern states than in the Eastern and lower Southern states or than at the Centre. Bullock capitalists are more significant in the economic and political life of the wheat-growing areas of the North and West than in the rice-growing areas of the East and South. In the North independent cultivators greatly outnumber agricultural labourers but they are evenly balanced in the lower South and Bengal. The ratios of independent cultivators using family labour to hired agricultural labourers in the wheat-growing areas of Punjab, U.P. and Haryana are 2:1, 3:1, and 4:1 whereas in the rice-growing areas of Tamil Nadu, West Bengal and Kerala they are 1:1, 1:1 and 1:2 (India 1975: Table 2–1(a)). These figures indicate the wheat-growing areas' greater propensity to utilize family labour and the relatively greater reliance on employed labour in rice-growing areas. Important rice-growing areas such as Than-javur district in Tamil Nadu, Hooghly and 24 Parganas in West Bengal, and Alleppey and Quilon in Kerala, for example, show a far lower proportion of family labour engaged in farm work than do important wheat districts such as Muzzafarnagar, Meerut, Amritsar, Ferozepur and Nasik.[31] Nevertheless, the fact of bullock capitalist

[30] Charan Singh, the authentic voice of bullock capitalism, made clear in his speech as Prime Minister of India to the Andhra Pradesh Kisan Advocates Forum, on 22 October 1979 that he hoped to forge some such alliance. He said that the percentage of cultivators had gone down from 51 to 43 while that of farm labourers had gone up from 17 to 26 as a result of the land reforms during 1961–71 (which is doubtful. See below). As U.P. Revenue Minister he said he had blocked such developments by not allowing the landlords to evict tenants on the pretext of resumption of land for self-cultivation. See *Hindustan Times* (1979: 23, p. 1).

[31] Thanjavur, 78 eight-hour days worked on the farm in the year per adult family worker; 87 Cuddapah; 42 Allepey and Quilon; 79 Hooghly and 24 Parganas; as against 263 in Meerut and Muzzafarnagar, 267 for Amritsar and Ferozepur and 239 for Nasik (India 1975: Table 2.1 ca).

cultivation and the appeal of its ideology remain powerful in the South too where many cultivators operate holdings that fully and remuneratively employ family labour.[32]

Bullock capitalists' political significance depends in part on their ability to maintain their economic base, i.e., the proportion of land under their operational control and the availability and use of technology that makes it as productive and profitable as large holdings using capital-intensive technology and hired labour. While the proportion of large landowners and the amount of land under their control declined between 1954–55 and 1970–71 (from 9 to 6 per cent and from 53 to 39 per cent, Table 1), the proportion of bullock capitalists remained stable and the amount of land under their control increased. In agricultural production, improved technology combined with improved human capital and entrepreneurship can cancel or reverse economies of scale. The commitment, reliability and quality of the self-employed labour available to bullock capitalists is markedly better than the wage or dependent labour on which large landowners rely. As between small holders, bullock capitalists and large landowners, we anticipate that over the medium term (the foreseeable future of about ten years) bullock capitalists will gain the advantage.

BACKWARD CLASSES

The mobilization of bullock capitalists as an economic class has been reinforced by the simultaneous mobilization as a status order of the 'other backward classes',[33] a euphemism for castes who by their own and the state's reckoning are socially 'depressed' or

---

[32] The figures for West Godavari, Andhra Pradesh and Coimbatore/Salem in Tamil Nadu show higher levels of adult family labour per year, i.e., 160 and 202 respectively, than the Southern district cited above. Marshall Bouton identifies two of five zones in Thanjavur District where cultivation based on family labour on middle-sized holdings predominates, and Joan Mencher too finds that many holdings in Chingleput support family labour. See Bouton (1980); Mencher (1978: 197).

[33] Officially, backward classes include the scheduled castes and tribes as well as 'other backward classes'. The Backward Classes Commission (Kalelkar Commission, 1955) identified 2,399 castes whose position in the ritual hierarchy, percentage of literacy and representation in public and private organized sector employment made them eligible for the benefits recommended by the commission. The central government reserved places in public employment and provided other benefits for the scheduled castes and tribes but not, as of this writing, for other backward classes.

'backward'. This layering of status and class interest enhances the political significance of both.

Marc Galanter in answering his own question, 'Who Are the "Other Backward Classes" ', has given as definitive an answer as the shifting career of the term allows (Galanter 1978; Dushkin 1961, 1971). It was initiated toward the end of World War I in South and West India when reservations for 'backward communities'[34] began to be made in public services and educational institutions. Today the term 'backward classes' loosely refers to about half of the 'Shudra' castes located below the traditionally literate upper twice-born (spiritually initiated) castes[35] but above the untouchables ('scheduled castes'). Backward classes have been estimated at between 20 and 49 per cent.[36]

Bullock capitalists are an economic class grounded in production; backward classes are a status order defined by traditional (*dharmic*) ritual ranking of castes and the state's official sociology of disadvantaged communities.[37] The two analytic categories refer for the most part but not entirely to the same people, i.e., empirically they

[34] The first wave of reservations began during World War I in Mysore and the Madras presidency but soon spread to the Bombay presidency and Kerala. Locally prosperous and prestigious landowning castes such as Mudaliars and Vellalas in Madras, Lingayats and Vokkaligas in Mysore, Naidus, Kammas and Reddis in the Andhra region of the Madras presidency, Nairs and, in a sense, Iravas in Kerala (Travancore and Cochin), and Marathas in the Maharashtra region of Bombay presidency pursued social mobility in anti-Brahman movements that challenged Brahman social ideology, established new caste names, histories, occupations and life-styles, demanded reservations of places in public employment and educational institutions ('communal awards' that established quotas) and sometimes, particularly in Madras, mobilized the overwhelming majority of non-Brahman caste communities by regional appeals to cultural nationalism (the Dravidian movement). See Rudolph and Rudolph (1967: I); Rudolph (1960); Hardgrave (1965, 1969); Barnett (1978); Irschick (1968); Dushkin (1974); Copland (1973); Omvedt (1976); Zelliot (1978); and Rao (1978) which contains useful bibliographies on peasant and social reform movements.

[35] The traditionally literate Brahman, Kshatriya, and Vaishya *varnas* or social orders.

[36] The 1951 census estimate was 20.5 per cent. The estimate of the Backward Classes Commission of 1955 was 31.8 (Galanter 1978: 1816). The second Backward Classes Commission of 1980 (Mandal Commission) estimated 49 per cent (*Times of India*, 13 December 1981).

[37] Galanter's figure: 'Various Denotations of the Term "Backward Classes" ' (1978: 1813) lists and locates spatially ten possible referents or meanings for the term 'backward classes'. His article details the official and unofficial contexts in which the ten meanings have been used.

are overlapping but not congruent populations. Some bullock capitalists are satisfied members of the backward classes. They succeeded during the first wave of reservations between the wars or in the immediate post-Independence period in gaining special benefits and economic assets to help them overcome their backwardness.

But many bullock capitalists, especially in the Northern Hindi heartland states, are part of the second incarnation of the backward classes movement that began in the late 1970s. The anti-Brahman ideology that helped after 1890 to mobilize mass support for reservations in the South and West against Brahman domination of public employment and educational opportunities did not penetrate the backward classes of the North. It may be that it did so in the South because the numerical balance between backward classes and twice-born upper castes in the South powerfully favoured the backward classes, while the balance in the North favoured the twice-born castes. The 1931 census, for example, showed 21 per cent twice-born in Uttar Pradesh, but only 3 per cent in Madras, and they were exclusively Brahmans (Rudolph 1967: 78). While in the South the twice-born were driven out of the bureaucracy and politics by the forties, they still dominate the public services in the North. As a result, a three-generation gap separates the two waves of backward classes movements, and the second faces stronger resistance from both above and below.

Organized caste communities of the backward classes seek reservations of places in public employment and educational institutions to improve their self and social esteem. By gaining access to opportunities in the organized sector of the economy, the bullock capitalist section of the backward classes can challenge the traditionally literate castes' hold on white collar salaried employment and gain the means to support or improve their circumstances as agricultural producers. Placing a son or even a daughter in service enables upwardly mobile cultivating families not only to enhance their income, security and status but also to pay for the costs of production and even to invest in more land and equipment. The typical small holder (below five acres) among the backward classes cannot use fully or employ remuneratively the five or six family members that a five to fifteen acres holder can. Income from organized sector employment can help to pay for the costs of production and the means to invest in more land and equipment required by backward class small holders seeking to become more prosperous bullock capitalists. Thus, the limited productivity and related low return to labour of many small holdings add an economic push to the pull of enhanced status in motivating backward classes to seek reservations.

In the late seventies, the political demands of the socially mobile backward classes of the Hindi heartland states of Northern India and a second wave among the socially mobile backward classes in the South and West under Devraj Urs and Sharad Pawar[38] reinforced the political coming of age of the bullock capitalists. In the 1977 parliamentary election backward classes and bullock capitalists contributed to and benefited from Janata's victory. Though Charan Singh, leader of the farm interest in the Janata Party, was himself a Jat, a caste not listed as backward, he thought of himself and was recognized as a leader of the smaller farmers and the backward classes, Ahirs, Kurmis, Gujars as well as Muslim cultivators. His earlier agrarian party, the BKD, had appealed to the common interests of backward classes as early as the 1967 and 1969 elections (Frankel 1978: 386; Brass 1965).

Following the June 1977 state assembly elections, leaders of backward classes became the chief ministers of India's two largest states, U.P. and Bihar.[39] Karpoori Thakur, Bihar Chief Minister and the leading advocate within the Janata Party of reservations for backward classes, succeeded in his efforts to obtain central government and state assembly approval for a measure reserving 26 per cent of all government posts (in addition to the 22.5 per cent already reserved for scheduled castes and tribes) for backward classes (*Keesings*, 8 December 1975: 29352; *India Today*, 16–31 Dec. 1978: 40–51). The measure benefits Bihar's relatively prosperous and well-organized backward class communities (Yadavas or Ahirs, Koiris and Kurmis) who constitute 18.5 per cent of Bihar's population and 60 per cent of its backward classes more than it does the disadvantaged 40 per cent among backward classes who lack comparable consciousness and organizational resources (Franda 1979: 148). Karpoori Thakur enacted his measure despite reluctance or opposi-

---

[38] The governments led by the late Devraj Urs in Karnataka (formerly Mysore) and Sharad Pawar in Maharashtra reflected in part the revival of backward class politics in the South and West by their displacement of 'satisfied' backward class community leadership and dominance (Lingayats and Vokkaligas in Karnataka and Marathas in Maharashtra) by mobilizing at the state level new entrants in the backward class category. See Bhat (1978) for a valuable account of a community involved in the 'second wave' in the South.

[39] Ram Naresh Yadav and Karpoori Thakur.

tion within the Janata governments at the Centre and in Bihar, and in the face of often violent upper caste and some scheduled caste and tribe resistance to a measure that seemed to threaten their hold on government jobs. The gain in the short run at least is more symbolic than material; the reservations provide no more than 2,000 jobs (*India Today*, 16–31 Dec. 1978).

The political vigour of the northern backward classes swept the issue of reservation back on the central government policy agenda, where it had not appeared since the mid-sixties. Between 1961 and 1963 the Nehru-led Congress government had made it clear that it would not take advantage of constitutional provisions permitting and encouraging compensatory discrimination on behalf of the backward classes.[40] It rejected the constitutionally sanctioned 1955 (Kalelkar) Backward Classes Commission's recommendations in support of reservations, refused to follow its injunction to draw up a national list of backward caste communities (as was done for the 'untouchable' scheduled castes and for the scheduled tribes), stopped funds sanctioned since 1949 for preferential educational programmes and urged the states to abandon caste for exclusively economic criteria of backwardness (Galanter 1978: 1819). By contrast, the Janata and, later, the Lok Dal articulated in their 1977 and 1979 manifestos the overlapping and complementary interest in reservations of bullock capitalists and backward classes. The manifestos revived the constitutional provenance of reservations, the 1955 commission's advocacy of caste criteria for backwardness and the allocation of benefits, and pledged to reserve at least 25 per cent of central government jobs for young men and women of the backward classes.[41]

To counter this policy initiative, Congress-I, whose upper caste

[40] Articles 15(4), 16(4) and 340 permitting the state to make special provisions for the advancement of any socially or educationally backward classes of citizens despite a provision against discrimination; permitting the state to make reservations of posts in public employment for backward classes of citizens despite a provision guaranteeing equality in matters of public employment; and providing for a presidentially appointed commission to make recommendations for improving the condition of backward classes. One commission (Kalelkar) was appointed in 1953 and reported in 1955, another (Mandal) in 1979 and reported in December 1980.

[41] For the 1977 and 1979 manifestos see Shakhder (1977: 41–2) and *Hindustan Times* (12 December 1979), which published the full text of the Lok Dal's manifesto. Janata promised to reserve 'between 25 and 33 per cent of all appointments to government service for the backward classes as recommended by the Kalelkar Commission' and the Lok Dal 'at least 25 per cent of Group A and Group B jobs

leadership, *noblesse oblige* attitude and upper caste support distances it from the outlook and interests of the backward classes, revived Nehru's ultimately unsuccessful effort to oppose caste-based criteria of backwardness. It again advocated the superficially attractive and simple but unworkable[42] economic criterion of the Nehru era, family poverty measured by income, as the test for backwardness and its associated benefits.[43]

By 1982, however, Congress had taken up a more equivocal stand on the issue, reflecting its strategic interest in recapturing bullock capitalist and backward class support that had eroded since 1967. A second Backward Classes Commission, chaired by the late B. P. Mandal, was appointed by the Janata government in December 1978 (*Hindustan Times*, 12 December 1979) but did not report until April 1980, soon after the Indira Gandhi Congress-I government took office. It estimated the proportion of backward classes at 49 per cent, 17 per cent more than the 1955 Kalelkar Commission estimate of 32 per cent. Its recommendation that 27 per cent rather than 49 per cent of jobs within the purview of the Government of India be reserved for backward class candidates was designed to avoid a conflict with the Supreme Court over the reservations question. The Congress-I government ignored the report for one and a half years,

---

in the Central Government services . . . as recommended by Backward Classes Commission appointed . . . by the Union Government itself under Article 340 of the Constitution.' Prime Minister Charan Singh's effort to get his caretaker coalition government to agree to reserve jobs for backward classes on the eve of the January 1980 election was blocked by the Congress-U ministers, 'because most of them hail from non-backward classes and a Government decision would cost them a great deal in terms of popular vote in the elections'. *Hindustan Times* (14 December 1979).

[42] Family poverty measures require accurate and reliable information about family income. For India's 240,000,000 poor (about 45 million families) such information is not available. State efforts to use income tests as the criterion for the benefits and privileges of backwardness by requiring affidavits from local officials can be (and have been) easily subverted by the 'purchase' of affidavits by upper literate castes more schooled in bureaucratic practice.

[43] Congress-I U.P.-PCC President, Dharam Vir, the state's most influential Harijan leader, reaffirmed Congress' position by stating that job reservations 'will cease to be based on backward classes but will be based on economic factors if the Congress-I comes to power'. He appealed to Congress-I twice-born support by observing that '. . . it would be immaterial if the person came from a backward class or from a Shravan [i.e., twice-born] family.' *Indian Express* (18 December 1979). In 1984, this Congress' position was reaffirmed by the Minorities Commission and a Secretaries Committee. See *Hindustan Times*, 18 and 19 January and 5 February 1984.

until June 1982, when it laid the Mandal Report before parliament. The Congress government's coolness and hesitancy arose in part from the conflict between its advocacy of economic rather than caste criteria as a test for backwardness and the Mandal Commission's thesis that there is sufficient congruence between caste (a *dharmically* defined status order) and class (an economically defined secular category related to income and property) to warrant treating them as identical for policy purposes.[44]

It is difficult to anticipate the ultimate policy outcome. Past principle and the requirements of maintaining upper and scheduled caste support suggest that Congress is not likely to support central government reservations for backward classes. But the shared interests of bullock capitalists and backward classes in reservations (and other benefits) mean that both, the class and the status order, can be mobilized over the next decade in support of policies that establish and fund reservations. Whether one or more parties will do so, and which ones, are among the unanswered questions of India's political future.

IV. *The New Agrarianism: Prospects for Single and Multi-Class Mobilization Strategies*

The new agrarianism is visible in the multi-class agrarian strategy of national, communist, and regional parties in the emergent politics of the agricultural sector. By late 1977, parties in or out of power from West Bengal to Haryana and from Kerala to Karnataka had abandoned single class agrarian mobilization strategies for multi-

[44] The Mandal Commission identified 3,257 caste communities as backward. The discrepancy between 27 per cent for reservations and 49 per cent backward class population proportion is the consequence of the Mandal Commission's pragmatic effort to live within the Supreme Court's finding in *Balaji* vs. *Mysore* (1961) that reservations, which already include 22 per cent for scheduled castes and tribes, cannot exceed 50 per cent. For the presentation of the report and an account of its leading findings and recommendations see *Times of India* (13 December 1981). For a defence of the view that caste and class are congruent, see Radhakrishnan (1982). Rajshekar [Shetty] (1982), a journalist and social theorist who represents Karnataka in the All-India Federation of Backward Classes and edits *Dalit Voice*, organ of the Dalit Sahitya Academy, Bangalore, goes beyond the congruence thesis of the Mandal Report in his new term 'caste-class' which, he holds, is a single (albeit hyphenated) social formation. His political objective is to unite the backward classes and scheduled castes for political action against the dominant twice-born and middle castes—higher

class ones. In part, the shift was a response to the electoral imperatives of parliamentary democracy in a federal system, in part to the rise of bullock capitalist power. The most dramatic instances are the CPI-M and CPI in West Bengal, Tamil Nadu and Kerala. After Independence, the West Bengal CPI tried to penetrate and lead the countryside by demanding the recording of share-cropper rights. The threat of implementation led to evictions of share-croppers by superior tenants and landowners who in turn became the CPI's enemies. After the second general election in 1957, the CPI adopted a more moderate multi-class strategy for rural mobilization by advocating policies that benefited cultivators generally such as insuring the availability of cheaper inputs and higher prices for agricultural commodities. In 1967, at the time of the fourth general election, the CPI-M led United Front put its multi-class support at risk by identifying itself with land grab and forcible harvesting movements against *jotedars* and lesser landowners. Once in power, it suffered from the contradictions involved in governing (e.g., maintaining law and order, protecting 'its' policemen) and maintaining multi-class rural support in the midst of the communist-led Naxalbari rebellion (Konar 1977). Since returning to power in 1977, the West Bengal CPI-M has adapted its agricultural policies and rural strategy to the electoral imperatives of party competition in a multi-class rural economy by seeking support from many varieties of share-croppers, tenants and landowners. It is not likely to expand its hard-won rural base without ideological and policy formulas that have a multi-class appeal. Short of revolution or secession, the best hope for communist parties seeking to adopt radical one-class or constrained multi-class agrarian mobilization strategies is to press for constitutional reforms that further decentralize India's federal system. Jyoti Basu's participation in a front of states seeking constitutional change along these lines reflects his acceptance of constitutional limits on radical strategies.

In Kerala and Tamil Nadu too communist and regional parties have had to adjust their agrarian mobilization strategies and policies to accommodate constitutional constraints and the imperatives of

income property owner class. Apart from a section of the Dalits, scheduled caste leaders and organizations have been unresponsive. They fear that the backward classes' demand for reservation will add to the increasingly evident 'Hindu' backlash against reservations for the scheduled castes. Namboodiripad (1981) disavowed Rajshekar's contention that he supports Rajshekar's caste-class thesis.

330 LLOYD I. RUDOLPH/SUSANNE H. RUDOLPH

party competition in rural economies and societies composed of a variety of classes and status orders. The CPI-M's capacity in opposition to mobilize from below and to bring pressure on government helps to explain why land and tenancy reform and the establishment of workers' rights and benefits has been more successful in Kerala than other Indian states. The CPI-M had to share the political rewards of these results with its rivals, the CPI and local bourgeois parties (including the Congress Party) because it was their coalition governments that adopted and implemented the CPI-M's programmes (Herring 1982: Ch. 7). Appeal to 'peasant masses' rather than an exclusive appeal to poor labourers and tenants in those states reflects both communist parties' recognition of the 'mixed' character of the agrarian economy. The CPI-M's objectives in Kerala have been redistributionist rather than collectivist. It has pressed for land reform and its effective implementation, rights and security for tenants and share-croppers, and for improved wages, working conditions and job security, not for the establishment of cooperative or collective arrangements.

The multi-class strategy also characterizes the new agrarianism of the Janata era. The agrarianism is 'new' in contrast to the 'old' agrarianism that Gandhi brought to the nationalist movement and to the Swatantra Party's agrarianism in the 1960s. Gandhi's agrarianism opposed industrialization in the name of village self-sufficiency. Simple tools and simple wants of local craft and agricultural economies would insure employment and pre-empt dependency on foreign and domestic capitalists. Swatantra's *kulak* and feudal agrarianism was linked to a conservative ideology of property rights and anti-statism (Erdman 1967; Frankel 1978).[45] The new agrarianism recognizes the interdependence of the industrial and agricultural sectors that thirty years of planned investment have brought into being and the critical role of state policy interventions on behalf of all agrarian classes. In purporting to speak for the agricultural sector, it does not so much oppose industrialization as challenge the al-

[45] Erdman details the pivotal role in 1959 of Congress' Nagpur resolution on joint cooperative farming in bringing about the formation of the Swatantra Party, India's only and now defunct conservative party. 'Anti-Congress sentiment was widespread . . . those . . . who had been in opposition for a long time were joined by those for whom the Nagpur resolution was the last straw—or who felt that it provided an opportunity for suppressed opposition to come into the open' (Erdman 1967: 73). For an extended discussion of the Nagpur resolution see also Frankel (1978).

legedly privileged position of industrial as against agrarian producers.

The new agrarianism first captured national attention in December 1978 when hundreds of thousands of *kisans* thronged to Delhi to celebrate the birthday of India's leading agrarian ideologue, Charan Singh (Singh 1978). The significance of the event did not escape Mrs Gandhi's attention. In 1980, soon after the electoral victory that brought Congress-I and Mrs Gandhi back to power, she too mounted a mammoth kisan rally only to be challenged by an equally large one staged on 26 March by the 'democratic' opposition's Central Kisan Coordinating Committee.

In the winter of 1980–81, the new agrarianism moved from urban spectaculars to rural agitational politics organized by interest groups supported by a wide spectrum of political parties[46] hoping to capitalize on or to control the new force. 'Farmers' in several states[47] were mobilized to demand remunerative prices for agricultural commodities, a demand that raised the broader issue of the terms of trade between the agricultural and industrial sectors.[48] The issue of remunerative prices had moved out of party headquarters, secretariat corridors and legislative chambers to the unmediated politics of *rasta roko* (road blocks), *gheraos* (sit-ins) and 'long marches'. In Western India, Sharad Joshi's Shetkari Sangathana adopted the Poujadist tactics of French petty merchants and farmers (Hayward 1973: 56) by blocking roads to enforce their demands.[49] Narayanaswami

---

[46] For example, the 23-day 'long march' from Jalgaon to Nagpur in December 1980 in support of price and wage increases was supported by a shaky six-party front composed of the Congress-U, the Janata Party, the Peasants and Workers Party, the Lok Dal, the CPI-M and the CPI.

[47] Farmers' agitations took place in Maharashtra, Gujarat, Tamil Nadu, Uttar Pradesh, Andhra Pradesh, Karnataka and other states. See 'Farmers' Agitation,' *Times of India* (20 December 1980); *Overseas Hindustan Times* (4 December 1980); *Statesman* (Overseas Edition, 13 December 1980); *The Hindu* (3, 13, 14, 17 January 1981); and 'Precarious Peace,' *India Today* (30 November 1981).

[48] According to the Government of India's Agricultural Prices Commission, the price index for agricultural products as a percentage of that for manufactured goods declined from 100.7 in 1974–75 to 83.5 in March 1980. 'Farmers' Agitation,' *Times of India* (20 December 1980). Except for 1951–52 (when the series begins), for twelve years (until 1963–64) the index was adverse to agriculture, ranging from 89.10 in 1955–56 to 98.85 in 1959–60 (1960–61 = 100). Starting in 1964–65, the index becomes favourable to agriculture, reaching a high of 134.13 in 1973–74 but declining thereafter. See Table 27, 'Indices of Prices Received and Prices Paid by Agriculture and Terms of Trade (1960–61 = 100)', *Boothalingam Report*, 19, p. 131.

[49] Joshi's agitations in 1980 led the Government of Maharashtra to raise the

Naidu's Tamil Nadu Agriculturist Association used similar tactics to press for cancellation of debts[50] as well as remunerative prices. Both organizations joined all-India industrial and commercial interest groups such as FICCI (Federation of Indian Chambers of Commerce and Industry) in the pantheon of influential and controversial organizations that shape national policy agendas and policies.

The language employed by the ideologues of the new agrarianism invokes tacit or explicit socio-economic theories. The terms they use differentially join or divide agrarian classes and urban and rural interests. Those who talk about 'farmers' usually include all agricultural producers involved in market relations while those who talk about peasants are likely to exclude rich farmers and large landowners. The two languages converge, however, by explicitly placing agrarian rural interests in opposition to urban industrial interests. The non-partisan new agrarian, Sharad Joshi, and partisan left new agrarian, Harikrishna Singh Surjeet, both hold that producers in the agricultural sector share a common interest in resisting the depredations of the industrial sector. Joshi's efforts to mobilize the countryside against the city are less constrained than Surjeet's because Joshi does not have to contend with an intellectual tradition that features class conflict and a strategic commitment to a peasant–worker alliance that attempts to bridge the rural agrarian/urban industrial division.

Sharad Joshi provided reasons for farmers to mobilize: the principal cleavage in Indian politics was Bharat vs. India, the countryside vs. the city. All rural families, from agricultural labourers to rich farmers, he believes, '. . . have a basic unity of interest on the

---

support price of onions and to give cash concessions to cultivators of cotton, sugarcane, paddy, *jawar* and *bajra*. 'Farmers' Agitations', *Times of India* (20 December 1980).

[50] The Tamil Nadu Land Development Bank reported in early 1981 that 90 per cent of its loans were in arrears. *Hindu* (3 February 1981). Like other government-sponsored credit agencies in Tamil Nadu, it found it expedient in the face of Naidu-led mobilizations to ignore its arrears. The M. G. Ramachandran AIDMK government subsequently risked the wrath of Tamil Nadu farmers when it cracked down on non-payment of electricity bills. The power of organized farmers in Tamil Nadu was already apparent in 1972 when the then Karunanidi DMK government enacted the Cultivating Tenants Arrears of Rents (Relief) Act cancelling past arrears on condition that current rents (1 July 1971 to 30 June 1972) be paid. This moratorium has been sporadically renewed in recent years.

issue of higher prices for agricultural products' (Omvedt 1981:
1937).[51] More broadly, all producers engaged in farming and related
occupations share a class interest. Farmer prosperity will 'free
blocked and warped productive forces of the country for new
industrial and agricultural development' (Omvedt 1981: 1937). Borrowing language from the dependency literature, Joshi holds that
the cause of national poverty is unequal exchange between India's
developed capitalist economy encompassing as much as 20 per cent
of India's almost 700,000,000 people and its producers of primary
products encompassing about 80 per cent, a view that has attracted
wide political and some ideological and scholarly support.[52] In
1980–81, all political parties, including those on the left (CPI, CPI-M
and CPL-ML) accepted the basic demand of the farmers' movement,
remunerative prices for agricultural products. Indeed, according to
Gail Omvedt, an astute critic of the new agrarianism, the mainstream left 'nurtured the soil in which the movement grows' (Omvedt
1981: 1937).[53] Because higher prices will bring prosperity to the
countryside, they become the key to alleviating the lot of the vast
majority of the poor who live and labour there.

A multi-class agrarian strategy has well-placed defenders on the
left even if not all leftists support it. Harikrishna Singh Surjeet, a

---

Already in the 1970s secure tenants and owner cultivators, not rent-collecting
landlords, were the dominant voice in Tamil Nadu agricultural policy. For
accounts of recent trends in Tamil Nadu's agricultural economy and politics,
including evidence of the re-emergence of Naxalite protest, see 'Myths and Facts
behind Agrarian Unrest,' *Economic and Political Weekly*, XVII (50) (12 December 1981), pp. 2027–29.

[51] Omvedt uses a recent publication in Marathi, *Yodh Shetkari*, edited by Vijay
Parulkar, that contains articles, conversations and speeches originally published
in *Manus* magazine, to depict Joshi's ideology, socio-economic analysis and
policy prescriptions.

[52] For example, Ronald Herring concludes an essay on Chayanovian vs. neo-
classical perspectives by arguing that tiny plots are more productive per acre than
large traditional farms. With substantially more consumers than producers, and
a limited amount of land, the only way to feed the family is to work harder, better
and longer. The policy implications for Herring are to 'correct the terms of trade
with agriculture' through price and input subsidy programmes, provision of credit
and infrastructure, raising labour productivity on small farms, reducing taxes, etc.
(Herring 1979).

[53] Omvedt (1981: 1940) castigates Joshi's attempt to divide urban from rural
workers, provides evidence to show how left union leaders have played a crucial
role in bringing sections of workers into alliance with the farmers' movement,

member of the CPI-M's politbureau and president for many years of the venerable All-India Kisan Sabha (AIKS), opposes Joshi's effort to lead the new agrarianism but argues along remarkably similar lines. Surjeet perceives the new agrarianism as a peasant uprising 'unparalleled in the history of free India'. 'The peasants are fighting for common demands—the most important being the demand of remunerative prices for their produce . . .' Surjeet also endorsed peasant demands for reduced prices for agricultural inputs, an end to increases in taxes and levies, relief from debt and found that 'in some states these movements were joined by agricultural labourers' demanding higher wages, more employment, debt relief and publicly distributed essential commodities at reasonable prices (Surjeet 1981: 12–13).

The cultivators who populate Surjeet's term, peasants, and Sharad Joshi's term, farmers, bear a strong family resemblance despite the two terms' very different ideological provenance. 'Every section of the peasantry', Surjeet holds, 'from the rich peasant to the marginal and small one, is affected . . .' by the Congress-I's anti-peasant price policy. He denies that remunerative prices for agricultural commodities benefit only landlords and rich peasant: 'Every section of the peasantry, including the poorest of them, is forced to sell a part of his produce . . . to purchase food grains for his family's consumption . . . and is therefore interested in such a level of prices as would meet the cost of production' (Surjeet 1981: 16).

The wide partisan and interest group support for new agrarian policy demands masks important differences over substance as well as language. Those who espouse the cause of peasant would like to exclude rich farmers and to mitigate or transcend the primacy of the Bharat vs. India cleavage. Surjeet dismisses Joshi as a spokesman for rich farmers who grow commercial crops even while he contributes to Joshi's successful mobilizations of a broad spectrum of producer interests and agrarian classes by swelling their ranks with mainstream left supporters. At the same time, ideology and the partisan struggle for power lead him to deny Congress-I's charge that farmer agitations are the work of the rich farmer lobby led by

---

e.g., *bidi* and tobacco workers publicly joined Joshi, the CPI and CPI-M provided the core of those participating in the 'long march' from Jalgaon to Nagpur in December 1980, and left propaganda tells urban workers with land that they will benefit personally from supporting farmers' demands.

kulaks and landlords. Surjeet's version of the urban–rural cleavage is qualified by his call for an alliance—not yet consummated— between peasants and workers who are meant to find common ground in their opposition to the Congress-I government's anti-peasant *and* anti-worker policies and in its repressive measures against both groups. Such difficulties arise for the left because the imperatives of competitive partisan politics lead it to embrace vote-winning multi-class agrarian strategies while its Marxian commit-ment leads it to affirm the politics of class conflict.

The pursuit of multi-class agrarian strategies by all parties, interest groups and movements bears witness to the political salience and strategic location of bullock capitalists. Whether one credits Gail Omvedt's view that other agrarian classes risk being coopted by the rich farmers or Surjeet's and Joshi's that all cultivators can benefit from remunerative prices, agrarian movements or parties that do not recognize the political salience of bullock capitalists and accord them a central place in their mobilization strategies are not likely to succeed.

Our argument for the possible establishment of bullock capitalists as a hegemonic class in Indian politics assumes that the class' eco-nomic base will remain stable or increase and that it will retain or enhance its competitive position in electoral and party politics be-cause all parties will continue to pursue a multi-class agrarian strategy. One cause of the erosion in Congress support since 1967 and, to an extent, earlier has been its inability to hold the support of bullock capitalists. Charan Singh's defection from the U.P. Congress Party in 1967 and the subsequent success at the expense of Congress of his BKD in the 1969 mid-term poll were manifestations of these developments.[54] The 1977 election not only repudiated authoritarian rule and restored constitutional democracy, it also signalled two less visible historical changes. First, as the Nehru settlement, which united urban and rural elites and interests behind a strategy of industrial self-reliance, lost cohesion and support; what Gregor Kotovsky calls tractor capitalists and Ashok Rudra (1978) large landowners began to yield their dominant political position in rural society to bullock capitalists. Second, Janata's 1977 successes in the March parliamentary and June state assembly elections revealed

[54] For recent electoral developments see Rudolph and Rudolph (1981) and Brass (1981).

the independent political influence of the agrarian sector.

Paul Brass (1980) and Ramashray Roy (1975) agree that Congress lost support in U.P. to Charan Singh's BKD. 'In U.P.', Roy found, 'Congress [in 1969] lost heavily to the Bhartiya Kranti Dal, a party made up of Congress defectors . . . a fresh entrant into the electoral battle . . . the BKD secured more seats than the total number of seats secured by the six national opposition parties . . . the BKD made major inroads into Congress territory and won 59 seats previously held by Congress' (37, 43). Brass' evidence even more decisively supports the hypothesis of emergent bullock capitalist dominance at the expense of Congress. He found that since 1962 Congress support in U.P. had become increasingly polarized. Its voters came more from among 30 acres and above and 1 acre and below agricultural producers than it did from the middle categories. By contrast, electoral support for the parties that later joined forces in the Janata, the Jan Sangh, the SSP and the BKD, came more from among 2 to 15 acre holders than from large landowners, labourers or dwarf holders (Brass 1980: 66).

The Nehru settlement favouring an industrial strategy came undone in 1977.[55] Its senior partners were India's proportionately small but politically powerful administrative, managerial and professional English-educated middle classes and private sector industrialists who welcomed the import substitution and to a lesser extent the industrial self-reliance strategies of the second and third five-year plans. The English-educated middle classes manned the bureaucracy, planned for, built and managed the state capitalist (public) sector and increasingly staffed firms in the private sector. Its junior partners were rural notables, mostly of the large landowner class. They consented to the industrial self-reliance strategy, urban control of the central

[55] The settlement began to unravel well before Charan Singh's Hyderabad speech of 22 October 1979 and his press statement of 27 October 1979 in which he attacked the policies and supporters of the Nehru settlement arguing, *inter alia*, that the settlement had 'de-industrialized' India (i.e., destroyed cottage and small-scale industry); enabled the organized sector, which constitutes about 10 per cent of the population, to blackmail the rest; given 'urban lobbies' a stranglehold over the country's governance; catered to the selfishness and *amour propre* of organized workers, bureaucrats and the parasitic intelligentsia; and through misconceived and wrongly implemented land reform unnecessarily increased the number of landless labourers while reducing the number of independent cultivators. See *Hindustan Times* (27 October 1979) and *Times of India* (28 October 1979).

government and the advantages that accrued to urban elites, interests and classes on condition that they remain in charge of the state governments and their resources and control the implementation of policies for the agricultural sector and rural society.

Mrs Gandhi's authoritarian regime under the emergency accelerated the demise of the Nehru settlement and its public philosophy by making victims of supporters and providing disparate opponents with a common cause. One consequence of Janata's massive victory in 1977 was to make bullock capitalists senior partners of the Janata ruling coalition. The election's only partially intended consequence was that, for the first time since Independence, agricultural interests were dominant at the Centre as well as in the states.

Janata took its mandate to mean not only restoring constitutional democracy but also replacing the Nehru era's public philosophy and policy settlement. Investment priorities and plan allocations were made more favourable to agriculture than to industry. Decentralization of economic and political institutions were favoured over centralized control of the economy and the state. Employment (via investment in the agricultural sector and encouragement of small-scale industry and 'appropriate technology'), income redistribution and the elimination of destitution were given priority over the growth of per capita income based on investment in capital-intensive industry. India was to be a nation of farmers more than it was to be a nation of bureaucrats, and industrial and office workers and state and private capitalists. Gandhi's public philosophy was to have precedence over Nehru's. These developments were slowed or modified when Indira Gandhi returned to power in 1980.

If bullock capitalists are to regain the kind of national influence they exercised in the Janata era, their alliance strategy and policy agenda will have to recognize the mixed class character of India's rural economy. The credibility of agrarianism as an ideology depends on its ability to make the rural agricultural/urban industrial cleavage more salient and meaningful than cleavages based on class, interest group or elite differences. If the parties under bullock capitalist influence make downward class and status order alliances and credibly pursue policies that promote redistribution with growth and the collective good of the agrarian sector, bullock capitalists will improve their chances for playing a hegemonic role. Downward alliances and the policies they entail require recognition of the demands and aspirations not only of labourers and small holders but also of the parallel but overlapping status orders, i.e., disadvantaged minorities and backward classes. Alternative strategies, alliance upward with large landowners or being a class for itself, are viable but foreclose the possibility of hegemony. In the world of day-to-day political struggles where personal ambition, group self-interest and short-term calculations seem to govern the course of events, all three strategies are evident at different times and contexts.

In the medium term a variety of regional patterns are evident. For example, in U.P. and Andhra Pradesh bullock capitalists have successfully pursued a class for itself strategy. Still there are signs that leaders of several parties in a variety of states have responded by pursuing downward class, caste and community alliances. In the 1970s, Karpoori Thakur in Bihar, the late Devraj Urs in Karnataka and Sharad Pawar in Maharashtra used downward alliances with backward classes, disadvantaged minorities, poor cultivators and workers to displace coalitions based on upward alliances of dominant castes (e.g., Bhumihars, Lingayats and Marathas) and large landowners. Thakur, Urs and Pawar may have shown India its longer if not its medium-term future.

Bullock capitalist hegemony depends then on the degree to which relations with small holders and agricultural workers are cooperative or conflictual. If small holders remain unconvinced that the ideology and policy agenda of bullock capitalists will enable them to benefit from the new technology and improved agricultural/industrial terms of trade, they may choose to make a downward alliance with agricultural labourers against bullock capitalists and large landowners. Both small holders and agricultural workers can benefit from enforcement of extant land ceilings legislation and from additional measures to lower ceilings further. Such measures will be at the expense primarily of large landowners but bullock capitalists will be affected too. Small holders are in a position to support the interests of agricultural labourers. As cultivators, they do not rely on wage labour and a substantial number work for wages. They can join forces with agricultural labourers in demanding from large landowners and marginally from bullock capitalists improved bargaining arrangements, working conditions and incomes. Such an alliance requires a kind of dual class consciousness on the part of small holders and agricultural labourers that encompasses their interests as actual or potential landowners and cultivators and their interests as wage labourers. Unless bullock capitalists can make good on their claims that small holders and labourers benefit from agrarian domination of state policy and from the benefits of new technology, their hegemonic aspirations will be frustrated. If they succeed, if agrarian power continues to become more manifest in politics and policy, agrarian productivity will benefit from the flow of resources they entail but it may do so at the expense of industrial investment. At the micro-level, bullock capitalist power promises to further increase agricultural productivity as improved human capital and entrepreneurship join forces with improved inputs and favourable factor costs and commodity prices.

REFERENCES

Ahluwalia, Montek (1977), 'Rural Poverty and Agricultural Performance in India', *Journal of Development Studies*.

Alavi, Hamza (1973a), 'Peasant Class and Primordial Loyalties', *Journal of Peasant Studies*, No. 1.

—— (1973b), 'Peasants and Revolution' in Kathleen Gough and Hari P. Sharma (eds), *Imperialism and Revolution in South Asia* (New York: Monthly Review Press).

Alexander, K. C. (1975a), *Agrarian Tension in Thanjavur* (Hyderabad: National Institute of Community Development).

—— (1975b), 'Genesis of Agrarian Tension in Thanjavur: Findings of a Research Study', *Economic and Political Weekly*, 10: 49 (6 December).

Azad, Maulana (1959), *India Wins Freedom* (Delhi: Orient Longmans).

Baliga, B. S. (1957), *Tanjore District Handbook* (Madras: Government Press).

Bardhan, Kalpana (1977), 'Rural Employment, Wages and Labour Markets in India: A Survey of Research', *Economic and Political Weekly*, I 12: 26 (26 June), II 12: 27 (2 July), III 12: 28 (9 July).

Barnett, Marguerite Ross (1978), *The Politics of Cultural Nationalism in South India* (Princeton: Princeton University Press).

Baruah, Sanjib Kumar (1978), 'Agrarian Structures, Economic Change and Peasant Political Participation', University of Chicago, South Asian Political Economy Seminar (mimeo).

Bendix, Reinhard (1977), *Max Weber: An Intellectual Portrait* (Berkeley and Los Angeles: California University Press Paperbacks).

Berger, Suzanne (ed.) (1981), *Organizing Interests in Western Europe: Pluralism, Corporatism and the Transformation of Politics* (Cambridge: Cambridge University Press).

Bhalla, Sheila (1976), 'New Relations of Production in Haryana Agriculture', *Economic and Political Weekly*, II, 13 (March)

Bharadwaj, Krishna (1974), *Production Conditions in Indian Agriculture* (Cambridge: Cambridge University Press).

Bhat, Chandrashekar (1978), 'The Reform Movement among the Weddors of Karnatak' in Rao (1978 I: 169–89).

Bhattacharya, N. and G. Saini (1972), 'Farm Size and Productivity: A Fresh Look', *Economic and Political Weekly* (24 June).

Béteille, André (1972), 'Agrarian Relations in Tanjore District, South India', *Sociological Bulletin*, 21: 2.

Boulware, Nancy (1960), 'The Search for Political Community in India, Congress–Muslim Relations, 1935–1939', B.A. Honours thesis, Radcliffe College.

Bouton, Marshall (1980), 'The Sources of Agrarian Radicalism: A Study of Thanjavur District, South India', Ph.D. dissertation, University of Chicago (forthcoming, Princeton University Press.)

Brass, Paul (1965), *Factional Politics in an Indian State; the Congress Party in Uttar Pradesh* (Berkeley and Los Angeles: University of California Press).

—— (1980), 'The Politicization of the Peasantry in a North Indian State', Parts I and II, *Journal of Peasant Studies*, VII, 4, and VIII (1) (July, September).

—— (1981), 'Congress, the Lok Dal and the Middle Level Castes: An Analysis of the 1977 and 1980 Parliamentary Elections in Uttar Pradesh', *Pacific Affairs*, 54, 1 (Spring).

Breman, Jan (1974a), 'Mobilization of Landless Labourers: Halpatis of South Gujarat', *Economic and Political Weekly*, 9: 12 (March).

—— (1974b), *Patronage and Exploitation: Changing Agrarian Relations in South Gujarat* (Berkeley: University of California Press).

Chauhan, Brij Raj (1967), *A Rajasthan Village* (New Delhi: Vir).

Chayanov, A. V. (1966), *The Theory of Peasant Economy*, edited by Daniel Thorner *et al.* (Homewood: Irwin).

Copland, Ian (1973), 'The Maharaja of Kolhapur and the Non-Brahman Movement, 1902–1910', *Modern Asian Studies*, 7, 2.

Das Gupta, Biplab (1977), *The New Agrarian Technology and India* (Delhi: Macmillan).

Dantwala, M. L. and C. H. Shah (1971), *Evaluation of Land Reforms; With Special Reference to the Western Region of India* (Bombay: Department of Economics, University of Bombay).

Dushkin, Lelah (1961), 'The Backward Classes', *The Economic Weekly*, 13, 44, 45, 46.

Dutt, Kalyan (1977), 'Changes in Land Relations in West Bengal', *Economic and Political Weekly*, 12, 53.

Eberstadt, Nick (1979), 'Has China Failed?', *The New York Review of Books*, 26, 5 (5 April). Part of a three-part series.

The Economic and Political Weekly (1979), Annual Number (Bombay).

Epstein, T. Scarlett (1962), *Economic Development and Social Change in South India* (Bombay: Oxford University Press).

Erdman, Howard L. (1967), *The Swatantra Party and Indian Conservatism* (Cambridge: Cambridge University Press).

Fainsod, Merle (1958), *Smolensk under Soviet Rule* (Cambridge, Mass.: Harvard University Press).

Franda, Marcus (1979), *Small is Politics* (New Delhi: Wiley Eastern).

Frankel, Francine (1971), *India's Green Revolution: Economic Gains and Political Costs* (Delhi: Oxford University Press).

—— (1978), *India's Political Economy: The Gradual Revolution* (Princeton: Princeton University Press).

Fremantle, Ann (ed.) (1971), *Mao Tse-tung: An Anthology of his Writings* (New York: Mentor).

Galanter, Marc (1978), 'Who are the Other Backward Classes? An Introduction to a Constitutional Puzzle', *Economic and Political Weekly*, 13, 43, 44 (28 October).

Galbraith, John Kenneth (1973), *Economy and the Public Purpose* (Boston: Houghton Mifflin).

Gent, John (1979), 'Cooperation, Conflict and Ideology', South Asia Political Economy Seminar (University of Chicago, mimeo).

Gough, Kathleen E. (1960), 'Caste in a Tanjore Village' in E. R. Leach (ed.), *Aspects of Caste in South India, Ceylon, and Northwest Pakistan* (Cambridge: Cambridge University Press).

—— (1974), 'Indian Peasant Uprisings', *Economic and Political Weekly*, 9: Special Number (August).

Government of India, Directorate of Economics and Statistics, Ministry of Agriculture and Irrigation (1975), *Indian Agriculture in Brief* (Delhi).

Government of India, Study Group on Wages, Incomes and Prices (1978), *Report* (New Delhi: Ministry of Finance).

Griffin, K. (1974), *The Political Economy of Agrarian Change* (London: Macmillan).

Habib, Irfan (1963), *The Agrarian System of Mughal India* (Bombay: Asia).

Harrison, James O. (1972), 'Agricultural Modernization and Income Distribution: An Economic Analysis of the Impact of New Seed Varieties on the Crop Production of Large and Small Farms in India', unpublished Ph.D. dissertation, Princeton University.

Hayward, Jack (1973), *The One and Indivisible French Republic* (New York: Norton).

Herring, Ronald (1979), 'Chayanovism vs. Neoclassical Perspectives on Land Tenure and Productivity Interaction' (mimeo).

—— (1980), 'A Paddy Field is Not a Factory; Production Relations and Redistributive Policy in South India' (mimeo).

—— (1982), *Land to the Tiller: Political Economy of Agrarian Reform in South Asia* (New Haven: Yale University Press).

The Hindu (Madras).

Hindustan Times (Delhi).

Hobsbawm, Eric J. (1959), *Primitive Rebels: Studies in Archaic Forms of Social Movement in the 19th and 20th Centuries* (Manchester).

India Today (Delhi).

Irschick, Eugene (1969), *Politics and Social Conflict in South India: The Non-Brahmin Movement and Tamil Separatism* (Bombay: Oxford University Press).

Januzzi, Tomasson (1974), *Agrarian Crises in India: The Case of Bihar* (Austin: Texas Press).

Juergensmeyer, Mark (1979), 'Culture of Deprivation: Three Case Studies in Punjab', *Economic and Political Weekly*, Annual Number (February).

342   LLOYD I. RUDOLPH/SUSANNE H. RUDOLPH

—— (1982), *Religion as Social Vision: The Movement against Untouchability in 20th-Century Punjab* (Berkeley and Los Angeles: University of California Press).
Keesings Contemporary Archives.
Khusro, A. M. (1969), *The Economics of Land Reform and Farm Size in India* (Delhi: Institute of Economic Growth).
—— (1974), 'Returns to Scale in Indian Agriculture', *Indian Journal of Agricultural Economics*, Annual Number (February).
Kolenda, Pauline (1978), 'Sibling-Set Marriage, Collateral-Set Marriage, and Deflected Alliance among Annana Jats of Jaipur District, Rajasthan' in Sylvia Vatuk (ed.), *American Studies in the Anthropology of India* (Delhi: Manohar).
Konar, Harekrishna (1977), *Agrarian Problems of India* (Calcutta: Jour Saha).
Ladejinsky, Wolf (1969), 'How Green is the Green Revolution?', *Economic and Political Weekly*, 8: 52 (December).
Mathew, George (1982), 'Politicization of Religion: Conversion to Islam in Tamil Nadu', *Economic and Political Weekly*, 17, 25 (19 June).
Mayer, Adrian C. (1960), *Caste and Kinship in Central India: A Village and Its Region* (Berkeley: University of California Press).
McLane, John R. (1977), *Indian Nationalism and the Early Congress* (Princeton: Princeton University Press).
Meisner, Mitchell (1977), 'In Agriculture Learn from Dazhai; Theory and Practice in Chinese Rural Development', Ph.D. dissertation in Political Science, University of Chicago.
Mencher, Joan (1978), *Agriculture and Social Structure in Tamil Nadu* (Bombay: Allied).
Metcalf, Thomas R. (1965), *The Aftermath of Revolt: India 1857–1870* (Princeton: Princeton University Press).
Minhas, B. S. (1974), *Planning and the Poor* (New Delhi: S. Chand).
Moe, Terry M. (1980), *The Organization of Interests: Incentives and the Internal Dynamics of Groups* (Chicago: University of Chicago Press).
Moore, Jr., Barrington (1966), *Social Origins of Dictatorship and Democracy: Land and Peasant in the Making of the Modern World* (Boston: Beacon Press).
Mutiah, C. (1971), 'The Green Revolution—Participation by Small and Large Farmers', *Indian Journal of Agricultural Economy*, XXVI (January, March).
Namboodiripad, E. M. S. (1952), *The National Question in Kerala* (Bombay: People's Publishing House).
—— (1957), *Kerala, Problems and Possibilities* (New Delhi: C.P.I.).
—— (1981), 'Once Again on Castes and Classes', *Social Scientist*, 9, 12 (December).
Newaj, Khoda and Ashok Rudra (1975), 'Agrarian Transformation in a District of West Bengal', *Economic and Political Weekly*, 10, 13 (March).
Oldenburg, Philip (1981), 'Rural Classes and Land Consolidation in Meerut District: A Report of Work in Progress' (New Delhi, mimeo).
Olson, Mancur (1965), *The Logic of Collective Action: Public Goods and the Theory of Groups* (Cambridge, Mass.: Harvard University Press).
Omvedt, Gail (1976), *Cultural Revolt in a Colonial Society: The Non-Brahman Movement in Western India, 1903–1930* (Bombay: Scientific Education Trust).
—— (1981), 'Rasta Roko [Block Roads], Kulaks and the Left', *Economic and Political Weekly*, 16, 48 (November 28).

Orenstein, Henry (1965), *Gaon: Conflict and Cohesion in an Indian Village* (Princeton: Princeton University Press).

Patnaik, Utsa (1972), 'Economics of Farm Size and Farm Scale', *Economic and Political Weekly*, Special Number (August).

Pradhan, M. C. (1966), *The Political System of the Jats of Northern India* (London: Oxford University Press).

Radhakrishnan, P. (1982), 'Backward Classes: In Defence of Mandal Commission', *Economic and Political Weekly*, 17, 27 (3 July).

Rajshekar, V. T. (1982), 'Mandal Report and Ruling Class', *Mainstream*, 20, 44 (23 July).

Rao, M. S. A. (ed.) (1978), *Social Movements in India*, Vol. I: *Peasant and Backward Classes Movements* (New Delhi: Manohar).

Ray, Rajat (1978), 'Mewar; the Breakdown of the Princely Order' in Robin Jeffrey, *Peoples, Princes and Paramount Power* (Delhi: Oxford University Press).

Rosin, R. Thomas (1978), 'Peasant Adaptation as Process in Land Reform: A Case Study' in Sylvia Vatuk (ed.), *American Studies in the Anthropology of India* (Delhi: Manohar).

Roy, Rameshray (1975), *The Uncertain Verdict: A Study of the 1969 Election in Four States* (Berkeley: University of California Press).

Rudé, George (1959), *The Crowd in the French Revolution* (Oxford: The Clarendon Press).

—— (1964), *The Crowd in History, 1730–1898* (New York: Wiley and Sons).

Rudolph, Lloyd I. (1959), 'The Eighteenth Century Mob in America and Europe', *American Quarterly*, XI: 4.

Rudolph, Lloyd I. and Susanne Hoeber Rudolph (1967, 1969), *The Modernity of Tradition; Political Development in India* (Chicago: University of Chicago Press; Delhi: Orient Longmans).

—— (1979), 'Authority and Power in Bureaucratic and Patrimonial Administration: A Revisionist Interpretation of Weber on Bureaucracy', *World Politics*, 31, 2 (January).

—— (1981), 'Transformation of Congress Party; Why 1980 was not a Restoration', *Economic and Political Weekly*, 16, 18 (2 May).

—— *In Pursuit of Lakshmi: Political Economy of the Indian State* (forthcoming).

Rudra, Ashok (1968), 'Farm Size and Yield per Acre', *Economic and Political Weekly*, Special Number (July).

—— (1978), 'Class Relations in Indian Agriculture', *Economic and Political Weekly*, 13, 22–24 (8, 10, 17 June).

—— (1981), 'Against Feudalism', *Economic and Political Weekly* (26 December).

Schram, Stuart (1967), *Mao Tse-tung* (Baltimore: Penguin Books).

Schultz, T. W. (1964), *Transforming Traditional Agriculture* (New Haven: Yale University Press).

Schurmann, Franz (1968), *Ideology and Organization in Communist China*, 2nd edn (Berkeley: University of California Press).

Schwartz, Benjamin I. (1952), *Chinese Communism and the Rise of Mao* (Cambridge, Mass.: Harvard University Press).

Sen, Amartya K. (1962), 'An Aspect of Indian Agriculture', *Economic and Political Weekly*, Annual Number (February).

—— (1964), 'Size of Holding and Productivity', *Economic and Political Weekly*, Annual Number (February).

Sen Gupta, Bhabani (1972), *Communism in Indian Politics* (New York and London: Columbia University Press).

Sengupta, S. (1970), 'Confusions Over Land Reforms: The West Bengal Experience', *Economic and Political Weekly*, 5, 26.

Sharma, Hari P. (1973), 'The Green Revolution in India: A Prelude to a Red One' in Kathleen Gough and Hari P. Sharma (eds), *Imperialism and Revolution in South Asia* (New York and London: Monthly Review Press).

Singh, Charan (1978), *India's Economic Policy: The Gandhian Blueprint* (New Delhi: Vikas).

Sinha, J. N. (1982), 'Census 1981 Economic Data: A Note', *Economic and Political Weekly*, 17, 6 (6 February).

Sirsikar, V. M. (1970), *The Rural Elite in a Developing Society: A Study in Political Sociology* (New Delhi: Orient Longmans).

Sisson, Richard (1969), 'Peasant Movements and Political Mobilization: The Jats of Rajasthan', *Asian Survey*, 9 (December).

—— (1977), *The Congress Party in Rajasthan: Political Integration and Institution Building in an Indian State* (Berkeley: University of California Press).

Skocpol, Theda (1979), *States and Social Revolutions: A Comparative Analysis of France, Russia and China* (New York: Cambridge University Press).

Smelser, Neil J. (1962), *Theory of Collective Behavior* (New York: Free Press).

Stern, Robert W. (1970), *Process of Opposition in India* (Chicago: University of Chicago Press).

Stokes, Eric (1978), *The Peasant and the Raj* (Cambridge: Cambridge University Press).

Surjeet, Harikrishna Singh (1981), 'Upsurge', *Seminar 267* (November).

Times of India (Bombay).

Toulmin, Stephen (1972), *Human Understanding* (Princeton: Princeton University Press), Vol. I.

Valentine, Charles (1968), *Culture and Poverty* (Chicago: University of Chicago Press).

Visaria, Pravin and S. K. Sanyal (1977), 'Trends in Rural Unemployment in India: Two Comments', *Economic and Political Weekly*, 12: 5 (January).

Vyas, V. S. (1976), 'Structural Changes in Agriculture and the Small Farm Sector', *Economic and Political Weekly*, 11, 1 and 2 (January).

Winner, Langdon (1977), *Autonomous Technology: Technics Out-of-Control as a Theme in Political Thought* (Cambridge, Mass.: MIT Press).

Wolf, Eric (1959), *Sons of the Shaking Earth* (Chicago: University of Chicago Press).

—— (1969), *Peasant Wars of the Twentieth Century* (London: Faber and Faber).

Zagoria, Donald (1971), 'The Ecology of Peasant Communism in India', *American Political Science Review*, 65: 1 (March).

—— (1972), 'A Note on Landlessness, Illiteracy, and Agrarian Communism in India', *European Journal of Sociology*, 13: 2.

Zelliot, Eleanor (1973), 'Mahar and Non-Brahman Movements in Maharashtra', *Indian Economic and Social History Review*, 7.

—— (1977), 'Dalit—New Cultural Context for an Old Marathi Word', *Contributions to Asian Studies*, 11.

Power Structure and Agricultural Productivity[1]

SUKHAMOY CHAKRAVARTY

I

Sustained increases in agricultural productivity, defined as increases in yields per acre measured in suitable units, have generally been regarded as crucially necessary to the growth of India's economy in the medium and long term. It can also be shown that important distributional objectives like meeting the calorie requirements of 'target groups' such as the lowest 40 per cent of the population can be more easily achieved when yields increase at rates which permit total agricultural production to grow at a rate which exceeds the rate of population growth by a reasonable margin. Exact calculations of such a margin are not necessary to our purpose; a detailed example was provided in the context of preparing the Draft Fifth Five Year Plan, whose methodological basis was displayed in a 'Technical Note' which the Planning Commission brought out in 1974.

Factors which can lead to increases in yields per acre in the Indian context have been discussed in numerous places. Amongst variables which have received repeated attention are irrigation, both public and private, drainage, improvement in the quality of seeds, fertilizers, organic and inorganic, the use of pumpsets and the availability of electricity and liquid fuel. These variables, which figure prominently in the so-called 'green revolution' strategy, have as-

[1] In preparing this essay, I have benefited from comments made by participants at the workshops organized under the ICSSR–SSRC auspices. I am particularly indebted to Hamza Alavi, Veena Das, Meghnad Desai, L. and S. Rudolphs and Ashok Rudra. Dr R. K. Das of the Delhi School of Economics also made helpful comments.

sumed considerable importance in Indian agriculture in the course of the last decade. While very spectacular increases took place in wheat, in more recent years the yields of some other crops have also been favourably influenced, e.g. cotton, rice. While a policy based on the above variables is generally dubbed as constituting a technocratic solution, certain other policies may also be mentioned which are based on the exploitation of regionally specific resource endowments and which involve better regional specialization of crop production, substitution of crop husbandry by animal husbandry in certain places and greater integration between crop production, poultry farming and livestock breeding, trying thus to achieve a production cycle based on ecological principles.

While much can be said by way of elaboration on these points—and the literature on Indian agriculture is full of detailed studies—our attention here will be focused on the relationship between existing power structures and the adoption of policies enumerated above. The first question, and a basic one, to ask is whether there exists a systematic relationship between power structures and changes in agricultural productivity. It may be argued that whatever may be the power structure, increases in agricultural productivity can take place provided there are appropriate economic signals. The question, then, reduces to one of determining whether appropriate economic signals are usually present in Indian agriculture. It was argued by Theodore Schultz (1964) in a widely influential book that, contrary to the prevailing opinion, the main problem facing Indian agriculture is not that the existing system of resource allocation is inefficient but is due to a syndrome that can be characterized by the prevalence of a high man–land ratio, which is getting worse every year, and the very low quantity of human and material capital invested per unit of land.[2] The general inference from this has been that what the policy-makers require is the maintenance of an economic *regime* which gives adequate return to the farmer on his investment, along with public investment in education and research. The basis of this whole approach is (1) that farmers are maximizing agents in the sense that neo-classical theory assumes; (2) that external effects pertain only to a few selected areas, if at all, which implies

[2] It may be mentioned here that Schultz's study of the question of rational behaviour of the peasant was foreshadowed in the work of the economists of Wageningen school in their criticisms of Boeke's work on 'dualistic economics'. See W. F. Wertheim (ed.) (1959).

that for most 'commodities' markets exist, and non-convexities are negligible; and finally (3) that imperfection in markets does not 'matter', in the sense that wastes that are the result of a departure from competition are insignificant.

This early formulation given by Schultz became the subject-matter of a very voluminous literature.[3]

While it is not to our purpose here to produce a survey of this literature, it is important to enquire whether the assumptions implicit in Schultz's policy conclusions can be held to be valid even as a first approximation. Since, for reasons that we cannot go into here, we do not accept the methodological position stated with great vigour by Friedman years ago,[4] it is necessary for us to examine how realistic these postulates are. On the first point, that farmers are maximizing agents, literature is extensive, ranging all the way from 'refutations' based on the alleged existence of a backward bending supply curve of labour to institutionally constrained behaviour based on 'reciprocity and redistribution'. It may be mentioned here that the so-called 'backward bending supply curve of labour' or of 'marketable surplus' was noted in the European context in the seventeenth and early eighteenth centuries, especially by Sir William Petty; and subsequently reaffirmed, in the context of nineteenth century expansion of trade, by European traders trying to commercialize traditional agriculture.[5] Whatever may have been its relevance in an earlier era, it is probably true to say that in India today farmers generally respond to differential price incentives in a positive manner,

[3] G. R. Saini (1979) provides a survey of discussions that were provoked by the framework of analysis provided by Schultz. Saini does not reject the general framework provided by Schultz but finds the evidence cited by Schultz deficient. While Schultz had relied almost exclusively on Hopper's analysis of Senapur, Saini provides a much more detailed analysis. He finds that farmers in Punjab were generally using resources efficiently while farmers in Uttar Pradesh could gain through adjustments which will move them over to the production possibility frontier. These adjustments would involve (*a*) change in crop-mix, (*b*) introduction of new crops, (*c*) change in input–output ratios, and (*d*) introduction of new inputs. Saini operates on the basis of short-run profit maximizing behaviour on the part of farmers. He utilizes disaggregated farm management data to find whether the behaviour predicted from his model agrees with facts.

[4] For a discussion of the relevant point, see E. Nagel (1963); Samuelson (1963). For a different critique of Friedman's position, see Hollis and Nell (1975).

[5] The following passage from Sir William Petty's *Political Arithmetic* is interesting: 'It is observed by Clothiers and others, who employ great number of poor people, that when corn is extremely plentiful, that the labour of the poor is

a point to which a very substantial amount of research effort was devoted in the sixties. However, in regard to the elasticity of agricultural supply as a whole to price changes, the evidence would point to a much lower figure, suggesting that 'other factors' may be more important than changes in the terms of trade between industry and agriculture, a point which is of critical significance in deriving a macro-economic theory of Indian agriculture.[6]

Furthermore, a distinction may even now have to be drawn between crops grown essentially for sale outside the village economy, such as tobacco, oilseeds, etc., and subsistence crops, especially certain food items (generally known as coarse grains) which are consumed within the village and which enter the exchange circuit in a context where products produced by village craftsmen are exchanged against these products, i.e., coarse grains and root crops such as tapioca. However, in certain parts of India where the degree of commercialization as well as monetization of the economy has progressed very far, as in the northwest, this distinction has largely disappeared. However, for large parts of the country, especially the central region as well as the north-eastern hill regions, this reflects a real distinction, a point which raises serious problems for regional planners.

We now come to the second point, the existence of markets. Standard economic theory operates on the assumption that economic units maximize their objective functions on the basis of 'given' production functions and 'given' prices of relevant inputs and outputs. This implies that markets exist for all or at least a very large number of these variables. This is a very big assumption. The point has been made repeatedly that the terms and conditions on which labour services are available are so varied that it is not meaningful to talk about a labour market, let alone a perfect labour market.[7] Free contractual labour is the institutional basis of rational

---

proportionately dear: and scarce to be had at all (so licentious are they who labour only to eat or rather to drink).' The same view was expressed in the eighteenth century. For an assessment of empirical relevance in the European context, see Jan de Vries (1976).

[6] The literature on 'terms of trade' has obviously power-theoretic implications even though it may not be caused by power-theoretic influences. For a whole-hogging approach which looks upon power as the key to the 'terms of trade' debate, see A. Mitra (1977). For an earlier and somewhat different treatment of the issue, see S. Chakravarty (1974).

[7] K. Polanyi (1975) put a great deal of emphasis on the creation of what he

calculation underlying standard theory, but labour encumbered with many restrictions is not compatible with standard formulations. This is where considerations such as the social existence form of labour enter, a point whose implications will be taken up a little later. This point can also be made in regard to the valuation of output if one takes note of the fact that, in the absence of an organized produce market, prices paid by the dealers for crops depend systematically on the amount of net wealth owned by the households, a point which is again strategically significant. In regard to material inputs other than labour, water is rarely priced on a commercial basis, and its availability is also a function of the general economic and/or social standing of the 'households'. Several studies, especially in West Bengal and Bihar, have emphasized the importance of the emergence of 'waterlords'. They have acquired considerable significance in regard to the cultivation of the summer 'rice crop'. This phenomenon is of significance for determining possibilities of multiple cropping and hence of agricultural productivity.

On the question of external effects, there are numerous illustrations ranging from groundwater exploitation to environmental degradation, through taking out more nutrients from the soil than are put into it. It is possible that in some of these cases price analogues may be conceptually constructed. But it is irrelevant from the point of view of actual economic decisions in so far as these markets do not exist and hence decisions are taken on a different basis.[8]

The question of (3) market imperfection should also be briefly considered. Standard literature on imperfect competition was based on the need to take care of the downward sloping character of the demand curve facing a producer. Under this assumption, price became an action parameter of the firm. Free entry took care of the equilibrium result in the so-called 'large-group' case studied by Chamberlin. All this is, of course, irrelevant in the context of Indian agriculture; in so far as we are dealing with food crops,

---

calls 'fictitious markets' involving land, labour and capital. He saw in the creation of these markets in the course of the seventeenth and eighteenth centuries the sources of all subsequent economic changes.

[8] Whether markets can be instituted for 'inputs' and 'outputs' which are currently allocated on a different basis is an interesting theoretical question. It takes us into the literature on 'transactions cost' and other related issues, an area which appears to me to hold out promise for more intensive work.

imperfections spring from the fact that poor peasants have to sell their produce at a very low price after the harvest and have to buy their requirements at much higher prices when they need it toward the end of the crop season. But technically there is no imperfection inasmuch as commodities at two time points are different commodities. The real source of imperfection lies in the fact that even when local markets are very well organized, a big farmer can sell his produce at a higher price as compared with a small farmer because of the latter's debt obligations or other forms of dependence on the trader. This takes us to an imperfection in a related market, which is the market for credit. In so far as agriculture is a business with a slow turnover, credit is a very essential variable, since the farmer has to support himself during the interval between the sowing and the harvesting of crops. Small farmers have proportionately greater difficulties in this regard. This implies that the condition on which credit is available becomes for the farmer a very decisive consideration which can influence his socio-economic status through a variety of ways which link together several markets. It is, however, true that the so-called credit market is a highly fragmented one with a very wide spread between the rates of interest. Besides, there are quantitative and qualitative differences as between credits available from different sources. While there has been a great deal of discussion on the question of formation of rural interest rates, it remains a moot point whether the phenomenon can be best viewed within a theoretical framework of imperfect competition or whether an alternative framework[9] is called for.

The upshot of the above discussion is that there is very substantial evidence that the assumptions underlying the standard economic

---

[9] Imperfection of the market is viewed à la Chamberlin–Robinson along 'the dimension of degree of control over output and prices by firms. At the end of the dimension are a perfectly free market and a completely monopolistic market respectively, with varying degree of imperfection between two extremes. We want to emphasize that the imperfection of the markets differs not only in degree but in *sociological type*. The market for consumer goods differs from that for labour, and both differ from capital funds. These markets differ in type primarily because the different markets connect the economy with different sectors of the society: these connections enforce qualitatively different limitations on the respective market conditions' (Parsons and Smelser 1956: 3). The point about a *qualitative* dimension to market imperfection is quite important, especially in regard to the distribution of power in different types of markets, i.e., a perfect market implying a certain symmetry in regard to the bargaining process.

view of the resource allocation process in the context of Indian agriculture are empirically untenable. Furthermore, it is not at all clear that one can rely on the principle of continuity of approximations which can justify our initial adherence to such a model. For that purpose, it is necessary to relax the assumptions and work out the consequent modifications in the results to find out what is the degree and direction of error involved. While a very interesting and analytically sophisticated literature is currently evolving which, by introducing features such as uncertainty, transaction costs and deficiencies in the signalling mechanism, seeks to provide a theoretical framework that can help explain phenomena such as share-cropping, the so-called inverse relationship between size and productivity, and the process of adoption of new technology, it is a little too early to pass any judgement on the robustness and/or fruitfulness of such an 'accretionist' procedure.[10] It is, however, important to note that as these reformulations are based on the principle of methodological individualism, they often tend to ignore the role of power exercised by an organized group in shaping the outcomes of economic processes. Nevertheless, it is not true to say that no power-theoretic considerations can be accommodated within the basic framework provided by a methodologically individualist position. One of these refers to the influence that individuals similarly situated with respect to a particular market or a group of interrelated markets can exercise collectively in getting a larger share of the total output for themselves than they would under conditions of perfect competition. The point

[10] From the analytical point of view, the most extensive discussion has centred on the presumed inefficiency of share-cropping. The initial Marshallian discussion in 'marginalist' terms pointed out the significant possibility that resource allocation under share-cropping will imply inefficiency, a point that was picked up in the Indian context by Sen. Since then, research done in India and abroad by Bardhan, Srinivasan, Newbery, Cheung and others has indicated the difficulty of arriving at general conclusions in view of the multi-dimensional nature of the rental contract that is involved. Furthermore, responses of share-croppers to changes in data cannot even be qualitatively predicted since the assumptions do not always ensure the existence of a competitive equilibrium, let alone guarantee that stability conditions can be validly assumed. This question acquires considerable importance in connection with adoption of technical changes of yield-raising character. Several scholars, both in India and abroad, have found that technical changes can bring about replacement of share-cropping by owner-management of farms with the help of hired labour. See particularly Ishikawa's work in the Philippines. Similar conclusions have been reported by scholars in India.

was well recognized by Mill when he was writing the third edition of his *Principles*. In discussing the question of wage determination he first talked about the principle of competition replacing the principle of power, a position from which he somewhat resiled in later writings without abandoning it altogether.[11] In more recent years, the Pigou–Robinson concept of exploitation was put forward to capture, at least in part, some aspects of market power. However, from the point of view of increase in productivity this concept of 'power' is relevant only to the extent that it implies inefficiency in resource use. That is to say, it refers to allocative inefficiency only. But in a situation where markets are relatively few in number, obstacles to an increase in productivity can stem from the fact that possession of the means of production by a selected few prevents a potentially more fruitful combination of factors of production being worked out in practice. Thus, the range of feasible (possible) input–output combinations is narrower in such situations, and this fact alone may be far more important from the point of view of increasing productivity than the extent of allocative inefficiency implied in an imperfect market setting. The more important question, then, turns around the problem of how markets get created. There is not much in neo-classical theory today to answer this question. For an alternative framework, one may then turn to Marxian political economy to find out whether it throws much light on this issue.

II

Marxian political economy is typically thought to be more concerned with problems of production than with problems of markets. This is true, but we should remember that it is *capitalist* production Marx had chiefly in mind. It is true that in his discussion of the logic of what may be described as 'pure capitalism', Marx operates with a fully articulated set of markets, but we should remember that he also discussed problems of pre-capitalist socio-economic formations as well as issues of transition from feudalism to capitalism. In this latter context, he talks about market creation involving at crucial

[11] See John Stuart Mill (1970: 219). It may be useful to recall that Marshall, who amongst all the marginalists was most sensitive to institutional questions, was also sensitive to this question of unequal bargaining power between employers and employees in determining the nature and terms of the labour contract (Marshall 1961: 335–6).

stages the application of force.[12] In particular, in Volume I of *Capital* Marx discusses the creation of a particular market, i.e., the market for labour power, on which all subsequent discussion turns. In Volume III, which was put together by Engels from various notes left by Marx, he devoted considerable attention to land, market and also, to a certain extent, to the credit market.

As an instructive example, we may take up Marx's analysis of the 'enclosure movement' in England. It is doubtless true that in recent years evidence that has been produced by Chambers (1953) and some of his associates makes it necessary for us to modify our understanding of the process in some details, as compared with what earlier scholars such as Tawney, Hammonds, etc. had written on the basis of the evidence provided by the contemporaries as well as by people such as Arthur Young. Furthermore, it is probably true that the role of the enclosure movement in effecting transfer of labour from the village to the town was greatly exaggerated by earlier authors. However, as an illustration of method, the analytical model based on Marxian lines and presented by Cohen and Weitzman (1975) shows how the exercise of power changed production relationships decisively in bringing about a structural transformation in English agriculture. The crux of the process lies in making land and labour into marketable 'commodities' so that capitalist accounting methods could apply. The transition was obviously a prolonged and in part a very painful one. But in the end one obtained a more efficient productive apparatus which was responsive to market stimulus.[13]

[12] It is useful at this stage to distinguish between the concept of 'power' underlying the Marxian system of reproduction of a specific system, of socio-economic relationships and the concept of 'power' involved in effecting transition from one system to another. As regards the former, Marx decided to meet classical economists on their own ground while carrying out his 'critique of political economy'. It has often been thought that Marx used a binary concept of power on an 'all or nothing' basis in carrying out such a critique. I believe that this position is overly strong and is not needed for Marxian political economy. It will be out of place, however, to attempt a demonstration of my position in this regard. As regards the concept of power involved in transitional societies, the nature of the State is a critical consideration. Marx's historical analysis is much too rich to permit of simple formalization.

[13] While this was true of England, the case of Germany was quite different. On this point, there has been considerable controversy. Debate has centred on the nature and consequence of the period of so-called 'second serfdom' which was introduced in the East Elbian Germany in the fifteenth century. But in both

It is worth recalling in what ways the power structure impinged on the organization of production. Basically, the process centred around the extension of 'property rights' over common land where no individual rights were previously exercised, with a view to creating large and compact estates which could profitably absorb investment in land and related facilities. This in its turn made it possible to turn them over to substantial tenant-farmers on a leasehold basis which could promote the development of capitalism in agriculture. It, therefore, paved the way for the typical organization of English agriculture which formed the basis of theorizing by English classical economists. This reorganization was brought about by local power structures acting in collusion with a parliament which was heavily dominated by landed interests. While the earlier generation of writers on the enclosure movement put a high degree of emphasis on the labour displacing aspect of this change, a point which linked up in their opinion with the formation of an industrial labour force, recent researches based on extensive use of regional demographic sources would seem to suggest that this might not have been the principal role played by enclosures. It is more in terms of sustaining higher levels of agricultural productivity that the significance of the process has to be sought.

We have discussed the question of enclosures in the context of showing how power can decisively shape the economic configuration, which in its turn can affect agricultural productivity. It may be mentioned, however, that the relationship between power and productivity is a reciprocal one. This means that power structures do not remain invariant with respect to changes in productivity. If a conjunction of unfavourable demographic and exogenous economic influences leads to a decline in productivity, we may have an example of 'agricultural involution' of the sort that was analysed with a great deal of penetration by Clifford Geertz (1968) in his study of Central Java, and for which parallels can be found in the Indian sub-continent, especially the Eastern Gangetic delta. Such changes, which are characterized by declining yield rates and a growing land–man

---

cases force was involved. In one case, it helped to dissolve the existing relations of production, whereas in the other, it strengthened the existing conservative elements, preventing the growth of industry in Germany in the seventeenth and eighteenth centuries. See Engels' letters to Marx in December 1882. See also Engels, 'The Mark', included as an appendix in *The Peasant War in Germany* (Moscow).

ratio, imply an immiserization process which need not and possibly cannot serve as a prelude to the transfer of labour from agriculture to 'industry' in sharp contrast with other situations where a growing agricultural surplus can lead initially to a stationary agricultural population, followed ultimately by an absolute decline in agricultural population as happened in the case of Japan. Power structures in such an involuted situation are apt to be much more oppressive. This shows itself in the nature of tenurial arrangements, wage rates and poverty indices. An important question that arises in this regard is whether such a situation can generate the necessary responsiveness to potentially yield-raising innovations. This is a point on which a certain amount of discussion has taken place in the Indian context under the general rubric of 'semi-feudalism'. To appreciate the debate properly, one has to understand the nature of the 'green revolution' which has taken place in the course of the last decade and a half.

Literature on the 'green revolution' is vast and sentiments and opinions expressed range from the most enthusiastic to the utterly condemnatory. It is neither necessary nor desirable to survey the literature here; furthermore, we are interested in it for what it shows of the power relationship and its effect on the spread and success of what is basically a biological-cum-chemical chain of innovations. The first point to note is that the success of the revolution has been both region-specific and crop-specific. While the crop-specific nature of the change has had much to do with the nature of the success achieved by agricultural research workers, region-specificity has had a great deal to do with questions of water management, including questions both of irrigation and drainage. This much is clear and non-controversial. The interesting question that needs to be looked into is whether differences in power structures have played an important causal role in the region-specific success of the 'revolution'.

It is well known that absentee landlordism is not a characteristic feature of the regions which have experienced the sharpest rates of increase. Secondly, owner-cultivators have a much larger role to play in these regions as compared with tenant-cultivators who operate largely on the basis of oral leases which are virtually renewed every year, a characteristic which is typical of the Eastern Gangetic region. Thirdly, medium and relatively large owner-cultivators have politically a much greater hold over the local and state administration in these areas. Fourthly, proximity to the seat of central government has also meant that certain national economic policies affecting the costs and returns of agricultural operations have maintained a certain incentive structure which influences attitudes toward risk taking in a favourable direction.

The net result of all these factors has been that the existing power structure has combined with the availability of certain investment options the adoption of which could lead to a sustained increase in productivity.[14] The crucial factor in this case has been credit, which was made available at a cheap rate in relatively abundant measure through the instrumentality of state and subordinate financial institutions; though such credit has been available on a skewed basis, the larger-sized farms gaining proportionately a greater share.[15] Unlike the West European case, the question of creating a free labour market has not played any significant role in this process. This is due to several reasons: (a) technological changes were not primarily labour-saving; (b) owner-cultivators can utilize labour reserves within the family, a point which figured prominently in the discussion between agrarians and Marxists in Russia; and (c) possibilities of migration from surrounding areas could be exploited as over time

[14] Readers will notice that what is being discussed here is the opposite of the question that is normally asked: did the 'green revolution' primarily benefit the powerful? I have chosen to discuss the causal consequence from power structures to increase in productivity. But it is good to recognize that there is an element of interdependence here. I believe that, by focusing typically on the question of distribution of gains in favour of the powerful, we have often forgotten to ask whether an increase in output to the recorded extent could have been generated in a different power context, a point to which we turn later on. It is doubtless true that in defining power I have concentrated on the relationship in which a group of people stand to the production process. This corresponds more closely to the Marxian discussion of 'classes' or 'fractions of classes'. But it is important to bear in mind that other forms of power are also involved in the process; in a more complete discussion of the 'green revolution', these will need to be taken into account. Our purpose here is to illustrate a methodological procedure with Indian data.

[15] The importance of credit as an essential input in agricultural production is, of course, very closely tied to the fact that the production process in agriculture has a slower turnover period than industrial processes. This is one major reason why in early modern Europe questions of credit attracted a great deal of attention. It is also notable that Tawney in his now classic study *Land and Labour in China* singled out the credit problem as the rural problem par excellence. While this would doubtless sound an over-simplification to many, it would no doubt serve as an important corrective to some contemporary analysis based on the use of hired labour alone.

the local reserve of low cost labour was showing signs of drying up.

However, the agrarian structure in the areas affected by the 'green revolution' has shown certain important changes which hold out potential for future changes in the power structure. First of all, there has been eviction of tenant-farmers, leading to resumption of cultivation by owners with the help of former tenant-farmers, now turned agricultural labourers. Secondly, the nature of tenancy has also changed, involving small farmers leasing out land to the richer farmers. These two processes have implied that the differences between the distribution of operational holdings and ownership holdings have diminished. Thirdly, mechanization is being resorted to on a larger scale to level out peak season rise in wage rates, over and above the migration factor mentioned earlier. Fourthly, the emergence of large marketable surpluses has induced mutations in the character of large farmers with changes in their behaviour patterns, including the adoption of life-styles which differentiate them more prominently from the rest of the village population.

While it is not within the scope of this essay to go into questions involving class consciousness, it is important to note that peasantism in politics has become a very pronounced factor in these regions, and also on the national level, albeit to a lesser extent.

While our attention has been focused on the role of power in inducing productivity changes, it must be mentioned that the distributional process had naturally been influenced by the same set of factors, as would be evident from various studies conducted on the incidence of poverty. A recent study by Ahluwalia which deals with the question of rural poverty and income distribution has come to the conclusion that the percentage of people living below the 'poverty' line has shown practically no alteration even in states like Punjab and Haryana which have been in the vanguard of the 'green revolution'. There are, of course, some economists who claim that the situation has in fact worsened even in these states. There is scope for doing considerable work for articulating a model or formulating a hypothesis which would enable us to identify the forces at work which cause income distribution to remain constant or worsen even in the presence of substantial growth. Unfortunately, the distribution theory in relation to rural societies still remains in a rudimentary state, although certain broad hypotheses can be formulated. While the problem of generating enough data to feed any quantitative model is doubtless very great, at least in the present stage, simulation models can be tried out to give us a somewhat better understanding of the strength of the relevant forces at work.

At this stage, we may be tempted to enquire whether the uneven character of agricultural growth in space may not have something to do with certain *specific* differences in power structures in different regions. Bhaduri (1973) and Prasad (1975) have argued that the presence of a 'semi-feudal' power structure has been responsible for the non-responsiveness of agriculture to innovational impulses in large parts of India, especially in Bihar. While Prasad's findings are of an empirical character, obtained from the field studies that he had carried out in Purnea and Saharsa districts in Bihar, Bhaduri has presented an analytical model based on his perceptions of the power relationships which prevail in certain districts of West Bengal. Bhaduri's model has attracted a considerable amount of attention, but much of this discussion has been directed toward refuting his conclusion that the so-called *jotedars* will be averse from introducing technical changes which will increase the productivity of land and, on his assumption, the productivity of labour. Even if Bhaduri's conclusion were to be regarded as an overly strong one, applicable in exceptional cases, several important points of an analytical nature emerge from his discussion. First of all, Bhaduri links up leasing-in of land to share-croppers very closely with interest income due to usury, since in his model the same set of people own land as well as liquid capital. Technically this looks like interlinking two different markets, a point of considerable interest in itself; but for Bhaduri, these markets are not two distinct markets in these regions because one cannot operate in disjunction from the other.[16] The reason for this is that Bhaduri considers 'attached' labour to be contractually unfree labour. Given this and the fact that *jotedars* do not by and large cultivate the land, labour is 'attached' to land if cultivation is to take place. This attachment process is not primarily carried out through an extra-economic process of coercion, although coercion may be present in several cases. Attachment comes through 'debt

[16] K. Bharadwaj and P. K. Das (1975a; 1975b) in their studies dealing with tenurial conditions and mode of exploitation based on the study of some villages in Orissa also place considerable emphasis on the existence of interlinkages amongst markets. Their studies are not concerned with the question of possible responses to innovations. Instead they concentrated on who leased out land to whom and under what conditions. The conclusions from these studies emphasized that the relative economic status of the tenant in relation to that of his landlord appeared to influence rents per acre under fixed kind and cash systems.

bondage', which in its turn is due to the inability of the cultivator or the direct producer to get a share of the net produce which will be adequate to cover his necessitous 'consumption'.

This form of agricultural organization can under certain circumstances permit the existence of a steady state configuration which may prove to be stable for a certain range of parameter values. Innovations would merely involve an increase in income from one source of exploitation (i.e. cultivation), which is compensated for by a decline in income from usury. Some critics have pointed out that if one were to allow for productivity-raising innovations to take place along with changes in the terms of the contract, e.g., change in the share of the net surplus accruing to the overlords, the innovation may well be absolved by the system, thus contradicting Bhaduri's conclusion.[17]

Secondly, there is an indication in Bhaduri's analysis, which comes out more clearly in Prasad's formulation, that overlords may prefer direct control over people to control over goods or a higher income because of the extra-economic advantages that it confers on them.[18] While the expression 'extra-economic advantages' suggests feudal privileges, in the present Indian context these may take the form of access to political power, which need not be inconsistent with acquisition of economic advantages as well, although in an indirect manner.

Thirdly, from the point of view of actual experience, it is no doubt an over-simplification to treat the entire eastern region as an area of stagnation. For example, in West Bengal, the substantial increase recorded in wheat production over the last decade suggests that even

[17] Bhaduri's analysis is based on the assumption that the share of the crop is a predetermined magnitude. He does not go into the question of determining the share itself. This is presumably due to the fact that in a state of stagnant output, shares are often customarily fixed around a conventional figure as in the case of the *metayage* system in France. However, it would be useful for further work to study the nature of share contracts much more carefully. One approach would be along the lines explained by authors who regard the relationship between tenant and landlord as being in the nature of an *exchange*, although a multidimensional one. The other would be along lines which emphasize bargaining. Bargaining approaches could in turn take two forms; a formal game-theoretic one studied by Bell and Zusman. The other could go into the highly asymmetric nature of the bargaining process based on the question of power and status. The latter approach is less formal but can nevertheless be put in testable forms.

[18] See P. H. Prasad (1975a).

in an area traditionally infested with share-cropping, technical changes can well take place provided proper water management and ancillary arrangements can be ensured. Thus the underlying theoretical model may be an overly restrictive one.

Therefore, while considerable scope for difference of opinion exists on the realism of the model postulated by Bhaduri and applied by Prasad to Bihar, from our present point of view the interest of the model lies in the fact that it focuses attention on certain power-theoretic issues. They are of two types. While the first has something to do with the nature of the objective function of the actors, in that they may not be interested in maximizing a usual type of utility function where income or consumption can serve as a surrogate for utility (compare Hicks' famous observation, 'The best of all monopoly profits is a quiet life'), the second has to do with the logic of economic arrangements. Thus, it is assumed that there exists a sufficiently high degree of cohesiveness on the part of individual *jotedars*, that they act as a homogeneous group in relation to the group of 'share-croppers', potential and actual, so as to forgo the individual gains that may have accrued to any *one* of them, if he alone were to go ahead with the proposed 'innovation'. The nature of this cohesiveness is, however, a factor which requires closer analysis if the inhibiting role of local power structure on the growth of agricultural productivity is to be comprehended.

Obviously, economic behaviour based on the principle of 'cohesiveness' which binds particular social groups is not consistent with the explanatory frameworks based on the principle of methodological individualism. Neo-classical economic theory would appear to be powerless to deal with such situations, at least on the face of it. Typically, if cohesiveness is seen to be a persistent phenomenon, neo-classical theorists can adapt their tools to deal with its consequences, in so far as they cause modifications in the supply–demand relationships, but in their existing formulations they are unable to deal with its genesis without invoking extra-economic relationships. The situation with Marxian political economy is different. The structural aspects of reproduction in Marxian economy require that exploitation be viewed as a feature inherently embedded in a capitalist system. This is, first, because labour power appears as a 'commodity' under capitalism, and secondly, because as a 'commodity' labour power possesses certain special features. Among these features, Marx himself emphasizes the fact that the use value of the 'commodity' labour power generally exceeds its exchange value. How is this inequality preserved in a directional sense?[19] One possible approach is to assume that with given technology, a given real wage basket defined in terms of commodities, and a stipulated vector of labour requirements by sectors, the relevant augmented matrix of input–output coefficients is a 'productive' one, i.e., capable of generating a vector of commodity surplus. The other approach is less mechanistic and tries to take into account the nature of the labour process, including factors determining the length of the working day and direction of technical change. Marx relies on the second approach in *Capital* (Vol. I). In doing so, he has to deal with classes, as is evident from the following observation on the question of the length of the working day. 'There is here, therefore, an antinomy, of right against right, both equally bearing the seal of the law of exchange. Between equal rights, force decides. Hence, in the history of capitalist production, the establishment of a norm for the working day presents itself as a struggle over the limits of that day, a struggle between *collective* capital, i.e., the class of capitalists, and collective labour, i.e., the working class' (Marx 1976: 344). The above quotation uses the concept of 'class' as an explanatory concept. How do we apply it to Indian agriculture? It appears that it is very necessary to do a great deal of further work before we get a workable model of Indian agriculture in Marxist terms. This is because classical Marxian theory in its well-developed form dealt with a historically specific socio-economic formation which prevailed in Western Europe. This limitation of the basic Marxian model became quite clear in the context of the Russian debate where Marx did admit in his letter to Vera Zasulitch that his analysis of the alleged historical inevitability was expressly confined to countries of Western Europe.[20] Marx's reservation arose from his basic perception that while in the case of Western Europe 'it is a

---

[19] In current debates on the 'value' problem, the length of the working day is not explicitly mentioned. Instead, reference is made to wider political factors. There are, in my opinion, sound historical and analytical bases for Marx's procedure.

[20] Different versions of the draft letter to V. Zasulitch show quite clearly that Marx did not find the question at all an easy one to answer. Of the four versions which are known to have been drafted, only three are extant. I am relying here on the text given in Marx–Engels, *Selected Works*, Vol. III, 1970, which was translated from the French. See also E. Hobsbawm (1964). See also the introduction to the Russian translation of the *Communist Manifesto*, published in 1882.

question of the transformation of one form of private property into
another form of private property', in the case of Russia 'one would
on the contrary have to transform their property into private
property'.

In the case of India, while the question of common property is
irrelevant and commodity production has invaded even relatively
remote rural areas, and labour power is fast becoming a 'commodity'
as Marx understood it, it is still inappropriate to use the model of a
full-blown capitalism. Some people have sought to conceptualize the
rural scene as a peasant economy, but not much has unfortunately
been done to deduce the laws of working of such an economy,
Thorner's attempt to revive Chayanov notwithstanding.

An interesting attempt has been made by Utsa Patnaik (1976) to
develop a more differentiated picture of the peasant society in terms
of an exploitation index which basically stems from the work of
Lenin and Mao carried out in rather different historical situations.[21]
Its theoretical roots can be traced to Marx's theory of rent, which
in its turn rests on the labour theory of value. The index is worked
out after adjustment for the presence of family labour in the cultivation process as well as for the phenomenon of leasing in and out of
land. Since the index is expressed in the form of the ratio of the net
use of outside labour to the use of family labour, both expressed in
days, there is an implicit equation between rent paid in cash and
kind and the number of labour days appropriated through rent. Such
an equation raises very serious conceptual difficulties which have
always posed a great problem to the Marxian theory of rent understood as an internally consistent doctrine, let alone for operational
use in the form of statistical estimates.

Further, Patnaik herself points out that in computing the index
she has excluded problems posed by market imperfections as well as
usurious practices, as she is not addressing herself to exploitation
in the circulation process.

It would, however, appear that by introducing a sharp distinction
between the production sphere and the circulation sphere, Patnaik
may here be distorting the real situation inasmuch as the process of
self-valorization of capital, which provides the rationale behind the
Marxian theory of exploitation, cannot be captured in the Indian
context without bringing in the question of interrelationship between

[21] Utsa Patnaik has recently restated the same points with minor modification.
See the interchange with Sen in *Economic and Political Weekly*, March 1980.

various circuits of capital. While Patnaik's efforts merit serious attention for their boldness and their basic perception that class analysis worked out most fully with regard to a situation involving machinofacture is much too simplified for doing justice to the Indian situation, much of which is characterized by a different mode of organization of the labour process, her contention that a synthetic index of the sort she has constructed can capture all the relevant dimensions is questionable. Further, to grasp the process at work, it is not enough to work out a merely typological analysis; it is also necessary to work out an economic framework based on the logic of a transitional system operating somewhere between a pre-capitalist system of exchange relationships and a developed capitalist economy.

As we have already seen, even the treatment of usurious capital, which has received a certain amount of attention, has not succeeded in specifying the conditions when moneylending succeeds in exercising a dissolving influence on the existing system of production relationships and situations when it 'appropriates all of the surplus labour of the direct producers, without altering the mode of production'.[22]

In my opinion, two crucial considerations have not received as much attention as they deserve from theorists with a broad Marxist persuasion: factors influencing the growth of demand, which can play an important part in changing techniques and relations of production, and the role of public investment in diffusing technical change as well as providing infrastructural facilities. While the first consideration was emphasized by Marx himself, as would be clear from the chapter of *Capital* which has only recently been translated into English,[23] the second did not have a parallel in European experience, although it played a major role in Japan.

While the question of the dispossession of the small peasantry is an important one from the point of view of demand, a fuller discussion will obviously require an analysis of rural–urban terms of interchange and of the extent of inroad made by the forces shaping the world market on the relations of production. Equally importantly, it will require an understanding of the forces that shape public investment and its distribution by categories of outlays and by

[22] See Marx, *Capital*, Moscow, n.d., Vol. III, p. 595.
[23] See Marx, 'Results of the Immediate Process of Production', *Capital*, Penguin Books, 1976, Vol. I.

regions. While the former set of issues will take us too far away from the present focus of discussion, it is important that we pay some attention to the second set. Since these require a somewhat extended discussion, we take them up in the next section.

Meanwhile, to round off our discussion, it is necessary to remind ourselves that our discussion so far has concentrated on the use of categories that may be described as economic in character, although they belong to different intellectual traditions. We have not taken into account the influence exercised on economic behaviour by such important factors as caste, which have figured so prominently in many studies carried out by social anthropologists, or factors like tradition and 'mores', which can reflect survival algorithms in a situation characterized by acute land-hunger and precarious rain-fall.[24]

III

Our discussion has so far been confined to the influence of structural economic power on the question of agricultural productivity. Even where we have referred to the effect of force in reshaping certain institutional features of an agrarian society, we have not paused to enquire into the nature and sources of authority of those who wielded force. In other words, we have not discussed questions relating to political power. In this section, we shall briefly describe this question, as it has been discussed in other essays in this volume.

On the descriptive level, a great deal of evidence has been collected to show that political power, as it has been articulated through the actions of political authorities including the government apparatus at different levels, has largely helped the rich and middle peasants to improve their productivity, with the richer farmer benefiting most from the deal. This policy has sometimes been described as a policy of betting on the strong, reminding one of Stolypin's famous 'wager' which was introduced in Tsarist Russia in the early years of the century.

Two interesting questions arise which deserve closer examination.

[24] For a discussion of these issues, we refer to Breman's outstanding study of the 'Hali' system in his book as well as to numerous studies by Bailey, Béteille and Kathleen Gough. There is a whole class of debates which pertain to the issues relating to the characterization of the 'mode of production' in Indian agriculture which I have not discussed here. This is primarily because the ground has been extensively covered by A. Rudra in a number of valuable critiques published in *Economic and Political Weekly*, 1977.

One of them relates to the causes underlying the phenomenon itself. The second relates to the possibility of doing any better, i.e., whether it is possible to reflect concerns regarding growth with those of equity in framing agricultural development policies.

Two kinds of answers are generally offered to the first question. One says in effect that, given the 'class character' of the Indian state, nothing better could have been expected. What, however, constitutes the class character of the Indian state has, in fact, never been spelled out with any great precision. We have already seen that a class characterization of Indian society cannot be deduced from the first principles of Marxian political economy. This point has been recognized by the more analytically inclined social scientists. It is notable that Marx's multi-class analysis of the French economic and political situation, especially in his '18th Brumaire', has come in for very favourable mention by some noted Indian economists such as Raj. To this date, however, no comprehensive study along these lines has been produced.

The second point of view considers that the failure has been not so much in terms of concepts as in terms of *implementation*. In this context, it is often mentioned that the first phase of land reform was successfully carried out in post-Independence India, involving the abolition of non-functional intermediary interests in the country, at least in substantial parts of it. There is little doubt that the change in the configuration of political power was largely responsible for this major change. It is now held that with a proper organization of the rural poor, it would be possible for a democratic polity to do much better in the direction of ensuring growth with equity in the rural sector. By implication, this provides us with a positive answer to the second question. In other words, while the adherents of the 'class theory' would be unwilling to grant autonomy to the sphere of 'political action' short of a complete change in the rules of the game, the latter group, sometimes described as 'populists', feel that the existing legislative framework, along with additional political 'inputs', can bring about a 'progressive' shift in the character of agrarian relationships.

One of the arguments which has been generally used to strengthen the 'populist' cause is the alleged existence of an inverse relationship between 'farm size' and productivity. Much has been written on this subject both in India and abroad. The first analytical formulation in the English language is to be found in the widely influential essay by N. Georgescu-Roegen (1960) which revived the older argument of agrarians of Eastern Europe. Unlike the classical and neo-classical economists, the agrarians were greatly concerned with the interaction between different property rights and the problem of relative factor endowments.[25]

They formulated their principal·policy prescription in the form of a double negation, 'neither capitalism, nor socialism'. This prescription rested on two basic propositions: (a) agricultural households generally act as output-maximizing entities, which leads to greater intensity of labour use and consequently higher yields per acre; (b) the ability of an interrelated system of agricultural households constituting a village community to engage in collective acts of capital creation which decentralized decision-making will not permit. In the Indian case, it was only the first proposition that was picked up by Sen in what purported to be an explanation of the data thrown up by Farm Management surveys. However, as early as 1968, Rudra had raised questions regarding the empirical base of the so-called findings from Farm Management studies. He found no systematic relationship between productivity, i.e., yield per acre, and farm size. He even found the occasional presence of a positive relationship. While this piece of evidence did not dispose of the issue, subsequent studies made by K. Bharadwaj (1974) helped to direct attention to the question of the cropping pattern as one of the crucial factors in explaining the existence of an inverse relationship between the total value of output and the farm size, even when the relationship did not hold for individual crops. Since then, there have been further attempts to probe the relationship which, in its initial version, rested on the simple point that labour use on a small farm was not determined by the requirement that a worker must be worth his keep, i.e., marginal productivity should be equal to the wage rate.

While there is sufficient warrant for the view that the nature of the 'economic calculus' employed by small farms is different in character from what prevails on large farms, due caution is called for in drawing far-reaching conclusions. Meanwhile, there is still scope for a detailed probing of the relationship.[26] What is interesting to note

[25] For a verbal restatement of the agrarian position, see D. Mitrany (1951).

[26] For a recent statement of the issues involved, see the article by A. Rudra and A. K. Sen (1980). Meanwhile, see a study on Pakistan by M. H. Khan (1979), which shows that larger farms are more efficient than small farms in the sense that they have greater output per acre.

is that while the first thesis of the agrarians became the subject of an intensive and heated debate, the second thesis did not attract much notice until fairly recently.[27]

This is because the logic of the second proposition was for a long time described as a mere problem in implementation. It was, however, thoroughly misleading to describe what amounted to a series of restrictions on property rights as a mere administrative problem. We have no theory as to how property rights change over time. Major changes in property rights have been sustained by, and in turn have helped to sustain, radical changes in the balance of political forces. But there have been cases where changes have been brought about by legislative measures without a violent change in the political fabric of a given society. Whether such a change is possible in the case of India is very much a moot question.

This takes our analysis into an area where possibly the least amount of analytical work has been done. It has been said often enough that what we require is an organization of the rural poor. But who are the rural poor? What are the occasions when they are likely to behave cohesively and in relation to whom? These questions require to be answered by economists who think in terms of mobilization of the poor as an answer to the problems of inequality stemming from power exercised through ownership of property, strategic location in the bargaining process and access to higher order administrative and political personnel.

What one knows of the broad profile of the rural poor would appear to suggest that they consist largely of agricultural labour and small and marginal farmers. Agricultural labour in the Indian context is still a heterogeneous category, differentiated by caste, tribal background, degree of attachment to employer and several other distinguishing features. There is little doubt that all this is changing, but changes are still slow, partly for economic reasons, and partly also for reasons which are political. It is well known that democratic processes have in several cases led to an intensification of primary loyalties, leading paradoxically away from homogenization and resulting in concerted political action on non-class lines.

As regards unity between agricultural labour and small and marginal farmers, there is the additional problem of status, even

[27] See S. Chakravarty (1975). For an articulation of the alternative policy approaches to Indian agriculture, see the Report of the ICSSR Working Group (1980).

though in terms of 'hired labour utilization' *à la* Patnaik it may fall in the same broad range.

It is also worth noting that in the original writings of Lenin, Mao and Chen Po Ta which deal with problems of differentiation within the peasantry, the main focus was on political mobilization involving the urban *proletariat* and the rural peasant. So far as the urban proletariat is concerned, the Indian situation presents a varied picture combining features of a pre-industrial economy with those of a highly capital-intensive pattern of industrial structure. Here again, it is easy to point out *à la* Emmanuel that workers in the high wage sectors are exploiting those in the low wage sectors, including agriculture. This is precisely what Dandekar has said in some of his recent work. The point here is not whether Dandekar is right or not. The point is that such arguments are being made by fairly influential economists. While Dandekar's is a recent contribution, some Indian and several foreign economists have been alleging for a long time that planners with an urban bias have been pursuing policies which have systematically discriminated against rural interests. An illustration of 'rural solidarity' which goes against traditional theories of political mobilization is provided by the recent agitation launched by farmers in Maharashtra and other places.

The upshot of all that has been said above is not to suggest that the organization of the rural poor is not a desirable aim in itself, but that we as yet know very little about how this can be done and what effect it is going to have in inducing changes in agricultural productivity. Obviously, this is an area where much more work needs to be done, although it is doubtful whether we can learn very much in this area from academic work, particularly if it is of a unidisciplinary type.

IV

This essay being in the nature of a critical survey of issues relating power to agricultural productivity, it does not need any conclusion. It may, however, be useful to highlight a few major findings as well as indicate the scope for further work. We have noted that while power relationships are a pervasive feature of rural economic relationships, most analytical work tends to ignore it. This is largely because analytical agricultural economics in India has largely been influenced by the standards and preconceptions of what goes in the U.S. and other Western countries as 'farm economics'. Farm economists generally use the principle of competition to replace the concept of 'power'. The sources for an increase in productivity are accordingly sought in improving the efficiency of resource use as well as the quality of inputs employed on the farm.

Power considerations can be introduced in this context by bringing in questions of differential access to 'credit', a very vital input in agricultural production because of its slowness of turnover, lack of marketing facilities and also of subsidization of purchased inputs such as chemical fertilizers, power, agricultural machinery, etc. In fact, most empirical work on the influence exercised by power structure on agricultural productivity has focused on these items.

There are occasional references to the element of imperfection in the labour market, which, it is sometimes held, favours the small farmers as against imperfections in the 'capital market', which are supposed to favour the large farms. Such discussion is used as a background to studies on dualism within agriculture, of which there is growing awareness.

Basing themselves essentially on this 'market determined' concept of power, policy-makers have often recommended the application of 'countervailing power'. In India, this has generally meant exhortation to the 'rural poor' to unite. But it has also included recommendation of a differential lending and interest rate policy, land tax exemption, etc. These policies have so far turned out to be unsuccessful, and the blame has been squarely placed on collusion between administrators and politicians.

However, there has been a growing feeling that the initial formulation of the problem may not only be inadequate but also seriously misleading. One point of view which is recently gaining ground is that in the Indian context the problem of interlinkages amongst markets for 'land', 'labour' and 'capital' needs to be very closely investigated before one can form a clearer picture of the functioning of the rural economy, let alone suggest effective policy measures. We have noted this point of view and there is little doubt that this set of questions needs much closer investigation.[28]

There is a second point of view which notes that in India we do not have 'farmers' but mostly peasants. A peasant economy, it is held, functions within a different logic. The late Daniel Thorner did much to focus attention on this concept of a peasant economy. He helped to popularize the work of Chayanov, although it is clear that

[28] See P. K. Bardhan (1980).

some aspects of Chayanov's work have little relevance to India because of the presence of acute 'land hunger'. But the main thrust has been to provide a theoretical underpinning of agrarian democratic policies. While this line of enquiry has to proceed somewhat further before one can judge of its fruitfulness, there is one important purpose that this approach can serve. This is to help provide us with a better comprehension of the production process in agriculture as compared with industry. There are reasons to believe that one distorts reality by assuming that 'labour process' in agriculture is fundamentally of the same type as in industry. One of Chayanov's main points, that small farmers can reap all the advantages of 'vertical concentration' if co-operatives are properly organized, is consonant with the point of view indicated by the ICSSR Working Group.

On the question of 'power', the central focus of our present study, the 'peasant' approach has, however, little to say. It is at this stage that a Marxist approach to the problem of rural economy appears to hold some promise. From a Marxist point of view, power is not derivative from a 'market' conjuncture, although certain types of market can heighten the power exercised by 'dominant classes' over the dominated. Domination is an asymmetric concept, rooted, in the Marxist view, in the nature of the underlying production process, at least according to its classical formulations. However, given the nature of the Indian economy, this classical formulation needs emendation in at least two major respects. One is the influence exercised by usurious capital on the production process, a point emphasized by those Indian economists who talk about the grip of the moneylender-cum-trader on Indian agriculture. The other is the extent of demographic pressure operating in a variety of agro-climatic contexts which has already produced a substantial measure of agricultural 'involution' in large tracts of India. The social and economic differentiation that such a process has created renders an advance toward higher sustainable levels of yields per acre extremely problematic, particularly in 'wet rice' regions. Marx's discussion of the institutional aspects of the 'land' question in Volume III of *Capital* is doubtless a considerable improvement over similar discussions of 'classical economists'.[29] But it is not quite adequate for our purposes.

[29] Compare the quality of the large volume of debate generated amongst classical economists on the Irish question. For this, see R. D. C. Black (1965).

The principal reason is that Marx's analytical structure dealt with a fully articulated system of markets. More particularly, it dealt with a specially 'privileged' market, i.e., 'the labour market', which at a certain stage of historical development acquires a critical importance in determining the economic system's overall functioning and growth. The dynamics of increase in productivity is shown to lie in an interplay between certain types of utilization of surplus and its continual regeneration on progressively higher levels. This is done by replacing Malthus' 'law of population' by a law specific to the 'capitalist' mode of production. Once the initial conditions are appropriate, the role of 'power' is confined to maintaining the 'rules of the game' which permit the process of self-valorization of capital to go on.

In the Indian context, there are several specific features which deserve to be carefully noted. First, the 'labour market' is not yet fully formed. Differences between agricultural labour and small farmers are in some respects quite important, especially if one takes into account the time structure of the production process in agriculture. Furthermore, empirical studies suggest various forms of attachment between 'labour' and employer, which in some areas take the form of patron–client relationship, making it difficult to treat 'labour power' as a commodity, at least in a straightforward sense. Secondly, while commercialization has made very substantial inroads, subsistence production is still very common, stemming in part from the existence of relatively small-sized farms.

Thirdly, the rapid and continuing growth of population implies the growth of a 'surplus population', which, in turn, implies less pressure on the capitalist to innovate. This leaves traditional Marxian 'dynamics' somewhat suspended in the air.

Neither the 'standard economic theory' nor 'classical Marxian' economics can be used to provide us with an adequate conceptualization of such a situation. We need a theoretical frame which can tell us under what conditions the economic system will 'reproduce itself' (the basic viability theorem) with a surplus, along with ensuring the compatibility between objectives pursued by different 'groups' in society which are involved in the production and circulation process.

While our survey has indicated that our understanding of the interrelationships has improved in recent years, the mere fact that policy interventions tend to produce many unintended consequences would seem to suggest that we do not as yet possess even a 'working theory', let alone the knowledge to explain all irregularities. It is my opinion that there is considerable scope here for innovative work by economists which can draw upon researches done by sociologists and political scientists. In addition, placing the Indian problem in a comparative historical perspective can also produce illuminating insights.

REFERENCES

Bardhan, P. K. (1980), 'Interlocking Factor Markets and Agrarian Development: A Review of Issues', *Oxford Economic Papers*, Vol. 32.

Bhaduri, A. (1973), 'A Study in Agricultural Backwardness under Semi-Feudalism', *Economic Journal*, Vol. 83, pp. 120–37.

Bharadwaj, K. (1974), *Production Conditions in Indian Agriculture* (London: Cambridge University Press).

Bharadwaj, K. and P. K. Das (1975a), 'Tenurial Conditions and Mode of Exploitation—A Study of Some Villages in Orissa', *Economic and Political Weekly*, Annual Number, February 1975.

—— 'Tenurial Conditions and Mode of Exploitation—A Study of Some Villages in Orissa: Further Notes', *Economic and Political Weekly*, Review of Agriculture, Vol. X, Nos. 25–6.

Black, R. D. C. (1960), *Economic Thought and the Irish Question* (London: Cambridge University Press).

Chakravarty, S. (1974), 'Reflections on the Growth Process in the Indian Economy', Foundation Day Lecture (Hyderabad: Administrative Staff College of India).

—— (1975), 'Mahalanobis and Contemporary Issues in Development Planning', *Sankhya*, Series C.

Chambers, J. D. (1953), 'Enclosure and Labour Supply in the Industrial Revolution', *Economic History Review*, Vol. V, No. 3.

Cohen, J. S. and M. Weitzman (1975), 'A Marxian Model of Enclosures', *Journal of Development Economics*, Vol. 1, No. 4.

Engels, F. (n.d.), *The Peasant War in Germany* (Moscow).

Geertz, C. (1968), *Agricultural Involution: The Process of Ecological Change in Indonesia* (Berkeley: University of California Press).

Georgescu-Roegen, N. (1960), 'Economic Theory and Agrarian Economics', *Oxford Economic Papers*, February, pp. 1–40.

Hobsbawm, E. (ed.) (1964), *Marx: Pre-Capitalist Economic Formations* (Lawrence and Wishart).

Hollis, Martin and E. J. Nell (1975), *Rational Economic Man* (London: Cambridge University Press).

ICSSR (1980), *Alternatives in Agriculture* (New Delhi: Allied).

Jan de Vries (1976), *Economy of Europe in an Age of Crisis, 1600–1750* (London: Cambridge University Press).

Khan, M. H. (1979), *Pakistan Development Review*.

Marshall, A. (1961), *Principles of Economics*, 8th edn (London: Macmillan).

Marx, K. (1976), *Capital* (Penguin Books), Vol. I.

Mill, J. S. (1970), *Principles of Political Economy with Some of Their Application to Social Philosophy* (Ashley edition).

Mitra, A. (1978), *Terms of Trade and Class Reflections* (London: Frank Cass).

Mitrany, D. (1951), *Marx Against the Peasant* (University of North Carolina Press).

Nagel, E. (1963), 'Assumptions in Economic Theory', *American Economic Review*, Vol. XII, No. 5.

Parsons, T. and N. Smelser (1956), *Economy and Society* (London: Routledge and Kegan Paul).

Patnaik, U. (1976), 'Class Differentiation within the Peasantry', *Economic and Political Weekly*, Vol. XI, No. 39.

—— 'Empirical Identification of Peasant Classes Revisited', *Economic and Political Weekly*, Vol. XV, No. 9.

Polanyi, K. (1975), *The Great Transformation* (New York: Octagon).

Prasad, P. H. (1975), 'Limits to Investment Planning' in A. Mitra (ed.), *Economic Theory and Planning: Essays in Honour of A. K. Das Gupta* (Delhi: Oxford University Press).

Rudra, A. (1977), 'Size Productivity—Revisited', *Economic and Political Weekly*, Vol. XII, No. 11.

Rudra, A. and A. K. Sen (1980), 'Farm Size and Labour Use: Analysis and Policy', *Economic and Political Weekly*, Annual Number.

Saini, G. R. (1979), *Farm Size, Resource-Use Efficiency and Income Distribution* (New Delhi: Allied).

Samuelson, P. (1963), Comment on Ernest Nagel's 'Assumptions in Economic Theory', *Papers and Proceedings of the American Economic Association*, May 1963; also reprinted in *The Collected Scientific Papers of Paul A. Samuelson*, edited by Joseph E. Stiglitz (M.I.T. Press), Vol. 2.

Schultz, T. W. (1964), *Transforming Traditional Agriculture* (New Haven: Yale University Press).

Wertheim, W. F. *et al.* (1959), *Indonesian Economics* (Leiden: Van Hoeve).

Index